Extending ecocriticism

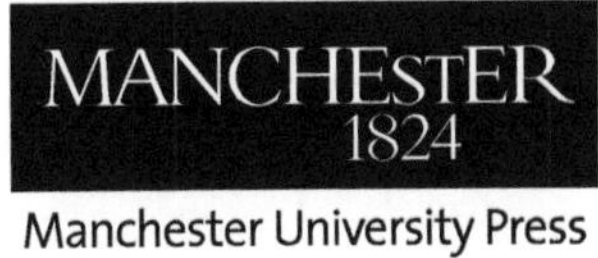

Manchester University Press

Extending ecocriticism

Crisis, collaboration and challenges in the environmental humanities

Edited by
Peter Barry and William Welstead

MANCHESTER
UNIVERSITY PRESS

Copyright © Manchester University Press 2017

While copyright in the volume as a whole is vested in Manchester University Press, copyright in individual chapters belongs to their respective authors, and no chapter may be reproduced wholly or in part without the express permission in writing of both author and publisher.

Published by Manchester University Press
Altrincham Street, Manchester M1 7JA
www.manchesteruniversitypress.co.uk

British Library Cataloguing-in-Publication Data is available

ISBN 978 1 7849 9439 6 hardback
ISBN 978 1 5261 4813 1 paperback

First published by Manchester University Press in hardback 2017

This edition first published 2020

The publisher has no responsibility for the persistence or accuracy of URLs for any external or third-party internet websites referred to in this book, and does not guarantee that any content on such websites is, or will remain, accurate or appropriate.

Typeset by Toppan Best-set Premedia Limited

Contents

Illustrations

All works of art are reproduced by courtesy of the artists or photographers unlessotherwise stated.

Plates

The plates appear in a section between p. 146 and p. 147.

Figures

Notes on contributors

Aaron S. Allen is Associate Professor of Music at the University of North Carolina at Greensboro, where he is also director of the Environmental and Sustainability Studies Program. A fellow of the American Academy in Rome, he received the PhD from Harvard with a dissertation on the nineteenth-century Italian reception of Beethoven. His BA in music and BS in environmental studies are from Tulane University. He is co-editor with Kevin Dawe of the collection *Current Directions in Ecomusicology* (2016).

Peter Barry is Emeritus Professor of English at Aberystwyth University. His books include *New British Poetry* (co-edited with Robert Hampson, 1995), *Contemporary British Poetry and the City* (2000), *Poetry Wars* (2006), *Literature in Contexts* (2007) and *Reading Poetry* (2013). He is also the author of *Beginning Theory* (1995, 4th edition, 2017, with translated editions in Korean, Hebrew, Ukrainian, Greek, Japanese and Chinese), and *English in Practice* (2000, and 2nd edition, 2013). He co-edited *English* (the journal of the English Association) for twenty years, and headed the 2012–15 Leverhulme-funded 'Devolved Voices' project on English-language poetry since 1997.

Clive Cazeaux is Professor of Aesthetics at Cardiff School of Art and Design. His research interests include the philosophies of metaphor and artistic research, and exploring alternatives to subject–object thinking. He is the author of *Metaphor and Continental Philosophy: From Kant to Derrida* (2007), and the editor of *The Continental Aesthetics Reader* (2011). He is currently writing a book called *Art, Research, Philosophy* for publication in 2017.

John Darwell works on long-term photographic projects that reflect his interest in social and industrial change, concern for the environment and issues around the depiction of mental health. He has had eighteen books published and has been shown in numerous international exhibitions.

His work is in the collections of the National Museum of Media/Sun Life Collection, Bradford, the Victoria & Albert Museum, London, and the Metropolitan Museum of Art, New York. In 2008 he gained his PhD for research into the visualisation of depression for his work entitled 'A Black Dog Came Calling'. He is currently Reader in Photography at the University of Cumbria in Carlisle.

Philip Gross is a poet, novelist and Professor of Creative Writing at University of South Wales. *The Water Table* won the T.S. Elliot Prize 2009, *I Spy Pinhole Eye* Wales Book of the Year 2010, and *Off the Road to Everywhere* the CLPE Award for Children's Poetry 2011. *A Fold in the River*, with artist Valerie Coffin Price, appeared in 2015, as did a new collection *Love Songs of Carbon*. His academic writing explores creative process and collaboration, as in 'Then Again What Do I Know: reflections on reflection in Creative Writing' in Richard Marggraf Turley (ed.), *The Writer in the Academy* (2011).

Patti Lean is an artist and art historian based in Dumfries and Galloway. She studied Art History at Edinburgh University and Fine Art at the University of Cumbria, where she is a currently a tutor and PhD researcher. Her art practice aims to respond to environment through the medium and materiality of paint. She is attracted to northerly, remote, 'pristine' places, and has developed a walking practice as means of generating and exchanging ideas. Fieldwork from walks combines with other sources, such as sound, memory, myth and literature, to inform abstract and semi-abstract paintings.

Mike Pearson is Emeritus Professor of Performance Studies in the Department of Theatre, Film and Television Studies, Aberystwyth University,. He creates theatre as a solo artist; with artist/designer Mike Brookes in Pearson/Brookes; with National Theatre Wales; and with senior performers' group Good News From The Future. He is co-author with Michael Shanks of *Theatre/Archaeology* (2001) and author of *In Comes I: Performance, Memory and Landscape* (2006); *Site-Specific Performance* (2010); *The Mickery Theater: An Imperfect Archaeology* (2011); and *Marking Time: Performance, Archaeology and the City* (2013). He is currently working with Michael Shanks on a new edition of *Theatre/Archaeology*.

Eve Ropek studied art and art history, beginning her career in adult education before turning to exhibition curating in the public arts sector. She developed the exhibitions programme at Aberystwyth Arts Centre, showing work by a wide range of contemporary artists including Paula Rego, Chris Drury, William Kentridge, Janet Cardiff and Ackroyd &

Harvey. When the Heatherwick-designed Creative Studios were opened in 2008 she also instigated and ran the Artist in Residence programme in which 66 UK and international artists took part until the project ended in 2016. She continues to work on a number of arts projects and is in the early stages of a community energy initiative.

Louise Squire was awarded her PhD by the University of Surrey in late 2014. Her doctoral dissertation examined a theme of ecological death-facing in contemporary environmental crisis fiction. She also has an MA in Philosophy (Nature Pathway). Her work falls broadly within the environmental humanities, crossing the fields of ecocriticism and contemporary literature. Her interests include critical and cultural theory, critical animal studies, European thought, globalisation and the discourses of the West, and speculative and post theory. Louise is currently completing a monograph based on her doctoral work. She is co-editor, with Adeline Johns-Putra (University of Surrey) and John Parham (University of Worcester) for an edited collection *Literature and Sustainability: Concept, Text and Culture* (forthcoming), and has published several articles, including in *The Oxford Literary Review* (2012). Louise currently serves as Treasurer for the Association for the Study of Literature and Environment, UK and Ireland (ASLE-UKI).

Harriet Tarlo's publications include *Poems 2004–2014*; *Poems 1990–2003* (2014, 2004); *Nab* (2005) and with Judith Tucker, *Sound Unseen* and *Behind Land* (2013 and 2015). She is editor of *The Ground Aslant: An Anthology of Radical Landscape Poetry* (2011). Critical work appears in volumes by Salt, Palgrave, Rodopi and Bloodaxe and in *Pilot, Jacket, English* and the *Journal of Ecocriticism*. Her collaborative work with Tucker has been shown at galleries including the Catherine Nash Gallery, Minneapolis, 20012; Musée de Moulages, Lyon, 2013; Southampton City Art Gallery, 2013–14; the Muriel Barker Gallery, Grimsby, and the New Hall College Art Collection, Cambridge, 2015. She is Reader in Creative Writing at Sheffield Hallam University.

Judith Tucker is an artist and academic. She has exhibited widely both in the UK and abroad. Recent exhibition venues include Cambridge, London, Brno, Czech Republic, Vienna, Minneapolis and Virginia. In addition to being an artist she spends part of her time at the University of Leeds where she is Senior Lecturer. She is co-convener of Land2 and of Mapping Spectral Traces networks and is part of contemporary British painting, a new platform for contemporary painting in the UK. She also writes academic essays which can be found in in academic journals and books published by Rodopi, Macmillan, Intellect and Gunter Narraverlag, Tübingen.

Jean Welstead is currently a PhD candidate at the University of Edinburgh following many years of working within the environmental sector for both charities and commercial consultancies in Scotland and Wales. Her research focuses on the social responses to renewable energy infrastructure and the possible influence environmental impact assessment processes have on these. She also continues to provide consultancy advice on sustainability and socio-economic issues in relation to the UK's transition to a low-carbon economy. Jean's other main interest is in photography, especially landscape and social documentary. She has exhibited at Aberystwyth Arts Centre and Fotofeis, the Scottish Festival of Photography. Earlier in her career, Jean studied Geography at the University of Edinburgh and Education at Aberystwyth University; she has recently completed an MSc by Research in Sociology at Edinburgh.

William Welstead has been variously a steelworks metallurgist, teacher, management consultant and Welsh hill farmer. In parallel with his formal career, he has followed academic interests in ecology, environmental justice, social science and literature. He received a PhD from Aberystwyth University in 2012 for an ecocritical reading of contemporary Welsh poetry in English. Since 2011 he has lived on the Isle of Tiree in Scotland where he now researches independently on the interplay between culture, ecology and literature. His publications include papers in *Green Letters – Studies in Ecocriticism*, and for the French Society for Scottish Studies. He is currently researching for a book on ecology, the animal turn and sheep in contemporary poetry.

1

Ecocriticism extends its boundaries

Peter Barry and William Welstead

Environmental literary criticism, usually contracted to ecocriticism, has advanced considerably since the term was widely adopted in the 1980s and 1990s. The aim of this book is threefold: firstly to consider examples of this advance across genres within literary studies and beyond into other creative forms; secondly to explore the ecocritical implications of collaboration across genres in the humanities; and thirdly to explore literary, artistic and performance production through direct collaboration between the creative disciplines and the sciences.

Although she was not the first to use the term 'ecocriticism' as a contraction of 'ecological literary criticism', its popularisation is attributed to Cheryll Glotfelty, who at a meeting of the Western Literary Association in 1989, proposed that the term 'ecocriticism' be used for what had previously been known as 'the study of nature writing'. Her proposal was seconded by Glen Love, who had been thinking along the same lines. In a 2003 essay on Willa Cather she suggested that 'the term ecocriticism for a critical practice that would take as its subject "the interconnections between human culture and the material world, between human and nonhuman"' (see Glotfelty 2003). It is perhaps significant that 'biodiversity' as a contraction of biological diversity was also adopted in the same decade, when W.G. Rosen suggested its use at the 1985 National Forum on Biological Diversity.[1] Both terms came into use at a time when it was becoming evident that we live in a world where there are great challenges to be faced if we are to avoid an environmental catastrophe.

In 1992 the United Nations Conference on Environment and Development in Rio de Janeiro reached the conclusion that 'nothing less than a transformation of our attitudes and behaviour would bring about the necessary changes' if such a catastrophe is to be avoided.[2] This conference, more popularly called the Rio Earth Summit, produced a number of statements and conventions focusing on sustainable development, biological diversity and climate change. In a rare moment of international agreement on such wide-ranging environmental matters, the academy in both arts and science was also challenged to rethink its priorities. It was in this context, also in 1992, that a group of scholars in North America formed the Association for the Study of Literature and the Environment (ASLE); sister organisations now include ASLE United Kingdom and Ireland (ASLE – UKI) and the European Association for the Study of Literature, Culture and the Environment (EASLCE).

Since these dates, researchers in the new discipline of ecocriticism have been busy. At first the concentration was on the literature of the American transcendentalists, including Ralph Waldo Emerson, Henry David Thoreau and John Muir, and in European literary studies of Romanticism, including William Wordsworth and Samuel Taylor Coleridge. Scholars have since extended ecocriticism to other literary genres and across the humanities, so that ASLE in its 2015 Strategic Plan:

> Seeks to inspire and promote intellectual work in the environmental humanities and arts. Our vision is an inclusive community whose members are committed to environmental research, education, literature, art and service, environmental justice and ecological sustainability.[3]

Laurence Coupe, editor of *The Green Studies Reader: From Romanticism to Ecocriticism* (2000), brought together contributors who illustrate the breadth and ambition of ecocritical practice. A section on the 'green tradition' discussed the legacy of Romantic ecology, and then moved on to a critique of modernity. The second section on 'green theory' explored the wide-ranging theoretical concepts available to ecocritics, from a social construction approach which claims that ideas about nature are constructed through such discourses as feminism, myth and (as Haraway terms it) 'the dualism of primatology'. Having available to it such a wide repertoire of theory, each thread of which is developing in parallel with ecocriticism, provides a stimulating – if challenging – intellectual environment for ecocriticism. In the third section contributors discussed 'green reading', showing how ecocriticism was then advancing across the literary canon.

At the outset theory was problematic for ecocritics. Greg Garrard discusses how ecocritics have been anxious to escape from the constraints of 'high theory' associated with 'impenetrable French philosophers' such as Jacques Lacan and Julia Kristeva, but notes that they have since embraced concepts developed by Martin Heidegger and

Raymond Williams and more recently by Bruno Latour and Donna Haraway (Garrard 2014: 9). The European approaches to ecocritical theory discussed by Goodbody and Rigby (2011) show that, far from being averse to theory, ecocritics have deployed an ever-widening body of knowledge and theorised approaches in their environmental reading of the humanities. Having such a wide range of theory is particularly necessary as ecocriticism continues to extend its scope across the humanities.

Karla Armbruster and Kathleen Wallace continued this advance of ecocriticism in their edited volume *Beyond Nature Writing: Expanding the Boundaries of Ecocriticism* (2001). A section of their book illustrated the scope for expanding ecocriticism across genres and disciplines with essays on science fiction, on film and on theatre. Literary examples showed the scope for re-examining criticism of texts that have informed Western attitudes to nature and looking again at writing from the nineteenth and twentieth centuries. Other authors have discussed the assumptions implicit in the green tradition.

For example Marris (2011) shows that wilderness is a constructed concept that has been achieved by erasing the habitat-modifying influence of traditional societies, both in the North American West and in supposedly primeval forests, such as Białowieża on the borders of Poland and Belarus. In the same way, Barney Nelson (2000) has shown how, in constructing their idea of wilderness, writers like John Muir have favoured wild animals over their domestic relatives. Nelson contrasts Muir's writing with that of Mary Austin (1868–1934) who wrote from first-hand experience of domesticated sheep. It is the task of ecocritics to explore the part that such texts have played in forming our view of the environment and in particular to uncover any dissonance between these views and the way we must now see the world if we are to avoid catastrophe. Deploying new theoretical approaches to ecocriticism is a powerful way to disrupt our assumptions about the world about us.

Such an eclectic approach to theory by ecocritics shows the scope for concepts to be enriched as they travel from one discipline to another. Of particular interest is the investigation by biologists into how the semiotics developed by Charles Saunders Peirce can be applied to living organisms, for example in *Towards a Semiotic Biology: Life Is the Action of Signs* by Claus Emmeche and Kalevi Kull (2011). Ecocritics have shown a particular interest in the development of semiotic biology (now contracted to 'biosemiotics') as evidenced by the inclusion of an essay on 'biosemiotic ecocriticism' by Timo Maran in the *Oxford Handbook of Ecocriticism* (Garrard 2014: 260–75). While biosemiotics is the study of signs between organisms, its extension back into culture has been called 'ecosemiotics' (Kull 2003: 54). Researchers at Tartu and Copenhagen Universities have shown how

> The notion of the semiosphere [can be seen as] as a larger 'bubble of meaning', encompassing multiple Umwelts. This made possible the examination of the relation between Umwelts and human culture, through Maran's model of the nature-text, which encompasses a landscape of four contexts: Environment, Text-Sign, Author, Reader. When intertwined with a physical region and a cultural community of place, a nature-text becomes an ecosemiosphere. (Siewers 2014: 8–9)

In *Re-imagining Nature: Environmental Humanities and Ecosemiotics* examples of such cultural landscapes include 'Estonian wooded meadows, constituted by interactions of village communities and physical environments across centuries, and the imaginary "Otherworld" or "green world" of Celtic and English landscape traditions in the British Isles'. Such an emphasis on meaningfulness is seen as redressing 'too dogmatic an emphasis on random struggle in approaches to nature, based on Darwinist or Neo-Darwinist science' (Siewers 2014: 9).

Fiona Becket and Terry Gifford, editors of *Culture, Creativity and Environment: New Environmentalist Criticism* (2007), include chapters on theatre, visual art and postcolonialism. They also introduce the distinctive approach in German animal stories and the challenge to our thinking from environmental philosophy. Graham Huggan and Helen Tiffin (2010) have taken ecocriticism into the study of postcolonial literature. Greta Gaard and Patrick Murphy have brought together readings from a feminist viewpoint in *Ecofeminist Literary Criticism* (Gaard and Murphy 1998). In broadening the literature covered, Gillian Rudd (2007) has shown how ecocriticism can be applied to late medieval English literature, and Helen Price (2013) has extended ecocritical enquiry back to Anglo-Saxon poetry. In addition to edited collections of essays that include consideration of cross-genre works, some book editors have explored ecocriticism within a single genre. As ecocriticism extends across literary studies, so it has also proved an effective approach to other genres in the wider humanities.

Ecocriticism is well established in film and theatre studies, particularly in North America, as exemplified by Paula Willoquet-Maricondi in *Framing the World: Explorations in Ecocriticism and Film* (2010). Gabriella Giannachi and Nigel Stewart in *Performing Nature: Explorations in Ecology and the Arts* (2005) bring together a wide range of essays on performance that cover similar ground to ecocriticism, but have little reference to the ecocritical canon. In contrast Wendy Arons and Theresa J. May's *Readings in Performance and Ecology* 'builds on critical and theoretical intersections between literary ecocriticism and theatre/performance studies that have been slowly but increasingly articulated over the past two decades' to explore how performance can help us to understand our relationship with the natural world (Arons and May 2012: 3). The power of environmental discourse since 1992 has penetrated each genre of the arts separately, as well as being augmented by cross-fertilisation from ideas developed in literary studies. Such is its reach across genres that some critics have adopted the term 'environmental humanities' to denote a field of study that covers the whole of both environmental discourse and humanities.

A practical example of environmental humanities is in Maja and Reuben Fowkes's *River Ecologies: Contemporary Art and Environmental Humanities on the Danube* (2015). This collection of essays came from the 'River School' project that took place mostly along the Danube, but also draws on a symposium at the Whitechapel Gallery in London on 'Navigating Ecological Times' and on various other exhibitions, excursions and study days. The Danube is rich in cultural associations and flows through some of the most civilised parts of Europe and, in its great delta wilderness, some of the wildest. The essays cover rewilding mentalities,[4] avian ethnographies, environmental histories and our responsibility for the biosphere. Interventions and excursions exposed members of the River School to the social and cultural aspects, as well as to environmental and climate change issues.

For Astrid Bracke, contemporary ecocriticism, although thriving, is still 'concerned with a limited set of nature-oriented or environmentally inflected texts [...] the cultural ubiquity of environmental issues is still not reflected in its relatively narrow canon' (Bracke 2014: 423). There is a risk that ecocriticism will not keep abreast of the full range of issues in environmentalist discourse, or with the development of thinking on environmental justice. The Intergovernmental Panel on Climate Change (as its name implies) produces periodic assessments of the pace and direction of climate change and the Fifth Assessment in 2013 confirmed the accelerating pace of such change.[5] The conclusion that humans are making profound and quite probably irreversible changes on the environment is now inescapable, with each assessment revising forecasts about climate change towards the upper range of previous forecasts. In 2000 P.J. Crutzen and E.F. Stoermer proposed that this change should be recognised as a new geological epoch, the Anthropocene (Crutzen and Stoermer 2000: 17–18). In 'The Anthropocene: an Epoch of Our Making', James Syvitski summarises the accumulating evidence for the Anthropocene to be formally adopted by geologists (Syvitski 2012: 12–15).

Defining a new geological epoch is a major event that would need to be ratified by the International Union of Geological Sciences. As presently defined, we are in the 'Holocene (Recent Whole) Epoch' that began 11,650 years BP with the start of the present post-glacial epoch. The case for adopting the term Anthropocene is being taken forward by scientists concerned that 'the magnitude, variety and longevity of human induced changes, including land surface transformation and changing the composition of the atmosphere' is such that a new epoch should be designated with the start date still to be determined (Lewis and Maslin 2015: 171–80). Candidate dates include the start of the industrial revolution or various dates in the twentieth century when human impact on the environment became marked. Although geologists have still to reach a conclusion, the concept of the Anthropocene has been adopted by ecocritics and in the environmental humanities. Timothy Clark considers how this concept can be applied to ecocriticism:

> Its force is mainly as a loose, shorthand term for all the new contexts and demands – cultural, ethical, aesthetic, philosophical and political – of environmental issues that are truly planetary in scale, notably climate change, ocean acidification, effects of overpopulation, deforestation, soil-erosion, overfishing and the general and accelerating degradation of eco-systems. (Clark 2015: 2)

In *Art in the Anthropocene*, Davis and Turpin bring together 'a multitude of disciplinary conversations concerned with art and aesthetics that are emerging around the Anthropocene thesis'. For these writers, 'becoming-geological undoes aesthetic sensitivities and ungrounds political commitments' (Davis and Turpin 2015: 3). Even before the Anthropocene has been formally ratified, it has proved to be a useful concept for ecocritics. It challenges our views about aesthetics and about the type of works that we should consider. Expansion across genres and the ever wider body of theory informing ecocriticism have demonstrated the versatility and relevance of this critical approach in questioning our cultural and material experience.

This present book follows the belief that ecocriticism has relevance across disciplines. The chapters that follow include those from contributors whose interest is in the visual arts or performance, as well as others from writers whose collaboration with other genres and disciplines has widened their perspectives, and those who take ecocriticism into the fields of environmental justice and ecological sustainability. Our aim has been to explore both praxis and criticism while drawing on the growing literature on ecocritical and environmental humanities theory.

Louise Squire, in Chapter 2, introduces the idea that the human denial of death has in part contributed to our approach to environmental crisis. She considers the possibilities for literary critique to account for these difficulties, focusing on contemporary environmental crisis fiction. The novels discussed are the three books of Margaret Atwood's MaddAddam trilogy (2003, 2009, 2013), Amitav Ghosh's *The Hungry Tide* (2004) and Jeanette Winterson's *The Stone Gods* (2007). Each of these books explores the notion of death-facing as an ecological imperative. She reads this fiction as being in dialogue with the question of today's environmental challenges. Squire argues that ecocriticism is a developing field in that the crisis and its literatures are still unfolding, so attention must continue to be directed at reformulating thought in the (also) still unfolding aftermath of high theory.

The next three chapters are all concerned with collaboration in the creative process. Philip Gross, in Chapter 3, explains how he started to explore the creative process at the same time as the terms 'ecocriticism' and 'ecopoetic' made an appearance. Although he writes about the natural world, he is wary of being seen as an eco-poet, on the grounds that it does not feel like his own experience of the writing process and that it implies a specific moral-political stance. In this chapter Gross looks at several collaborative projects that he has been drawn to, sensing that they too hold clues to this process, not just in the subject matter but in the process itself. In one such collaboration he joined a multidisciplinary group that brought him into contact with people with a professional interest in ecology and the social sciences as well as with a visual artist who bases her work on walking. Subsequently he walked together with the same artist at the Newport Wetlands. He uses examples of his own poetry to explore how the creative process works for him.

In Chapter 4 poet Harriet Tarlo and artist Judith Tucker discuss their collaboration over several years on a number of place-based projects. This dialogue between them was born of close observation of each other's practice, and of their shared exploration of the similarities and differences between producing texts and producing images, both in and out of place. Examples of this collaboration show Tarlo's radical landscape poems side by side with Tucker's landscape drawings. One such place is an abandoned mill-owner's garden, near their homes in the South Pennine landscape, where the house and mill have long been submerged in a reservoir. Further away from this familiar landscape, Tarlo and Tucker explored unfamiliar landscapes on the Lincolnshire estuarial coast, where they contributed to the multidisciplinary *Excavations and Estuaries* project. Within this chapter ecocritical ideas are integrated with the discussion of how this creative partnership has led to a body of work and the subsequent exhibitions and readings in which it has been taken to the public.

Artist Patti Lean, in Chapter 5, gives an account of a walking and camping tour of Iceland in the company of two other artists. Here the collaboration was in sharing the experience of close contact with the sublime landscape of the island, with each artist responding in their own way to produce art work. Lean's art practice focused on this compelling landscape, but all three artists also engaged with the rich Icelandic culture and the chapter includes discussion of writer Halldór Laxness, film maker Benedikt Erlingsson and artist Louisa Matthíasdóttir. The challenge for Lean is to reconcile her training in Art History and the narrative of the sublime with the environmental concerns that she met during this tour, for example the failure of breeding for arctic terns as climate change has left too little food in the surrounding sea.

Eve Ropek in Chapter 6 claims that, to approach any art work ecocritically, it is necessary to bring to it some knowledge of current scientific thought regarding the biosphere. Indeed the breadth and complexity of the ideas and issues of humans' place within the Earth's ecosystems encourage an interdisciplinary approach; to join together methods and insights in order to inform the next steps at what is seen to be a crucial global point is an urgent and daunting task. Artists working today are very well aware of the narrative of change and of environmental issues. Ropek considers how this interdisciplinary approach can be applied to some art works by British artists Heather Ackroyd and Dan Harvey, who practise in partnership as Ackroyd & Harvey. The examples she discusses include such artefacts as: photographs in which the negative image is projected on to grass as it grows, so that the resulting portrait is developed on the grass itself; an artificial diamond made from a polar bear bone; and an installation based on the skeleton of a minke whale. These artists create works that are directly related to climate change and its impact on the biosphere.

Peter Barry in 'The word among stones', Chapter 7, explores poems about stones, on stones and stones which are the poem. He shows how our ancestors have had a special regard for stones particularly those that seemed out of place, for example where a glacier has carried an erratic to another place. The Ringing Stone on Tiree is one such erratic that has numerous cup marks on its surface from Neolithic times. He considers how poems have been placed in the environment on trails and paths, sometimes with a didactic purpose as part of an environmentalist interpretive scheme. Some of these poems are printed on stone rather as they would be on the page, but others have taken advantage of the expressive potential of the stones themselves, and of letter carvers who blend this with their own artistic heritage. It is the examples where collaboration between carver and poet can make best use of the space between the words that come closest to Barry's interest in avant-garde or neomodernist poetry (especially 'concrete' and 'visual' poetries). Barry also considers poems in urban settings where the words have been incised on pavements, as by Alyson Hallett in Bath, and for the same artist where the stone poem has been carried across the world, becoming an erratic through human agency.

Photographer John Darwell, in Chapter 8, reminds us that big environmental issues and *Homo sapiens's* problematic response to them are also evident in the mundane experience of our day-to-day environment. Darwell, who until fairly recently had based his photographic practice on postindustrial landscapes of Sheffield and Manchester, and the area around Chernobyl, has now turned his attention to the 'edgeland' of his twice daily dog walks. This immersion in the landscape throws up new subjects for his work. One aspect that stands out is the phenomenon of discarded dog-shit bags. Dog owners have taken the trouble to clean up after their pets, but then discard the bags by hanging them in trees or just throwing them away. Bringing photographic aesthetics to what is a disturbing subject has allowed him to develop a typology of this practice. While we may prefer to look away, these images do pose big questions for environmentalists. How can we solve the big issues of climate change and loss of biodiversity, if we can't even carry through to its conclusion this modest attempt not to despoil the environment?

In Chapter 9 Clive Cazeaux argues that eco-art poses a problem to classification because its two terms have such a broad meaning: after conceptual art, there are no restrictions on the material form art can take, and ecology covers notions of environment, nature, interactions with nature, interconnection and a fundamental, ontological condition of belonging. He considers recent attempts to classify the field, and suggests that, while they can be helpful, the full force of the problem of categorisation is better addressed by turning to the position given to aesthetics by phenomenology. This takes categorisation down to the level of how categories can be applied to experience when conventional, subject–object frameworks have been suspended. Although this leaves the classification of eco-art open, it nevertheless shows that the openness is a result of the complexities of our aesthetic rootedness in the world, where 'aesthetic' is understood in sensory, causal and metaphorical terms.

Wildlife art does not receive the critical attention that it deserves. In Chapter 10, William Welstead considers how the images made after close observation in the field incorporate the signs and visual clues that enable us to identify the species, have some idea of what the individuals are doing and how they relate to the wider environment. These are all important factors in building an informed view of the non-human world and establishing how we feel about it. Wildlife artists tread a difficult path between serving science and catering for the affective response of viewers and between the representational and the abstract depiction of their subject matter. Welstead suggests that the way we recognise wild-life by its overall look or 'jizz' means that drawings and paintings can capture in a few lines and shapes the essence of the creature. This eco-nomical application of lines and colour therefore allows for at least some level of abstraction. The subject would merit further attention from ecocritics.

Our experience of the environment relies on all the senses. There is a growing interest among musicologists across a wide variety of music genres in the way that music engages with the natural world. Aaron Allen in Chapter 11 introduces us to the relatively new field of ecomu-sicology. He argues that, for musicology, the genre or idea of the sym-phony is laden with prestige; for ecocriticism, the pastoral has similar stature and is a genre or mode central to the discipline. In the concise juxtaposition of these two terms, Allen illustrates ecomusicology, which connects ecocritical and musicological scholarship, and further outlines a brief critical history of selected symphonies in relation to the pastoral. He makes the case that symphonies – ostensibly a textless genre of music conceived as abstract – can relate ideas about nature. Such connections between disciplines, approaches and materials contribute to the larger effort in the environmental (post)humanities to break down humans' problematic and self-destructive nature-culture binary.

Mike Pearson in Chapter 12 takes us to Antarctica. This continent is a vital record of past climate patterns and holds our future in the fate of its covering of ice. Pearson considers how international treaties have imposed strict environmental controls on what is permissible on the continent, and its unique status as an area where military activity is banned. These controls cover the scientists who are stationed there and the relatively small number of visitors who will visit from cruise ships. He notes that science holds an unchallenged hegemonic position and that the Treaty makes no acknowledgement of the arts and that the advent of tourism is unforeseen. In this context, he considers how more recent programmes have aimed to promote understanding and apprecia-tion of the values of Antarctica through the contribution of writers, artists and musicians. He considers how such initiatives as the Antarc-tica Pavilion at the 56th Venice Art Biennale have challenged the scientific domination of the continent by claiming Antarctica as a cultural space.

One of the most ubiquitous features of the official countryside is the proliferation of interpretation boards that inform and enhance our experience of the natural world. Writers, artists, performers and story tellers will often play an active role in the interpretation process. The products of heritage interpretation can be considered as cultural objects in their own right. In Chapter 13 William Welstead makes the case for an ecocritical eye to be turned towards the practice and products of heritage interpretation, which is big business in which its practitioners have their own professional organisation. This chapter looks at how interpretation practice constructs a way of looking at the natural world, which will inform those coming to the usual creative works that are already within the domain studied by ecocriticism. The narratives of interpretation are influenced by inputs from the creative arts, but they would merit further work to establish whether this is a two-way process in which the works studied by ecocritics have themselves been influenced by interpretation narratives.

At about the same time as the literary establishment was getting very concerned about how environmental issues, such as climate change, biodiversity loss and sustainability were leading to the formal emergence of ecocriticism within the academy, wind turbines started to be seen in the countryside. Jean Welstead in Chapter 14 explores how photomontage has been used during the planning process to address concerns about the aesthetic appearance and community acceptance of turbines and wind farms. As this practice has developed from simple Letraset techniques superimposed on photographs to computer-generated images, photomontage has started to converge on to ground that is the concern of ecocritics. Welstead discusses how the cognitive nature of the official landscape-character assessment approach is often in contrast to the perceptions of those who live and work in the area, and other 'communities of interest', for example, those who visit for recreation or creative practice. Both these groups, by the very nature of their activities, are likely to experience a more immersed and engaged relationship with the landscape.

Collectively, these chapters, with their considerable biodiversity, show how an ever-widening creative practice, together with rapidly advancing knowledge about ecology, both creates problems for ecocritics and allows for new insights from outside the traditional domain of the environmental humanities. Science and art can and should work together and ecocriticism is well placed to mediate a common understanding between these two cultures.

Notes

1 UNEP, Biodiversity Glossary, www.unep.org/tunza/youth/Events/Biodiversity Glossary/tabid/3937/language/en-US/Default.aspx accessed 6 December 2015.
2 www.un.org/geninfo/bp/enviro.html accessed 9 November 2015.
3 www.asle.org/discover-asle/vision-history accessed 9 November 2015.
4 Rewilding initiatives aim to restore to nature land that has been heavily managed by humans. It takes many forms: for a discussion of different approaches see Branson (2009).
5 www.ipcc.ch/report/ar5/wg1 accessed 14 November 2015.

References

Armbruster, Karla and Kathleen R. Wallace (eds) (2001) *Beyond Nature Writing: Expanding the Boundaries of Ecocriticism*. Charlottesville: University Press of Virginia.

Arons, Wendy and Theresa J. May (2012) *Readings in Performance and Ecology*. New York: Palgrave Macmillan.

Becket, Fiona and Terry Gifford (2007) *Culture, Creativity and Environment: New Environmentalist Criticism*. Amsterdam and New York: Rodopi.

Bracke, Astrid (2014) 'The Contemporary English Novel and Its Challenges to Ecocriticism', in Greg Garrard (ed.), *The Oxford Handbook of Ecocriticism*. Oxford and New York: Oxford University Press, pp. 423–39.

Branson, Andrew (ed.) (2009) 'Naturalistic Grazing and Re-wilding in Britain: Perspectives from the Past and Future Direction', *British Wildlife* 20:5 (special supplement)(June).

Clark, Timothy (2015) *Ecocriticism on the Edge: The Anthropocene as a Threshold Concept*. London: Bloomsbury.

Coupe, Laurence (ed.) (2000) *The Green Studies Reader: From Romanticism to Ecocriticism*. London and New York: Routledge.

Crutzen, P.J. and E.F Stoermer (2000) 'The "Anthropocene"', *Global Change Newsletter* 41: 17–18.

Davis, Heather and Etienne Turpin (2015) *Art in the Anthropocene: Encounters among Aesthetics, Politics, Environments and Epistemiologies*. London: Open Humanities Press, freely available online at http://openhumanitiespress.org/books/art-in-the-anthropocene accessed 8 November 2015.

Emmeche, Claus and Kalevi Kull (eds) (2011) *Towards a Semiotic Biology: Life is the Action of Signs*. London: Imperial College Press.

Fowkes, Maja and Reuben (eds) (2015) *River Ecologies: Contemporary Art and Environmental Humanities on the Danube*. Budapest: Translocal Institute.

Gaard, Greta and Patrick D. Murphy (1998) *Ecofeminist Literary criticism: Theory, Interpretation, Pedagogy*. Urbana and Chicago: University of Illinois Press.

Garrard, Greg (ed.) (2012) *Teaching Ecocriticism and Green Cultural Studies*. Basingstoke: Palgrave Macmillan.

Garrard, Greg (ed.) (2014) *The Oxford Handbook of Ecocriticism*. Oxford and New York: Oxford University Press.

Giannachi, Gabriella and Nigel Stewart (eds) (2005) *Performing Nature: Explorations in Ecology and the Arts*. Bern: Peter Lang.

Glotfelty, Cheryll (2003) 'A Guided Tour of Ecocriticism, with Excursions towards Catherland', in Susan J. Rosowski (ed.), 'Willa Cather's Ecological Imagination' *Cather Studies 5*. University of Nebraska-Lincoln, www.unl.edu/cs005_glotfelty.html accessed 6 December 2015.

Goodbody, Axel and Kate Rigby (2011) *Ecocritical Theory: New European Approaches*. Charlottsville and London: Virginia University Press

Huggan, Graham and Helen Tiffin (2010) *Postcolonial Ecocriticism: Literature, Animals, Environment*. London and New York: Routledge.

Kull, Kalevi (2003) 'Thomas Sebeok: Mister (Bio)semiotics', *Cybernetics and Human Knowing* 10:1: 47–60.

Lewis, Simon L. and Mark A. Maslin (2015) 'Defining the Anthropocene', *Nature* 519 (13 March): 171–80.

Maran, Timo (2014) 'Biosemiotic Ecocriticism', in Greg Garrard (ed.), *The Oxford Handbook of Ecocriticism*. Oxford and New York: Oxford University Press, pp. 260–75.

Marris, Emma (2011) *Rambunctious Garden: Saving Nature in a Post-wild World*. New York and London: Bloomsbury.

Nelson, Barney (2000) *The Wild and the Domestic: Animal Representation, Ecocriticism, and Western American Literature*. Reno: University of Nevada Press.

Price, Helen (2013) 'Human and Non-human in Anglo-Saxon and British Post-war Poetry: Reshaping Literary Ecology', unpublished PhD thesis, University of Leeds.

Rudd, Gillian (2007) *Greenery: Ecocritical Readings of Late Medieval English Literature*. Manchester and New York: Manchester University Press.

Siewers, Alfred Kentigern (ed.) (2014) *Re-imagining Nature: Environmental Humanities and Ecosemiotics*. Lanham: Bucknell University Press.

Syvitski, James (2012) 'Anthropocene: an Epoch of Our Making', *Global Change Magazine* 78: 12–15.

Willoquet-Maricondi, Paula (ed.) (2010) *Framing the World: Explorations in Ecocriticism and Film*. Charlottesville and London: University of Virginia Press.

2

'I am not afraid to die': contemporary environmental crisis fiction and the post-theory era

Louise Squire

For an evanescent moment within the history of the Earth, *Homo sapiens* sought its own exclusion from the laws of the universe. No matter the wider cost, humanity would overcome its mortal limitations. The outcome, however, of this refusal to die – this rejection of natural laws – turns out to be death itself, since the abuses of planetary resources upon which death denial relies cause the promise of death to rebound upon humanity. Or as Claire Colebrook – discussing the Anthropocene as a 'doomsday device' – puts it, the very act of our 'intentionality' or 'mastery', in developing the technē of life enhancement, has 'the tragic quality of coming back to destroy us' (pers. com. 2013).

This view of humanity's journey to date, as underpinned by a denial of death, points to the need to repair our relations with death – an idea of some contemporary currency, as this chapter will indicate. Yet it is also just one version of events. Today's environmental crisis might be put down to any number of causes – social, political, behavioural, biological and so on. Its origins, similarly, might be relegated to the immediate or the distant past. Where did we go wrong? When we set out on the path of industrialisation? When we built the first plough? When we lit the first fire? Even this notion of 'we' is problematic since not every mode of human habitation is detrimental to the planet, while those most responsible for the crisis may not be the first to feel its effects – as recently acknowledged at the 2015 United Nations Climate Change Conference in Paris (COP 21), which culminated in the Paris Agreement.[1] One of the challenges of eliciting a contemporary response to the crisis is that of its sheer scale alongside the fact that no singular narrative can cater to its complexities. This of course has implications for ecocriticism, posing certain risks. As Timothy Clark – referring to the disparate demands of various environmental questions – remarks:

'Many of the tensions and intellectual fragilities of ecocriticism come from the drive to reconcile increasingly incompatible claims under one diagnostic framework, despite a context that must render them more and more at odds with one another' (2015: 12). Yet ecocriticism is a developing field, the crisis and its literatures still unfolding. Much attention so far has been invested in reformulating thought in the (also) still unfolding aftermath of high theory, countering such difficulties as its foregrounding of culture over nature, or its viewing of 'epistemological closure [as] [...] necessarily a form of domination' (Elliott and Attridge 2011: 2). The emergent conceptual frameworks to which Clark refers, such as new materialism in its various guises, often enact a contemporary drive against 'theory' as understood in its high form, repositioning our conceptions of ourselves, the planet and everything in between, redistributing agency in order to make ethical, epistemological and indeed narrative room for nonhuman forms of vitality and matter (Iovino and Oppermann 2014: 1–17). These new modes of thought vastly open up the field to possibility and offer new ways to reflect on the difficulties of our times. At the same time their ontological grounding can reduce the heterogeneity that poststructuralism underscores. Meanwhile, as the global community attempts to unite in addressing the environmental challenges of today's world (COP 21), what becomes plain is the stark gap between divergent discourses as differing views collide, for example, over the strength of the deal (Bawden 2016, *Independent*) and the scale of lifestyle changes needed (Nelson 2016, *Guardian*).

My broad focus in this chapter is on the possibilities for literary critique with regard to accounting for such difficulties. Focusing on contemporary environmental crisis fiction, I pursue a route that takes the text as its starting point – not in order to prioritise text over environment but to read its 'environing' (Bergthaller et al. 2014, Sörlin and Warde 2009: 23). I accordingly read this fiction as being in dialogue with the contemporary, post-theory era on the question of today's environmental challenges.[2] In recent years, a number of established contemporary writers have turned their hand to writing novels that deal with the environmental crisis – a crisis that has also been referred to as a crisis of reason (Plumwood 2002, Morton 2007: 27). Many of these novels employ the trope of *death* in dealing with this crisis. This reflects the way the notion of an environmental crisis evokes the possibility of humanity's ends. Yet death might also variously function in these novels, less ominously, as a thinking device. My specific focus in this chapter, therefore, is on the thematic use of death in a particular strand of environmental crisis fiction. This strand is one I identify as producing its own device for thinking through the challenges we face – one, furthermore, which is open-ended since it pivots on a notion of death as underlying all life. Novels such as the three books of Margaret Atwood's MaddAddam trilogy (2003, 2009, 2013), Amitav Ghosh's *The Hungry Tide* (2004), Jeanette Winterson's *The Stone Gods* (2007) and various others each explore a notion of death-facing as an ecological imperative. Taking death-denial as the root cause of environmental crisis, they consider a conscious turning towards death, depicted as the recognition and acceptance of humanity's mortal status. This theme of *ecological death-facing*, as I refer to it, thus signals a fundamental shift towards more ecological modes of being, opening up the possibilities for new narratives. As such, this fiction appears in some sense to share the contemporary quest among ecocritics to move beyond the limitations of high theory in the exploration of ecological ideas, thereby also countering a trajectory of Western thought that precedes the advent of a crisis. But, as I will illustrate, these novels also undermine death-facing in certain ways, disclosing a somewhat postmodern caution against investing absolutely in any singular idea. In this, they make room for the way discourses interweave and collide in the envisioning of ways forward, while underscoring the risks to which any given solution is subject. As such, their thematic use of ecological death-facing might be said to evoke possibilities for the ways we might go forward from here, while highlighting the difficulties faced in doing so. My aim in this chapter is to illustrate this fiction's thematic use of death and to explore its commentaries on today's challenges and on the possibilities of reading change at a time of environmental crisis.

There are of course any number of ways to think about death, a topic that carries an extensive scholarly history – not least within a philosophical domain. One way to understand the appearance of ecological death-facing as thematic device is therefore, simply, as a point of reflection that opens up to all the possibilities to which death gives rise. Reflecting on death has of course long been a means by which to consider life, hence the importance of the study of burial practices to archaeology and anthropology. As the crisis of environment materialises, undermining – it seems – all that we conceive ourselves to be, it is perhaps unsurprising that contemporary writers turn to death in reconsidering our modes of living. Yet this turn is also a feature of a specific moment: that (for us) of the contemporary. Since it moves against the death-denial of the modern West – a phenomenon widely discussed by late twentieth-century poststructuralists, historians, psychoanalysts and others – this turn towards facing death can be said, at least in part, to reflect today's shift away from related late twentieth-century preoccupations, such as with the power of language. Parallels thus become apparent between the ecological possibilities of death-facing, as explored in the narratives of this fiction, and the new conceptual forms emerging today – particularly those of the new materialisms, which in recent years have appeared across the humanities and social sciences, and contemporary philosophy's new movement referred to as speculative realism. Similarly, this fiction's refusal to relinquish the insights of poststructuralism altogether has some correspondence with the way these emergent forms move against while at times also extending prior modes of thought. This correlation opens up the possibilities for the analysis of this theme in fiction. In considering ecological death-facing, in this fiction, I therefore call upon a selection of the many ideas it explores, drawing mainly on contemporary thought but also on earlier thought at times – by no means utilising every possibility.

The central and underlying narrative emphasis in the novels I examine is the turn towards facing death as a means to elicit or open up ecological possibilities. Of the various ideas this fiction evokes, in this chapter I consider that of death's material role (discussed alongside the work of late environmental philosopher Val Plumwood (2008)); death's participation in the unfolding of temporal becoming (discussed alongside the work of contemporary speculative realist Martin Hägglund (2011)); and death as a loss to be acknowledged in the valuing of lives and the living world (discussed alongside an essay by contemporary scolar of queer, feminist and material ecology, Catriona Sandilands (2013)). Also important is the way this fiction, at times, conversely questions the very idea that death (as such) can be faced. This is reflected, for example, in a comment by the narrator, Billie, in Winterson's *The Stone Gods*. At the point when she realises the imminence of her own death, she states: 'The mind will not believe in death, perhaps because, as far as the mind is concerned, death never happens' (97). This highlights the problem of facing death in actuality, in that death is ungraspable by the living mind. It also revisits the more formal difficulty that arises in the attempt to represent death in written form. The work of Jacques Derrida (as I have identified elsewhere)[3] is helpful for considering this fiction's grappling with the conceptual difficulties of death-facing, since it seems at times to counter poststructuralism precisely at the point of its refusal of an absolute referent.[4] As such, contemporary thought might be described as evoking 'a turning to the object' (Morton 2013: 22, 174) – a turn which, like death, performs an exit from the bounds of a textual domain. In discussing the difficulties of death-facing I call, albeit lightly, on Derrida's late work on death in *Aporias* (1993), in which he interrogates Heidegger's notion of death as the 'possibility of impossibility' (36). Identifying death as an aporia, he insists on the impossibility of explaining death per se, despite our endless accounts of it. He thereby points to the way our stories are always stories among stories. This matter appears in all the novels I discuss, as in attempting to designate death they each come into eventual narrative collision with their own discursive form. Through identifying and exploring these differing facets in these novels, it becomes apparent that their uses of death are far subtler and more nuanced than it might at first seem.

In considering death's thematic use in environmental crisis fiction, one might initially turn one's attention to apocalypse, the use of which, in general terms, has become widespread in popular discourses of environment. Such fetishising of doom and disaster in contemporary environmental crisis fiction and other media has, however, been viewed as unhelpful (Dobson 2007: 103, Morton 2007: 185, Squire 2012: 212). Even if we might potentially be rendering the planet inhospitable to us, such focus on our inevitable ends seems to overwrite attention to the subtleties of the problem and of the possibilities for change. There is also the matter that 'the end of the world', as Timothy Morton suggests, has already occurred (2013: 99) – if by 'the world' we mean some discrete phenomenon that once existed in state of pristine completeness, untrammelled by human action. Of course, death and destruction are features of all life, not just human life. Our problem is not that we are distinct from nature but that in thinking ourselves so we have facilitated our own journey to dominant species, destroying nonhuman lives and habitats in the pursuit of our own interests. The loss of the pristine world is therefore not so much a loss we fear, since it has already occurred, as a loss we (or some of us) regret. These observations seem to undermine the logic of apocalypse with regard to the contemporary crisis of environment. They therefore also, potentially, problematise readings of environmental crisis fiction and other media as apocalyptic or as holding the Sword of Damocles over us with the threat of the end of our species should we fail to change our ways.

Of the novels that employ ecological death-facing as a thematic device, some, such as the three books of Atwood's trilogy, nonetheless do make certain use of environmental apocalypse, linking the ends of humanity, or of the Earth that sustains us, to our environmentally destructive behaviours. Yet they also tend to play off this apocalyptic trope, employing it as a device by which to introduce layers of ambiguity. In the MaddAddam trilogy, the question of perspective is raised in the entwining of two different narratives around the trilogy's one apocalyptic event. The Gods' Gardeners – the eco-cult central to *The Year of The Flood* (book two) – predict the end of the world in the form of a waterless flood, understood as God's just punishment upon a humanity that has failed to change its ways. But parallel to this, scientist Crake in *Oryx and Crake* (book one) makes the decision to eliminate all humans as fatally flawed, which he achieves by distributing a lethal virus, replacing them with his geo-engineered eco-hominids, the Crakers. Since the first two novels are simultaneal, working their narratives around the single event of Crake's act of destruction, this act when it occurs (in book one) appears to the Gardeners (in book two) as the act of God they had predicted. This has the effect of emphasising, on the Gardeners' part, the limitations of perception and the extension of belief beyond the surface of events. This phenomenon is relatable to death through Derrida's notion of *trespass* discussed in *Aporias*, by which he means the extension of our explanations of death beyond that which is knowable, or beyond a border that is not really there (1997: 43). The encounter with the opacity of the singular event (death) is accordingly dispersed into discourse in the process of meaning-making, out of which cultural form arises.[5] This illustrates death-facing as a turn towards opacity and thus towards the unrepresentable, drawing attention to the plurality of life and living. Yet this opacity is also that which forms the question mark out of which new forms of theorising arise, seen for example in Morton's turning to the object. The implication of this, for ecocritique, lies in the possibilities for investigating the complex nuances to which this bifurcation gives rise. Thus, while the Gardeners point to notions of the ecological through their brand of Epicurean, close-to-the-land living, which retains a degree of narrative approval throughout the trilogy, the validity of their subject mode is also undermined, appearing as discursive, partial and reliant on the recognition of its contingency within the world of the present.

If apocalypse is a feature of some environmental crisis fiction, the thematic use of *death* also infiltrates the narratives of this fiction where the apocalyptic trope is entirely absent, as well as performing alternative roles within an apocalyptic frame. This is subtle at times. For example, Maggie Gee's *The Ice People* (1998) speaks little of death, since the novel is about living on in a climate-changed world. Even so, first-person narrator Saul, whose story the novel follows, opens the narrative by looking back on his story from the standpoint of his old age. The very first page includes his line: 'I am not afraid to die' (13). He then philosophises briefly on death before going on to make the somewhat literary point that his life will live on, in any case, in the story he is about to tell.

This 'I am not afraid to die' rings out as a sentiment variously reiterated across the strand of fiction to which I refer. It is often, although not always, depicted in terms of death's material role. In Atwood's trilogy, while the Gardeners invest in the belief of themselves as survivors of a broadly Judaeo-Christian apocalypse, they also promote the idea that humans must learn to accept our place in the natural scheme of things, recognising the material substance of our physical bodies as nutrient returnable to the soil. The sermons of head gardener, Adam One, constantly remind the Gardeners that they play a role in nature's wider cycles of life and death, through such phrases as: 'Shall we not repay the gift of Life by regifting ourselves to Life when the time comes?' (*The Year of the Flood*, p. 193). A similar idea is seen in Winterson's *The Stone Gods* through the reflections of Spike, a female android whose main function is to reflect upon the human condition. In the first of the novel's three interlinking stories – in which three iterations of Spike and her queer lover Billie appear – narrator Billie (who is female and human) meets Spike at the point when Spike is due to be dismantled. As it turns out, Billie helps Spike to escape; but prior to this she asks her how she feels about being dismantled, remarking: 'It's a kind of death, isn't it?' Spike responds saying: 'I think of it as recycling, which is what Nature does all the time. The natural world is abundant and extravagant, but nothing is wasted. The only waste in the Cosmos comes from human beings' (37). Here, Spike dismisses the thought of her own ends as nothing more than a return to cosmos, a closure of one phase and the start of another. Death is not personal, for Spike, nor is it something to fear. Since Spike is an android, her aligning of material recycling with the processes of biological death is also illustrative of the novel's negation of dualistic modes of thought – a negation further accentuated when Spike develops a beating heart. Spike's quest to understand the human condition by experiencing love closes the gap between human and android. Her conception of death and her experience of human love bring to mind Donna Haraway's (1991) cyborg – a conceptual figure for whom affinity is prioritised over essentialist ideas, and binaries such as the natural and the artificial are annulled. Spike also describes the universe (in the novel, but indicated to represent our own) as quantum, evoking the new materialism of Karen Barad, for whom 'matter is enfolded into itself in its ongoing materialization' (2007: 180). This relinquishing of the boundaries of the human into the nonhuman and the cosmos renders human agency partial and non-hierarchical, localising the practice of reading. As such, this novel, like others in this strand, decentres the language-base of human discursivity. Spike's view of death as a form of recycling in a quantum universe runs parallel to the Gardener's more organic conception of death. In both cases, the notion of the human as discrete object is released into one of wider participation in the material becoming of life and the cosmos.

Hence, somewhat differently but with clear correspondences, the three books of Atwood's trilogy and Winterson's *The Stone Gods* each propose a notion of death-facing that affirms its material role.

This very materialist conception of death has clear ecological implications, since it deals with humans in terms of our bodies as natural substance, as participating in wider cycles of life and death. One is reminded of Plumwood's (2008) 'food-based approach to death' – the topic of an article in which she reflects on her experience of being 'seized as prey by a crocodile'. This experience leads her to consider her valuing of her own life, and thus to question her own incredulity at the idea of relinquishing her life to become crocodile food. Accordingly, she calls for a 'reconception of death' that might 'honour the dissolution of the human into the more-than-human flux' (329–30). The implications are striking if one considers the human practice of burial as going far back into history. The very inception of the need to perform acts of burial signals the emergence of the theorising of death, arising in a negotiation of the (envisaged) borders between the living human subject and the nonhuman world. Our contemporary sense of having distinguished ourselves from nature is thus by no means recent, even if it has been amplified by Cartesian and subsequent ideologies. It is nonetheless worth noting a trend that has emerged more recently that favours natural burials. These are burials that facilitate the decomposition of the body into the soil in order to release nutrients – often for a complementary tree. A recent study of this phenomenon has identified a common motive in this choice of burial to be the desire to 'give something back' (Davies and Rumble 2012: 61). This signals a shift towards a conception of the human body as a physical link in the food chain, an idea Plumwood remarks on as being intolerable to the individualised modern liberal subject (2008: 324). In evoking these various ideas from the domains of contemporary philosophical and popular thought, ecological death-facing can therefore be said to facilitate the exploration of materialist notions of the human subject, where this subject is regarded as only notionally distinct from other material forms. In this sense, one of its thematic roles is to undermine the values of the modern liberal subject, pointing to a material levelling that forms one facet of the contemporary extension of concern beyond the immediate domain of the human.

For all its ecological merits, however, this materialist conception of death-facing can run into difficulties. At a base-line level – that is, with no recourse to any form of exceptionalism – life (as that which death concludes) is not just the material body but is also, in itself, a value. The vast majority of living beings, human and nonhuman, hold on to and fight for life, life being perhaps the ultimate possession on both instinctive and aesthetic grounds. The significance of this is that it reframes the difficulty to which death-facing is a response in the first place, reconfiguring death-denial and its associated behaviours as natural or instinctive, therefore undermining our conception of ourselves as having deviated from nature. Hannes Bergthaller (2010) reads the first two books of Atwood's trilogy in such a way. Drawing attention to Crake's 'terrifying perspicacity' (in viewing humanity as irretrievably flawed), Bergthaller discusses our destructive behaviours as already symptomatic *of* our naturalness, thereby countering the oft-held ecocritical view that literature – like death-facing – helps us engage *with* the natural world (735). As such, the envisioned shift towards an acceptance of one's mortal state in recognition of wider planetary needs, as seen in the thematic use of ecological death-facing in this strand of fiction, now appears as a rejection of unmoderated behaviours. Death-facing understood this way is ecological where it introduces, rather than abandoning, a transcendent mode – as suggested in Bergthaller's eponymous 'housebreaking the human animal'.

This possibility for a reversal is perhaps the most fascinating feature of ecological death-facing with regard to its thematic use in contemporary fiction. Underlying this reversal is a pivotal turning of two faces of 'death': the material and the discursive. Death is material in the sense that everyone and everything inevitably dies – a matter concealed from everyday life in the course of modernity (Ariès 1974). Material death-facing thus brings death out of concealment and back into view, repositioning its corporeal function as participatory in the wider world – a world in which matter comes to 'matter' (Barad 2007). Death is discursive in the sense I have derived from Derrida, who insists that our explanations of death are always to some extent 'contaminated' by the workings of our mind, our beliefs, our experiences and so on (1976: 158); death, in this sense, is anthropological. Thus, as ecological death-facing evokes or enacts a shift towards the material, it both counters and extends twentieth-century thought. It is here that the theme of ecological death-facing is operative, pointing to a re-engagement with our material participation in the material world while retaining an emphasis on the contingency of this turn.

As such, this fiction both responds to and questions new-materialist integrations of the discursive into the material. Barad sees 'discursive practices' as defining 'what counts as meaningful statements', thus as including but not being limited to written and spoken language (2007: 146). Similarly, Iovino and Oppermann identify 'an implicit textuality in the becoming of material formations' (2014: 6). While much of the fiction discussed here actively points to such posthumanist levelling of discourse, it nonetheless, as I next illustrate, retains a concern with the implications of text. While exploring the vital ecological ethic that arises in the recognition that human language is just one mode of meaning-making amongst many, this fiction also alludes to the risk of a collapse into the reductive where one stands and arbitrates amid these various modes. While consideration of that which exceeds humanity is an important task of the present, the question of human practice and behaviour nonetheless also remains an important site of critique – one which itself operates on many levels and at differing scales (see Clark 2015). Accordingly, observing how this fiction actively pivots between death's material and discursive modes allows one to track the way it makes visible while questioning the difficulties we currently face.

Ghosh's novel *The Hungry Tide* is noteworthy for such treatment of ecological death-facing and the difficulties it discloses. In particular it performs a close interrogation of both death's material and discursive faces. In the novel, the call for the human to face its own mortality on ecological grounds is imported by protagonist, Piya, into the Sundarbans region of West Bengal. Piya is an environmentalist of Indian heritage who travels from her US home to the Sundarbans to study the rare Irrawaddy dolphin. The region is characterised by a tidal ecology and is also home to the Bengal tiger, among other predators. The Sundarbans' human inhabitants are therefore vulnerable both to the tides and storms that encroach upon their lands, and to the tigers that prey on them at times. A key scene in the novel depicts Piya's extreme distress at the killing of a tiger, which is trapped, speared in the eye and then burned alive, having wandered into a village. Horrified at the brutality of the attack, but also concerned with the plight of tigers as an endangered species, in objecting to the killing Piya declares her own willingness to die, should such an act save the Irrawaddy dolphin. But her companion, Kanai, points out that these people have had to 'learn to take such killings in their stride' (297). Illustrated here is the incongruence of her insistence on a preparedness to face death in a region where death is already immanent in people's lives. This episode highlights the way death-facing, while signalling an emergent ecological perspective, is also itself also operative as discursive form. In pointing to the risks inherent to ecological death-facing, it highlights the way environmentalisms might so easily reconvene as neo-colonialisms (see Clark 2011: 120–2). As such, it points to the need to address environmental questions across conflicting domains, paying close attention to the differing levels on which environmental harms occur, and in which death-facing potentially operates.

Even so, the ecological aspect of death-facing retains much of its affirmative value in Ghosh's novel. The question becomes one of how to distinguish its value from its configuration as that which Morton, borrowing from Hegel, refers to as 'beautiful soul syndrome' – the 'beautiful soul' being one who, in 'washing his or her hands of the corrupt world', does not admit how 'in this very abstemiousness and distaste he or she participates in' its creation (2007: 7). While Piya embraces a discursive conception of ecological death-facing as advocate for the nonhuman, she herself is repeatedly forced to face death's material possibility within her life's temporal unfolding. She nearly drowns falling off a boat, she narrowly misses being seized by a crocodile and she fails to seek shelter in a violent storm – surviving at the cost of her guide, fisherman Fokir, who dies saving her. Hägglund, who revisits and revises Derridean thought, argues that death is inherent not only to all living beings but to life at as it unfolds on a temporal plane. Therefore, it is not, for Hägglund, that we live and then we die, but that death pervades life at every moment (2011: 115–16). From this, he extrapolates his notion of 'radical atheism', the idea that all forms of knowing – all religions; all belief systems; all discourses – are predicated on the hope not for immortality but for survival (2011: 129). This idea functions as an equaliser, undermining the advancement of any one discourse over another, locating all positions as forms of response to death's immanence. Thus, as Piya undergoes a journey that distils her death-facing sentiment to an experiential mode predicated on survival, her guide Fokir illustrates a life in which death's immanence is already given. The value of this is it brings forward the way the novel complicates easy solutions to difficulties posed. Our concern for the loss of the natural world, in this case the loss of Bengal tigers, is pitted against a parallel concern for human lives, legitimising all voices while dismissing partial or one-sided views.

So far, I have demonstrated how ecological death-facing pivots on a dual axis of material and discursive death, illustrating how this becomes a means by which to explore the challenges arising at a time of environmental crisis. Yet this may still be too simplistic a picture. How exactly does one position death-facing? As already indicated, to accept death's inevitability is one thing but to face death in actuality is quite another. Likewise, death-facing as personal journey has egalitarian connotations, yet when proclaimed to others – potentially amplifying a left politics – might equally reconvene as a new mode of power. There is also the question of our responses to the loss of another, which in ecological terms equates to the loss of the nonhuman, or that of planetary wellbeing – other human lives not excluded. Common to several novels in this strand of fiction is their depiction of environmental loss as a loss to regret.

The question of our response when faced with such loss is central to the storyline of Winterson's *The Stone Gods*. Largely pessimistic on this matter, the storyline revolves around our tendency to repeat the same mistakes, based on a flawed assumption that there will always be a way out. In the quantum universe of the novel's first story, planets are repeatedly burned out by human inhabitation. This story is set on Orbus, a planet so abused that only fifty years remains of its capacity to support human life. All attention is focused, however, not on Orbus but on the planned relocation to the pristine Planet Blue. Catriona Sandilands considers the problem of a failure to acknowledge environmental loss in terms of a failure to value. Her concern is with bourgeois and capitalist 'imperatives to forget', to move on, to transfer attention to another object (2010: 354). Using Judith Butler's conception of mourning as accepting loss that 'will change one forever' (340), she draws a comparison between environmental loss and loss through HIV, both of which involve a failure to value. Accordingly, she identifies a queer response to loss as one that refuses to forget or deny – a refusal that allows environmental loss to become grievable and therefore meaningful, keeping open the possibilities for action. In Winterson's novel, these latter two elements are played out in the love between Spike and Billie. It is Billie who repeatedly draws attention to loss, resisting the high-tech, commodity-driven world she inhabits by remaining on her farm, 'the last of its line – like an ancestor everyone forgot' (2008: 13), and by refusing to 'fix' her age, the novel's genetic means of halting death's temporal role. In refusing to forget, Billie upholds the value of a close relationship with the land and of the natural processes of decay. Meanwhile, it is Spike who, in opening up new narratives, keeps open, too, the possibilities for action, helping Billie to see loss not as something to forget, since everything 'is imprinted forever with what it once was' (105), but as an aspect of life in its quantum becoming. Thus '[t]rue stories', she tells Billie, 'are those that lie open at the border, allowing a crossing, a further frontier' (106). Death in this novel is therefore acknowledged, valuing that which has been, and which therefore remains intrinsic to possibilities going forward.

It becomes clear through these differing analyses that ecological death-facing, as thematic device, facilitates this fiction's explorations of a range of ideas as it considers the challenges of the environmental crisis. Through its reflections on death as that which is universal, inevitable and yet also unrepresentable, this fiction illustrates many facets of the challenges we face whilst demonstrating that there are no easy answers.

This unresolvability is nowhere more apparent than at their endings. For all their innovations and evocations, each of these novels in some way falls back on a self-conscious discursivity in the last instance – indicating perhaps that the environmental message they convey can have traction only in the real world, and not the pages of a book. This message, as they indicate, is itself discursive, variable, multifaceted and contingent, while that to which it points is inescapably real, but no less complex. Thus Atwood's trilogy closes with a return to the question of writing, Ghosh's novel with Piya's memorialisation of Fokir through the integration of his dolphin knowledge into her GIS system, and Winterson's with Billie's narration of her inner world beyond the point of her death, evoking a Derridean 'trespass' beyond death's material border. As such, these novels point to that which they cannot in themselves achieve: a tangible engagement with death and the natural in all its guises, while at the same time naming the human subject as both the problem and the solution.

Much ecocritical scholarship to date has been driven by a concern with the global community's failure to take sufficiently seriously the environmental challenges of today's world. As such, it has tended to home in on the question of how literary scholarship, and indeed literature, might contribute to alleviating this worrying state of affairs. This has included a range of approaches that seek to close the gap between text and world – a project that has parallels in various domains, as I hope to have illustrated. Indeed, the ecocritical concern with 'the reinstatement of the environmental or nonhuman referent' as Kate Rigby puts it (2015: 122), in disclosing some correspondences with emergent new materialist and speculative realist ideas, seems to move with the zeitgeist of the era – one which this fiction itself also contemplates. Fiction that employs a theme of death in dealing with environmental crisis might therefore be read as enacting a leverage for change or as evoking a recognition of our ultimate corporality. Yet this fiction also draws on the complexities to which death, as concept, gives rise. As such, it fluidly embraces an explorative approach with regard to who we are and who we might yet be, but maintains a firm eye on the risks of inducing such notions of being.

What, then, does this suggest about the possibilities for extending ecocriticism with regard to contemporary fiction? It would seem that this fiction itself pre-empts this question. In identifying its use of ecological death-facing as thematic device I stake no claim on the ways this fiction might be read, except to highlight its invitation to a radical openness to possibility, even as it reminds us of the dangers of reductive approaches. This fiction seems to enter into a dialogue with ecocritics in today's post-theory era. Do we still need theory? As argued by some, we should perhaps not be too hasty in disregarding it (Johns-Putra 2010, Oppermann 2011, Phillips 2003). While the issues of the day require us to extend our ethical, ontological and epistemological horizons, this fiction prompts us, too, to be mindful of our starting point as mortal beings who can always, ever, only go so far.

Acknowledgments

My grateful thanks go to Dr Adeline Johns-Putra (University of Surrey) for her helpful comments on this research at various stages of its development.

Notes

1 The Paris Agreement achieved a historic consensus on the reduction of emissions. According to Amanda Little (2015) in an article in the *New Yorker*, members of the Alliance of Small Island States, and Least Developed Nations are feeling hopeful, following the agreement (which includes the provision that developed nations should provide financial support to developing nations to a collective sum of US $1 billion per year; Clause 54; Article 4.5, UN FCCC), but uncertainties remain with regard to how funding for adaptation, for these countries, will be fulfilled and administered.

2 On this point, see Bergthaller et al., who insist on the importance, for the environmental humanities of remaining 'relentlessly and deftly historicist'. Texts, they argue, 'are historically produced and can be historically productive, too'; they both 'reiterate established protocols of environing' and 'in doing so [...] expose them to our scrutiny and make it possible for us to imagine alternative' (2014: 273).

3 See my 2012 article 'Death and the Anthropocene: Cormac McCarthy's World of Unliving', *The Oxford Literary Review* 34:2: 211–28.

4 I refer here to Derrida's *il n'y a pas de hors-texte* (there is no outside-text) (1976: 158).

5 On this point one might consider the work of Jean Baudrillard, who describes culture as built upon conceptions of death, and identifies what he refers to as a Western 'de-socialisation' from death (1993: 147).

References

Ariès, Philippe (1974) *Western Attitudes towards Death: from the Middle Ages to the Present*, trans. Patricia M. Ranum. London and Baltimore: The John Hopkins University Press.

Atwood, Margaret (2004) *Oryx and Crake*. London: Virago Press.

Atwood, Margaret (2009) *The Year of the Flood*. London: Virago Press.

Barad, Karen (2007) *Meeting the Universe Halfway: Quantum Physics and the Entanglement of Matter and Meaning*. Durham, NC: Duke University Press.

Baudrillard, Jean (1993) *Symbolic Exchange and Death*. New York: Sage.

Bawden, Tom (2016) 'COP21: Paris deal far too weak to prevent devastating climate change, academics warn'. *Independent*, 8 January. Retrieved from www.independent.co.uk/environment/climate-change/cop21-paris-deal-far-too-weak-to-prevent-devastating-climate-change-academics-warn-a6803096.html accessed 3 March 2016.

Bergthaller, Hannes (2010) 'Housebreaking the Human Animal: Humanism and the Problem of sSstainability in Margaret Atwood's *Oryx and Crake* and *The Year of the Flood*', *English Studies* 91:7: 728–43.

Bergthaller, Hannes, Rob Emmett, Adeline Johns-Putra, Agnes Kneitz, Susanna Lidström, Shane McCorristine, Isabel Pérez Ramos, Dana Phillips, Kate Rigby and Libby Robin (2014) 'Mapping Common Ground: Ecocriticism, Environmental History, and the Environmental Humanities'. *Environmental Humanities* 5: 261–76. Retrieved from www.environmentalhumanities.org accessed 25 November 2015.

Clark, Timothy (2011) *The Cambridge Introduction to Literature and the Environment*. Cambridge: Cambridge University Press.

Clark, Timothy (2015) *Ecocriticism on the Edge: The Anthropocene as a Threshold Concept*. London: Bloomsbury Academic.

Davies, Douglas and Hannah Rumble (2012) *Natural Burial: Traditional – Secular Spiritualities and Funeral Innovation*. London: Bloomsbury.

Derrida, Jacques (1976) *Of Grammatology*, trans. Gayatri Chakravorty Spivak. Baltimore: Johns Hopkins University Press.

Derrida, Jacques (1993) *Aporias*, trans. Thomas Dutoit. Redwood City: Stanford University Press.

Dobson, Andrew (2007) *Green Political Thought*. Fourth edition. London: Routledge.

Elliott, Jane and Derek Attridge (eds) (2011) *Theory after Theory*. London: Routledge.

Ghosh, Amitav (2005) *The Hungry Tide*. London: Harper Collins.

Hägglund, Martin (2011) 'Radical Atheist Materialism: a Critique of Meillassoux', in Levi Bryant et al. (eds), *The Speculative Turn*. Melbourne: re.press.

Haraway, Donna (1991) 'A Cyborg Manifesto: Science, Technology, and Socialist-Feminism in the Late Twentieth Century', in *Simians, Cyborgs and Women: The Reinvention of Nature*. New York: Routledge, pp. 149–81.

Iovino, Serenella and Serpil Opperman (eds) (2014) *Material Ecocriticism*. Bloomington: Indiana University Press.

Johns-Putra, Adeline (2010) 'Ecocriticism, Genre, and Climate Change. Reading the Utopian Vision of Kim Stanley Robinson's Science in the Capital Trilogy', *English Studies* 91:7: 744–60.

Little, Amanda (2015) 'What the Paris Agreement means for vulnerable nations'. *New Yorker*, 15 December. Retrieved from: www.newyorker.com/news/news-desk/what-the-paris-climate-agreement-means-for-vulnerable-nations accessed 12 December 2015.

Morton, Timothy (2007) *Ecology Without Nature: Rethinking Environmental Aesthetics*. London: Harvard University Press.

Morton, Timothy (2013) *Hyperobjects: Philosophy and Ecology after the End of the World*. London: University of Minnesota Press.

Nelson, Arthur (2016) 'Europe's climate change goals "need profound lifestyle changes"', *Guardian*, 15 February. Retrieved from www.theguardian.com/ environment/2016/feb/15/europe-climate-change-goals-need-profound-lifestyle-changes-european-commission accessed 2 March 2016.

Oppermann, Serpil (2011) 'Ecocriticism's Theoretical Discontents'. *Mosaic* 44:2: 153–69.

Phillips, Dana (2003) *The Truth of Ecology: Nature, Culture and Literature in America*. Oxford: Oxford University Press.

Plumwood, Val (2002) *Environmental Culture: The Ecological Crisis of Reason*. New York: Routledge.

Plumwood, Val (2008) 'Tasteless: towards a Food-based Approach to Death', *Environmental Values* 17: 323–30.

Rigby, Kate (2015) 'Ecocriticism', In Julian Wolfreys (ed.), *Introducing Criticism in the 21st Century*. Second edition. Edinburgh: Edinburgh University Press.

Rozelle, Lee (2010) 'Liminal Ecologies in Margaret Atwood's *Oryx and Crake*', *Canadian Literature* 206: 61–72.

Sandilands (Mortimer), Catriona (2010) 'Melancholy Natures, Queer Ecologies', in Catriona Mortimer-Sandilands and Bruce Erikson (eds), *Queer Ecologies: Sex, Nature, Politics, Desire*. Bloomington: Indiana University Press.

Sörlin, Sverker and Paul Warde (2009) 'Making the Environment Historical – an Introduction', in Sverker Sörlin and Paul Warde (eds), *Nature's End: History and the Environment*. London: Palgrave Macmillan.

Squire, Louise (2012) 'Death and the Anthropocene: Cormac McCarthy's world of unliving', *The Oxford Literary Review* 34:2: 211–28.

United Nations (2015) *Framework Convention for Climate Change* (FCCC), 12 December. Retrieved from unfccc.int/resource/docs/2015/cop21/eng/ l09r01.pdf accessed 14 December 2015.

Winterson, Jeanette (2008) *The Stone Gods*. London: Penguin.

3

Halfway-to-whole things: ecologies of writing and collaboration

Philip Gross

Driving over the Second Severn Crossing, some ten years ago, did something to my writing life. (With a shameless abuse of the term, you might call it a *watershed*.) What nudged that change was not so much the coming to Wales – first to take up a job, then to live – as the compelling presence of the Severn estuary itself. With its massive tidal range, the emergence and melting away of vast tracts of mud flats and stone grounds, the waterscape altering with every change of weather, wind or light, it defied my concepts of 'river' or 'sea', and indeed of 'place'. It was simply, and with enormous subtlety, itself. Nor was its meaning for me that of a national boundary. By comparison with this 'betweenland', the nation-states and complicating cultures on either side seemed arbitrary, recent. After living for a few years in the depths of the South Wales Valleys, I was drawn back to the edges, facing out across that potent space-between.

Writing poems informed that choice. It was only on reading through my working notebooks for the first two years in Wales that I saw on the page what my mind had not yet registered – that the writing itself kept looking away from the Valleys, back towards the estuary. Though a handful of poems in the previous book, *The Egg of Zero* (2006) had hinted at that direction, it was in *The Water Table* (2009) that a book-length meditation-cum-fantasia on the estuarine landscape took shape. That book was widely received in ecocritical terms, leaving me with a certain unease. Was I an eco-poet? An environmentalist? Really? That unease increased when subsequent collections, *Deep Field* (2011) and *Later* (2013), were received in terms of their biographical content (my father's old age, dying, language loss). For all their apparent change of subject, these successive books seemed all of a piece to me … not just in the pervasive imagery of water, water-margins or migrating wildfowl but at some deeper level. Might ecological thinking be a fruitful way to make sense of what was emerging through this poetry, in a way that does not necessarily depend on being *about* ecological issues in themselves?

On the way to an answer, I will look at several collaborative projects I have been drawn to, sensing that they too hold clues – again, not just in the subject matter but in the process itself. If that is so, then the tools of ecology, its understandings of interdependent living processes in a system, might make a contribution to our knowledge of Creative Writing, that practice-led discipline that stands alongside literary study in the university, familially linked to it, but distinct. If I do this through consideration of my own work, this is in the spirit of the sceptical reflectiveness Creative Writing advocates (Gross 2015a). For a writer to say 'What I meant to say was …' is of passing interest; what the writing itself seems to have been doing – what we can catch it *up to* – is the point.

Crossing the water

Indefinite grounds:

constant inconstancy.
Birds appear, condensing

from the sky where they had been

and not been, incipient, un-
formed, latent, like silt,

say, in this ever-flexing water.

Indefinable grounds:

don't try to set foot,
not even if some craft

could steady in these mud-thick shallows

(almost ground) by ground
almost as loose as water. Don't

count on your fine distinctions then.

(Gross 2009: 47)

If this is ecological writing, there is an irony in it from the start. The ambiguous (and ambiguously named) 'grounds' featured in *The Water Table* are a place where I, the observer, cannot be. The only reason I can get this perspective on it at all is that I am driving in a petrol-powered car across a tremendous (and, I have to say, beautiful) construction of concrete and steel. In ecocritical terms this is a compromised perspective. At the same time, what that up-in-the-sky perspective gives me is, incidentally, a bird's-eye view – a well-worn phrase that has its own life for me with associations of migration and a radical defocusing of human boundaries.

So far, so paradoxical ... since books acquire their own life in the world, these were paradoxes I was obliged to explore. After the publication of *The Water Table*, what would I say about the Severn Barrage plan? Would I oppose it, for the sake of those birds and their endangered wetlands? Would I endorse it as a massive renewable energy source? Or would I stand up and say 'Sorry, you're asking the wrong poet. Don't assume I am an environmentalist, just because I write about ... well, the environment.'

The terms 'eco-poetics' or 'ecocriticism', emerging into the critical domain as they did in a time when I began thinking about writing, never felt to me like a description of my writing process. It is hard to find a definition of ecocriticism that does not declare itself fuelled by a moral-political stance. I might even share such a stance, but the notion of writing poetry that is defined either by its moral or political designs on the reader (like, say, Christian poetry) or by its subject matter (poems about sport) felt alien to the ways that, for me, poems came about. The poems in *The Water Table* seemed to be investigating something else.

> A body of water: water's body
>
> that seems to have a mind (and
> change it: isn't that what makes
>
> a *mind*, its changing?) not much
> prone to thinking – rather, thoughts
>
> curl through it, salt or fresh, or hang
>
> between states; sometimes gloss
> the surface with their oil-illuminations.
>
> (10)

Such poems gives attention to the water, mainly to find their own reflection given back, with added questions about just how the observing self, or any self, can be defined. Sometimes it is hard to tell whether it is the water or the watcher on its banks that is being described. If the test is that of Deep Ecology – whether this writing speaks for nature *in itself* – this writing fails it, unapologetically.

> Only catchment, maybe, is a sort
> of *self*, a notional line
> within which nothing is alien to a river:
> runoffs and bosky rivulets, storm drains
> and spills, precipitation filtered though
>
> our million bodies. And the mouth
> debouches – all our secrets …

(27)

Reflections, refractions, impurities that float down on its surface: that is how water appears in *The Water Table*, as much as a carrier for what surrounds it or dissolves or floats in it as a thing in itself.

Not surprising, then, that the estuary began to behave like the sentient ocean in *Solaris* which gives back to its viewers images from their own concerns and memories. In my case it began to reflect the deepening old age and aphasia of my father. This seamlessly became the matter of the next collection, *Deep Field*, whose central sequence 'Something Like The Sea' revolves around the question of what *self* might mean as we lose memory and language.

> ### John, you are the sea
>
> I stare into, until my eyes maze, flicker-bits
>   of sunlight running hither and from
>
> without moving – any single point
>
> as steady maybe as a lighthouse's one-
>   pointed name for itself, but who
>
> could know? From here, it's jizzle and slur,
>
> our particles (reshuffled slightly
>   to make up a you, me or anyone)
>
> scarcely material …

(Gross 2011: 59)

Surely by now I have talked myself out of any claim to eco-poetry? Rather than the escape from the human that has motivated many eco-poets, my obsessive contemplation of the water seems to bring the focus back to *us*. The question then might be: yes, but as it brings our sense-perceptions back inside the self, what does it *do* to us? The answer might be the same as W.S. Graham's, addressing a passing cloud: 'Gently disintegrate me / Said nothing at all' (Graham 2004: 216).

Not only the personal self is dissolved at the edges. In the opening poem of a subsequent collection, *Later*, an aeroplane passenger is startled out of an effort to comprehend Wales as nation or as landscape by the setting sun suddenly making luminous every glimpse of ground-water. In place of human boundaries, this moment hints at wider, subtler connections:

> ... we see
> what the birds see
> with their thousand miles to fly
> and steering by the flicker-compass
>   in the genes: the stateless
> state of water, on the frontier between day and night.
>
> (Gross 2013: 9)

The resonances of this moment nod towards my deeply internalised family history, including my father's status as a Second World War refugee, officially a Displaced Person, coming from a Northern culture in which the flight of migratory birds had been a point of reference from the earliest prehistoric artefacts. In the birds'-eye view, as in my own work, water seems a more potent force than the land on either side of it, and one that tends to connection, not to separation. That viewpoint sees the natural world as an integrated system that has scant regard for human boundaries.

Collaborations at the margins

In December 2011 a multidisciplinary group walked by the Gloucester and Sharpness Canal – a cultural ecologist, a social anthropologist, a natural resource economist and geographer, a visual artist whose working practice grew from walking in a landscape, and myself. In a sense it was the natural world that had made the first move, with catastrophic flood events of late 2009 prompting government funding for academic research into flooding and resilience, including the AHRC's Researching Environmental Change initiative.

Our intention was to walk together through an area of wetland beside the Severn, sharing our different perceptions and knowledge of how communities have managed living in such (literally) marginal environments. Our self-set challenge was one of 'therapeutic deconstruction: [...] to reconsider our assumptions about land, water, and the relationship between the wet and the dry'. Or more precisely: 'a thought-experiment in what it might mean to "think like a wetland" [...] not simply treating these habitats as resources to be managed, but as sites of dwelling which have agency in their own right' (Dillon et al. 2013: 100).

My joining that group was a result of an ongoing collaboration with the artist and letterer Valerie Coffin Price that had begun when she incorporated text from *The Water Table* in an installation, *Estuary* (2011). She and I then walked together at the Newport Wetlands, a site created by Natural Resources Wales, Newport City Council and the RSPB as 'compensation land' for losses of wildlife habitat from the Cardiff Bay Barrage. The ground, with reed beds laid on a base of the 'Pulverised Fly Ash' waste created by the coal-fired Uskmouth power station, is crossed by a cat's-cradle of power lines that leave no doubt about its cheek-by-jowl-ness with the human world. With the sweep of the estuary and indefinite mud shores it has some of the qualities of wildness, yet seemed at a far remove from the 'wilderness' to which ecocritical writing, in the USA especially, has often been drawn. For someone brought up near the edges of Dartmoor, an apparent wilderness actually shaped by grazing, mining and deforestation, this compromised ground could feel like home.

> *Between …*
>
> the grey-on-grey
>   sky (steam
>
> breathed off the power station
>   into wisht November)
>
> and the Pulverised-Fly-Ash slurry
> settled to a wan grit,
>
>   layer me;
>
> between the shuffle-and-thrill
> of reed beds, party
> children getting ready for
>   *Surprise!*
>
> and the cool
>
> rococo of the pylons,
>   the chitter of voltage
>
> like grasshoppers never
>   where you bend to see,
>
>   inter-layer these two
>
> worlds walking, look
> and word and look and word and
>
>   silence, me and you;

> between the many vague retractions
>   of the tide
>
> (for now, for now) and small
> stunned bird cries, tattered flightpaths,
>   archaeology …

(Gross 2017: 63–4)

This is not an observer wanting to stand apart from any aspect of the 'layered' environment. The will to see oneself as part-of, not apart-from, might be the defining step towards an ecocritical stance. Reading those lines now I notice how the 'layered' of this poem would become the 'folded' of a later collaborative book, *A Fold in the River* (Gross and Price 2015) where the working together the artist Valerie Coffin Price took a step further towards an 'integrative' collaboration, in terms we will explore below.

What did feel certain was that seeing the place alongside a different perspective – being 'between look and word and / silence' – stood a chance of opening a *space between* our viewpoints, which might be creative in itself. This way of figuring collaboration between art forms had begun to crystallise five years earlier, in work with the engraver Peter Reddick on a project published as *The Abstract Garden* (2006). The villanelle that acted as a prologue to that book explored 'the word, the image, and the space between' – a space-between in this case humanly represented by the publisher and book designer Nicolas McDowall of the Old Stile Press, whose role it was to judge the relationship that pieces of text and image would have on the page. In some cases we looked at three or four possible configurations for a page, and realised that the balance, the dynamics and even the meaning of the whole was affected by that choice. In the villanelle, the repeating partner for the line above was 'what's meant is more than it was meant to mean'. The creative outcome is neither the sum of the parts nor a compromise between them but the way that they relate across – the way they shape – that space-between. This thought is itself a product of collaboration – learned from years of facilitating workshops alongside visual artists who teach the ability to see the form of the space between things as the key fact in a composition.

Meanwhile another collaborative project was taking place on the banks of the River Taff in Cardiff. Two film makers from Glamorgan University's Faculty of Cultural and Creative Industries collaborated in one case with a performance artist, in the other with a writer, myself, on a project called *In and Between*. In each case they were observed by one or more academic critics; the focus of the project was not so much the place or the river as the collaboration between creative and critical modes of knowing.

The film maker Wyn Mason and I were closely observed by poet and critic Kevin Mills. The original intention was for there to be an objective, outside viewpoint on the process. The work proved otherwise, as the critical gaze on us, even from the far side of the supermarket car park where we filmed, became more and more tangibly one of the forces shaping what emerged. The work between Wyn and myself went through several iterations, from straightforward poetry-film, though narrative and on to interactive website – a journey charted in the article 'Surface Tensions' (Gross and Mason 2013). At the same time an active conversation took shape between Kevin and myself, around the well-known line ascribed to Heraclitus: 'You cannot step into the same river twice'. Again, as with *The Water Table*'s ruminations, a body of water acquires a kind of selfhood, and becomes the field for questioning ideas of self. At the outset, we were testing the terms 'flow' and 'frame' as ways to conceive of experience, but the exchange was also between manners of approach – between the theoretical, deconstructive method and the more cavalierly sensual, performative and playful manner of the poetry. It became an investigation of how we could talk across different modes, the conversation too as a collaboration.

> We could be staring at this flux,
>   trip and back-rip, this ever-
>   self-troubling surface,
>   until kingdom come ...
>
> till something pocks it, up
>   from under, where the water
>   spreads from the pinch
>
>   of the bridge, and slows,
> and stills; the shadow
>
>   makes it visible, a vis-
>
>   -itation from its own dimension.
>   Splash. There. And again.
>
> Fish (or String Theory)
>   might account for this
>   irruption of one process
>
>   into, in and through
> another ... much as this
>   rippling shiftless shift
>   of interference patterns, con-

> -versation, moves
> of itself, without moving, as
> silk flows, its waves
>
> of *moiré*, something of
> us and between us, made of
>
> you and me, yet neither me nor you.
>   (Gross and Price 2015: 54–5)

This image of the *moiré* effect is indebted to a former collaborator, Alexis Nuselovici, formulated in the context of translation and the technology of film (Mason and Nuselovici 2012). In practice, it makes little difference whether the betweenness is imagined as a space conditioned by the figure-selves on either side of it, or as the overlap between the two that acquires, like that 'rippling' of silk, a 'life' of its own.

The ecology of space-between

How far has this discussion strayed from ecocriticism? In all these collaborations, a sense of actual place remained central. The parallel strand of *In and Between* was later described by Jodie Allinson in terms of changing the perceptual habits of the performer *vis-à-vis* the landscape, and exploring a different experience of the relationship between them. (Allinson 2014)

The landscape in question for her work with Inge Burrows was another water-marginal space, a disused tidal swimming pool on Barry Island, and the filmed performance showed a sense of place embodied and enacted as a range of characters.

We have seen already how natural phenomena and processes may offer themselves as a way to see the process of an individual's self – to imagine the self, in fact, as an ecology, with disparate elements in shifting but interdependent relationships with each other. What emerged in the course of several collaborations was that the same might be true of the *collective* 'self' of a collaboration – that 'living space-between'. In the multidisciplinary wetlands project, this became part of our agenda, consciously. To 'think like a wetland' was the self-set project. A prose-poetic piece of mine, 'Wetland, Thinking', became a point of reference for all the contributions, as it responded to the different subject viewpoints of the scientists and the artist's sketches, to a passing bird-flock and the texture of the ground beneath our feet:

I … Well, I wouldn't say 'I', to begin with. If I think, I think *I* am a *we*.

*

Water is only one of the voices, though the most volatile, the most apt to come at you with threat, or gift, or glitter. Earth is the quieter partner. It inheres.

*

And plants, the children of this (shifting, this uneasy) marriage made ... if not in heaven, in the actions of the moon? They're what holds us together, all the way from marram grass in sand dunes to the sphagnum moss that feeds on, and feeds itself into, the body of the bog.

*

No one governs the 'we' in 'wetlands'. OK, maybe the moon, but is she really looking, does she really care?

*

We're family, then, born into webs of connection? Root hairs, rhizomes, obligations. Channels worn, entrenchments. The awful relations whom we rub along with after all.

*

You don't know, do you (ah, this human language) whether this 'we' is the kind including 'you'?

*

Or are we crowds of strangers, jostling in the customs hall, towards border control? The rich melange of voices. Tongues as many as grass. You have to bend down very close to hear.

*

You hope we're a pack, like the old drovers' sleek canny black and white dogs, lolloping their own way home. Those dogs grown to be part of *your* pack, your purpose, only closer to the ground and to the sheep. You can do business with that.

*

We're not so different from you, maybe – you singular, who call yourself a personality. You too let your memories, your meanings, bank and veer and flow to cohere with their neighbours, following their wingtips, the whole flock of you lightening, darkening, scarfing and furling in flight.

*

What do we want of you? You, who've elected yourself first cousin to the old ones, tide and moon ... and yet, so childlike, touching really, the way you gaze into us, wanting to see words like 'want', like 'think, like 'I'. Reflections of your own face in our standing water.

*

But we level with you, all the same.

*

You can do this by taste. This blank page of surface water, where the beasts graze, is it salt or sweet? You could take a sample bottle of it for analysis. Or chance it, to know us that close. Our languages, there, on the tip of your tongue.

(Dillon et al. 2013: 101)

In previous explorations of collaboration, the work of Vera John-Steiner had been a valuable tool, with her distinctions between different levels of closeness in collaboration. Using examples from science and mathematics as well as a range of creative arts, she maps a spectrum between the 'distributed' mode of co-operation, with individuals having control of separate tasks within a wider pattern, through the 'complementary' to the 'integrative' mode, in which the work itself takes on a new and shared identity. None of these states should be confused with compromise, which is what people nervous of collaboration rightly fear.

Any living collaboration is likely to have an element of all these modes, and healthy ones move fluidly between them. Nor is there a value-judgement involved. For myself, I have been excited by the moments when an artist-collaborator has allowed me access to their sketchbooks, and has been keen to see mine; the work emerging gains autonomy in direct proportion to our willingness to relax our individual ownership. It seems a natural extension of this insight to include not only other human agencies but the non-human, landscape, place and living things, in that collaborative space-between.

This is not the self-denying ordinance of the writer who attempts to leave behind the human and represent the thing or creature in itself, without human referents. (The project of doing this *in language* is doomed from the start, though fine creative provocations like Les Murray's *Translations from the Natural World* can result from pushing at that edge.) It is to embrace *relationship*, with people and with things, as fundamental to writing *from the starting point of* one's position in the world.

A criticism any poet faces, at least any one for whom metaphor is the most natural way of thinking, is that metaphor and simile themselves may be acts of control, compelling the world into the shape of our perceptions. It may be rather flattering to have our power as writers overestimated in this way, but a much more realistic way to see it would be that a likeness, an association, is an ongoing thought-experiment. We and our readers go on living, and our poetry gets reality-tested all the time, both by the reader's direct observation and by the growing fund of scientific knowledge in the public domain. We know, collectively, that the pelican does not in fact feed its young with the blood of its own breast, as medieval mythology held; we have no excuse now for thinking that a chimpanzee is laughing when it bares its teeth. And then there is the case of birdsong:

> *The myth,*
> the metaphor, that this is music ...
> Just because our toys (the bone flute

from a cave bear femur, or the first
time a boy feels a grass blade shriek

between his thumbs) approximate
to the sounds of the forest machine

– cogs in operation; the friction
as much as the mesh is what we hear.

Or the creak of the world's pipes,
morning, evening, its small seasons:

the rough adjustments of space
against space, warping

the matter round it. Stress patterns
that it pleases us to hear as harmonies.

(Gross 2017: 27)

A metaphor is invariably an angle – a resemblance that holds for a moment, from one point of view. Its job might be to play against another metaphor, as some of the tropes here do against a romantic figuring of birdsong as joyful utterance or indeed as 'song' at all. These extracts come from a sequence exploring a dingle, a small urban-feral wooded valley at the end of my street, as a space shaped into an integrated system by the different natural presences that make themselves felt, most especially by their sounds. But the poem's way of working is itself a space shaped by the multiple bids for attention – an image figured this way or that, in shifting relationship to each other. This does not compel the world. By standing round at many angles, the different 'takes' on it allow the world its space to be itself.

Is this collaboration? Yes, if the thing observed itself has agency, and in my experience it does. To think ecologically is to grant the natural world the power to change the way one sees not just it but how one sees oneself – to put us, arguably, *in our place*:

To the birds
in the three dimensions of the dingle
I am flatfoot
down here in the silt.

At their pitch I am low
as underground, the premonition
of an earthquake. In their time I am slow

as a trilobite shuffling to my station
in Jurassic mudstone
even when I think I'm running for the train.

(Gross 2017: 21)

Bringing ecology inside

So we are not exempted, not as physical creatures or as thinking minds. I approached this chapter with the brief of showing an ecocritical approach in poetry extending outwards into wider areas of cross-arts collaboration. In the event, it seems to have revealed the insights of ecology extending inwards, into the creative process, shared or individual, and into the ways we understand the self.

I hope it has seemed natural to recognise no boundary between creative work done on one's own or in collaboration. The individual process brings together sense perceptions, memories, other reading, mental operations too quick, vague or deeply stored to be noticed consciously, and the accidents of the moment as you write. Part of the work of writing is to hold open the space in which these come together, often not in the way you intend. Much of the way this takes place is also vague and flickering; it is only when you share this space with another person, in collaboration, that you have to make the elements explicit, or at least visible, so they can pass across. The more 'integrative' the collaboration, the more intuitive that communication gets to be, but still it is communication. And the exchange depends, of course, on the two of you being different. Sameness is not collaboration, nor is it creative; it is just the same thing twice.

Working with another person is a choice. To work creatively alone is also to allow a space inside the self for disparate elements to relate. This might take practical form in the writing of work in multi-angled, multivocal sequences; it might be visible at the notebook stage; it might be simply the adoption of an inward stance. The metaphors that suggest themselves for this reveal it to be, potentially, an ecological thought.

> How to address them, that seethe
> of loose connections – half ink, half itch in the neurones?
>   For every halfway-to-whole
>   thing that gathers its membrane
> in the evolution gloop, to slouch up the shores of the page,
>   hundreds stay fluid, indistinguishable
>
>   from what they breathe, eat and excrete,
> mulching into each other. Or perhaps they slope off, deeper
>   in their element, to be ... what
>
>   I can't name.

(Gross 2012: 20)

There is, in Geoffrey Bateson's phrase, an *ecology of mind*. His argument is part of the resource of ecocritical thought, dissolving the boundaries between the inner, mental operations and the world around us to which they relate. Meanwhile, however our minds might theorise about the role of language, our physical bodies insist on their place in the ecology – by their appetites, their aches, and unavoidably, their decay. My father's loss of language in old age was a result of events in the physical tissues of his brain. The fact that medical science can now intervene, in once-unimaginable ways, in these processes, complicating even the boundary between life and death, means that living in (no, *as*) our bodies needs to be seen as an ecology.

Being alongside one person's ageing and dying in *Deep Field* and in *Later* opened a perspective on the human mind and body that applies unavoidably to my own. The poems in a new collection, *Love Songs of Carbon*, set themselves to inhabit and, yes, celebrate this fact. Many of them are literally love songs; relationship is at their heart, and whether that is a collaboration in creative writing or in living (or both) makes little difference.

> See our two (do we even
>
> own them?) bodies sense each other,
> waking in the dark; each would know if the other was gone.
> We give out presence,
>
> weather, transpiration. Life
> is work and work
>
> is heat, the one
> sheer gift; we hold it here between us, just to spend
> on, subcontractors to the sun.
>
> (Gross 2015b: 11)

Ecocriticism was defined by William Rueckert early on as 'the application of ecology and ecological concepts to the study of literature' (Rueckert 1996: 107). Less has been said about its application to creative writing – in the sense not only of the subject matter or political commitment of the work but of the study of creative process in itself. There is potential in the systems thinking of Csiksentimihalyi and other theorists of creativity that points this way. The 'halfway-to-whole' things in the last but one extract are conceived of in a more organic way than 'notes' or 'drafts'. The notebooks in which they take shape consist of wide and unlined pages, littered with fragments often unconnected in any way that I know; they contain a good deal of deliberately cultivated space. This is both a practical tool and an image of the stages before any words are written. The poems I have quoted here are often from multifaceted sequences that bring together different voices, viewpoints and registers, held at a deliberate distance from each other, to invite connections rather than to reconcile them in a single point of view.

To prescribe a working method based on my own would be counter to the spirit of the approach I am describing here, which depends on encouraging a creative biodiversity. I suggest, though, that to conceive of our work in ecologically informed metaphors might be a thought-experiment worth undertaking for the discipline. Ruekert's article, mentioned above, echoes Ian McHarg's suggestion that 'perhaps the greatest conceptual contribution of the ecological view is the perception of the world and evolution as a creative process' (Rueckert 1996: 111). The converse of this statement – that creative process is best perceived as an ecology – might be simultaneously the case.

Is this chapter an argument against the moral or political imperatives of environmental writing and criticism? It is neither for nor against, though any evidence that an ecological understanding is clarifying and creatively productive both in an individual's working and collaboration must tend to an argument *for*. It implicates us, metaphorically and actually, as thinking and creating bodies, in the constant experiment of organisms round us, diverse, interacting in a bounded space, arriving at provisional coherence in the act of living. The contribution of creative work and our reflections on it are also provisional, not so much suggesting answers as provoking questions, widening the range of possibility. If I once worried that an ecocritical approach must mean self-denial, with a stern subordination of creative play to political ends, what a liberation it might be to know that ecology simply describes what is the case, around us and inside us, and includes us, creativity and all.

Twenty Questions about Green

1. What, so close to the thickening heart-knot of the country's motorways, could be the meaning of this garden – the meaning of *green*?
2. Is a lawn an exercise – yes, and a groundsman's labour – in concentrating all our minds on that: clipped, kept, to concentrate its colour: green?
3. What is it we feel, even if it isn't our own memory, is being *remembered* by this gathered meeting of a hundred greens?
4. How far back do we have to peel the history before the water, the brook in the wood, would recognise its 'own face before it was born'?
5. And if it did, would it have anything to say to us any more, or be off, in itself, and away?
6. Does it mind, this water, that we have detained it here, delayed it on its way, to call it 'lake'?

7. And the dragonfly's glint, metallic before we had metal, or the damselfly's, neon before neon, whose dream is that: ours, the water's or their own?

8. Don't they fly lighter not weighed down with memories – of the grand *Meganeura*, say, of the Carboniferous, not yet come down to our time's jewelled toys?

9. But when did the concept of *lawn* first step out of the trees, onto the stage of itself, and take a bow?

10. Something might safely graze, it whispers to our Sunday School selves – ah, but what, or who?

11. How much closer might I get to *that*, what as kids we called Dinosaur Rhubarb, if I knew its proper name?

12. Or if I knew that name – which it, itself, does not – how much further apart might we be?

13. What shuffling and dealing took place round the edges of their habits, so many species, before their ornamental rooming-house became a home?

14. And if we should turn our back on them for a year, for ten, for a hundred, what would the meaning of green be then?

15. How much more of the brown, the greyish, the mould-blue, the lichen-yellow, does there truly want to be?

16. Isn't green itself a strenuous gesture, all that striving for the sunlight, just another kind of hungering?

17. If we ask every species here to name itself to us, just once, in the language in which anyone or thing first named them, do we have ears to hear?

18. Could we bear it, that awful laying-down of language, uncountable as leaves themselves, as dying, at our feet?

19. What might we be asked to lay at *their* feet, roots and tendrils, in return?

20. And when we did, when we stepped out, over it, into the silence, into green, together, then what would we be?

(Gross 2017: 38–9)

References

Allinson, J. (2014) 'Training Strategies for Performance and Landscape: Resisting the Late-Capitalist Metaphor of Environment as Consumable Resource', *Theatre, Dance and Performance Training* 5:1: 4–14.

Bateson, G. (1972) *Steps to an Ecology of Mind*. Chicago: University of Chicago Press.

Dillon, P, P. Gross, R. Irvine, V. Coffin Price and C. Staddon (2013) 'Thinking like a Wetland', *Journal of Arts and Communities* 4:1–2: 100–26.

Graham, W.S. (2004) *New Collected Poems*. London: Faber.

Gross, P. (2006) *The Egg of Zero*. Tarset: Bloodaxe.

Gross, P. (2009) *The Water Table*. Tarset: Bloodaxe.

Gross, P. (2011) *Deep Field*. Tarset: Bloodaxe.

Gross, P. (2012) 'The White Bit round the Edges', in H. Ivory and G. Szirtes (eds), *In Their Own Words: Contemporary Poets on Their Poetry*. London: Salt.

Gross, P. (2013) *Later*. Tarset: Bloodaxe.

Gross, P. (2015a) ' "Roots in the air": Teaching of Creative Writing in UK Universities', *Scriptum Creative Writing Research Journal* 2:1: 23–45. Available online http://urn.fi/URN:NBN:fi:jyu-201502041249 accessed 17 January 2016.

Gross, P. (2015b) *Love Songs of Carbon*. Tarset: Bloodaxe.

Gross, P. (2017) *A Bright Acoustic*. Tarset: Bloodaxe.

Gross, P. and V. Coffin Price (2015) *A Fold in the River*. Bridgend: Seren.

Gross, P. and S. Denison (2009) *I Spy Pinhole Eye*. Blaenau Ffestiniog: Cinnamon.

Gross, P. and W. Mason (2013) 'Surface Tensions: Framing the Flow of a Poetry-Film Collaboration', New Writing: *International Journal for the Practice and Theory of Creative Writing* 10:3: 323–5.

Gross, P. and P. Reddick (2006) *The Abstract Garden*. Llandogo: Old Stile Press.

John-Steiner, V. (2000) *Creative Collaboration*. New York: Oxford University Press.

Mason, W. and A. Nuselovici (2012) 'Continental Drift: Europe and Translation, Poetry and Film'. *Journal of Adaptation in Film & Performance* 5:1: 79–92.

Murray, L. (1993) *Translations from the Natural World*. Manchester: Carcanet.

Rueckert, W. (1996) 'Literature and Ecology: An Experiment in Ecocriticism', in C. Glotfelty and H. Fromm (eds), *The Ecocriticism Reader: Landmarks in Literary Ecology*. Athens and London: University of Georgia Press.

4

'Drawing closer': an ecocritical consideration of collaborative, cross-disciplinary practices of walking, writing, drawing and exhibiting

Harriet Tarlo and Judith Tucker

The short poem in Figure 4.1 was written by the poet Harriet Tarlo, watching artist Judith Tucker draw, very early on in our collaborative place-based practice. In the subsequent years since we began to work together, this poem has become talismanic. It has been read aloud in numerous galleries, university lecture theatres and art galleries at openings, papers, talks and readings. Like all the place-based work we have made together, it has travelled a distance, on paper and in performance, from its origins outside, where we sat in September 2011, on the crumbling stone step of a long-deceased mill owner's garden. The garden is only just discernible through decades of subsequent growth, and leads down to a house and mill long buried under a reservoir in the South Pennine Yorkshire landscape.

This short piece pointed to the beginning of a dialogue between us born of close observation of each other's practice, but also to our shared exploration of the similarities and differences of producing text and image both in and out of place. Composed in deceptively simple everyday language, it seemed to acquire new meanings each time we cited it. As such, it reflects the simplicity and complexity of putting pencil to paper in the landscape. The idea that a drawing or piece of writing 'cuts landscape off' implies the inevitable artistic imposition (even violence) upon place when we begin to work outside, while the gentler phrase, 'seam or folded', references ways in which this might perhaps be ameliorated through attentive and collaborative practices. In the space before the word 'lead' lie many unanswered questions, not least the question of how our practices might disturb and disrupt our understanding of social, environmental, temporal and spatial relations with place.

The 'line in space' that ends our opening poem is where we both begin. Although we touch on painting here, we pay particular attention

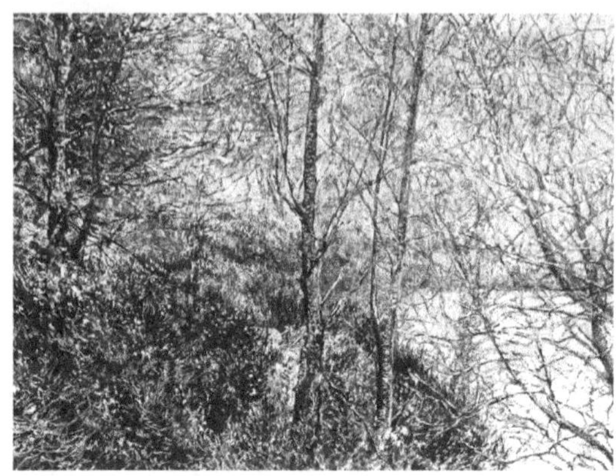

Figure 4.1   Judith Tucker (monochrome drawing) and Harriet Tarlo (open-form poem), Excerpt from *Tributaries*, 2013

to drawing, both literally and as a conceit, as our title suggests. To attempt to define drawing would inevitably lead us, as Petherbridge argues, to enter the trap of an 'all-embracing and inevitably flawed definition' (2010: 3). In contemporary work distinctions between drawing and painting have become imprecise. Tucker's paintings, although they do make use of colour and shimmery, uncertain surfaces, emerge from a drawing tradition. Here we retain a sense of 'the current open-ended exploration and discourse about drawing [that] intensifies its irresolute and fluid status' (Petherbridge 2010: 27). We are particularly interested in the line and the horizon and how they function in poetry and drawing, specifically in our collaborative practice. This chapter is as much a product of these explorations as the creative work itself. It begins with introducing our work in ecocritical context, moves on to its origins in the field and then returns again, with insight gained, to the line in practice on the page (the production of the work itself), and finally to its presentation in gallery, performance and book spaces.

We present the poem above in relation to an image of a drawing, which is in turn, of course, an image of a place. This prompts us to ask what relation does the practice of drawing have with place and how might that feed into our collaboration when we work in place? The feminist geographer Doreen Massey proposes an open, unstable, fluid, provisional and contested approach to 'place' and she aims 'to evoke place as meeting place rather than as always already coherent, as open rather than bounded, as an ongoing production rather than pre-given' (Massey 2006: 33). In many ways drawing, so often considered to be fluid and evolving, might be considered an ideal medium through which to explore place as ongoing. In Brian Fay's essay 'A Continuous Incompleteness', he explores the sort of thinking through making that drawing with its 'properties of contingency, intermediacy, in-betweenness and becoming' makes possible (Fay 2013: 20).[1]

Central to this essay is the way that creative practice not only informs critical analysis but is a critical tool itself, a thinking through making. We interrogate not only how ecocriticism might feed into the combined, collaborative practices of poetry and drawing but also what ecocriticism might learn from practice. As the opening suggests, the writing of poetry might be close to the drawing of place within such a context. In situating the word 'drawing' next to the word 'closer', we highlight the intensity and intimacy of our joint practice and point to perhaps the most important aspect of our work together, our attempts to 'draw closer' to place through parallel explorations, not just for ourselves but for our audiences.

As Petherbridge (2010) suggests, 'drawing is a site of inquiry, response, and invention, and in that sense becomes a philosophical activity' (169). For us, our joint practice of drawing, and writing together, is an ethical, even eco-ethical, activity in which we move, together, away from the simply representational towards an investigation of the relationship between things, including our differing disciplines, rather than an attempt at unproblematic integration. Defying binary models of thinking about writing and drawing, we experiment with the radical possibilities for how these practices might operate together. We refer to two such experiments here in the form of case studies of two place-based creative projects based in northern England: *Tributaries*, close to home on Black Hill, near Holmfirth in the South Pennines, and *Excavations and Estuaries*, located a little further away, on the estuarial coastline and Fitties Holiday Park, Cleethorpes.[2]

Working from practitioners' perspectives, we attempt to test out the arguments of critics such as Jonathan Skinner and Timothy Clark that it is interdisciplinarity and off-the-page work that is becoming increasingly important in eco-poetics, what happens 'where the work is sited and performed, as well as what methods of composition and decomposition, precede and follow the poem' (Skinner in Hume 2012: 760). However, as Clark notes, 'The breakdown of normal disciplinary frames is exciting but also vertiginous […] in practice, this breakdown of barriers between intellectual disciplines can become too easily a breakdown of intellectual standards' (Clark 2015: 145–6). Wary of such charges, in our case we prefer the term cross-disciplinary to interdisciplinary as we each emerge from individual art practices and creative and academic contexts.

Our two disciplines remain separate in presentation, rather than superimposed on each other, and we use them to conduct open conversations with each other and our viewers and readers. It is through the spaces between that the greatest challenge can come. Similar ideas emerge in conversation with other artist collaborators. Thomas A. Clark talks about how his partner Laurie enters the work in ways he does not expect, even when asked simply to illustrate. Clark says (in conversation with us): 'What we try to do is have the drawing provide something that is not in the poem, another suggestion or extension. Maybe we could say it is an accompaniment rather than an illustration.' Like the Clarks, we value adjacency and difference. The idea of expansion or augmentation both for practices and for place might be elucidated by this excerpt from our *Tributaries* suite, which also acts as an introduction to our work. The text and image of figure 4.2 appeared in close relation to each other in various exhibitions and in *Sound Unseen* (2013), our artists' book (as it is shown here). Having text and image together in an open space abutting each other at a similar scale allows a viewer to make connections and to appreciate what happens when there is apparent divergence between the two practices. It is perhaps on these occasions that the unexpected aspects of our collaboration emerge. These aspects cannot be overdetermined or planned: silent, static drawings might become filled with sound and movement and somehow the density of the drawing is counterbalanced by the spaces between the words. In this way, both symbiotically help to emplace the other.

In this example, a viewer or reader might in the first instance find relief in literal recognition that that white shape there is the 'ice slabbed gritstone' but then the following 'where we can, where we cannot see / underedge water curling against land' hangs over the drawn marks and

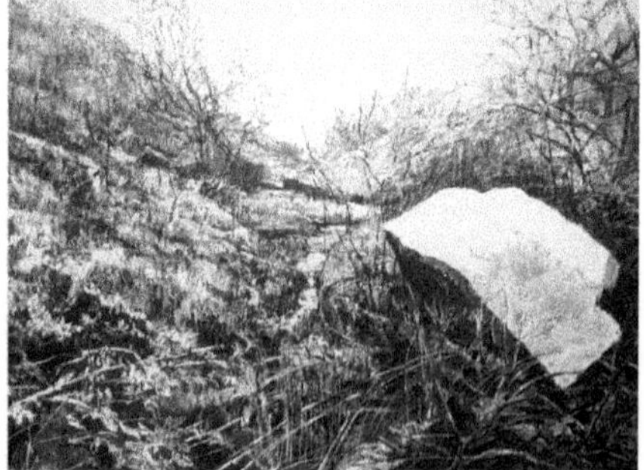

Figure 4.2 Judith Tucker (monochrome drawing) and Harriet Tarlo (open-form poem), Excerpt from *Tributaries*, 2013

changes their emphasis. There is reference to the defunct quarry through the solitary 'ice slabbed gritstone', the shape of which is unmistakably hewn by artificial means, a small example of a subtle eroding away at notions of the nature/culture binary, which will be explored further in the next section. However, both the poem and the drawing also provide evidence of 'having been there' of direct experience of place, of bodies moving and then being still in the landscape. We return now to our beginnings where we are walking and working in place, the move from 'delicate blue line on a pathfinder map' to slipping in the fast-moving water.

Fieldwork

Our joint fieldwork in place begins with an acceptance that we cannot of course *know* place – as Massey suggests, it is always mysterious, our grasp always tenuous. We are always attempting to counterbalance our individual and joint expectations of and investments in particular places and place as concept. This understanding is explored and underpinned by principles distilled from the earliest days of ecocritical thinking. For instance, while elements of Thoreau's sauntering, countercultural philosophy might inspire our movement through landscape, others we resist. We might celebrate and respond to his claim that, through walking, he would 'fain return to my senses', a term he uses in reference to sanity, but we might extend to thinking about the senses as early ecocritics such as Merleau-Ponty might refer to them. The phenomenological approach fosters a heightened awareness of 'being in place'.[3]

More recently, ideas from environmental criticism and philosophy about being 'enmeshed in a dense network of relationships' can further intensify our engagement with the nonhuman and encourage us to erode away at the human/nonhuman binary (Bennett 2010: 13.) Jane Bennett explores these relationships through a theory of distributed agency, of which more later, but the notion of being 'enmeshed' emerges from a zeitgeist of 'mesh-thinking', as we might call it. This includes Timothy Morton's 'the mesh' and Tim Ingold's 'meshwork'. Ingold extends this into a more encompassing concept in *Lines: A Brief History* (2007) in which he writes of an 'entanglement of lines', arguing that 'the lines of the meshwork are the trails along which life is lived' (2007: 81).

When we bring phenomenological awareness and 'mesh-thinking' to how we think about place, it further contributes to our discomfort with the pastoral traditions of working outside which we inherit. As so many of his romantic and transcendentalist predecessors do, Thoreau thinks within a binaristic perception of the world, a pastoral idea of retreat and return to wilderness from the home, village or city with insights gained. Early in our respective careers, both of us were influenced by Kate Soper's book, *What Is Nature?* (1995), in which Soper argues that, if nature is only that which is independent of culture, then there would be very little nature. She favours maintaining the awareness of the difference between human and nonhuman effects and constantly assessing and reassessing the positions of nature and culture, rather than indulging in simplistic defence or denial of this familiar Western dualism (11).

We cannot understand the evolving and complex topography of the areas we work in in terms of such binary distinctions. Both places remind us that every exploration of a small 'local' area is steeped with wider-reaching and interweaving aspects. Black Hill in West Yorkshire, now regarded as recreational semi-wilderness, is a locale haunted by industrial and farming history – only traces remain of prior farms, mills and quarries. There are lanes and paths, now used only by walkers, which would have once been busy thoroughfares, and others which are faint tracks just discernible through the bracken. The mills are long-gone, their place taken by reservoirs, but the grouse-shooting begun in their mid-nineteenth-century heyday remains. The depletion of the sphagnum moss bogs, due to acid rain partly caused by the Lancashire mills over the Pennines, is being redressed to some extent by environmentalist groups such as 'Moors for the Future'.[4]

The coast between Cleethorpes and Tetney is a low drained landscape where marsh, beach and farmland border on each other. Here we find traces of ancient salt production and, in the more recent past, industrial and commercial relics from the glory days of the Tetney–Louth canal. Concrete embrasures from the Second World War line the raised path we took regularly as one of our journeys. Like all localities then, this is a changing place where human interventions and priorities intersect with the short- and long-term, large- and small-scale nonhuman changes such as the recent reshaping of land by water in tidal surges. This more nuanced way of thinking about so-called rural places offers a different perspective, even a check, on the contemporary penchant for 'edgelands' as sites of the marginal par excellence.

This is informed by past artists and writers who have often been too easily pigeonholed as pastoral and retrogressive, such as the neo-romantics, whose work Tucker has recently returned to as a surprisingly radical inspiration.[5] Our world may appear to be a very different place, with its digital and global developments, but there are unexpected parallel concerns too. Working in an analogous period of transformation, change and potential loss, artists such as Nash, Piper and Sutherland were always nuanced in their blurring of natural and cultural distinctions, exploring place in all its complexity as we attempt to do. Graham Sutherland in particular might have relished our places for, when he worked in the War Artists' Scheme, he worked from landscapes marked by bombsites, mines and quarries. The hill in his painting *Red Landscape* is thought to be Carn Llidi whose slopes house Second World War defensive installations and are adjacent to quarries.

More recently Donna Haraway has coined the term 'natureculture', as in the 'rich naturalcultural contact zones' between dog and human (2003: 7). Running these two key words together perhaps takes Soper a step further, and certainly feeds into our thinking about our cross-disciplinary practice. Arguably, the naturalcultural has become intrinsic to contemporary ecocritical thinking per se. Greg Garrard for instance, in his recent Critical Idiom guide to the subject, notes that 'reciprocal shaping networks of nature and culture are bound to be complex to the attentive eye' and aims 'to balance the constructionist perspective with the privileged claims to literal truth' (Garrard 2011: 10). As practising artists, we take up the challenge of this 'attentive eye', a concept that recurs frequently in the writings of artists and ecocritics interested in this area. We attempt to remain always aware of these issues *in practice and in place*, rather than just in theory.

All these considerations affect our decisions about where and when to visit the landscapes where we work. We quickly realise that the scale of working needs to be small in order for us to attempt to respond to place with any kind of subtlety of awareness, to maintain precisely the attentive quality of our work. Moving from map to land, we find ourselves honing in on a smaller and smaller geographical spaces and also needing to revisit the same places, not keep going to new ones. We both take zigzag notebooks into the field and stop intermittently in order to fill one small surface each with drawing and writing from the same location. In this sense, we are not epic walkers but slow walkers, repetitive walkers. Each individual walk is a slow way of being in place. The process of seasonal revisiting is also slow – we cannot see the autumn again until it is autumn again. Much that characterises contemporary life runs counter to this approach with its opportunities for international travel, the transporting and purchasing of produce from across the world and the central heating and air conditioning that we use to regulate the atmosphere around us. We also need to attend to these realities of course, but we should not allow them to mask other temporal and spatial rhythms, but attempt to hold them together in tension in our work. Just offshore from Cleethorpes, oil is pumped in from ships into pipes which run under the delicate sea lavender of the marshes.

In the painting in Plate 1 the tanks holding the oil appear to float above the fields between land and sky, obscuring the horizon. We know that there is a pipeline under the earth being filled from a distant boat. We cannot see it in this painting; it is behind us on the horizon, but it is depicted in another. We *can* see the wind turbine, the subject of much local controversy. Those palest green crops might be harvested by migrant workers and headed for supermarkets, but the fields are only fertile as the 'soils of the area were also extensively modified from the mid-18th Century onwards by the practice of warping i.e. the seasonal impoundment of tidal silts' (Anon. 2009: 33).

The artist and academic Iain Biggs acknowledges the difference between working near where one lives and at a distance:

> We enter [place] in one of two ways: either by living in a place as an inhabitant or by moving through it as an attentive traveller. Either process involves us in engaging with multiple temporal and spatial dimensions, in understanding both human and natural activity. Our entry is finally achieved only through the marriage of many kinds of knowledge and experience. (Biggs 2008: 24)

He is careful not to privilege one method over the other; rather he draws attention to what he terms elsewhere a 'polyvocal' approach to drawing that helps him explore ideas, often about landscape or place-related issues (Biggs 2008: 7). Thomas A. Clark, also integrating reference to bodily senses, has argued that working from within one's own locality might in itself be a stepping-off point that is resistant to a dominant culture:

> voice must involve some sense of being embodied, of speaking from where you are and who you are. If some of us, at least, are disenchanted with the dominant culture, with the way it has blighted the planet and blighted individual lives, then it may be that the beginning of an answer is in the local. By local I mean not only a small area but an immediate area, what is to hand, what in terms of nature and culture is available, to a community or a person. (Finlay, interview with Clark, n.p.)

As much as Tarlo had always worked immersed in her locale, working locally was a change of practice brought about through collaboration for Tucker. Whilst acknowledging the materiality from which it originated, she often built into her methodology, and the work itself, a deliberate distancing from her source. Working on the east coast near Cleethorpes was the opposite challenge for Tarlo, and she was to learn from Tucker's longstanding artistic practices of working in places as an 'attentive traveller'. It is partly in the shifting of established methodologies such as these that we see how collaboration changes practice and perspective. For us, encountering place as inhabitant in *Tributaries* and as attentive visitor for *Excavations and Estuaries* has led us to interrogate our ideas of place more intensely.

For the east coast project, we were invited to revisit a previously unknown place over eighteen months. We quickly honed in on four small patches of land between Tetney and Cleethorpes; we visited these regularly and timed our visits carefully in order to attempt to 'capture' seasonal changes, changes which were of course just as likely to 'capture' us. Watching a jerky, 1930s black-and-white film of Cleethorpes's promenades, we could not help but be struck by the vast crowds marching up and down the 'fine sea front', the pier, the quantity of trolley buses and charabancs. There is a sense of nostalgic security in such images of familiar, everyday tourist landscapes. What might an ecocritical sensibility bring to a 'working class playground' such as Cleethorpes (Walton 2000: 29)? Cleethorpes's history is closely linked to industrialisation and the rise of the railways. Its long links with Yorkshire, especially around Sheffield, had their origins in a time when tourism for most was restricted to the times when the mills were closed for Wakes Weeks and whole communities made for the seaside. In its heyday it was the destination of miners, steel workers and mill workers. For these people, seaside resorts were places to encounter the 'natural' for therapeutic, mental or physical replenishment. They are all about interaction between humans and environment. Visiting the seaside from Yorkshire, we embraced this history, staying in the Humberston Fitties.[6] The Fitties plotlands were, like much of the low-lying land around the mouth of the Humber estuary, carved out of saltmarsh. They lie low behind marshy beach and dunes, a quirky domestication of land always liable to flood, to a return to its former state. Here, since the early part of the twentieth century, local people and visitors have erected their diverse dwellings with individualistic names and styles, in order to enjoy seaside life.

In the work itself we were influenced by our previous practices, which in both cases laid great emphasis on fieldwork and process. Tarlo has evolved a form of working in place and writing poetry that draws on the open field tradition developed in American Black Mountain poetics, in particular William Carlos Williams's 'The Poem as a Field of Action' (1948), Charles Olson's 'Projective Verse' (1950) and Robert Duncan's *The Opening of the Field* (1960). In an essay on 'Open Field: Reading Field as Place and Poetics' Tarlo writes:

> The cycle of working the land is referenced here, the listening, seeing, writing, editing of the work: land work, poetry work, 'Groundwork', to

> cite the title of two of Robert Duncan's late books. It is a place to think
> about thinking, to perform, to enact and embody our physical relationship
> with the world. It is a micro-environment. It is an energy field, a trajec-
> tory, Olson's threshing floor, Duncan's dance. (2013: 114)

This is a process-led form of working simultaneously in place, language
and page space, exploring the connections between each element.

In common with many other artists, Tucker had also always thought
of making work on location as a kind of fieldwork, not in a strictly
geographical sense but as a suggestive rather than overdetermined methodology. Stephen Daniels, Mike Pearson and Heike Rom consider the
significance and reverberations of fieldworking as 'a richly resonant
term [that] recalls traditions and techniques of open-air research and
teaching, field studies, field trips, field trials, field walking and field
notes' (2010: 3). For us, walking, writing, drawing, painting and producing work together involve an open, responsive and flexible approach
in which we decide our moves in the field rather than beforehand; this
helps us to try to diminish the undue influence of our own prior encap-
sulations of place.

This openness leads us to change our foci as the projects developed.
For instance, we became increasingly interested in working around and
about the Fitties themselves, rather than just on beach and marsh, and
this has developed into a new body of work exploring this celebration
of an alternative, restorative form of simple seaside living through found
poems and small, quirky paintings. Here Tucker evokes the past and
present, exteriors and half-hidden interiors of the holiday chalets,
always liable to flood and weather damage, and to the threat of the
dominant culture, as the painting and accompanying poem entitled
'Once Was Holiday' in Plate 2 show.

We set these paintings beside much larger paintings of the saltmarsh
itself with its suppressed but resurgent life, paintings in which Tucker
attempts to integrate our ideas of process and seasonality that would
operate in counterpoint with poetic text. These paintings developed out
of processes of layering and meshing; they focus on surface, yet they
also evolve out of the viscosity and liquidity of the paint. These processes sound like a description of the saltmarsh itself: what is always at
stake in representational painting is the tension between the materiality
of substance and its metaphor. In looking as attentively at the marsh as
at the Fitties, and placing the two adjacent to each other and to accompanying texts, we have a greater chance of avoiding the landscape
clichés of bleak sublime invited by marsh, and of picturesque suggested
by the Fitties.

In her poetic voice, Tarlo also strives to avoid romantic lyricism, attempting not to subsume localities into an all-encompassing sublime or sentimental rhetoric. Her modernist influences go back to the 1930s American objectivist poets (particularly Lorine Niedecker, George Oppen and Louis Zukofsky), all poets who combined formal experimentation with ethical considerations. These poets attempted to find not an interiorised landscape but an externalised self, one that goes out in search of particulars.[7] Objectivism laid emphasis on 'sincerity and objectification', the rejection of lyricism, verbosity and 'strained metaphor' in favour of the clear image, the 'bringing of the rays of an object into focus'.[8] Objectivism was clearly in Olson's mind when he defined his own 'objectism' in 1950:

> Objectism is the getting rid of the lyrical interference of the individual as ego, of the 'subject' and his soul, that peculiar presumption by which western man has interposed himself between what he is as a creature of nature [...] and those other creations of nature which we may, with no derogation, call objects. (Olson 1997: 247)

We hold in common the desire to modify what Olson called 'the lyrical interference of the individual as ego,' ever-present in the past landscape practices we inherit. This is an ongoing process that we know can never be entirely successful, though, as collaborators, it is perhaps possible to act as check and balance for each other. We have explored some of the ideas of 'Vital Materialism' in relation to this process (Bennett 2010). Jane Bennett, like us, worries about whether all the responses to the material world she cites are just human, subjective and intersubjective and explores this via a fascinating discussion of Adorno and her own concept of 'thing-power' (10–17). She answers her own conundrum with the idea that the 'swarming' inside her head is itself vital materiality; human power is not so distinguishable from thing-power, being a lively and self-organising minerality of bones, metal of blood, electricity of neurons (10). The crucial ambition for the vital materialist is *'to raise the status of the materiality of which we are composed'* (12). The ethical task is to recognise ourselves as part of vital materiality, to discern non-human vitality (13–14).

Bennett's repeated emphasis on the word 'attentiveness' in this context resonates with us and many of the artists we engage with, and demands a revaluation of the body and the limitations of perception (14–16). In the field, through attention to particulars and to our own particularity, we begin to imagine ourselves, and to create from that place of imagining, as part of the ever-changing meshwork of that specific naturalcultural nexus we call place. When we stop to draw and write from the same location, our work is quick and immediate but very focused – the presence of the other body working alongside enhances the sense of concentration. We accept that notions of time and place are human constructions, but also that they create these moments of placing that are moments made up of the materiality of things (including us) in relation to each other. We are amongst things that are not reducible to the culture of objects but, drawing again on Bennett, as Latourian actants, which do not have to be classified as either human or nonhuman and are in fact often both/and/and. In poetry and art, it is perhaps possible to hold in creative tension the sense of interconnected actants whilst not excluding the sense of the human consciousness with all its elaborate mobilities and constructions.

Our attentiveness extends not only around us but back into the material histories of our landscapes and ourselves. For many years, Tucker has explored both how we might be inhabited, not only by our own histories, memories, and experiences but also by those of others, and the ways in which places too bear traces of others, both visible and invisible. Her paintings and drawings became places between these psychic traces and the actual traces in the landscape. Working and walking in collaboration only multiplies these possible inhabitations as we layer into our practice individual and collective past and present readings of textual, visual and critical texts, as well as archival local researches into the naturalcultural pasts of these landscapes.

This process, which runs parallel to work in the field itself, could be seen as akin to deep-mapping practices such as those advocated by Pearson and Shanks, who call on us to record and represent the grain and patina of place and landscape 'through juxtapositions and interpretations of the historical and the contemporary, the political and the poetic, the factual and the fictional, the discursive and the sensual' (Pearson and Shanks 2001).[9] Tarlo has always used found text in her poetry in an attempt to avoid a usurpation of place into her own voice. Fragments of stories and documents, little pieces of found text and speech, work their way into her poetry. The following piece draws on the history of the mills that once stood in the valleys below Black Hill. It is stitched together from entirely found text and we often incorporate it into *Tributaries* events to allow that history to resurface:[10]

You see. I had to go into the mill.
I never wanted to go into the mill.

>Methodists and Primitive Methodists
>we sung at the tops of our voices
>we used to sing 'sweet is thy name'
>and do you know, I can hear it now

but we never stopped working, we knew
if we didn't work, there was no pay

we couldn't mend holes at that age
we hadn't learned to mend holes

        rubbing your fingers along, feeling
        the pieces for knots; after a few weeks
        they bled; they said you're becoming
        menders

we'd to knot as well as mend
hundreds and thousands of knots

        we'd ten minutes morning and afternoon
        to go out, play at hide and seek between
        those big bales of wool: we stopped
        so quiet

In much of our work together, the fruits of our researches are not so obvious at first glance. The reader or viewer is also asked to be attentive in order to discover the diverse ways in which we suggest the specificities and complexities of these localities through the materiality of language, graphite, charcoal and paint. This attentiveness, as theorists of defamiliarisation in all its forms have often argued, has the potential to stimulate, if not change itself, at least a rethinking of consolidated ideas and habits of perception, in this case of place, locality, landscape and natureculture. Whilst we might offer sufficient contextual material through talks, catalogues and essays to suggest what cannot be seen in the images and words offered, we are ever wary of the didactic, wanting to allow always for multiple readings of the work to coexist.

In Figure 4.3, whilst the ostensible focus of much of the work is in the lush and entangled foliage, hedge, ditch and feral plants, the low perspective of the footpath lures the viewer's eye on to the edges of the

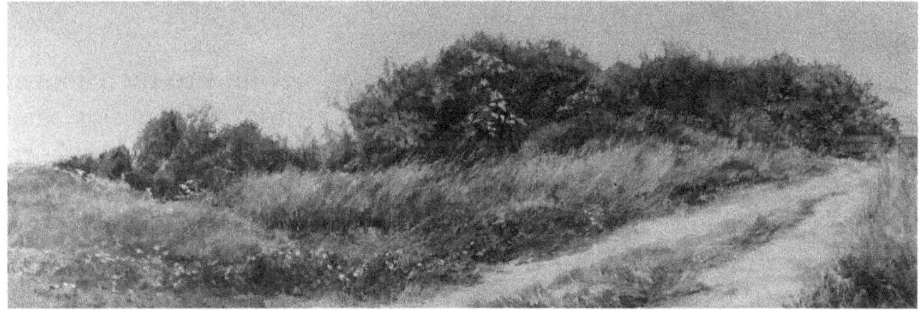

Figure 4.3   Judith Tucker, *Either Side*, 2014. Oil on canvas, 60.1 × 183 cm

canvas. On one side, almost hidden in the greenery is a concrete pill box and on the other is the pipeline emerging to cross the drainage channel. The industrial and military appear as tiny incidental events, on the periphery of the jumble of tangled weeds, crops and grasses.

The line in practice

Joseph Beuys argues that:

> Drawing is ... the first visible thing of the form of the thought from the invisible powers to the visible thing ... it is not only a description of the thought ... you have also incorporated the senses ... the sense of balance, the sense of vision, the sense of audition, the sense of touch. (Beuys in Petherbridge 2010: 109)

As we have discussed above, our fieldwork involves a conscious and unconscious gathering of material through our senses as we move through the landscape.

We suggested at the very start of this chapter that drawing and poetry share the conceit of lines and their relation to the space of the page or ground. We can explore how they interrelate through considering the horizon. The phenomenologist Edward Casey considers that 'place is what takes place between body and landscape. Thanks to the double horizon that body and landscape provide, a place is a locale bounded on both sides, near and far' (Casey 1993: 29). Here, crucially, not only does locale refer to the way a place looks but also implicit in the word is that it is where something happens. The object that is art begins with the line, the line that connects the hand (body) to the place to the page in a process of embodied triangulation. In her introduction to *On Line: drawing through the twentieth century* Catherine de Zegher writes that:

> A kinesthetic practice of traction – attraction, extraction, protraction – drawing is born from an outward gesture linking inner impulses and thoughts to the other through the touching of a surface with repeated graphic marks and lines. (de Zegher 2010: 23)

Perhaps the greatest challenge we faced when we came to the Humber estuary was the horizon lying low and absolutely uncompromising, suggesting infinity. Our lines, drawn and written, needed to find new horizons. For most of our paintings, drawings and poems-for-the-wall, and for the artists' book, *Behind Land* (2015), we decided to use an extended landscape format. We both celebrated the way in which so many of the points of interest line up on the horizon. Tucker counteracted the

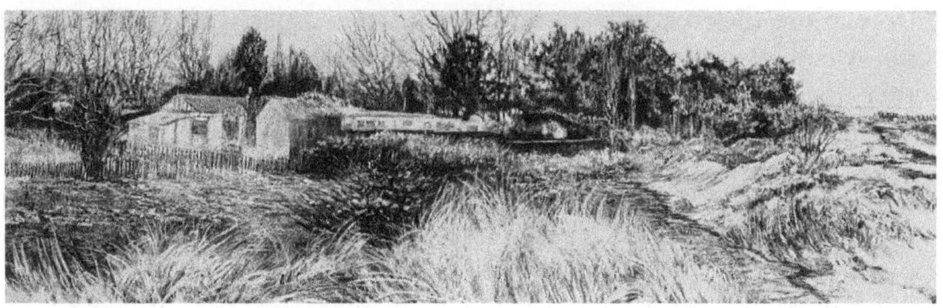

Figure 4.4 Judith Tucker (monochrome drawing) and Harriet Tarlo (open-form poem), Excerpt from *Excavations and Estuaries*, 2014

associations of the horizon with romantic, sublime landscape by various destabilising techniques: high horizons, a flattening of pictorial space through mark making and thus a bringing of the horizon to the surface of the picture plane, countering both the expected depth-of-field and aesthetic distancing. Some of the work thus appears almost as if it is an aerial view or a view from inside the land looking out.

As in 'Either Side', in Figure 4.4 there are at least three ways a viewer's eye might imagine entering, and more often than not the focus is right at the edge, encouraging the viewer to scan from side to side. The way that the words create their own horizons, or lines, their spacing on the page encourages a similar scanning process and, through particulars, unsettles in a complementary manner to the way that the marks counteract a sense of distance. Through this we invite our viewers or reader to focus on, precisely, the reverse of the sublime, rather, what can be seen, heard, smelt and experienced, what is near, to invite them into the mesh or work. As the texts and images of the east coast show, when it comes to the production and editing of our work in the field, we are led to explore, beyond methodology, how our lines can mirror each other. It is in the subtleties of interplays such as this that the work challenges conventional landscape writing, painting and drawing. However, we also explore difference in our collaborative practice with regard to the line. A consideration of the way in which these art forms imagine each other now, and in the past, helps us do this.

In particular we are interested in how poetry can be considered in terms of lines of sounds through space and the process of drawing may incorporate imagining lines of sight through the air from an implied horizon to the eye. It is easy to see how our drawing and writing made in place conform to what Badiou terms:

> true Drawing, a creative one, the marks, the traces, the lines, are not included or closeted in the background. On the contrary, the marks, the lines – the forms, if you will – create the background as an open space. They create what Mallarmé names, 'the empty paper which is protected by its whiteness'. (2011: 65)

Here we see Badiou turning to a poet to help make his point – Stéphane Mallarmé was arguably the prime originator of modernist *vers libre*, as well as one of the first poets to open up the page in his *Un coup de dés jamais n'abolira le hasard* (1897). He escaped the strictures of the classical alexandrine to discover that space lay at the back of all marks.

Like many poets writing in the modernist tradition, Tarlo included, Mallarmé's inheritors long for language to be more of an embodied, material practice, something closer to drawing, painting and sculpture. The objectivists (and later, the concrete poets) often referred in their poetics to other art forms such as sculpture and drawing, but also to the melodic powers of music. Michael Heller talks about the objectivist vision being one 'which uses language as a painter might use paint to create a structure of relations, a spatio-linguistic object' (1985: 2). Yes, space lies at the back of all marks and a poem might attempt to be a material object, but *at the same time*, in *the same poem*, silence lies at the back of all sound, as Lorine Niedecker attests in these lines from 'Wintergreen Ridge':

> Nobody, nothing
>   ever gave me
>   greater thing
>
> than time
>   unless light
>   and silence
>
> which if intense
>   makes sound

(Niedecker 2002: 253)

The spatial and sonic attention that is brought to the forming of these lines speaks for itself.

The lines of thought, conversation, of drawing, of poetry that we compose when out in the field are the closest we can come to engaging with the world in sincerity as fact, to employ Objectivist terminology:

> In sincerity shapes appear concomitants of word combinations, precursors of [...] completed sound or structure, melody or form. Writing occurs which is the detail not mirage of seeing, of thinking with things as they exist, and of directing them along a line of melody. Shapes suggest themselves, and the mind senses and receives awareness. Parallels sought for in the other arts call up the perfect line of occasional drawing. (Zukofsky, 'An Objective' (1930), in Zukofsky 1981 [1967]: 12–18)

Here Zukofsky turns to drawing to explore poetry as a thinking, responsive art that produces things. His simultaneous emphasis on the visual and sonic qualities of poetry, the 'line of melody', shows again that desire to make language material, to make it MATTER, printed matter such as we might see in a gallery alongside the drawings of a visual artist, but also to make it sound, lines of difference.

It is in the differences that emerge from the space and silence between them that our finished works hold their power to provoke the imagination. Our lines contrast with each other, even as they hold in common an acute awareness of space. Tucker's richly textured and dense drawings, though apparently opaque, reveal their surfaces to be translucent, composed of a lattice of lines revealing the layers beneath. Hidden drawings below are visible and what is underneath all the layers, the texture of the paper itself, is incorporated even on the very top surface, becoming both one time and an enmeshed time in a way that which relates to place. Even though, at first glance, the surfaces of these drawings are intense, they are far from impenetrable. There is 'breathing' space in these drawings, not the white space of the paper but pictorial space, apparent space between the skein-like layers that do not coalesce on the surface.

Both poems and visuals address how we move through landscape; size, space and viewpoint are key to this. In the very short poems she writes for the wall and artists' books, Tarlo focuses on the condensation principles of modernist poets such as Lorine Niedecker. Next to Tucker's drawings and paintings, these sparse pages, prints, vinyls or canvases 'create the background as an open space' and can be looked at as drawings, line drawings perhaps, which enliven and open up space. It is possible to see all the words at once and to move between them in different ways, as one does when walking through landscape and when looking at drawings. The dense surfaces of the drawings employ dramatic tonality in combination with the use of more delicate marks. They simultaneously invite the viewer's eye to explore the space and remind us that it is a surface, thus implying distance, but also proximity.

We are moving on here to consider our audience, whether viewers, listeners or readers, more closely here. They are our final collaborators whom we invite into our sense of movement, our pauses of production in exhibition and publication. Jill Bennett argues that certain 'images have the capacity to address the spectator's own bodily memory; to touch the viewer who feels rather than simply sees the event, drawn into the image through a process of affective contagion' (2005: 36) This 'affective contagion' is both augmented and disturbed precisely in the gap between words and drawn marks, as the viewer's or reader's eye moves back and forth between them. Defying obvious boundaries and binary ways of thinking about art and poetry, our collaborative works are experiential. Both more and less descriptive or topographical, they play with the recording of presence or encounter, acknowledging and yet questioning this possibility, both for ourselves and for our audiences, not least because of the multiplicity of perception we present and the multiple forms in which we present it.

We do not move smoothly from reading the text or image of landscape to production of our own texts and images. We are engaged in all these processes at once. We continue to talk and make work about these now much-visited places and to exhibit, read and publish in a series of productions from drawings, paintings, texts to exhibitions, to papers, to books, all of which interrelate in a flow of production involving the disembodied space of virtual communication as well as conversations outside and in the studio. Time is spent producing our own work, considering each other's work and considering the responses of our various audiences to the work, thus allowing other voices to enter the conversation. This kind of fluidity is resonant of Ingold's exuberant finale to his book *Lines: A Brief History:* 'Lines are open-ended, and it is this open-endedness – of lives, relationships, histories, and processes of thought – that I wanted to celebrate' (2007: 169–71).

Often newcomers to open-form or concrete work that so evidently engages with poetry as spatial, even as object, do not at first realise that the work is also a score, that all poetry worthy of the name brings deep feeling, not through rhetoric but through suggestion, not simply through words but through the delineation of sound in space. Basil Bunting, the northern British modernist poet, talked of poetry as 'lines and patterns of sound drawn in the air which stir deep emotions which have not even a name in prose' (Williams and Bunting 1968: n.p.). This is one of the reasons why, wherever possible, we include readings in front of the work in our presentations of it, if only at the opening of an exhibition. In performance it is often possible to bring alive the collaborative, multilayered and insistently cross-disciplinary, unintegrated nature of our work. For instance, at the Trembling Grass festival in Exeter, Tarlo read the text of *Sound Unseen* while Tucker projected images from the book on to a large screen. Effectively we were turning the pages live, but avoiding, as the concertina structure of the book itself does, the direct equation of one image to one text as pairs. In the multiple fold, there is a democracy of units – drawing is not privileged over poetry or vice versa, each page is entire unto itself or may be read sequentially. There are infinite ways of folding and unfolding the book to reveal different combinations.

The constraints of exhibition spaces have often led to the presentation of text and image as pairs; this has a degree of flexibility as pairs can change and be presented one on top of the other or side by side depending on the space. Here we work to avoid the sense of duplication, description or illustration. The two art forms should rather complement each other, speaking to each other as we have throughout the working process and allowing a viewer to appreciate the connections and divergences between the practices that we have elaborated on here. Recent decisions about how to present the work have been designed to increase the involvement of audiences, to create greater freedom of interpretation, but also to challenge conventional notions of place and environment. In some iterations of the east coast work, we used vinyl text so that the poetry can be placed around the images more freely, rather as birds transcribe the sky space around them, and we have thus escaped the notion of pairing altogether.

Ultimately, our aspiration is that out of difference come connections bringing new imaginings to our audiences, imaginings that mirror our own discoveries made through collaborative cross-disciplinary practice. What might happen in the minds and bodies of the audience if our embodied lines meet – the poet's reaching into space through lines of sound drawn in the air, as Bunting puts it, and the artist's lines of sight from the implied horizon to the eye viewing the finished painting or drawing? As De Zehger suggests, 'the eye manages to discern what has become a trace on the paper from a gesture in the air' (de Zegher and Newman 2003: 82). Perhaps when poetry and drawing work as companions together there is a ricochet effect, where lines of sound come off the written page and lines of movement have coalesced on to the drawn page; perhaps this is one of the ways that we (artists, audiences and ecocritics in collaboration) might all be able to 'draw closer' to

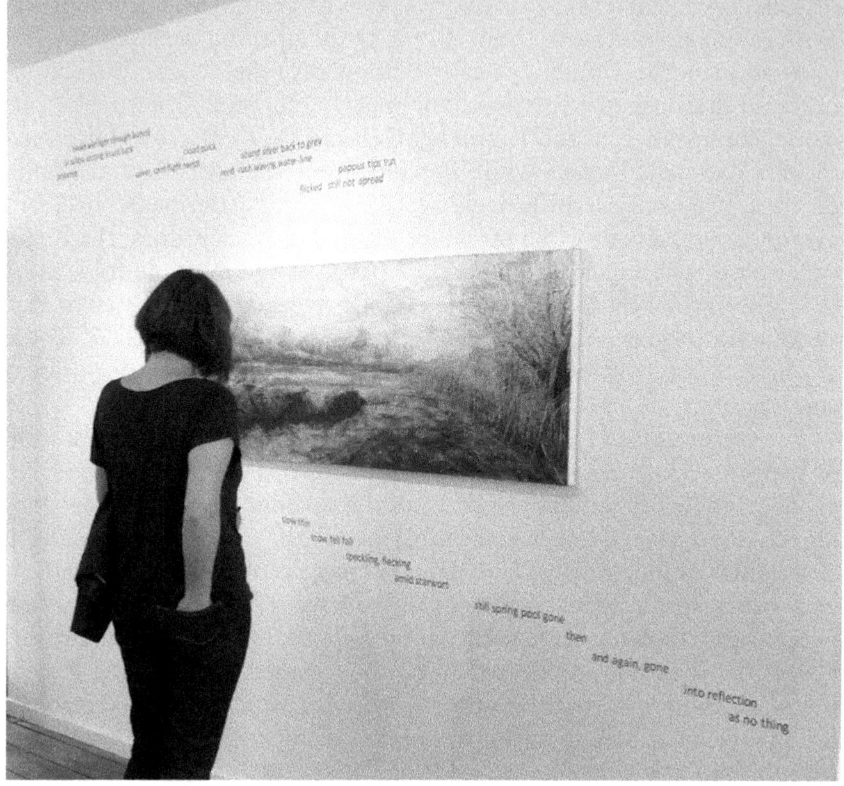

Figure 4.5   Judith Tucker and Harriet Tarlo, *Excavations and Estuaries* at Bank Street Arts, Sheffield, 2014

place and, through this, to begin to reimagine new relationships to wider landscapes and environments.

Notes

1   This title is derived from Norman Bryson, 'A Walk for a Walk's Sake', in Catherine de Zegher (2003: 149–58).

2   The *Excavations and Estuaries* project was curated by the independent curator Linda Ingham and, although we worked mainly with each other, there were other artists involved. Our collective work was brought together in seminars, workshops and group exhibitions. In this context however we focus on our joint work within this.

3   Tucker has explored this approach extensively in relation to drawing in 'Brooding on Bornholm: Postmemory, Painting and Place' (2012) and 'The Lido in the Forest: Painting, Memory and Subjectivity' (2010).

4 See www.moorsforthefuture.org.uk accessed 29 January 2016.

5 The geographer David Matless and the English scholar Alexandra Harris share an interest in examining the mid-century phenomenon of trying to bring together the romantic and the modern in relation to locale. In *Romantic Moderns* Harris (2010: 291–2) argues against Christopher Wilk's assertion (2006) that Englishness and modernism were antithetical, arguing, rather, that British artists were differently modern.

6 These were part of the plotland settlements which cropped up all over the UK coastline. 'These were unplanned, self-built, knots and straggles of seasonably occupied dwellings featuring creative adaptations of old tram cars, railway carriages and later bus bodies which sprang up on the shoreline [...] offering a foothold to bohemian seekers after the simple seaside life or, increasingly working class families whose only hope of affording a seaside holiday [...] was via this makeshift and independent route' (Walton 2000: 36).

7 The word 'particular' is also important to Thomas A. Clark who calls one of his early collections *Some Particulars* (1971).

8 These principles and phrases are distilled from Louis Zukofsky 1931a and 1931b.

9 An example of another poet and artist pairing, Frances Presley and Tilla Brading's work *Stone Settings* (2010), in which they collaboratively explore the Neolithic stone settings, rows, longstones and circles of Exmoor, we find a texture of work which reflects a similar process, including the incorporation of maps, music, diagrams and archeological material. Here the two poets' actual text is as minimal and fragmentary as some of the stones themselves.

10 Found Poem from the direct speech of Grace Hinchcliffe and June Peabody in Eileen Catchell's *Tales of the Mills* (no date).

References

Anon. (2009) *North Lincolnshire Landscape Character Assessment*. Scunthorpe: North East Lincolnshire Council.

Badiou A. (2011) *Drawing*. http://lacan.com/sypmtom12/?p=65 accessed 28 March 2016.

Bennett, Jane (2010) *Vibrant Matter: A Political Ecology of Things*. Durham, NC, and London: Duke University Press.

Bennett, Jill (2005) *Empathic Vision: Affect, Trauma, and Contemporary Art*. Redwood City: Stanford University Press.

Biggs, I. (2004) *Between Carterhaugh and Tamshiel Rig: A Borderline Episode*. Bristol: Wild Conversations Press.

Biggs, I. (2008) 'Extract from a Presentation on "Polyvocal" Drawing', in Judith Tucker and Jayne Bingham (eds) *All over the Place: Drawing Place, Drawing Space*. Bristol: Wild Conversations Press.

Bryson, Norman (2003) 'A Walk for a Walk's Sake', in Catherine de Zegher (ed.), *The Stage of Drawing*. New York: Tate Publishing and The Drawing Centre, pp. 149–58.

Casey, Edward S. (1993) *Getting Back into Place: Toward a Renewed Understanding of the Place-World*. Bloomington: Indiana University Press.

Catchell, Eileen (n.d.) *Tales of the Mills*. Holmfirth: Friend to Friend.

Clark, T. (2015) *Ecocriticism on the Edge: The Anthropocene as a Threshold Concept*. London: Bloomsbury Publishing.

Daniels, Stephen, Mike Pearson and Heike Rom (2010) 'Editorial' of the Special Issue: Fieldworks. *Performance Research: A Journal of the Performing Arts* 4: 1–5.

De Zegher, Catherine (ed.) (2003) *The Stage of Drawing*. New York: Tate Publishing and The Drawing Centre.

De Zegher, Catherine (2010) *On Line: Drawing through the Twentieth Century*. New York: Museum of Modern Art.

De Zegher, Catherine and Avis Newman (eds) (2003) *The Stage of Drawing: Gesture and Art*. London: Tate Publishing.

Fay, B. (2013) *What Is Drawing – A Continuous Incompleteness*. Dublin: Irish Museum of Modern Art.

Finlay, Alec (1995) 'Standing Still and Walking in Strath Nethy: An Interview with Thomas A Clark'. *Edinburgh Review* 94 (Autumn). Accessed online www.cairneditions.co.uk/thomasaclark/interview.pdf accessed 28 March 2016.

Garrard, G. (2011) *Ecocriticism* Second edition. London: Routledge.

Haraway, Donna J. (2003) *The Companion Species Manifesto: Dogs, People, and Significant Otherness*. Chicago: Prickly Paradigm Press.

Harris, Alexandra (2010) *Romantic Moderns: English Writers, Artists and the Imagination from Virginia Woolf to John Piper*. London: Thames and Hudson.

Heller, Michael (1985) *Convictions Net of Branches: Essays on the Objectivist Poets and Poetry*. Carbondale: Southern Illinois University Press.

Hume, Angela (2012) 'Imagining Ecopoetics: an Interview with Robert Hass, Brenda Hillman, Evelyn Reilly, and Jonathan Skinner', *ISLE* 19:4: 751–66.

Ingold, Tim (2007) *Lines: A Brief History*. London: Routledge.

Mallarmé, Stéphane (2006) *Collected Poems and Other Verse*, trans. E.H. and A.M. Blackmore. Oxford: Oxford University Press.

Massey, Doreen (2006) 'Landscape as a Provocation: Reflections on Moving Mountains', *Journal of Material Culture* 11:1–2: 33–48.

Matless, David (1998) *Landscape and Englishness*. London: Reaktion Books.

Niedecker, Lorine (2002) *Collected Works*, ed. Jenny Penberthy. Berkeley and London: University of California Press.

Olson, Charles (1997 [1950]) 'Projective Verse', in *Collected Prose*, ed. Donald Allen and Benjamin Friedlander. Berkeley and London: University of California Press.

Pearson, Mike and Michael Shanks (2001) *Theatre/Archaeology: Disciplinary Dialogues*. London: Routledge.

Petherbridge, Deanna (2010) *The Primacy of Drawing: Histories and Theories of Practice*. New Haven and London: Yale University Press.

Soper, Kate (1995) *What Is Nature?* Oxford: Wiley-Blackwell.

Tarlo, Harriet (2013) 'Open Field: Reading Field as Place and Poetics', in Ian Davidson and Zoe Skoulding (eds), *Placing Poetry*. Amsterdam and New York: Rodopi.

Tarlo, Harriet and Judith Tucker (2013) *Sound Unseen*. Leeds: Wild Pansy.

Tarlo, Harriet and Judith Tucker (2015) *Behind Land*. Leeds: Wild Pansy.

Thoreau, H.D. (2006 [1862]) *Walking*. New York: Cosimo.

Tucker, Judith (2010) 'The Lido in the Forest: Painting, Memory and Subjectivity', in E. Anderson, A. Maddrell, K. McLoughlin and A. Vincent (eds), *Memory, Mourning, Landscape*. Amsterdam: Rodopi Press, pp. 191–218.

Tucker, Judith (2012) 'Brooding on Bornholm: Postmemory, Painting and Place', in O. Jones and J. Garde-Hansen (eds), *Geography and Memory*. Basingstoke: Palgrave Macmillan, pp. 68–84.

Walton, J.K. (2000) *The British Seaside: Holidays and Resorts in the Twentieth Century*. Manchester: Manchester University Press.

Wilk, Christopher (ed.) (2006) *Modernism: Designing a New World: 1914–1939*. London: V&A Publications.

Williams, Jonathan and Basil Bunting (1968) *Descant on Rawthey's Madrigal: Conversations with Basil Bunting*. Lexington: Gnomon Press.

Williams, William Carlos (1954 [1948]) 'The Poem as a Field of Action', in *Selected Essays of William Carlos Williams*. New York: Random House.

Zukofsky, Louis (1930–1a) 'Program: "Objectivists" 1931', *Poetry* 37:5: 268–72.

Zukofsky, Louis (1930–1b) 'Sincerity and Objectification', *Poetry* 37:5: 272–85.

Zukofsky, Louis (1981 [1967]) 'An Objective' (1930), in *Prepositions: The Collected Critical Essays of Louis Zukofsky*. Berkeley: University of California Press.

5

ARTlines: three walking artists in Iceland

Patti Lean

In August 2015, I made a month-long camping and walking journey in Iceland, in the company of co-artists Julie Livsey and Lesley Hicks. This is a record of that journey, and of ways in which it informed our practice as artists. Drawing from examples of our own work, and other works of visual art and writing encountered through the journey, I position our activities within a historical, practical and theoretical framework, and I also investigate contemporary interdisciplinary practice and ways in which artists work with delineations of 'nature in Iceland' in the face of serious environmental concerns.

To artists attracted by 'nature' and 'wilderness', Iceland can represent a particular view of northerliness; its mountains and glaciers attracted artists and writers, including John Ruskin, William Morris, W.G. Collingwood and W.H. Auden, for whom 'the glitter / Of glaciers, the sterile immature mountains intense' (Auden and MacNeice 2002 [1937]: 23) conveys an Iceland, or a vision of it, that is remote, transcendental and otherworldly, where you can lose yourself in the power of nature. With these suprageographical powers, Iceland's landscape exemplifies and taps into theories that often come under the aesthetic category of the sublime in the history of art and literature. For Edmund Burke (2015 [1756]: 33–4, 53) the sublime is a response to natural sights and occur-rences, an experience during which the mind is filled with a mixture of delight and terror, to the extent of feeling completely overwhelmed. Expanding on Burke's theories, Immanuel Kant (2011 [1764]: 16–17) identifies the attributes of sublimity as the terrifying, the noble and the magnificent, and develops Burke's differentiation of the sublime from the more anodyne 'beautiful'. Moreover Kant ascribes a strong moral constituent to the sublime, as he separates 'true' virtues from more contingent ones, concluding that 'true virtue alone is sublime' (22). So, the elemental landscapes of Iceland would seem inextricably linked with narratives and mythologies that conflate landscape and terrain with characteristics and behaviours attributed to its inhabitants, both human and nonhuman.

As regards the sublime, nowadays, as Simon Morley (2010: 19) points out, contemporary artists might 'shy away from describing their work in such terms' and are 'wary of attributing to their practices lofty or grandiose intentions'. Notions of Iceland as a northerly Utopia are tempered by a growing body of evidence that anthropogenic climate change is permanently and visibly altering ecosystems: in Bill McKibben's words:

> We have changed the most basic forces around us. We have changed the atmosphere, and that is changing the weather. The temperature and the rainfall are no longer entirely the work of some uncivilisable force but instead are in part a product of our habits, our economies, our ways of life. (McKibben 2003 [1989]: 47)

Environmental considerations can be seen to cut across 'traditional' aesthetic categories like 'sublime' and 'landscape', and, in contemporary practice, artists tend to work in interdisciplinary ways that elide boundaries between 'nature' and 'culture', and that look outside art-historical tropes into other fields and disciplines. It can be argued however that art-historical categories underpin and frame what is happening nowadays, even as we dismantle them: as Morley (2010: 19) observes, 'there is a field of ideas that the sublime generates'. Given that it is hard to talk about Iceland without invoking mountains, volcanoes, glaciers, waterfalls, whales and sagas, my discussions take place in these contexts.

For the three of us, walking in Iceland has become integral to making work. Walking allows us to explore at a pace and rhythm in which ideas can play out in terms of sense-data. Through the line of the walk it's possible to conceptualise our real and imagined trajectories in place and time. In his 2015 book *The Life of Lines* Tim Ingold proposes life and knowledge as a mesh of lines. In order to live, beings – human and nonhuman – must put out lines to one another through the atmosphere: knots, loops, arteries, streams, sounds, voices. Moreover, we acquire knowledge by means of the body-action of walking:

> For the walker, movement is not ancillary to knowing – not merely a means of getting from point to point in order to collect the raw data of sensation for subsequent modelling in the mind. Rather, moving is knowing. The walker knows as he goes along. (Ingold 2015: 47)

As a metaphorical representation, according to Ingold, 'personal' knowledge operates 'in-between' shifting lines or 'articulations' of pre-existing knowledge (148–9). As a visual artist I'm fascinated by these ideas, partly because artists tend to think and produce with the drawn line, and partly because, during our physical journeys, we are constantly putting out as-yet-unknown lines to unpreconceived experiences, that will unfold through the chance delineations of the journey. On this trip to Iceland, a second for me and third or fourth for the others, our project is to travel for nearly a month, camping and walking as mood, energy and weather conditions take us. Our aim is vibrant, ideas-generating lines: art-lines that will depend on other physical and conceptual lines: tent-ropes, trajectories, bus-routes, footpaths, trails, rivers, shorelines, crevasses, lines that link through time and place to other artists and writers: all of which, we hope, will loop back into our own explorations and art practices.

Our destination and specific area of enquiry is the Westfjords, the sparsely-populated mountainous peninsula that protrudes from the north-west of Iceland, like a troll's hand. In my bag I have basic drawing and painting materials, notebooks and a copy of Nan Shepherd's *The Living Mountain*, a prose-poem about walking in the Cairngorms that continues to inform and inspire my work. Although it adds extra weight, nevertheless I carry it up and down mountains like a talisman. We wear strong boots and layers of warm lightweight wind- and-waterproof clothing. We each carry a large rucksack containing necessary outdoor kit: tent, sleeping bag, inflatable mattress (very necessary protection from ground-chill, we find), survival bag, guidebook, map, compass, GPS, first aid kit, mobile phone, camera, sound recorder, laptop – all this 'gear' a pertinent reminder that technology has helped bring increasing numbers of visitors, mainly from affluent countries, to bear on Iceland's ecosystems. On arriving at Keflavík airport we trudge to the exit to find a bus; 'trudge' because, like the majority of our fellow passengers, we wear our hiking boots on the flight. Inside the terminus we pass billboards that state, 'Everything is nice that is green' and, more enigmatically, 'There are many wonders in a cow's head'.

Since the *kressa*, the bank collapse of 2008, Iceland's economic recovery is predicated in no small part on the marketing of mountains, glaciers, snow, ice, geysirs: as if 'nature' were a prime destination you could travel to.

Which in a sense perhaps it is, if you travel along the trajectories of your own memory. One Icelandic painter who did so was Louisa Matthíasdóttir (1917–2000), whose work offers a very particular vision of

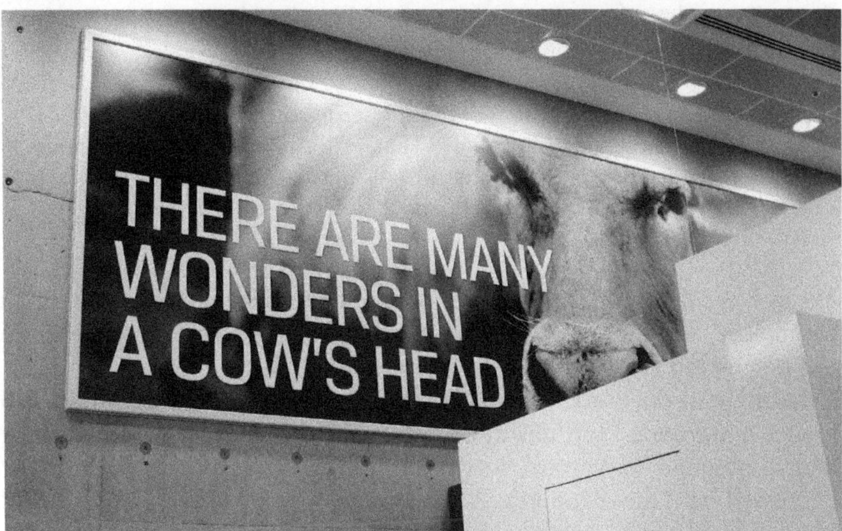

Figure 5.1 Patti Lean, *Many Wonders*, 2015. Digital photograph, arrivals hall, Keflavík airport

Iceland, conceived partly from reconnection and partly from memory, echoing Merleau-Ponty's statement that 'Quality, light, colour, depth, which are there before us, are there only because they awaken an echo in our bodies and because the body welcomes them' (Johnson and Smith 1993: 125). Although Matthíasdóttir studied in Paris before heading to New York in 1942, going on to become part of the postwar avant-garde in that city, she revisited Iceland both physically and artistically all her life, drawing on deep childhood knowledge: 'I guess when one is born somewhere or is young in a particular place, one knows that part of the world better than any other and is more attached to it than any other. So it seems natural that I should want to paint Iceland' (Perl 1999: 133). In New York Matthíasdóttir studied with the modernist painter and teacher Hans Hofmann, an important figure in abstract expressionism: perhaps this is why sheep, horses, mountains, fjords, farmhouses, people are levelled to near-abstractions in her paintings. For Perl her work is 'a vision of Iceland as a hieratic, austere, magical place. The country becomes a series of impregnable images: sharp, clear, absolute' (140).

It is difficult to assign Matthíasdóttir's work to any specific classification in art, like the sublime or the picturesque, the abstract or the realist – although all these terms might apply in some measure. Known to be down-to-earth and sparing with words, Matthíasdóttir succinctly echoes the formalism of her education:

> I don't do shapes and colours without seeing them in nature. Either it looks like a landscape or it doesn't. That's all. And also, either a form fits in the painting or it doesn't. After all, a painting isn't really a still-life or a landscape, it's a mere canvas. It can never be real life. It must be a painting. (99)

Yet in ways that somehow do not seem incongruent with Greenbergian formalism[1] and modernist ideals, Matthíasdóttir's sheep do what sheep do; they stand still and stare at you (see Plate 3).

Looking at the work within contemporary ecocritical discourses also invites congruity: Matthíasdóttir's interplay of place, material, human and nonhuman in her work would seem to correspond with a view expressed in Jane Bennett's 2010 book *Vibrant Matter: A Political Ecology of Things:*

> Humanity and nonhumanity have always performed an intricate dance with each other. There was never a time when human agency was anything other than an interfolding network of humanity and non-humanity; today this mingling has become harder to ignore. (Bennett 2010: 31)

Matthíasdóttir articulates all this through surgically accurate colour that is inseparable from form: 'The reason I paint is because I want to paint what I see. But to paint what I see, I must build from color' (Perl 1999: 99). Grassy pasture is a sweep of blue-green, the colour of vitriol or copperas; venetian red and *caput mortuum* denote deposits of ferrous oxide and haematite in the rocks. These alchemical-sounding substances that derive from rock-pigments are also the colour of shadows on a lamb's tail, or the delineation of a rider's leg. Matthíasdóttir's working methods offer insight into her clarity of vision: she 'paints rapidly in long horizontal strokes and using a loaded brush' preferring 'to paint successive versions of the same subject rather than to labour for weeks on the same canvas', a 'visible process that laid bare the act of painting, with its numerous decisions and nullifications of those decisions' (Sawin 1999: 76).

Another artist's work percolates our journey, that of Benedikt Erlingsson, director of the 2013 film *Of Horses and Men (Hross í oss).*[2] The film portrays similar subjects to those of Matthíasdóttir: horses, riders, sheep, mountains, rural life, but in a bleak and edgy comic idiom that draws on both Greek tragedy and the Icelandic sagas. Episodic plotlines interweave separate lives and individual passions against a backdrop of sublimely harsh landscapes: feuding families, love, loss, sex, death, killing. It all happens for horses as well as humans; as a keen horseman Erlingsson is fascinated by the reciprocity of human/horse relationships through time.

I interview Erlingsson by Skype. He says that the remoteness of the landscape contains 'a very beautiful paradox': 'If people have a space around them, if there is a distance around people, they tend to be very interested in each other. But when you press people together, like in a big city, they are not interested, they close up.'[3] Mutual interest seems key to horse/human interplay in Icelandic life, bringing to mind again Bennett's ideas of 'intricate dance' and 'interfolding networks of humanity and nonhumanity' (2010: 31). Each seems to inform the other in ways that blur boundaries between human and nonhuman, or perhaps in this case, 'horse' and 'nonhorse', both social creatures with an extreme interest in eyeing up others. Humans observe their neighbours' every move through binoculars that glint across valleys, while the camera zooms in large to the eyes of the horses in which the viewer sees reflections of human foibles and idiosyncrasies.

We talk about Erlingsson's next film, which will be about climate change, 'the most important subject of all, and I think politics should not be about anything else'. We also talk about lines: the first settlers in the ninth and tenth centuries established a horse-based system of roads that criss-cross the whole country. Erlingsson is proud that Icelandic horses are not 'broken': there is 'negotiation' and the horse must be 'willing' – this latter term is apparently much used by Icelanders, often as euphemism for an over-energetic horse. What it comes down to in the end is, you either 'have a slave or have a companion'. I ask if breaking or taming horses is a metaphor for breaking or taming nature: 'Taming nature or breaking nature – if nature is strong enough it will hit you back, or you break it and you lose the spirit'. According to Erlingsson, the bridle-paths were made with great economy of design, and there is beauty in the knowledge that riders today are using the same paths as the characters in the sagas.

Over a millennium of negotiating rough ground, Icelandic horses have developed *tölt*, a gait unique to the breed. All Icelandic horses are born with the ability to *tölt*, a gait additional to walk, trot, canter and gallop. In *tölt* the feet follow the same four-beat sequence as in walk: left hind leg, left front leg, right hind leg, right front leg. There is high knee action and at least one foot is on the ground at any one time, making the *tölt* smooth and comfortable for the rider: William Morris refers fondly to 'my own little red among them the softest-paced of the whole train' (Greenlaw 2011: 77). *Tölt* is thought to derive etymologically from the Hungarian *telik* 'to pour': riders and goods are less likely to topple and undergo damage, and a horse with good *tölt* is highly prized by riders and breeders. When you look at the terrain it is easy to see why, although nowadays the four-wheel drive replaces the horse for all but recreational purposes.

Iceland's terrain is new, geologically speaking, and moves around a great deal. According to *Geology of Iceland,* 'If we take the age of the earth as one year, then Iceland was only born less than two days ago' (Thordarson *and* Höskuldsson 2014: 1) and 'The forces of nature that constantly mould and shape the face of the Earth operate faster in Iceland than in most other places. The rocks are shattered by the frequent change of frost to thaw, and the wind, seas and glaciers laboriously grind down the land' (1). Travel can be difficult and dangerous in this environment, even in cars and jeeps. For Hjallmar Sveinsson in his 2011 essay 'Songlines of the Jeeps', 'the disastrous journey is a literary genre unto itself in Iceland' (Sveinsson 2011). Iceland's Nobel Prize-winning, and, arguably, national-identity-forming, work of literature, *Independent People* by Halldór Laxness (1955) contains several spectacularly perilous journeys, starting with one in which the central character Bjartur makes a very big mistake that will inform everything that subsequently happens. Ólafur Elíasson's exhibition *Bílar í Ám / Cars in Rivers* (2009)[4] is a contemporary iteration of the perilous journey. Following a call for photographs of cars stranded in rivers, the artist received more than a hundred images from members of the public, from which a final piece was curated. My favourite image is pure Monty Python: a floppy-haired 1970s dude squares up to the deluge from the bonnet of his semi-submerged red Land-Rover.

If *tölt* seems a perfect example of interplay between human, nonhuman and environment, there are times on our walking journey when I sincerely wish we could *tölt* our way through this landscape. On long hikes this leads me to muse on exactly what it is we *are* doing. If, as Rebecca Solnit (2014 [2006]: 272) observes, 'the simple gesture of walking can tie the walker to the surface of the earth', then the recent proliferation and diversity of walking practices as strategies of artistic production seem good indicators of environmental connectedness. But what are we doing? Despite our array of 'gear' and equipment, the *ad hoc* nature of our forays would suggest we are not 'mountaineering' in the sense of attaining summits or conquering peaks. '*Flâneur*' ('stroller' or 'saunterer') contains the correct sense of purposeful aimlessness and slow travel, allowing for possibilities of place ... but we are neither young men nor urban, so *flâneur* doesn't quite cut the mustard. I look to Nan Shepherd for guidance. The Aberdeen mountaineer-writer and teacher-training lecturer spent many of her eighty-eight years exploring mountains with mind and body inseparable and sensate: as she puts it,

'I can teach my body many skills by which to learn the nature of the mountain' (Shepherd 2011 [1977]: 90). Shepherd's poetic eulogy to the Cairngorms, *The Living Mountain*, written in the mid-1940s but not published until 1977, combines practical mountain-sense with sharp clarity, acuity of observation and a zen-like approach: 'The mountain gives itself most completely when I have no destination, when I reach nowhere in particular, but when I have gone out merely to be with the mountain as one visits a friend with no intention but to be with him' (Shepherd 2011 [1977]: 14). The Scots '*stravaig*' keeps coming to mind as a suitable descriptor that has undertones of digression beyond normal limits of thought and speech, in addition to physical terrain, and it is good to think we are '*stravaiging*' new ideas and projects.

En route to the Westfjords, we camp in a field of new-cut grass on Flatey Island. I buy fresh eggs from the farmer, and ask where the shop is. 'There is no shop, but if you're still hungry tomorrow, come at five and I will give you some cod.' Still hungry indeed, we arrive next day to watch the farmer-fisherman gutting cod under a shrieking umbrella of arctic terns (onomatopaeically named *kría* in Icelandic). Like so many undersized harpies, the terns skim our heads, all pointed beaks and scarlet claws on hair.

The fisherman carefully cuts small cubes of fish, and places them on the side of his board. By now the terns are hysterical. From the small crowd of onlookers someone asks, why the little cubes? '*Kría* can't eat anything bigger. Their beaks are too small and pointed. And the chicks are starving; parent birds have to fly too far to get food.' One tourist asks for a cube of the fresh fish. 'But you are not a bird.'

Half of all Iceland's seabirds, twenty-three species, nest on Flatey and surrounding islands in Breiðafjörður Bay. Terns were once prolific but nowadays studies show drastic loss of numbers, both here and throughout the circumpolar north. According to researcher Freydís Vigfúsdóttir, 'There are just dead chicks everywhere. Not only do you have to provide your field assistants with food and shelter, but also some psychological help after many, many days of collecting dead chicks' (Katz 2014). Breeding has been poor not only for the terns but also for fulmars, kittiwakes, puffins and guillemots.

On the mountain we give in to the temptation of attaching meaning to our interactions with birds. A whimbrel follows us for hours, gurgling like water over rock; this augurs well (oh! lucky; it must *like* us). A raven caws overhead (not so lucky; isn't the collective name 'unkindness'?). On one walk at Ólafsfjörður, a snow bunting perches and ruffles (oh! sweet! It's so tiny, it must be cold or hungry etc.). Halldór Laxness's 1968 novel *Under the Glacier* is an unsettling tale of animistic

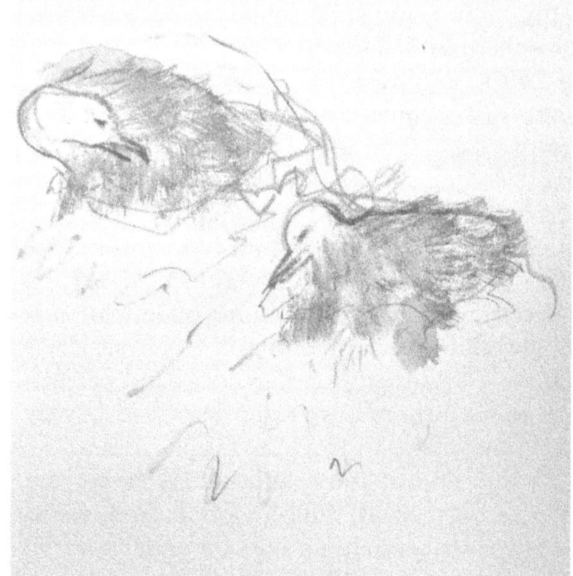

Figure 5.2　Patti Lean, *Fulmar Chicks on Grímsey Island*, 2014

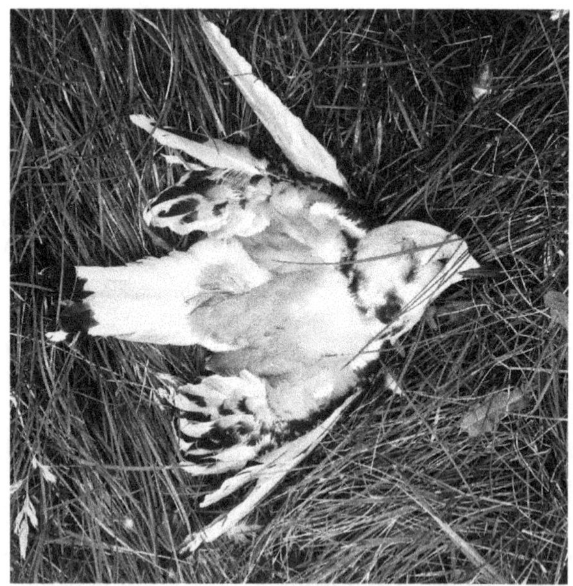

Figure 5.3　Patti Lean, *Dead Fulmar Chick, Grímsey Island*, 2014

goings-on in a remote parish. To the dismay of the bishop of distant Reykjavík, the priest has boarded up the village church and appears to have become a nature-worshipper:

> Pastor Jón: Often I think the Almighty is like a snow bunting abandoned in all weathers. Such a bird is about the weight of a postage stamp. Yet he does not blow away when he stands in the open in a tempest. Have you ever seen the skull of a snow bunting? He wields this fragile head against the gale, with his beak to the ground, wings folded close to his sides and his tail pointing upwards; and the wind can get no hold on him, and cleaves. Even in the fiercest squalls the bird does not budge. He is becalmed. Not a single feather stirs.
>
> Embi: How do you know the bird is the Almighty, and not the wind?
>
> Pastor Jón: Because the winter storm is the most powerful force in Iceland, and the snow bunting is the feeblest of all God's conceptions. (Laxness 2005 [1968]: 82)

Julie was taken with these ideas on a previous trip, and begins to pull connections through into the objects and materials that she constantly collects.

On this trip, the text, the imagery and the idea are realised in site-specific text-pieces made from dandelion seeds, laboriously glued on to buildings with egg or yogurt (See Plate 4). Julie's work involves minimal waste, minimal harm, and artistic control is relinquished on completion, 'It's not supposed to last very long. I have no control over how long it lasts' (Livsey 2015: 3). The work returns to its environment through effects of time and weather.

Julie is a lifelong horsewoman and keen gardener, with expert knowledge of alpine plants. Bringing these knowledges to bear, she circumnavigates the mountain landscape continually scanning and sizing up the terrain. For Julie, 'Sculptors are people who are interested in matter. It just so happens that the matter that I'm using is very delicate [...] very fragile [...] and I use this because I feel that it reflects the vulnerability of the natural world – and that's something I'm interested in' (3). A self-described hunter-gatherer, Julie collects things that might go unremarked by most walkers: eiderdown snagged on a beach-pebble, dandelion clock-seeds, horsehair, sheep wool, sedge-grass, 'For me, bog cotton is as much a sculptural material as stone or steel' (4). Material undergoes weighing, measuring, sketching, being thought-upon, temporary transformations in often cold and uncomfortable places. 'It's very slow [...] it is a bit like a penance. It is both penance and salve, but that slow way of working suits me very well' (6). In Laxness's 1957 novel

Fish Can Sing, the boy Álfgrímur listens to the ticking of his grandparents' clock and comes to a realisation:

> How did it ever come about then, I wonder, that I got this notion that in this clock there lived a strange creature, which was Eternity? Somehow it just occurred to me one day that the word it said when it ticked, a four-syllable word with emphasis on alternate syllables, which was et-ERN-it-Y, et-ERN-it-Y. Did I know the word, then?
>
> It was odd that I should discover eternity in this way, long before I knew what eternity was, and even before I had learned the proposition that all men are mortal – yes, while I was actually living in eternity myself. It was as if a fish were to discover the water it swam in. [...]
>
> 'Grandfather,' I said. 'Is eternity a living creature?'
>
> 'Try not to talk nonsense, my boy,' said grandfather. (Laxness 1957: 5)

Julie's 'penance and salve' echoes Laxness's spiritual dimension, and on return from Iceland she reworked *et-ERN-it-Y* as part of a community project at Coanwood House, a Quaker meeting house in Northumberland, during Haltwhistle walking festival.

One day, about halfway through our journey, we *climb to a high plateau* above the town of Tálknafjörður, a small town in the Westfjords that boasts several facilities, including a beautiful contemporary church of glass and timber, and an organic cosmetics company. Julie is testing out and filming a piece of sculpture, a balance. Lesley and I sit down to paint and sketch. The cold is excoriating; our trail has petered out to what Nan Shepherd (2011: 51) aptly refers to as the 'unpath' and, while not exactly lost, neither are we exactly certain where we are.

Here on the high plateau, the sediment-bare terrain is scattered with basaltic rocks and huge glacial erratics, single boulders balanced often-precariously with no obvious provenance, as if a giant troll dropped them down just yesterday. I photograph them, and several months later, in the studio, test out ideas of bulk and balance in a series of new, large paintings. Vegetation has adapted to be effective at growing close to the ground: vision zooms beyond its accustomed fields to take in both the vastness of the rocks and mountains and the micro-world of tiny hardy alpine plants; saxifrage, butterwort, sedge, moss campion, as well as masses of miniature aromatic wild thyme in shades from blood crimson to pastel-pink. There are spongy beds of the grey-green lichen called Iceland moss (*Cetraria islandica*) and we tread carefully because we've heard that, in Iceland, lichen can take up to ten years to recover from a footprint, 'As Lichen, I work with time, great stretches of time. I know time is my friend. I give you that patience for the long haul. I would relieve you of haste' (Seed et al. 2007 [1998]: 87). As I imagine the

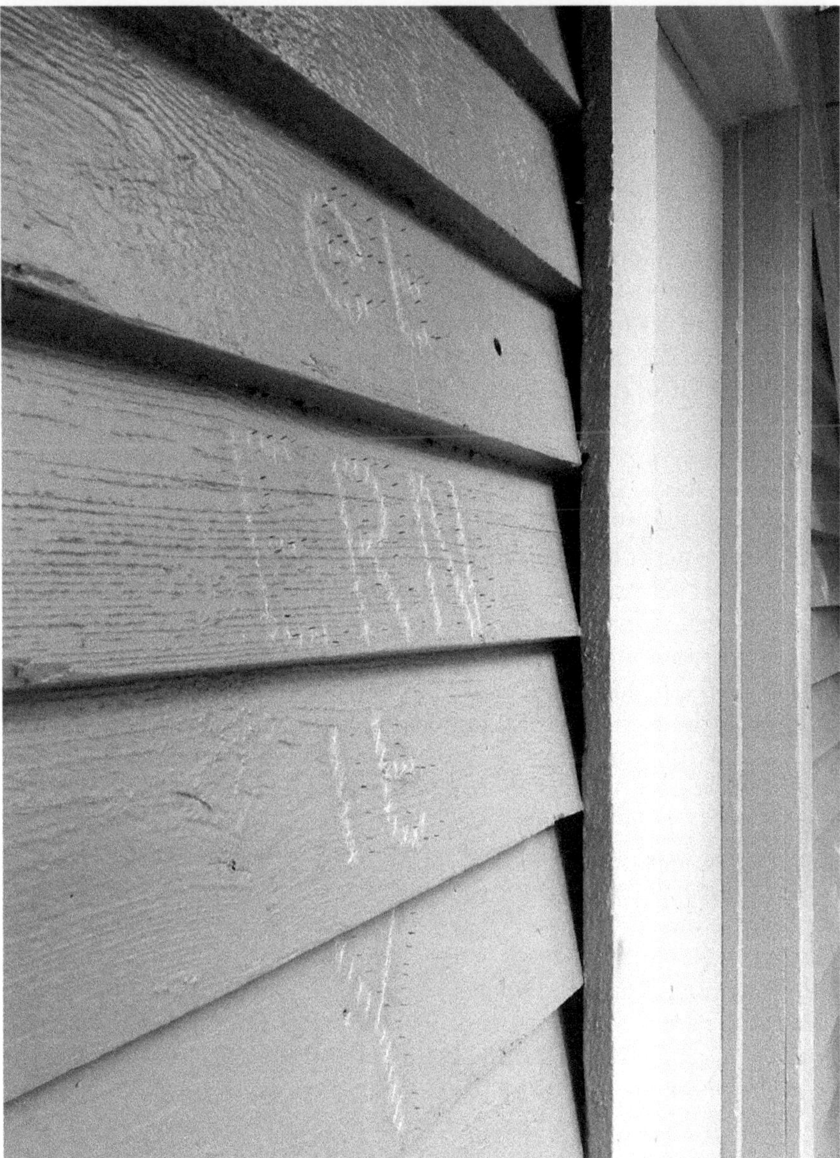

Figure 5.4 Julie Livsey, *et-ERN-it-Y*, 2015. Installation view, Coanwood Meeting House, Northumberland

lichen wincing beneath our boots, I think how it would feel, to be relieved of haste.

The smaller varieties of lichen on the scattered basalt rocks are in hot, tender pastels: tangerine and mango, pistachio and coconut, as if in a Venetian ice-cream parlour. I sit in the shelter of a stone cairn, and manage two rapid watercolour sketches before numbness takes over fingers. On the way uphill we have seen vivid citrus orange, red and yellow arctic poppies, facing to the sun's trajectory, and low-growing bilberry bushes in final hot-flush before the winter snow sets in. Blaeberries, as I call them, are normally found where there's snow cover in winter, Icelandic ones smaller than Scottish ones, but more plentiful, and are often harvested with a blueberry comb, a tool resembling a dustpan with wire prongs. In this landscape – because of the cold, illogically – I'd expected bleak monotones, but colour confounds my senses as I try to both 'copy' in paint and commit to mental image. Chill encourages speedy decision-making and I feel pleased at the beginnings of a new-to-me colour palette, much lighter and airier than first anticipated. Later I learn that 'subarctic tundra' is the term designated by WWF to denote this part of the ecoregion.[5] 'Tundra' comes from the Finnish word *tunturi*, meaning 'treeless plain' but at the same time, curiously, the region is designated as boreal birch 'forest'. Where there is forest, it hugs the ground, mimicking lichen or moss, in the form of horizontally-growing networks of the woody dwarf variety of birch (*Betula nana*). Apparently there's a joke: Q. 'How do you find your way out of an Icelandic forest?' A. 'You stand up.' For me, 'boreal' and 'tundra' are more than descriptors, they are romantic words resonant with notions of 'north', and being 'away in a *dwam*' (dream). As a teenager in the *dreichness* of 1970s suburban Paisley, I would daydream around words such as these, imagining undefined wildernesses; chilly, snowy, remote. Many years later, reading Nan Shepherd, 'I am a mountain lover because my body is at its best in the rarer air of the heights and communicates its elation to the mind' (2011 [1977]: 72), it all starts to make sense.

The air's 'rareness' can trick perceptions as to what's 'over here' and what's 'over there', as Lavinia Greenlaw (2011: 76) observes, apropos William Morris's travels in Iceland, 'Nearer to it / The unreachable landmark is seen as a picture still. It cannot be here and you cannot be there'. On this same walk Lesley and I head towards a waterfall that tempts us, wavy like a horse-tail and luminous against rust-red layers of basalt and sediment. After more than an hour, our goal appears not a bit closer. We have noticed this before and find it to be a recognised phenomenon due to the cold dry atmosphere. According to our *Rough Guide*, 'mountains and glaciers seem to stay the same size, or even shrink, the closer you come to them' (Leffman and Proctor 2013: 330).

There turns out to be a large crevasse between ourselves and the waterfall, so we give up and clamber over gravelly moraines to photograph a pair of partially collapsed snow-bridges. These form over steep gullies when fast-flowing meltwater undercuts the winter snowdrifts, chiselling wavy arch-spans in the underside of the snow-slab. For Nan Shepherd, 'The mountain has an inside' (2011 [1977]: 16), and sometimes I've crawled under a snow-bridge to look, listen and record the splashing and gurgling of the mountain's innards. When I do this I am high on fear, 'so close to death, I've never felt more alive' (Söderberg 2014). I am in thrall at the resonance of sound under the snow-vault, while on edge at the uncanniness of having snow waves above your head. Later in the studio, I paint to the sound of these watery recordings. They trigger memory's images in the manner of Marcel Proust's famous tea-dipped madeleine (2003 [1913] 1, 60–4) and captivate my own 'structure of recollection' (64) so that subsequent studies and paintings become a combination of memory and desire: Proust again, 'When an idea – an idea of any kind – is left on us by life, its material pattern, the outline of the impression that it made upon us, remains behind as a token of its necessary truth' (4, 275).

Questions of seeing and looking are of central concern to Lesley Hicks's work. Through years of observing a walking practice, Lesley treads lightly on the earth, both literally and metaphorically, effecting a graceful, precise, gentle and efficient covering of ground. Lesley was recently 'converted' to walking poles, and rehearsed technique at home in Newcastle before the trip. When the time, the terrain, wind direction and light seem right, she stops, sits down and works from direct, concentrated observation. Her painting kit consists of a small, well-used box of watercolours, a tube containing brushes, two bottles of ink, a pad of good-quality cartridge paper, a water bottle and a bulldog clip. Lesley paints with complete focus, fully present, for as long as wind and weather will allow, producing two, three or more small finished paintings in a sitting. Lesley's paintings don't discount the obviously artificial: there is an interest in road signs as artefacts in the landscape, as sources of information, injunction and warning of potential catastrophe. Recent work investigates digital iterations of the road sign. In Iceland a live traffic channel plays continuously in service stations, shops and offices throughout the country, as it is advisable for drivers to check conditions before setting off on any road journey outside the capital. Even in summer, there is often the possibility of violent storms, flash-floods, mudslides or rock-falls. Webcams are situated at many sites, including the mouths of Iceland's numerous long road-tunnels. At night, the grainy images seem unspeakably remote and other, yet viewing onscreen has the uncanny effect that Heidegger terms 'de-severance', a phenomenon of spatiality 'making the farness vanish – that is, making the remoteness of something disappear' (2013: 138). For those who derive wistful or melancholy pleasure from such things, there is much to be said for viewing in warmth and safety at home, café or office, from the nearness of the digital screen (see Plate 5).

Derived from these slow-moving images and expressed as small-scale intensely rendered pencil-and-watercolour drawings, distant car headlamps seem strange and otherworldly behind a screen of hand-drawn lines. In these terms it is difficult to differentiate between the familiar and the unfamiliar, self and other. For the eighteenth-century Romantic painter Caspar David Friedrich, writing *circa* 1830, painting was a projection of the artist's psyche: 'The painter should paint not only what he has in front of him, but also what he sees inside himself. If he sees nothing within, then he should stop painting what is in front of him' (1998 [*c.* 1830]: 54). Lesley's contemporary take on Friedrich's nature-as-human-nature positions the looker as a sort of weather-voyeur. In an age of remotely controlled surveillance, who is the watcher, we wonder, and who is being watched? And in a country with a population of just over three hundred thousand, there seems more than a *frisson* of likelihood that those headlamps belong to someone you know, a friend or relative – an adulterous mate perhaps?

The medium of paint and the activity of painting are seldom at the forefront of discussion about art informed by ecological concerns. For painters such as Lesley and myself, 'It is near impossible to escape the weight of canonical art history bearing down on those (brave or foolhardy these days?) who deal with the painted surface' (Williams 2012). For Linda Weintraub, the term 'landscape' is problematic for several reasons:

> The word *landscape* is absent from ecocentric considerations because painted representations disregard the components of ecosystems that enable them to function: drainage patterns, ranges, biotic regions. They also ignore the interactions occurring within and among rivers, shorelines, mountain ranges and meadows. These elements of the planet's locations are included in ecological terms like *watershed*, *habitat* and *biome*. Such terminology considers locations according to their ability to provide resources, manage wastes, and perform dozens of additional services that determine the destination of their populations. (Weintraub 2012: 16)

A painter engaged with environmental processes may therefore struggle with the question, how can painted representations of place seek to extend the category of 'landscape'? In critical practice, the term 'landscape' may be imbued with history and subjectivity, either a 'window-on-the-world' sort of experience or a backdrop to human actions. Tim Ingold refers to landscape as visual 'surface', containable and contained in time and space:

> We treat the landscape as a view, and imagine that we see the world in pictures, optically projected into our minds as upon the white walls of the interior room. In this picture-landscape there is no weather: the wind does not blow, nor does rain ever fall. Clouds are forever arrested in their growth. (Ingold 2015: 41)

For postmodernists and beyond, ideas of 'beauty' and 'nature' have given way to representations of nature damaged and depleted, and, for us, the question arises again, what is it that our work is *doing*? To paraphrase the words of contemporary painter and my teacher, John Skinner: painting is a way of going from 'not-knowing' to 'knowing' in reciprocal engagement by and with environment.[6] The materials, the movement and the sensibility of the painter are observances in the transformative work of painting, of turning greasy messy material 'stuff' into paintings. While painting in response to landscape doesn't necessarily result in a 'view' in terms of illusion or illustration, it is also not necessarily abstraction in the sense of 'pure feeling' or 'painterly gesture'. Ecological and ecocentric concerns may be embedded both within the work, in terms of research-as-practice, and in the critical discourses surrounding the work.

Meanwhile, at around 10.00 pm most nights, the temperature plummets, and my sleeping bag is hopelessly inadequate. Still wearing my day clothes – thermal 'technical' layers, down jacket, ski socks and woollen hat – I push into the sleeping bag, then I push the sleeping bag into a silver-foil survival bag and close the top, apart from a small breathing hole, so the result resembles a giant oven-ready turkey. This way I wake up extremely warm, if slightly damp. In the early mornings, I amuse myself by manipulating the 'view' inside my tent, using knees, elbows and fingers to mould and fold back the foil into miniature mountains, valleys and rivers. As Ingold points out: 'every mountain is a fold in the ground not a structure that is placed upon it' (2015: 32–5). I push my creations from above and below, creating new landscapes in the tent. I photograph self-made rivers of condensation in self-made crevasses. I am both inside the mountain and on top of it. Rather grandiosely, I imagine, I *am* the mountain:

> Humans! I, Mountain, am speaking. You cannot ignore me! I have been
> with you since your very beginnings and long before. For *millennia* your
> ancestors venerated my holy places, found wisdom in my heights. I gave
> you shelter and far vision. Now in return you ravage me. (Seed et al. 2007
> [1998]: 87)

This feeling sits very uneasily amongst other feelings about mountains.
As a lifelong skier, I'm addicted to the hedonistic mix of fear and pleasure brought about by sliding down mountains at speed, a sensation
difficult to express to deep-green friends. Emily Brady (2008) addresses
this ambivalence: 'I'm not suggesting that extreme sports are in themselves experiences of the sublime, but they offer opportunities for aesthetic experience of this kind because of how they situate people in the
environment' (51). In some places, including parts of Iceland in summer,
mountain recreation has developed to near-industrial levels, and, as
with other forms of 'wilderness' tourism, there is the fear and the prob-
ability of irrevocably altering and destroying the things with which we
seek interface.

The journey back to Edinburgh, and everyday life, takes us over the
moonscape of the Reykjanes peninsula, through liquorice-black lava-
fields extending beyond the shoreline and forming a boundary between
the diverging North American and Eurasian tectonic plates. This line,
the Mid-Atlantic Ridge, marks where the continental plates which have
been moving apart for seventy million years continue to diverge at a
rate of about two centimetres a year. The rift and associated ridge 'can
be viewed as a suture where the crust is being pulled apart and molten
rock (i.e. magma) wells up from below to fill in the gash' (Thordarson
and Höskuldsson, 2014: 4). Hot molten material rises up along fracture
zones, resulting in eruptions such as the flight-disrupting ash-clouds of
Eyjafjallajökull in 2010, and the Holuhraun lava-fields of Bárðarbunga
in 2014–15. I think of the Eldfyallasafn volcano museum in Stykkishól-
mur, where we saw Athanasius Kircher's 1664 *Mundus Subterraneus*,
an engraved cross-section of the earth illustrating a web of interconnected fires, *pyrophylacia*, under the Earth's surface, connecting with a
large and Dantesque central inferno.[7] Then I visualise sponge cake
erupting in a too-hot oven, and the thought occurs that this is everyday
normality if you're an Icelander.

Later, back in my Dumfriesshire studio, in Timothy Morton's words,
'here is shot through with there' (2010: 39). We have gathered material,
sketched, filmed and photographed; we've climbed a glacier, thrillingly,
and borne witness to the ice-field's recession, sadly. We have eaten
hákarl, fermented shark meat. I have changed in myriad small ways:
now I drink coffee black (milk is an unnecessary hassle); I prefer to

briskly rub-dry with a hand-towel (big towels are a hassle). My legs and spine have realigned to be at their most comfortable in hiking boots; I carefully save plastic bags and elastic bands (precious to the camper). My head and sketchbooks contain new colours, shapes, relationships, movements, directionalities; a clean-cut geometric terrain, slabs and slices of rock, snow and light. I feel a renewed sense of working with matter going from one state into another state. All this material will inform another activity, that of pushing and pulling the connections into studio paintings.

The nature of the frustrating-but-joyful activity of painting means that for me it can take hours, days, weeks, months or years for a painting or a series of work to come together. Initial responses usually involve copying, fiddling, overdeliberation, feeling overwhelmed by the amount of 'stuff', the sensory material, to take into account. I experiment with media such as raw earth-pigments, carbon, and Japanese paper, and think about things like performance, movement, rhythm, directionality, theme, variation. I make drawings from boot-print monoprints tramped in the mountains, and I collage them on to paintings. With luck, time, and daily observance, I will stop over-thinking, and the work will begin to take on its own life in a reciprocal, call-and-response sort of way. Like many artists I try to stick to a daily routine – yoga, coffee, walk, more coffee, mark-making – with the idea that the fewer decisions there are to make in daily life, the more energy there will be for decisions concerning the work. The stripping-down of life to practical necessities around eating, sleeping, washing and walking in Iceland's environment allowed for fruitful collaborations and exchanges of ideas (see Plate 6).

In reflecting on the art *praxes* of Julie Livsey, Lesley Hicks and myself, I place emphasis on contingency of bodily experience in encounters with place, in terms of camping and living 'in' the landscape and the repetitive rhythms of our walking. While 'nature' in Iceland is more forceful, unpredictable and potentially dangerous than in most countries, it was and is increasingly mediated by human activity. Art-historical tropes in the categories of romanticism and the sublime have produced works of visual art, poetry, music and literature that predispose us to construct and reproduce notions of place that have become inextricably linked with 'nature'. In our collaborative walking, our artistic interests interface with literature, geology, botany, ecology, tourism, horse breeding, sheep farming, traffic websites. In the face of irreversible and catastrophic environmental change, artists can put out lines, literally and figuratively, to other disciplines, engaging artistically and critically with what it means to be and to act in 'nature' at this time.

Notes

1 In his 1940 essay 'Towards a Newer Laocoön', US critic and writer Clement Greenberg (1909–94) advocates 'purism' or 'pure sensation' in painting, arguing that realistic imitation through perspective must be resisted in acknowledgement of the picture plane's essential flatness. Greenberg promoted the work of the abstract expressionists, including that of Matthíasdóttir's teacher, Hans Hofmann.
2 Image available at: http://hrosss.is/the-film/ accessed 16 April 2016.
3 Benedikt Erlingsson in interview with the author. (Transcript: Patti Lean, 4 September 2015).
4 Ólafur Elíasson 2009. *Bílar í Ám / Cars in Rivers*. Available at: http://olafureliasson.net/current/148 accessed 16 April 2016.
5 WWF Global species. Available at: www.globalspecies.org/ecoregions/display/PA0602) accessed 6 February 2016.
6 John Skinner 2016. Artist's talk, 29 February 2016. Seawhite Studio, West Sussex. Notes taken by the author. Further information available at: www.johnskinner.me.uk/ and Seawhite Studio http://emilyball.net/ and www.emilyballatseawhite.co.uk/ accessed 6 February 2016.
7 Athanasius Kircher 1665. Mundus subterraneus. Available at: https://ouhos.org/2011/09/14/athanasius-kircher-mundus-subterraneus-1665/ accessed 10 April 2016.

References

Auden, W.H. and Louis MacNeice (2002 [1937]) *Letters from Iceland*. London: Faber & Faber.

Bennett, Jane (2010) *Vibrant Matter: A Political Ecology of Things*. Durham, NC, and London: Duke University Press.

Brady, Emily (2008) in Aesa Sigurjonsdottir (ed.) *Dreams of the Sublime and Nowhere in Contemporary Art* [exhibition catalogue]. Exhibition at Reykjavic Art Museum May–August.

Burke, Edmund (2015 [1756]) *A Philosophical Enquiry into the Origin of Our Ideas of the Sublime and Beautiful*, ed. Paul Guyer. Oxford: Oxford University Press.

Friedrich, Caspar David (1998 [*c.* 1830]) 'Observations on Viewing a Collection of Paintings Largely by Living or Recently Deceased Artists', in C. Harrison, P. Wood and J. Gaiger (eds), *Art in Theory, 1815–1900: An Anthology of Changing Ideas*. Oxford: Wiley-Blackwell.

Greenlaw, Lavinia (2011) *Questions of Travel: William Morris in Iceland*. London: Notting Hill Editions.

Heidegger, Martin (2013 [1927]) *Being and Time*, trans. and ed. J. McQuarrie and E. Robinson. Oxford: Blackwell Books.

Ingold, Tim (2015) *The Life of Lines*. London and New York: Routledge.

Johnson, Galen A. and Michael B. Smith (eds) (1993) *The Merleau Ponty Aesthetics Reader*. Evanston: Northwestern University Press.

Kant, Immanuel (2011 [1764]) *Observations on the Feeling of the Beautiful and Sublime and Other Writings*, ed. Patrick Frierson and Paul Guyer. Cambridge: Cambridge University Press.

Katz, Cheryl (2014) 'Iceland's seabird colonies are vanishing, with "massive" chick deaths', *Environmental Health News*, 28 August. Available at: http://news.nationalgeographic.com/news/2014/08/140827-seabird-puffin-tern-iceland-ocean-climate-change-science-winged-warning/?rptregcta=reg_free_np&rptregcampaign=2015012_invitation_ro_all# accessed 15 September 2015.

Laxness, Halldór ([2001] 1957) *Fish Can Sing*, trans. M. Magnusson. New York: Vintage Classics.

Laxness, Halldór (2005 [1968]) *Under the Glacier*, trans. M. Magnusson. New York: Vintage International.

Leffman, David and James Proctor (2013) *The Rough Guide to Iceland*. London: Rough Guides Ltd.

Livsey, Julie (2015) *et-ERN-it-Y: An Installation at Coanwood Meeting House*, Coanwood, Northumberland, 9 September 2015 – 3 January 2016 [exhibition catalogue].

McKibben, Bill (2003 [1989]) *The End of Nature*. London: Bloomsbury Publishing.

Morley, Simon (ed.) (2010) *Documents of Contemporary Art: The Sublime*. Cambridge, MA: MIT Press.

Morton, Timothy (2010) *The Ecological Thought*. Cambridge, MA: Harvard University Press.

Of Horses and Men (Hross í oss) (2013) Directed by Benedikt Erlingsson [DVD]. Reykjavík: Hrossabrestur

Perl, Jed (ed.) (1999) *Louisa Matthíasdóttir*. Reykjavík: Nesutgafan Publishing.

Proust, Marcel (2003 [1913]) *In Search of Lost Time*, volumes 1–7, trans. C.K. Scott-Moncrieff and T. Kilmartin, revised by D.J. Enright. New York: Modern Library Classics.

Salander O'Reilly Galleries (2003) *The Paintings of Louisa Matthíasdóttir*. Exhibition 1–26 April 2003. New York: Salander O'Reilly Galleries [exhibition catalogue].

Sawin, Martica (1999) 'Early Years in New York', in Jed Perl (ed.) *Louisa Matthíasdóttir*. Reykjavík: Nesutgafan Publishing.

Seed, J., J. Macy, P. Fleming and A. Naess (2007 [1998]) *Thinking like a Mountain: Towards a Council of All Beings*. Gabriola Island, BC: New Catalyst Books.

Shepherd, Nan (2011 [1977]) *The Living Mountain*. Edinburgh: Canongate Books.

Söderberg, K. and J. (2014) 'Waitress Song', *Stay Gold* by First Aid Kit. New York: Columbia Records.

Solnit, Rebecca (2014 [2006]) *A History of Walking*. London: Granta Books.

Sveinsson, Hjallmar (2011) 'Songlines of the Jeeps', *Bílar í Ám / Cars in Rivers*. Exhibition by Ólafur Elíasson, at National Gallery of Iceland, Reykjavík, 16

September 2010 – 7 November 2010. Reykjavík: National Gallery of Iceland [exhibition catalogue].

Thordarson, Thor and Ármann Höskuldsson (2014) *Iceland: Classic Geology in Europe*. Edinburgh and London, Dunedin Academic Press.

Weintraub, L. (2012) *To Life: Eco Art in Pursuit of a Sustainable Planet*. Berkeley: University of California Press.

Williams, Robert (2012) 'Patti Lean – Thin Places'. Exhibition essay, Studio Eleven, Hull, June 2013.

6

Nature matters: notes on Ackroyd & Harvey, ecocriticism and praxis

Eve Ropek

A small painting from the 1950s hangs on a friend's wall. A Welsh landscape, little sky is visible; the bold black simplified shape of a train cuts across the painting, whooshing through the greens. One could describe the vigorous way the paint has been applied, or place the work in art-historical context. Considering what the work might reflect of *Homo sapiens*'s relationship to the land, sky and co-creatures – the 'natural' world we inhabit – brings another perspective. Ecocriticism or an 'earth centred' (Glotfelty and Fromm 1996: xviii) approach to culture is a well-documented but relatively new discipline which sprang from awareness of environmental issues arising in what has become termed the 'Anthropocene' epoch (Crutzen and Stoermer 2000); and, arguably, the desire to address these issues. Scientific information suggests that human industrial-era lifestyles, allied to our species's global population growth, are creating changes which are not only altering aspects of the entire biosphere but risk wiping us off the Earth's face for good. Nature can no longer be seen as an inexhaustible resource and separate 'other' to which we can retreat or to use at will; nor does science now view it as a system which will inevitably regain equilibrium, but as one subject to change, including chaos and catastrophe.

The story of how human ingenuity and desire are causing ecological crises worldwide has become a key narrative for our time. Environmental changes, including those caused by human behaviour, require not only scientific but also cultural analysis; inevitably implicit or explicit within this are political and ethical standpoints. The practice of ecocriticism certainly has a broad base; as EASLCE's online introduction has it:

Nevertheless, the term ecocriticism has stuck as the name for what is, today, a rather large tent, where work on nature writing can sit comfortably next to animal studies, and postcolonial theory rubs shoulders with ecofeminism.[1]

While ecocriticism encompasses many approaches and theories, central to it is the desire to critically examine the relationship between human and other species and the world we all inhabit, and to evaluate and question accepted norms.

To approach any art work ecocritically, it is necessary to bring to it some knowledge of current scientific thought regarding the biosphere. Indeed the breadth and complexity of the ideas and issues of humans' place within the Earth's ecosystems encourage an interdisciplinary approach: to join together methods and insights in order to inform next steps at what is seen to be a crucial global point. Artists working today are very well aware of the narrative of change and of environmental issues; the text that follows considers some art works by British artists Heather Ackroyd and Dan Harvey, who practise in partnership as Ackroyd & Harvey.

With their artistic interests grouped around the ideas and realities of transformative biological processes, of change and decay, and with deep interest in ecology and biology, much of Ackroyd & Harvey's work engages with environmental and scientific concerns. The artists are far from didactic, however; they do not set out to deliver a homily nor is the work received primarily as such – it is too visually complex and too extra-ordinary to be easily read in this way. The works for which they are probably best known have used grass, that most ubiquitous plant, in extraordinary ways – growing over buildings, within rooms, covering the fly-tower of London's National Theatre; bright and green, signalling fertility, cultivation and renewal. Uniting photosynthesis with traditional darkroom techniques, the artists have also used growing grass to make massive portraits of people by projecting a photographic image on to a vertical wall sown with grass seed. The watered surface over days produces the miracle of the likeness, grown in fresh, soft, green grass. The photosynthetic processes of the grass plant replace the silver bromide in the traditional photographic darkroom, with a result as magical-seeming as that of early photography. The images in grass are fragile and relatively fleeting; this work does not translate well into a commodity. Left alone, these grass portraits would fade and crumble. Wanting to 'fix' the resultant images, as one would fix a photograph, Heather Ackroyd and Dan Harvey worked alongside scientists at IBERS at Aberystwyth University, who had discovered a mutant strain of grass with a stay-green character.[2] Grass usually senesces and loses chlorophyll as it dries, turning yellow; but, by using this stay-green strain, the artists' photographic grass images can be better preserved.

The stages of making the grass portraits are thrilling – the growing stage intensely magical, seeing the picture emerge in the various shades of green of living plants, creating an image determined by the projected negative and dependent on how much light is received by the seedling. There follows the arresting period where the grass dries out – a slice of the earth with human faces imprinted on it. The grass portraits are in the main very large, dwarfing the viewer. The images are calm and direct, with an intensity which reflects a human closeness, at-homeness, in the 'nature' they are fashioned from. The essentially fleeting quality of the medium lends a poignancy; the intimate connection between human face, earth and plants reflecting human mortality and biology. Writer Barbara Ehrenreich recalls longing to roll on lawns as a child: 'Wasn't I made of the same stuff myself, although a little heavier on the carbon than the silicon?' (Ehrenreich 2014: 43). Ackroyd & Harvey have made portraits of people of all ages, not necessarily 'famous' people but individuals with relevance to the artists and their work: the artists and their daughter; workers from the Domaine de Chamarande; random sunbathers on Aberystwyth beach – our fellows, enjoying the world in a way very familiar and every day to our first world life (see for example Plate 7). These people are not known to us but could be us; loving the sun's warmth which leads to life, photosynthesis, food. It is exhilarating to see this use of cultivated grass to make images in our likeness; images which like us grow, flourish briefly and dry away. Human ingenuity has allowed Ackroyd & Harvey to retain the images, fix them; that same amazing human curiosity and ingenuity has, on a larger scale, fundamentally altered our lives in many ways – by, for example, giving us YouTube to waste our time and allowing the vast majority of our children in this country to survive infancy.

Green grass is a significant plant. Herbaceous grasses as a family (Poaceae) are hugely important for humans – for food as pasture or grains, for beer and whisky or for practical uses including fuel, clothing and construction. Ackroyd & Harvey's works use new growing seedlings, fresh and uncut. These soft, bright seedling grasses bring to mind lawn grass; labour-intensive and appearance-conscious, it is an aspirational, joyous grass to lift the spirits. A green lawn celebrates the delight in aspects of the natural world beyond the utilitarian. The verdant grass which people covet for their gardens is a characteristic bred by humans. Similarly, the stay-green grass which was developed has a valuable place in the market; people like their decorative lawns to look green even in dry conditions. Copied in miniature from the estates of the ruling classes, green lawns signify the boundary of an individual or family's personal space, a transitional area between public and private; a symbol of belonging, of community and a happy way to control a small part of the natural world. The effect, like many desirable objects, is quite hard to achieve – it is difficult to keep a lawn looking green and lovely, though many attempt it as their public face.

The relationship of power between human will and natural forces in Ackroyd & Harvey's grass works, portraits and others, is interesting to think about. The works cause a catch of the breath; they are uplifting to see, whether in the gallery or chanced upon in an alleyway – a celebration both of people's creative ability and of natural processes. Yet the grass portraits will die back and eventually fail; the green tower of grass will dry and crumble; 'for you are dust, and to dust you shall return' (Genesis 3:19). Despite the innovative stay-green grass, change is an integral part of these works. They do not treat of the natural world in a romantic or idealised manner. At a time when we understand that there is no part of the world that has not felt the effect of humans' lifestyle (Andreae et al. 2015: 42), we cannot think of a return to any storybook 'natural' past. There is no longer any wilderness. Ackroyd & Harvey's works reflect what appears as a fast stream of capability carrying *Homo sapiens* onwards. There is no doubting the creativity and ingenuity of what humans have achieved; it is also necessary to question the wider implications and consequences. We can celebrate and marvel at what we humans can set our minds to and achieve, but also take a warning – bright stay-green grass is very much a human construct. High-status green lawns, hungry for water and fertiliser, are grown as a monoculture; mown before being allowed to flower or seed, they are of little use to the pollinators needed for 75 per cent of global food crops. In pursuing certain characteristics and human desires within the natural world, there are risks – such as reducing the biodiversity which Julia Whitty (2007) called 'life's only army against the diseases of oblivion'. Simon Estok finds the need to direct and control nature by 'compunctions to lawn care' as a kind of 'ecophobia [which] is all about fear of a loss of agency and control to nature' (Estok 2010a: 79). These portraits in grass reflect people as one with and bordered by plants, by nature, by our biological reality which must be acknowledged and negotiated with.

Ackroyd & Harvey explore nature and natural processes; the story they tell of our place in the natural world is one of glory and enormous potential, but also of instability and transience. The individuals whose grass portraits are exhibited in the cool, dim galleries are each unique, different, valuable in their own way in terms of what they are and do and in terms of their genetic and biological material. These images portray individuals who have both 'selfhood' in the Western liberal sense and are intrinsically linked to the rest of the natural world. The individuals portrayed in grass are part of nature. Their portraits offer the potential of strength, of power and of individual agency; bounded by biology yet able to choose the terms of a relationship with the natural world. Ackroyd & Harvey's use of photosynthesis allied to the photographic technique brings home our intimate relationship to the biological processes of the world of which we are a part; and to the two way potential of effect. We are part of one biosphere, even though we often act as though we are insulated from it. Ackroyd & Harvey land lightly on various aspects of our points of contact with other creatures, plants, biological processes. They create works which are in the main vastly positive; which alert us both to the extent of our powers and the individual and collective responsibility this confers. They touch on the extraordinary ability to effect change which is now in our grasp, alongside a wonder at the processes of nature and at ourselves, our place within them.

Polar Diamond was created by Ackroyd & Harvey as a result of taking part in an expedition to the Arctic with Cape Farewell, an artist-led campaigning organization.[3] Cape Farewell's expeditions bring together artists, scientists and communicators to experience the effects of climate change at first hand; stimulating cultural responses with the aim of more effectively communicating abstract, global issues on a human scale. *Polar Diamond* was made for a gallery: a sparkling diamond, spot-lit; sealed within the kind of case a robber creeps towards in a heist film (see Plate 8). This signals value; something covetable, costly and worthy of attention. Diamonds are loaded with meaning in our culture. They have an aura of glamour and excitement – think Marilyn Monroe, thrillers, celebrity dressing; and, due to the international importance of the diamond market, think also of conflict diamonds with their chilling sobriquet 'blood diamond'. An allotrope of carbon, diamond is very hard and can be cut and polished to reflect light; it is used to make cutting tools and we humans love its sparkly form. Its relative rarity makes it a key commodity with a high exchange value. However, this isn't Tiffany but an art gallery – so something has to be different about this rock. When displaying a work like *Polar Diamond* in a public gallery, information is often supplied to the visitor; there is a plurality of approaches in contemporary art, and the viewer often wants some guidance as to the artist's standpoint. The information relates that Ackroyd & Harvey's *Polar Diamond* is human-made; this diamond was not mined from the ground. The artists played god, using technology now readily available, to create this diamond from a polar bear's leg bone; from a mammal like ourselves.

Mined diamonds are made from carbon; probably, science tells us, carbon trapped inside the Earth when the planet was formed and which was then subjected to high pressure. The diamonds we mine today are hundreds of millions or even billions of years old. To create *Polar Diamond*, Ackroyd & Harvey took a polar bear leg bone that they had been given by the Governor of Svalbard following their Arctic expedition, and cremated it; turning it into a form of carbon. The billion-years-long geological process needed to make diamonds was then circumvented by use of technology, which created a 'laboratory-grown' diamond from the bone. Scientists tell us that most of the carbon supporting life on Earth came from stars that turned into white dwarfs instead of exploding; that the carbon, nitrogen and oxygen atoms in human bodies essentially came from stars billions of years ago. So as Ackroyd & Harvey point out (and as Moby sang) we are all truly, including polar bears, humans and diamonds, made of stars.

Polar Diamond uses a found bone. During their Cape Farewell expedition to the Svalbard Arctic Archipelago in 2004, the artists were shown a polar bear leg bone kept in an office by the Environmental Manager at Svalbard; necessary permissions were eventually granted and the leg bone was sent to the UK, there was no killing or conquering of another creature. The art work does not reflect on the natural bone itself but uses it and alters it to make something different. This isn't a gentle intervention in the natural world but technological knowhow shaping a piece from another species to reflect human wishes. The polar bear is attractive (in the abstract – not many would want to meet one on a dark night), as is the diamond attractive; each prized by humans for sensual visual appeal and for rarity. The bears have become poster creatures for the climate change debate; a symbol for the complex range of conditions which appear to be reflecting anthropogenic (i.e. human-caused) change. Science, as is popularly known, shows us that humans' excessive carbon emissions are endangering and altering ecosystems across the Earth, and that the polar bears' habitat and their very survival are seriously endangered. Envisage these enormous creatures, who have now been listed as a threatened species in the USA under the Endangered Species Act, at our mercy as ice melts; we are each complicit in destroying them. Ironically, perhaps, the polar bear is deadly dangerous to humans; the largest land-living carnivore, it is a quick, curious, aggressive hunter. Moreover, because bears are starting to spend greater periods of time on land as a result of longer ice-free seasons, their contact with people is likely to increase – with dire consequences for one or the other. *Homo sapiens*'s technological knowhow has altered the balance of power at an overarching level; with many unintended consequences. Polar bear communities, like people in poorer countries, will most likely continue to suffer losses because the richer countries in the world make choices which do not consider wider wellbeing. Similarly diamond mining, as well as supplying the deep pockets of Hatton Garden, can cause environmental problems both in methods of extraction and in dumping of refuse. The industry blights the lives of many miners through poor working practices, and child labour is still common. The technological method of making *Polar Diamond* is an example of the ever more ambitious possibilities open to us to satisfy desire and curiosity as well as need; of human improvements and alterations to nature. The true cost of the miraculous technology and processes now available – from solar tech to latest iPhone gadget – includes many unforeseen developments.

Perception of the *Polar Diamond* must alter once we know what it is made from. Recently cremated bones are not desired in the same way as a billion-year-old diamond, but likely to invoke revulsion or pity; or perhaps just amazement at the technological feat. The pleasing nature, the beauty of the result – the diamond – and its associations, including economic worth, are all tempered and questioned by the knowledge that this was recently part of a living creature. Moreover the reminder of the common roots of life on the planet, the biogeochemical cycle of atoms such as carbon between the living and inanimate, throws values into question. Which is more valuable – either intrinsically or to us today – diamond or bear?

Polar Diamond uses a familiar lovely and coveted object to evoke associations in the viewer allied to ideas of beauty and value. The information offers the intellect the reality that science and technology have shaped this diamond from a creature's carbonised bone rather than inert carbon in the earth; a creature moreover whose habitat, as we are very well aware, is daily more threatened and curtailed. The widely publicised threat, through climate change, to polar bears' very survival as a species can cast humans not only as despoilers but also as potential 'saviours' and controllers of the natural world. The extent to which humans are within nature, or alienated from it, can be argued in different ways. Essentially humans have never not been part of nature; we are living out who we are, *Homo sapiens* – but as Ian McEwan (2005) wrote:

> We are a clever but quarrelsome species – in our public debates we can sound like a rookery in full throat. We are superstitious, hierarchical and self-interested, just when the moment requires us to be rational, even-handed and altruistic. (McEwan 2005: 4)

Ackroyd & Harvey's *Polar Diamond* both enacts and exposes our ability and desire to alter and shape the environment. It inspires wonder at the possibility of natural processes and human ability to harness them – with consequences both foreseen and unexpected. It is a celebration of possibility, of power; and a direct warning.

An interesting footnote, not usually offered as part of the experience of viewing *Polar Diamond*, is the fact that the first diamond Ackroyd & Harvey had made fractured at the end of its manufacture and was actually put together in pieces. The roots of the word diamond come via an old Greek word, meaning unbreakable or untamed. The verdict on human diamond v. nature: must try harder. Our attempts to outperform the natural world are certainly not yet foolproof.

Just like Yorick 'to this favour [we] must come';[4] death and return to the sod awaits each of us. Another work by Ackroyd & Harvey uses animal bones more explicitly; *Stranded* elicits an immediate visceral response in the viewer. The skeleton of a minke whale, bones picked clean and sparkling with chemical crystals, it is offered respectfully on a large low plinth within a gallery's white walls (see Plates 9 and 10). An initial response is to the size; this was a large creature – one would think twice about approaching any animal this size in life. The bones are assembled in a recognisable shape; a vertebrate, another mammal something like us, with a ribcage and backbone. The skeleton is reassembled much as one would see in a natural history museum; perhaps a long extinct dinosaur. It is a very beautiful object to experience – clean white bone with a surprising growth of sparkly alum crystals; the remains of a creature both powerful and, like all creatures, fragile in face of death. The elegant white bones on the plinth were once alive, plump with insulating blubber, swimming and communicating in a group, a family, of other whales. These fine, still bones are a contrast with the minke in life, in deadly earnest need of food, of habitat. The crystal growth on the bones is fragile, delicate, a beautiful temporary chemical adornment.

The minke's remains were boiled clean in a lengthy, fairly disgusting process described by the artists in a film shown alongside the work; the bones were then dipped into an alum solution to grow the crystals – a beautiful, artificial, chemical growth. We humans like to decorate, to embellish, to alter; this growth mimics creation where life leads to decay and growth in a cycle, but there is sterility, a full stop, in this chemical growth. One of the early uses of alum was to purify water; it also proved to have many uses in industry, and in order to produce it (from shale and human urine) large areas of Yorkshire were cleared of trees and mined in the seventeenth century and the land was polluted with sulphuric acid and ash. The artists learned during the process of making *Stranded* about the extent of human-produced carbon dioxide absorbed by the oceans since the start of the industrial revolution, which has caused the water to become increasingly acidic. The – unintended – effects include a decrease in oxygen levels: killing algae, disrupting food chains and depressing the immune systems and metabolic rates of some aquatic organisms. The acidification and warming of the oceans has clear implications for much marine life. Coral reefs are intricate, living ecosystems which support a rich biodiversity; the warming water bleaches and weakens them while acidification causes the coral to dissolve; while creatures such as whales are threatened through the disruption of the food web, those that are dependent on cephalopods and certain planktivores may be especially vulnerable (Bass et al. 2006).

The whale of *Stranded* is a young minke male, not yet full grown. It was recovered by the artists, with permission, from a beach in Skegness; its cause of death is unknown. The minke is one of the smaller whales; this young adolescent would have weighed around five tonnes in life and could have had a life span of forty to fifty years. Minkes are thought of as inquisitive creatures, choosing to approach ships for example; and people have identified their vocal communication system, which appears to differ between groups. There is a suggestion that minkes increased in number recently as food became more available following the sustained hunting by humans of larger whale species; but minkes, once considered too small to bother with, are now also targeted for whaling.

Displaying bones raises interesting thoughts. Even ancient bones of our own species are now subject to carefully drafted codes of conduct aimed at showing respect and care to long-dead people. This has often not been the case of course – for example the bones of dead soldiers and their horses from the battlefields of Austerlitz, Leipzig and Waterloo were shipped to bone-grinders in Britain to be used as fertiliser. There would no doubt be outrage if a recently deceased human body were to be treated as the minke whale's body has been – an exhibition in Scotland which included two recently unearthed medieval skeletons was declared (admittedly by a minority) a 'moral abuse'.[5] However, the skeleton in *Stranded* has been reconstructed and displayed with care and respect, expressing the close links between whale species and our own; as well as a keen curiosity and a desire to provoke change. Moreover, animal bones are commonplace to carnivorous humans, though not perhaps of this scale; the chicken carcass from lunch is certainly not treated with any modicum of respect. Indeed, human cruelty to other species in much food production is truly shocking. Animals are, for example, routinely regarded as insensate when planning operations such as testicle removal or method of death; millions of redundant male chicks are ground up alive or suffocated, each year. The fact that these processes of food production are opaque to most of us does not absolve us of our society's practices. Human attitudes to other species are certainly inconsistent. The death of Cecil the lion,[6] shot by a gung-ho dentist tourist, caused an internet storm; while news reports reflecting that many scientists believe we are on the edge of a sixth mass extinction trigger mainly feelings of helplessness.

Choices need to be made. Not many would privilege the hungry polar bear, prowling the edge of a settlement, over the humans; but what of the effects of intensive farming on other species? We have moved further than ever in questioning attitudes to 'others', certainly human others; although a cynic might suggest this is largely shape-shifting by capitalism to embrace a non-threatening new market – the Williams Institute 'think tank' suggests that the legalisation of same-sex marriage for example will be worth $2.6 billion to the US economy over the next three years.[7] Whales and oceans do not buy stuff. The artists describe *Stranded* as 'here where the gleaming crystals encase his bones lies a *memento mori* for our time' (Ackroyd & Harvey 2006). *Memento mori* – a reminder of mortality – was used in medieval Britain to emphasise the vanity of earthly possessions and of striving for human power. Like this minke we must individually die, that is our biological reality, and reflect that, if we cannot consider the total picture of the biosphere in which we live and the implications of the actions we carry out, our future reign as a species may be short indeed.

Ecocriticism was born out of a concern with *Homo sapiens*'s imagined and enacted relationship to the earth and to other species, and central to this are the – often unintended – implications and effects of our lifestyle on the biosphere in a wide range of ways including, arguably, species extinction, warming of the climate, acidification of the oceans and so on. The facts and issues surrounding the anthropogenic effect on the planet are complex. In our society we rely on scientists and data; this is the truth the vast majority of us accept, much as in some societies morals and ethics were and are driven by religious belief. Ecocriticism as a practice is also orientated towards scientific data and opinion. Scientists themselves stress how difficult it can be, for example, to extrapolate data with any certainty; or to predict future events from current happenings, given the complex interactions and feedbacks within the biosphere. There is also of course the possibility that the scientific prognoses are not quite accurate, that factors will come into play which negate or rebalance or even exacerbate anthropogenic effects. Nevertheless the overwhelming majority of scientists agree that the carbon-intensive lifestyle humans are pursuing is unsustainable, magnified by population increases, and that the effects have now permeated to every corner of our shared planet (see IPCC 2014 and Andreae et al. 2015). The consensus among the international scientific and policy community is that change in our behaviour is both needed and inevitable.

Concerns over the imbalances caused by industrial capitalism have been voiced and debated worldwide over a relatively long period and information has increasingly been in general circulation. An immediately pressing and debated issue worldwide is that of the 'green-house gas', largely carbon dioxide and methane, emissions which underpin Western lifestyles and which are precipitating global changes. Back in 2007/8 a Gallup poll indicated that awareness of climate change in the UK was already at 97 per cent of the sample; the global median at the time was 62 per cent, with the vulnerable countries most in danger of suffering in the near term at a far lower level of awareness – for example Niger at 24 per cent and India at 35 per cent (Pelham 2009).[8] There has been no shortage of cultural responses in recent years reflecting environmental concerns. In 2015 Jason de Caires Taylor's *Rising Tide*, showing four horses and riders swallowed daily by the tide, was installed on Vauxhall Embankment – tantalisingly close to the Houses of Parliament at Westminster.[9] So apparently we in the UK have gained reasonably good understanding of this pressing problem in our relationship with the rest of the natural world; our consciousness has been well and truly raised. Yet, surprisingly, climate change was not a key issue in, for example, the 2015 UK election; and the elected Tory government's policies have led former US Vice President and climate change campaigner Al Gore to politely declare he was 'puzzled' by the UK government's decisions which reduced support for renewable energy.[10]

Humans are risk takers, and with increased technological and biological capability the risks appear to carry ever more destructive potential consequences. Just as fairy tales like 'Red Riding Hood' have in the past warned children about the perils of taking a new path in the woods, dystopian prediction and imagery in our adult arts reflect anxiety at global events apparently beyond human control, and also at the very pace of change; a warning call that ethics and behaviours must develop for the new realities precipitated by ingenuity and technology. The natural world apart from us humans is both a cultural construct and an objective reality; I may romanticise the life of the bees in my garden, but the sting in my arm is painful. A challenge for ecocriticism is to try to separate these two and understand the difference; the better to create stories to live by that can support life rather than destroy it. Lawrence

Buell articulated a variety of approaches before deciding that a 'myth of mutual constructionism' would prove most acceptable (Buell 2003: 6).

It is a dominant narrative for our time – the idea that humans are destructive and voracious even if at times unintentionally. A story in current culture about humanity's place within nature sees our species as the dominant partner overwhelming the rest of the world, the despoiler objectifying nature to dominate and exploit; so that in the Arctic we need to repent and become the caretakers – caring for the rest of the natural world through invention and brain power, safeguarding (certain) species and habitats. Implicit in this colonial narrative is also the fear of the vulnerabilities of all human societies against forces of nature; including forces manipulated by people. The symbolic Dooms-day clock was started in 1947 by leading scientists to reflect the threat to humanity from nuclear war; since 2007 it has included climate change among its indicators.[11] This clock (which at its best has been only seventeen minutes from the midnight of apocalypse) now stands at three minutes to twelve, due to 'Unchecked climate change, global nuclear weapons modernizations, and outsized nuclear weapons arse-nals'. This relationship between us, 'wise' *Homo sapiens*, and the rest of the world is a big change from an idea where people could step out from human society into relatively benign areas of a 'natural' state or a wilderness. What constitutes a 'natural' state can be articulated in many different ways through time, but a natural state today cannot be conceived of as outside the person. The links between human behav-iours and the rest of the Earth's populations and environments are seen as so overwhelming that other stories have emerged. Nature is no longer the ever-present provider to which we can turn as necessary. Strongly current is a biocentric narrative whereby humans acknowledge that we are inextricably part of the natural world – we too are the wild. Implicit in this is the need to grasp the bigger picture, to understand some of the implications and consequences of what we do, in order to inform our decisions and actions.

Relatively diverse as the tenets of ecocriticism appear to be, one key aspect is the imperative, the impetus to action: praxis. This is funda-mental to ecocriticism, with much of its roots clearly within the envi-ronmental movement and so part of the narrative whereby humanity needs to assess and, crucially, alter its relationship with the rest of the natural world. As Simon C. Estok phrased it, 'ecocriticism has always sought to uncover connections and offer readings that are committed to praxis and engagement' (Estok 2010a: 76). It can be argued that simply carrying out ecocriticism is a kind of activism by raising aware-ness; that, since it requires interdisciplinary research, ecocriticism can contribute to the ongoing debates about the relationship between *Homo sapiens* and our world both past and present, while potentially examining links with other key social and political questions. Patrick Murphy develops this point:

> Ecocriticism is a form of aesthetic praxis that is not by itself a form of activism in the sense of direct immediate and local actions. But being propagandistic and agitational it does contribute to the potential success of activism through its effect on the social consciousness. (Murphy 2015: 16)

For Estok: 'Praxis – real praxis – starts with theoretical connections that allow us to see how we participate in the systems we critique' (Estok 2010b: 147).

Artists who engage with environmental concerns can offer insights and experiences which challenge and lead to greater understanding; and potentially to some change. Artists in the UK, like most individuals in Britain, are well aware of the issues of anthropogenic effects in our world and many, like Ackroyd & Harvey, engage with it in their work. The question of what the implications of environmentally ethical artwork can be for 'real life' is a thorny one. Marina Abramović has it that 'Art can't change the world [...] It can only bring the consciousness and ask the questions'.[12] The 'art world' is a part of our society; an artist's function is not to become a lonely martyr to a cause, any more than the rest of us. Gary Hume, who took part in a Cape Farewell project, commented ruefully in a newspaper interview:

> The people who do the most damage [environmentally] buy my work, and I'm not using ecologically sound paint. I feel like apologising – I can't help the world. Climate change is too big for my art. My painting is a small thing, like a child might do. (Quoted by Madeleine Bunting 2009)

As Fredric Jameson has it, much art produced 'has become integrated into commodity production generally'. Laura Cumming noted sharply in her review of the 56th Venice Biennale that it 'is nothing if not explicitly critical of capitalism, consumerism and filthy lucre while relying upon them all for its very lifeblood'.[13] There is indeed a possibility that art can be safely neutralised in what Robert Smithson termed the 'cultural confinement' of the gallery (Smithson 1972): remaining an isolated experience and losing connection in the artist's and the viewer's mind with the world outside. In addition, despite all efforts to the contrary, much of what our culture identifies as the arts remains, as the *Guardian* reported following the recent Warwick Commission's report, an 'overwhelmingly middle class' pursuit.[14] Yet talking to a section of the population is better than none; and the 'chattering classes' are where the power to influence is more likely to be located:

> When the corporate bosses, the MPs, the journalists – and authors of books such as mine – all go to the same dinner parties and social events ... an insular ruling class develops ... it is democracy in name only. (Steve Hilton quoted in *i* newspaper by Yasmin Abihai-Brown, 18 May 2015)

Or, as George Orwell put it in a very non-PC way, 'in almost any revolt the leaders would tend to be people who could pronounce their aitches' (Orwell 2001 [1937]: 45).

The desire to do good, to do the right thing, will not necessarily translate into any tangible benefit to human society or the biosphere. Scientific 'measurability' is hard to apply to the arts, and concern about the lack of resultant practical effect following strong cultural engagement with environmental issues is entirely understandable. Currently the Climart Project is attempting to determine whether 'visual art affects viewer perceptions of climate change'; Adam Chodzko's video *Deep Above*, about to be released at the time of writing, questions why we can understand climate change yet remain paralysed from taking action. Simon C. Estok notes the lack of data explicitly showing that studying 'green' texts leads to increased environmental activism, referring to David Mazel's questioning in 'Ecocriticism as Praxis' (2008); but Estok also, crucially, warns against relying only on science to validate ecocriticism – as if it were the only site and type of knowledge (Bruckner and Brayton 2011: 240, Oppermann et al. 2011: 33). As Richard Kerridge and others have put it, the environmental crisis is also a crisis of representation; and it is clear looking at the history of our species that the stories we adhere to in any given society are key to its successful functioning (Kerridge and Sammels 1998,: 4). If a majority of us stopped 'believing' in banks or the rule of law, for example, imagine the chaos. The move to transversal knowledge, to a broad multidisciplinary approach, the links being made between science and the humanities – these are key in preparing for a shift in priorities. It can be said with confidence that people are persuadable of many different things – culture has changed many times – and a key strength of the 'big tent' of ecocriticism is its messy but fertile cross-disciplinary licence.

Despite the knowledge which artists and public have about aspects of the anthropogenic effect, the move to action or change can be problematic. A political climate and social system which encourages consumerism and arguably personal greed will struggle with changes which threaten short-term profit. Richard Kerridge summarises that environmental issues are neglected because they are 'either too vast or easily peripheralised', and uses Žižek's Lacanian analysis to describe how people avoid addressing the crisis, from disbelief to panic to breast beating (Kerridge and Sammels 1998: 4). An individual sense of agency, of the power to make a difference, is missing. Globalisation compounds the deficiency in what Fredric Jameson calls our cognitive mapping abilities – we struggle to understand from our everyday experience the complex structures driving contemporary life; our attentional filters are overloaded and the scale of problems overwhelms and hinders action. We are nevertheless each complicit in a system which mostly ignores the wider picture; as George Orwell noted about capitalism, in order for us to live in comfort, others – poorer countries, animals, oceans – must suffer a price: 'an evil state of affairs but you acquiesce in it every time you step into a taxi or eat a plate of strawberries and cream' (Orwell 2001 [1937]: 148).

The seminal 1960s experiment on 'Bystander Apathy' by Latané and Darley[15] suggests some factors which can inhibit people's reactions to emergencies, including the idea of a 'diffusion of responsibility' and 'pluralistic ignorance' – or 'why should I act when they do not?' We are more easily moved by first-person stories even though this may well be a statistically flawed approach. Cecil the lion falls into this category. More dramatically, the single image printed in most newspapers of a young, dead, refugee child[16] – after many thousands had perished, as we all knew – resulted in a sea change in opinion as well as a deluge of practical help from the public, leading to a small shift in government action. In a similar way, art works can focus knowledge, feelings, ideas in an assimilable way. Art can help the movement towards a new paradigm, not necessarily in any didactic way but through the alchemy of imagination, conjuring possibilities and hopes. At base we are all short-lived individuals with fears and worries, experiencing a rush of feeling, of thought, of experience. Ackroyd & Harvey's work lights on aspects of our interactions within the physical environment and produces an effect in the viewer which touches beyond rationality or logic; triggering multiple associations and offering visual delight. Daniel Levitin suggests that two key properties of the human brain are 'richness and associative access' (Levitin 2014: xi), referring to the huge amount of data of all kinds which people store in their brains and which can be accessed in many different, often unexpected, ways. Complex and affecting, art works like Ackroyd & Harvey's can provoke reflection and an expansion of vision, of ideas, rather than a cerebral confrontation with a single issue. Many of their works involve a changing, taming, alteration of an aspect of the natural world; this is approached not in an aggressive or conquering way but in a delight of possibilities and a fascination with shared biology. Their art is ambiguous and unsettling; it takes humans' place within nature and allies it to the amazing technological world that has been created.

Ecocriticism is often associated with celebration of the natural world; Ackroyd & Harvey's work certainly celebrates nature, but also celebrates human capabilities and potential, offering hope and possibilities when confronting apocalyptic scenarios. As Margaret Atwood aptly phrases it, unlike other animals 'we suffer from the future perfect tense'.[17] So we can imagine into being better futures; making cultural choices with the new understandings we have. When the objective reality of nature apparently depends in part on the whim of human choice, it is probably time to take our individual and joint responsibility with some seriousness of purpose. After all, as Dickens's Mr Jarndyce points out, 'the universe makes rather an indifferent parent, I'm afraid'.[18]

Notes

1 EASLCE is the European Association for the Study of Literature, Culture, and the Environment. www.easlce.eu/about-us/what-is-ecocriticism/ accessed 2 January 2016.

2 IBERS is the Institute of Biological, Environmental and Rural Sciences at Aberystwyth University.

3 Cape Farewell www.capefarewell.com/ accessed 3 January 2016.

4 William Shakespeare, *Hamlet*, Act 5 Scene 1.

5 The *Courier* newspaper ran a story by Charlene Wilson, on 1 March 2014, about an exhibition displaying two recently unearthed medieval skeletons with the title 'Exhibition featuring human skeletons branded "moral abuse"'. A former president of Dunfermline Heritage Trust, Sheila Pitcairn, is quoted as saying: 'It is not good practice to retain human remains. There is a very clear code of professional conduct relating to the treatment of human remains [...] I object strongly to these skeletons being put on display.'

6 Cecil was a thirteen-year-old lion living in Hwange National Park, Zimbabwe; he was killed by Walter Palmer, an American 'recreational big-game hunter' on 1 July 2015.

7 MarketWatch www.marketwatch.com/ 26 June 2015: 'Marriage equality nationwide could mean a $2.6 billion spending boom over the next three years.'

8 Gallup, 22 April 2009. *Awareness, Opinions About Global Warming Vary Worldwide* by Brett W. Pelham.

9 Hannah Ellis-Peterson. 'Underwater sculptures emerge from the Thames in climate change protest', *Guardian*, 2 September 2015.

10 Widely reported in the *Guardian* and the *Independent* newspapers among others, 22 September 2015.

11 *Bulletin of the Atomic Scientists*, January 2007: 'Global warming poses a dire threat to human civilization that is second only to nuclear weapons. Through flooding and desertification, climate change threatens the habitats and agricultural resources that societies depend upon for survival. As such, climate change is also likely to contribute to mass migrations and even to wars over arable land, water, and other natural resources.' http://thebulletin.org/press-release/doomsday-clock-moves-two-minutes-closer-midnight accessed 2 January 2015.
12 Marina Abramović, interviewed by Nancy Groves in the *Guardian*, 18 June 2015, www.theguardian.com/profile/nancy-groves accessed 16 January 2016.
13 Laura Cumming, 10 May 2015 review in the *Guardian*.
14 *Guardian*, 17 February 2015, Mark Brown: 'Warwick commission report finds fewer pupils taking GCSEs in design and drama, and describes arts audiences as overwhelmingly middle class and white.'
15 B. Latane and J. Darley, 'Bystander apathy', *American Scientist 57* (1969): 244–68.
16 On 2 September 2015 poignant images of young Aylan Kurdi, found dead at Bodrum seashore, Turkey, were published in newspapers and online.
17 Margaret Atwood, in a review of *Brave New World* in the *Guardian*, 17 November 2007.
18 Charles Dickens, *Bleak House* (1853), ch. VI.

References

Ackroyd, Heather and Dan Harvey (2006) 'Stranded', in *The Ship: The Art of Climate Change*. London: Natural History Museum.

Andreae, M.O. et al. (2015) *The Amazon Tall Tower Observatory (ATTO): Overview of Pilot Measurements on Ecosystem Ecology, Meteorology, Trace Gases, and Aerosols*. Göttingen: Copernicus Publications on behalf of the European Geosciences Union.

Bass, Claire L., Mark P. Simmonds and Steve J. Isaac (2006) *An Overview of the Potential Consequences for Cetaceans of Oceanic Acidification*. Cambridge: International Whaling Commission, Scientific Committee document: SC/58/E10.

Bruckner, Lynne and Dan Brayton (2011) *Ecocritical Shakespeare*. Farnham: Ashgate.

Buell, Lawrence (2003) *Writing for an Endangered World: Literature, Culture and the Environment in the U.S. and Beyond*. Cambridge, MA: Harvard University Press.

Bunting, Madeleine (2009) 'The rise of climate change art', *Guardian*, 2 December.

Climart Project: www.climart.info/ accessed 9 January 2015.

Crutzen, P.J. and E.F. Stoermer (2000) 'The "Anthropocene"'. *Global Change Newsletter* 4: 17–18.

Ehrenreich, Barbara (2014) *Living with a Wild God: A Non-believer's Search for the Truth about Everything*. New York: Twelve.

Estok, Simon C. (2010a) 'An Ecocritical Reading, Slightly Queer, *As for Me and My House*', *Journal of Canadian Studies / Revue d'Études Canadiennes* 44:3 (Autumn).

Estok, Simon C. (2010b) 'Narrativising Science: the Ecocritical Imagination and Ecophobia', *Configurations* 18:1–2: 141–59. Sungkyunkwan University, Project Muse. http://muse.jhu.edu accessed 16 January 2016.

Glotfelty, Cheryll and Harold Fromm (1996) *Ecocriticism Reader: Landmarks in Literary Ecology*. Athens: University of Georgia Press.

IPCC (2014) 'Summary for Policymakers, Synthesis Report: Contributions of Working Groups I, II and III' to the *Fifth Assessment Report of the Intergovernmental Panel on Climate Change*. Geneva: IPCC. www.ipcc.ch/report/ar5/syr accessed 16 January 2016.

Jameson, Fredric (1991) *Postmodernism, or, The Cultural Logic of Late Capitalism*. Durham, NC: Duke University Press.

Kerridge, Richard and Neil Sammels (1998) *Writing the Environment: Ecocriticism and Literature*. London: Zed Books.

Levitin, Daniel (2014) *The Organized Mind: Thinking Straight in the Age of Information Overload*. New York: Dutton.

Mazel, David (2008) 'Ecocriticism as Praxis', in Laird Christensen, Mark C. Long and Fred Waage, *Teaching North American Environmental Literature*. New York: MLA.

McEwan, Ian (2005) 'An Essay for Our Time', in British Council, *Let's Talk about Climate Change*. www.opendemocracy.net/globalisation-climate_change_debate/article_2439.jsp accessed 6 January 2015.

Murphy, Patrick (2015) *Persuasive Aesthetic Ecocritical Praxis: Climate Change, Subsistence, and Questionable Futures*. Lanham: Lexington Books.

Oppermann, Serpil, Ufuk Özdağ and Nevin Özkan (2011) *The Future of Ecocriticism: New Horizons*. Newcastle-upon-Tyne: Cambridge Scholars Publishing.

Orwell, George (2001 [1937]) *The Road to Wigan Pier*. London: Penguin.

Pelham, Brett W. (2009) *Awareness, Opinions about Global Warming Vary Worldwide*. Gallup, 22 April.

Smithson, Robert (1972) *Cultural Confinement*, Artforum, October. www.robertsmithson.com/essays/cultural.htm accessed 11 January 2015.

Whitty, Julia (2007) 'Animal Extinction – the Greatest Threat to Hankind', *Independent*, 30 April, www.independent.co.uk/author/by-julia-whitty accessed 16 January 2016.

7

The word among stones

Peter Barry

<blockquote>
While myths might be narrative fossils from unimaginably long ago […] they offer themselves to us as rich objects for reverie and conjecture, becoming the 'shore of dreaming' ('l'orée du songe'), as Roger Caillois called his own collection of stones. Like dream stones, the myths are puzzles, and they keep inviting new thoughts. (Warner 2015: 46)
</blockquote>

The title of this chapter is taken from the title-poem of a poetry booklet containing the work of Patricia M. Ball, which was published after her death by two of her colleagues at London University (Ball 2000). Ball was a specialist in Romantic and Victorian poetry, on which she published three influential books, and, as a sideline, she was herself a fine and private poet. I became interested in the topic of 'stone poems' about a decade ago, without really knowing why, and have found her formulations very helpful in reaching some understanding of their appeal. 'Stone poems' are roughly definable as poems on stones, or about stones, or among stones, or even stones viewed as in themselves poems. They are usually placed or encountered outdoors, sometimes as isolated individual items, and sometimes grouped together as part of a 'trail', or 'walk', or 'garden'. If they are in an urban, semi-urban or 'edgelands' locale, they may form part of a monument, or a memorial, or they may be an element in a self-proclaimed or de facto 'localising feature'. Sometimes they are arranged in strategic locations across a wide stretch of terrain, or they may be globally positioned, as determined by some schema, which might be shamanistic or cabalistic (involving ley-lines, for example, or the course of an underground river) or placed in locations pinpointed by up-to-the-minute electronic tracking data, or by some combination of such ancient and modern forces. What these stone poems 'say', or embody is usually, or, at least, often, conjectural, for they seem to lie on 'l'orée du songe', sometimes obscured by mist or ice, or just by the workings of time, for constant friction with the elements always threatens to remove them from the record, as if the stone with a poem on it were doing its best to revert to just being a stone. As to how we might attempt to interpret them, I will quote in full the first stanza of 'The Word Among Stones' (7):

> It is never the obvious;
> and so you must be always expectant
> or never. Either will do.

At first, stone poems seemed to bear no evident relation to my interest in avant-garde or neomodernist poetry (especially 'concrete' and 'visual' poetries), seeming, if anything, to run counter to it. But if it is 'never the obvious' that stone poems convey, then perhaps there is a distinct link with avant-garde aspirations (which always involve some form of pushing language towards the edges of signification), and the final stanza of the same poem reinforces this possibility, emphasising the stone poem's resistance to meaning, to closure, to smoothness:

> It is a pebble,
> learnt by unprejudiced touch
> to be, not smooth
> but pocked; ridged; rough,
> and never wholly round.
> Only so hard
> that the bruised fingers grip
> in this alone permitted to rejoice.[1]

Further, stone poems are necessarily the opposite of wordy, the reasons for which are obvious when they are, or are on, stones – they tend towards a verbal minimalism, which the contrasting bulk of their sheer presence seems to emphasise. Likewise, they are 'disjunctive' by nature, placing word by word without linkage, paratactic rather than syntactic, often 'grammarless' even, to take a word from another of Ball's poems ('The Corpse Way, Swaledale', *The Word Among Stones*, p. 12), in which water, mist and rocks become 'inconsequent facts / for grammarless words'.[2] In the remainder of this chapter, I will look first at some prehistorical and historical examples of individual stone poems, then at examples of stone poems grouped together in landscaped settings, then at four urban examples and finally at the practice of a single poet in greater detail.

Prehistorical and historical stone poems

The Ringing Stone on the Island of Tiree, in the Inner Hebrides is a glacier-borne granodiorite erratic originating from the island of Rum, about 65 kilometres away, and 'balanced on other rocks like an egg on a spoon'. It derives its name from the fact that it 'emits a metallic ring when struck', and it bears 'a number of cup markings generally associated with the period of the Megalithic Builders'.[3] There are 'at least 53' of these 'circular or oval depressions', and 'there can be no doubt that these markings are artificial and, while several of them are unusually large', 'the whole assemblage may be prehistoric in origin' (Royal Commission on Ancient and Historical Monuments in Scotland 1980 cited by Fagg 1997: 85). The cup marks are clearly visible in Plate 11 and the round pebble placed on top has been left there to strike the stone with to make it ring. Rocks and stones are traditionally emblematic of permanence – at meetings we talk of things not being 'set in stone', meaning that they are not yet fixed, decided, and permanent, but notions of fixity and permanence depend on what timescale we are using. As well as being a traveller, this rock is unrock-like, in that it performs actions – it rings, and rocks, moves and balances, and bears on itself the marks of human culture, though what purpose or significance these markings had is unknown. The nearby information board has some lurid speculations, but the tightly descriptive official accounts resist interpretation, so that the rock poem (though in this case neither 'mute' nor 'motionless') has to embody the formula 'A poem should not mean / But be.' These are, of course, the last two lines of Archibald MacLeish's 'Ars poetica', a poem that prescribes several things that a poem 'should' be – including 'mute', 'motionless', and 'wordless' – but perhaps the very word 'should' implicitly concedes that these attributes are merely ideational (see MacLeish 1990: 106). Other aspects of the traditional emblematic spectrum of rocks include their maintenance of an inscrutable silence, but this rock is a silent witness only in the forensic sense – we can read its history by the marks upon it, both human marks, and the indications of the type of rock it is, which tell us where it travelled from.

The Tiree stone itself *is* the poem, so that the term 'stone poem' seems entirely appropriate, whereas in the case of the second example we have a poem *on* a stone, and the poem's meaning is intensified by the nature of the stone, and by its positioning. The stone itself is a modern 'transported erratic' (that is, one which has been moved by human agency) originating from the region of Laconia, also known as Lacedaemonia, in south-eastern Greece, where the city of Sparta was situated. The stone has been shaped into a square slab with the smoothness and regularity of the stones used to construct buildings: it has been placed at the Pass of Thermopylae in northern Greece to commemorate the Spartans who defended the pass against the invading army of Xerxes in

480 BC. On it is carved an elegiac couplet by Simonides which can be translated:

> Go tell them, back in Sparta, passer-by,
> That in accordance with their wishes, here we lie.[4]

The text of the stone poem plays on the idea of the innate silence of stones in order to emphasise that the now-voiceless dead lie for ever far from home, like the erratic on which their posthumous plea is carved. So poem and stone seemingly 'speak' as one, transgressing the defining silence of both the dead and stones, and reaching out across the divide, to enlist the required assistance of the passing reader-stranger, rather like Coleridge's self-composed epitaph in St Michael's Church, High-gate, which begins 'Stop, Christian passer-by! Stop, Child of God'.

The third historical example is Trajan's Column in Rome, which can be seen as a stone poem without words, again foregrounding (in the present context) notions of silence. The column (115 ft high, including the pedestal) is faced with a sequence of bas-relief images which spiral upwards around it, telling the story of the Emperor Trajan's two military campaigns in Dacia (modern Romania) in AD 101–2 and 105–6 (for the most readable and comprehensive account of the Column see Pollen 2010 [1872]). The modern 'codex' book form (in which separate sheets are joined together, 'hinged' at one side, and placed within covers) had already been invented in Trajan's time, but the dominant form of the book for the next couple of centuries remained that of the continuous scroll, read by gradually unwinding the text from the spool to which it was attached. So Trajan's Column is in the form of an upended Roman book, and, since the column is stationary, a notional reader would have to spiral round it until reaching the end of the story, which is the statue of the victorious emperor that surmounts it. Of course, the height of the column renders most of the visual text unreadable – even in the full-scale cast of the column cut laterally into two halves, which is in the Victoria & Albert Museum in London, it is impossible to 'view' the whole of it. But the very height of the column which renders the text 'illegible' itself embodies or encapsulates the primary 'message' of the text, for the height is a visual correlative of the two arduous and lengthy campaigns successfully concluded, the column 'says', because of the Roman virtues of perseverance, steadfastness, determination and meticulous planning. So the column, with its endless train of soldiers, carpenters, engineers, provisioners etc., communicates a sense of 'Romanness' as a relentless and unstoppable force moving in a characteristically methodical and rational manner towards its goals and achievements. The visual 'text' around the column is supplemented by a capitalised inscription placed over the entrance in the base that leads to the spiral staircase in the hollow interior of the column. The inscription informs the reader that a hill as high as the column itself was removed to make way for Trajan's Forum, which effectively says again what the column itself 'says' about Roman character and identity.

A final historical example is closer to modern times: it is the memorial known as The Brothers' Parting Stone, placed at the spot near Cofa Pike in Cumbria, where William Wordsworth parted from his brother John on 29 September 1800. John died as Captain of the East Indiaman *Earl of Abergavenny*, when it was wrecked off Portland at the start of a voyage to India and China in 1805. The voyage was to have made the family fortune, so that William could devote his life to poetry. The site is marked by a metal sign (above the stone) which reads 'The Brothers' Parting', followed by the name Wordsworth, and the rock-face below has eight lines from Wordsworth's commemorative poem 'Elegiac Stanzas' carved into it. The lines used are the first four of Stanza III and the first four of the last stanza (VII), reading:

> Here did we stop; and here looked round
> While each into himself descends,
> For that last thought of parting Friends
> That is not to be found.
> ...
> Brother and friend, if verse of mine
> Have power to make thy virtues known,
> Here let a monumental Stone
> Stand – sacred as a Shrine.

The extract from the poem is now mostly illegible, perhaps making the sense of loss and absence all the more poignant and easier for the 'reader' to inhabit. In this instance, the stone poem has the traces of words, and fragments from a poem, but the words are not completely legible *in situ*. Making the wish expressed in the poem into a literal fact was not Wordsworth's act, nor his desire, as one might deduce from the fact that, though surviving his brother by forty-five years, he never did anything to bring it about. Perhaps he felt that the 'monumental stone' already existed and had been consecrated as shrine to his brother by the poem. In this sense, the stone poem becomes more *of* a poem as it enters the condition of wordlessness. It was only some thirty years after Wordsworth's own death, that is, in the 1880s, that Canon Hardwicke Rawnsley (1851–1920), one of the co-founders of the National Trust in 1895, arranged for an extract from William's memorial poem to be inscribed on the rock. As is well known, it wasn't just the brothers who parted on this spot, but brother and sister too, for Dorothy Wordsworth was also present, though, as on other occasions, she was written out of the account: she wrote in her diary:

> [*September*] *29th on Monday.* John left us. Wm & I parted with him in sight of Ullswater. It was a fine day, showery, but with sunshine and fine clouds. Poor fellow my heart was right sad. I could not help thinking, we should see him again, because he was only going to Penrith. (Clark (ed.) 1978: 71)

So the vanishing stone poem echoes many absences, and omissions both textual and personal, as well as foreshadowing its own. Wordsworth wrote that 'thoughts which should be fixed in language upon a sepulchral stone' were suited to 'epitaphic composition' (quoted in Swaab 2014). Whether he meant this to be taken literally of the words extracted by Rawnsley and inscribed on the 'parting stone' it is impossible to know.

Contemporary stone poems grouped within landscapes

In recent years stone poems have often been placed in groups or clusters within landscaped settings and forming a 'walk' or 'trail'. Perhaps the best-known such site in the UK is the garden called the Little Sparta Trust, in the Pentland Hills near Edinburgh, originated by the Scottish poet Ian Hamilton Finlay (1925–2006). Here stone poems and formal sculptural objects, with many classical and naval motifs, are arranged within discreetly managed rustic environments. It is a setting which is both 'authored', as Finlay's son, Alec, describes it in the 'TateShots' short film about Little Sparta, and yet also natural-seeming.[5] These opposed and yet complementary elements are embodied in a stone poem, carved on a stepping stone across the stream in the Wild Garden at Little Sparta.[6] This is a practical and weathered object, embedded within its rural surroundings, but culturalised, as the stone has carved into it (by the letter carver Michael Harvey) a dictionary definition of the word 'ripple' in a lapidary form which evokes the inscription style seen on Roman monuments, thus: RIPPLE: n, A FOLD. A FLUTING OF THE LIQUID ELEMENT. The formality of the lettering contrasts with the untreated nature of the stone itself, an example of what the art critic Stephen Bann calls 'wild stones', which are irregularly shaped and marked 'boulders taken from the sea-shore' or other locations (see Bann 2014: 20). A clue as to the possible meaning of this object is provided by a Finlay item in the collection of Kettle's Yard, Cambridge, as described by Bann, the foremost Finlay scholar (20). Bann notes that the motif of the formally inscribed wild stone is used in miniature in the idea of 'Unnatural Pebbles', the title of a 1981 exhibition in Edinburgh to which Finlay had contributed a series of statements called 'Detached Sentences on the Pebble', forming an appendix to the catalogue. One of these statements reads: 'Kettle's Yard, in Cambridge, England, is the *Louvre* of the Pebble.' The sentences were conceptual pieces only, but this one became a physical reality in 1995 for an exhibition at Kettle's Yard. The sentence was inscribed on a much smaller irregular wild stone than the Little Sparta stepping stone, carrying the inscription in this form (with oblique strokes added here merely to indicate the lineation): 'KETTLE'S YARD / CAMBRIDGE / ENGLAND IS THE / *LOUVRE* OF THE / PEBBLE'.

The juxtaposition of the Louvre and the pebble encapsulates the culture/nature dichotomy which is central to, and unresolved by, Little Sparta. A ripple (in the natural and fluid medium of water) and the fluting evident in the columns used in classical architecture, or seen in the folds of suspended curtain fabric, are linked together by a visual pun – if we can imagine them viewed in cross-section, the ripples, flutes and folds all have the same undulating linear form. Furthermore, flutes and fluting are recurrent elements in Little Sparta, and several examples are collated in Victoria Emma Pagan's 'The Afterlife of Little Sparta' (Pagan et al. 2015: 164–5). For Finlay, the blade and the flute stand, respectively, for conflict and harmony, and are united in the image of the machine-gun on the plaque which commemorates the 'First Battle of Little Sparta' in 1983 when bailiffs from Strathclyde Regional Council struggled unsuccessfully with Finlay's supporters to remove items from the site in lieu of alleged non-payment of local rates – the Council maintained that the garden's 'temple' (a place of worship) was actually a profit-making visitor facility. On the commemorative plaque at the spot where the 'battle' took place, there is a supposed analogy between the sleeve vents on the machine-gun barrel and the finger stops of the flute, and the plaque also carries the words (from Virgil's Eighth Eclogue) 'Flute, begin with me Arcadian notes': likewise, the wooden gate across the entrance driveway to the site has carved into the wood the words '*das gepflugte Land*' ('the fluted land'), possibly because the field, when ploughed, takes on the undulating linear cross-section referred to above. As the Kettle's Yard catalogue says, 'the natural surroundings [of Little Sparta] now became his page' (53), on which Finlay explored 'his ongoing interests in ancient philosophy, Classicism, and the French Revolution'. Against the 'Athens of the North' title claimed by Edinburgh, Finlay identified with the Spartans who were the archetypal antagonists of Athens. Here it was the now-defunct Strathclyde Regional Council centred on Glasgow that was seeking to impose its cultural definitions on him. The long-running economic and cultural rivalry between Edinburgh and Glasgow makes for a triangular set of antagonistic relationships. So the apparent pastoral innocence and tranquillity of the stepping stone are transformed by its own verbal echoes, and the contextual reverberations of its containing 'page' into something altogether more unsettling and troubled.

In contrast with Little Sparta, the poems featured in the Ted Hughes Poetry Trail, set up in 2006 at Stover Country Park in Devon, are on 'sixteen specially-designed "poetry posts", each displaying a poem by Ted Hughes on a theme relating to the natural world'.[7] The poems are in the open air, and on fine-grained black granite, set within a supporting wooden frame. The sixteen poems are perhaps reminiscent of the fourteen 'Stations' of the Cross, in the sense that they are contemplative stopping points on a mapped-out progression round a dedicated space which cannot easily be traversed in any other way. In the case of the Stations, the progression follows a narrative timeline, whereas the poems on the Trail each relate to something in its immediate vicinity – thus, the poems 'An Otter', 'Cormorant', 'To Paint a Water Lily' and 'The Lake' all have a lakeside position. Inscribed in white on wood-framed granite, and in a conservative 'typeface' of the Times New Roman kind, the poems seem to mimic a printed page in negative reversal, without using the stone itself in any integrated or expressive way. The walking has to stop so that the poem can be read, and one effect is to make us wonder what exactly a 'trail' is: the two basic relevant senses seem to be (1) a path or track through countryside, lakeside, forest or mountain area, 'often one made for particular uses or purposes', a dictionary says, and (2) the traces left behind which provide evidence of the passage of someone or something (such as the trail of destruction left by a flood or a tornado). Usually, poems evoke the presence of something not actually present (a moment in the past, for instance, a fox, a sense of foreboding), so if there is actually a lake in front of us, stopping to read a poem about a lake may seem anomalous.

It is worth adding, in relation to Hughes, that Devon is particularly rich in 'trails': this one intersects with the Templer Way, run by Devon County Council, and named after the Templer family which once owned the Stover estate. It follows the route of the granite tramway that transported the stone from the quarry (which is possibly the source of the granite used in Hughes Trail poetry posts) to the Stover canal, to Teignmouth and then on by sea to London and elsewhere. This granite was used to build London Bridge, which was dismantled in the 1960s and transported stone by stone to Arizona, where it has been reassembled.

There is not much that is poetic in this moving-bridge saga, but plenty about 'migrating stones'.[8] The Hughes Trail is a garden-like 'authored' space within a wider country space, blurring the boundaries between the two (as the term 'country park' implies). By contrast, at Little Sparta, poems are embedded in the landscape or the garden, with words or emblems that are usually legible or identifiable from a distance, so that to look at *it* is to look at *them*, rather than having to close out the environment to read poems which are simply 'posted' there. A blended form of these two approaches is seen in the next example.

The 'Poetry Path' at Kirkby Stephen in Cumbria is on 'the south boundary of the officially designated North Pennines Area of Outstanding Natural Beauty' (Capel n.d.: 28). To some extent, it seems to combine the better features and characteristics of both Little Sparta and the Hughes Trail. It tells the story of the agricultural year, month by month, in a series of twelve stone poems, so this is something like the 'stations' aspect of the Hughes Trail – there is a narrative and a set track to follow – but the poems are not 'posted' and page-like, but 'embedded' in the landscape, as at Little Sparta, but more informally. The aim of the Poetry Path, as stated in the guidebook, is 'to introduce a permanent and integrated interpretive experience into the landscape *that is assimilated as part of the heritage it promotes* [my italics] and conveys a powerful message about the farmer's role in the countryside'. So the didactic element is quite strongly emphasised (Little Sparta-like) – it is about interpreting the environment, but it isn't providing this actively for us to accept passively, but is offering an 'interpretive experience', an internal process of collaborative empathy, just as universities these days offer a 'learning experience', rather than just teaching. The word 'heritage' is used without embarrassment, and the modern-day farmer's triple role in 'nature conservation and recreation as well as food production' is foregrounded by Project Manager Dick Capel 'in conjunction with a local steering committee consisting of local people in partnership with landowners' (Capel n.d.: 1). The landscape itself is a 'local resource', and there is an 'economic need to attract more visitors to an area where the main resource is its beautiful landscape'. There are also carved decorative motifs with poems for some of the months, depicting the activities associated with that month of the hill-farmer's year (all these details from the guidebook).

Some of the poems are set alongside a 'holloway', defined by Robert Macfarlane, Stanley Donwood and Dan Richards as 'A sunken path, a deep & shady lane. A route that centuries of foot-fall, hoof-hit, wheel-roll & rain-run have harrowed into the land. A track worn down *by the traffic of ages & the fretting of water,* and in places *reduced sixteen or eighteen feet beneath the level of the fields*' (Authors' italics, 2013: 3) The holloway on this path is only waist-deep, but that is sufficient to create an intimacy with those poems set on this section of the path. The poems are discreetly placed within their settings, so that they might conceivably be missed in certain conditions of light, season or weather, and in any case will provoke different reactions (or 'interpretive experiences'), depending on which are being viewed 'in-season' and which not. The April poem, for instance, is positioned at ground level and set within a drystone wall, not concealed in any sense, since the wall has been breached for the poem to be set within it, and the shape and size of the stone poem breaks the fractal patterning of the stones in the wall, set by master wall-maker Steve Allen. April's poem (Plate 12) is carved in the same limestone as the wall, but the poem for May is incised in red sandstone in sharp contrast to the limestone wall. The use of locally quarried stone is a key feature of this installation. In April's eight-line poem Peacocke starts with reference to the wild flowers of the season and then paints a word-picture of twin lambs rushing bleating to their mother where 'they jostle the ragged ewe / boosting each split hoof / high off the bitten turf'. This is a sight that a visitor from April onwards might see for themselves as they look over the wall housing the poem. As they grow, twin lambs frequently lift the ewe off the ground when they feed one at each side. The bitten turf reflects the grazing habits of sheep which at peak demand during lambing reduces the grass to a lawn-like smoothness. As can be seen in Plate 12, the words are not Times-Romanised and aligned to a left-hand margin, like words on a page, but undulate across the stone.

It is worth adding here a word on the complexities of the collaborative energies at the heart of such large-scale projects, which is a marked feature of the various poetry walks and trails now in existence. Pip Hall (with her apprentice Wayne Hart) is also the letter carver of the Stanza Stones Poetry Trail, the 2012 Cultural Olympiad Project of the Ilkley Literature Festival. Six poems on stones by Simon Armitage are situated along a trail stretching 47 miles across Yorkshire, from Marsden to Ilkley, the poems 'inspired by the language and landscape of the Pennine Watershed and carved onto stones along the upland'. Each poem describes water in one of its forms, 'the element which gave shape and form to this region'.[9] The project included extensive collaborative work with groups of young writers, dancers and film makers from the region. This element – the engaging of younger generations of aspirant practitioners in stones projects – is emphasised by Pip Hall in a local newspaper article about her published while the Olympiad project was still in progress in 2012. It begins with her meticulous account of the provenance of her own letter carving skills: 'The skill goes back to one person a hundred years ago, Edward Johnston, the father of modern lettering, who taught Eric Gill; Gill taught David Kindersley, who taught his own son Richard, who taught Alec Peever, who was my teacher.'[10] Tarlo and Tucker, in the present book, quote a phrase about being 'enmeshed in a dense network of relationships' in collaborative working, and this makes it clear that the mesh is both synchronic (taking in all those artists, practitioners, amateurs, professionals and users one is actually working with throughout the project) and diachronic (encompassing all those who inducted, instructed or collaborated with those through whom our skills and outlook came into being).

The didactic and officially funded element of such projects ought to be irritating, perhaps, as the poems have a 'palpable design' on us, but somehow it isn't. It is anomalous, maybe, that a committee once met and decided that a particular place is an 'an area of outstanding natural beauty' (an AONB), and then took the decision to have it 'officially designated' as such, conferring upon it entitlement to certain protective measures and to the allocation of extra 'resources'.[11] Across the nation there is a 'canon' of such places, just as there is a pantheon of canonised writers, and a body of experts who look after their interests. Actually, the places I most like to be in, and would most like to see kept more or less as they are, are quasi-industrialised, or formerly industrialised, rather than National Trusty, but it might be hard to persuade others, en masse, that they are places of outstanding beauty. Again, then, stone poems, especially when assembled outdoors in a worked setting, can raise difficult questions.

Stone poems in urban or 'edgelands' settings[12]

The next set is made up of four examples of stone poems in settings which might not be considered places of outstanding beauty. The first is the monument in Dunraven Street, Tonypandy, in the Welsh Valleys, which commemorates the town's mining past. Sculpted by Howard Bowcott, working in collaboration with Tim Rose of the Bath-based landscape architecture firm Macgregor Smith and Rhondda Cynon Taf Council, it was unveiled in 1999. It takes the form of a narrow stone column, shaped rather like the tapering blade of a Stanley knife, and 'made from hundreds of small, individually shaped pieces of thin sandstone, stacked and graded by colour', and arranged in narrow bands around a concrete core. The height of the column is 460 cm, each millimetre of which 'represents a million years in the evolution of the earth'.[13] In the top third of the shaft, near the apex, is a circular hole, representing the pithead wheel above the mineshaft. In the lower third of the shaft or column of the monument is set a band of Welsh slate which is 80 cm thick, which represents the 2 ft 9 in height of the coal seam beneath the town in which the miners worked, and where thirty-one of them died in 1965 in the last pit explosion in Welsh mining history.

Superimposed on the Welsh slate section are poems by Gillian Clarke (in English) on one side, and by Menna Elfyn (in Welsh) on the other. Clarke's poem, shown here at Figure 7.1, is circular in form, representing an access tunnel to the coal face, and the poetic format is the one known as specular form or mirror form, associated with (among others) Julia Copus.[14] Thus, the first eight lines are formally mirror-imaged by the last eight, so that each of the first eight lines is longer than the previous one, and each of the last eight is shorter than the one before. Similarly, the rhyme scheme is mirrored, 1 going with 16, 2 with 15, 3 with 14 and so on. The 'northern' apex of the Clarke poem is the near-present, when the mining industry was at its height, and the remainder traces the geological processes which produce the coal, the seas that come and go over aeons, trapping the sea-creature fossil traces now

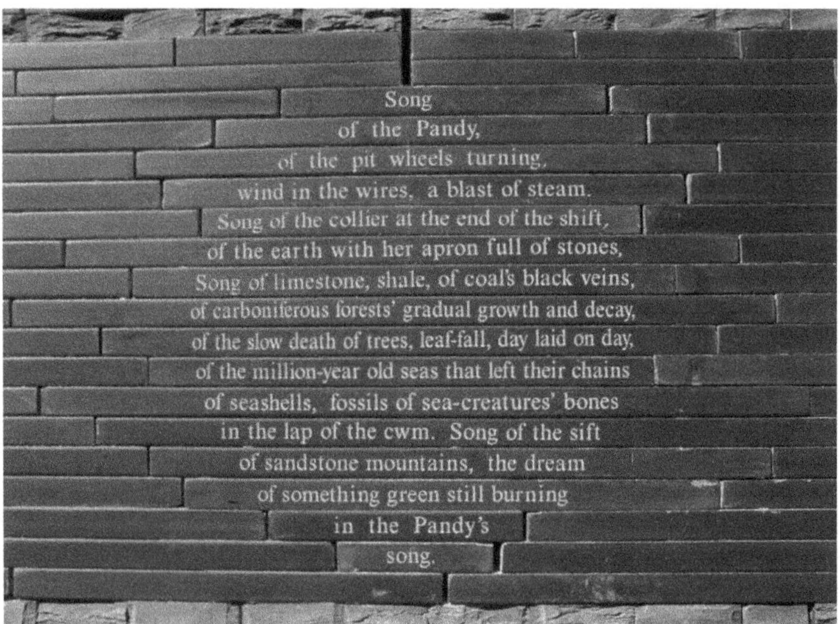

Figure 7.1   Gillian Clarke, poem on Howard Bowcott's Tonypandy monument to commemorate the town's mining past

embedded in the stone. In the same way, the coal is embedded in the people who mined it, and all those who lived in the town, whose lives, and those of their descendants, are for ever enmeshed with it – or, as Menna Elfyn's Welsh poem expresses it, 'Ynom ni bydd glo o hyd' – 'In us, there will always be Coal'.

The civic setting and public partnership elements prominent in the miners' monument are seen on a larger scale in recent work from the Dundee-born poet Bill Herbert, currently (2016) professor of poetry and creative writing at Newcastle University. He has 'engaged in numerous public art and cross-media projects [...] [and] is the poetry consultant for the Westpark project, originating text and co-ordinating artworks across this development in Darlington, one of the largest public art projects in the North East'.[15] The Darlington West Park project is the first public park constructed in the area for over a century. For the poet, the brief is not an end-stopped, one-off commission but an ongoing commitment to extensive public engagement with a typically contemporary mix of potential users and beneficiaries, and involving contact with various layers of professional committees. The poet also worked with children from a local primary school, producing texts referring to the town's historical significance in relation to the Stockton and Darlington Railway, the world's first public railway to use steam locomotives, which opened in 1825. As with all recent arts finance, the 'reach' of a project of this kind has to go well beyond the comfortable parameters of contact with habitual visitors to art galleries, frequent concert-goers and committed book-buyers. The implications, in terms of redefining what it means to be a poet (or painter, or sculptor), are profound.

The *West Park Management & Maintenance Plan* gives a detailed account of the project (Darlington Borough Council 2013). Herbert's work is a crucial part of several features within West Park, including the amphitheatre, described on p. 12 of the plan, which has central stone features placed within a ring of COR-TEN® steel (a steel alloy which, unpainted, develops a weathered and protective patina). The ring is about the size and height of the low wall round a circus ring, and the words of a three-line poem by Herbert about the town of Darlington are cut through it in capitals, so as to be read clockwise from inside the ring, and possibly to be also decipherable in reverse from outside:

> This is Locomotion town, where the railways first ran
> This is Quakertown, where sharing took root
> This is Darlingtown, that wears its heart within its name

The 'lineation' in the ring-poem, as cited above, is provided by the three breaks in the ring which provide entrances into the amphitheatre. The Quakers ('line' 2) were a major eighteenth- and nineteenth-century force in the town's key industries (wool, linen, railways and banking).[16] In the words of the booklet, the amphitheatre 'is surrounded by the Trinity Stones comprising of three sets of three stones. The Trinity Stones display the smallest of text, haiku celebrating three species that were found in the original site – the dingy skipper butterfly, the little ringed plover, and the water vole.' The three haiku are:

> **Water Vole Haiku**
> Diver from the bank
> Pearls of air catch your fur
> And scatter in silt
>
> **Little Ringed Plover Haiku**
> Straw-legged sprinters:
> Who's the third eye, yellow-ringed,
> Helping your chicks thrive?
>
> **Dingy Skipper Haiku**
> Steer this limestone ark
> Rapid pilot, Dingy brown
> Rare as principles
> (reproduced at Darlington Borough Council 2013: 10)

The Trinity Stones each weigh ten tonnes and are 'from the Catcastle quarry, which supplied the stone for the [nearby] railway viaduct'. Also, at the centre of each stone is 'a bronze bowl displaying the name of the creature as well as poetry relating to the creature', these bronze bowls being illustrated on page 10 of the brochure.

One of the assumptions about projects of this kind, which Bill Herbert mentioned to me in conversation, is that public art, whether sculpture, poetry or hybridic forms, is seen as having the potential to exert a civilising or socialising influence, especially on younger people growing up in post-industrial locales where hitherto career choice was pre-decided, because a town was identified with (for example) steel-production, cotton mills, railways or mining. Instead of the actuality of daily work and careers which take youngsters from the age of fourteen or fifteen to their sixties, there are now 'schemes', and 'initiatives', and postindustrial expanses, or commemorative tourist attractions where the 'yards' or the 'works' used to be. Whatever public art, and its associated stone poems, can do to combat that communal sense of loss of identity is surely well done. Certainly the poet's enthusiasm for commissions of this kind, and his fascination with the artistic challenges and problems involved, were obvious. He also emphasised the importance of 'peripherality', defining it as 'the idea that the artwork shouldn't intrude or present a dominating narrative', and stressed the high value of 'engagement with unintended consequences', meaning that poets and artists cannot foresee all the effects of a work until it is onsite and up and running. Some works may prove to have unenvisaged potential, 'for instance, the extraordinary acoustic properties of the circle [of the West Park amphitheatre] which are now being picked up for a piece in Phase 2.'

Alyson Hallett's pavement poem, with its 'outlying' word clusters, in Milsom Street, Bath, is another public-art, Council-sponsored urban example. This major city-centre street has not been pedestrianised, but the width of the pavements has been much extended to alter the balance between pedestrians and traffic in favour of the former. Stone carver Alec Peever (who, as discussed above, was the teacher of stone carver Pip Hall) was invited to provide art work, and he collaborated with Alyson Hallett to make a 'poetic pavement' around her poem, which seems to drift or flow across the linear patterning of the flagstones: it reads:

> Arise from the earth like water
> give birth to your sacred dreams
> this world's an ocean of mirrors
> an invitation to create and be seen

In the illustration, given at Figure 7.2, the shadow of the head of the passing person-with-a-bag falls across the 'd' of the word 'dreams' in the second line.

The poetical pavement, says the website, 'draws on the city's beginnings and future as a spa': the poem has been hand-carved 'with hammer and chisel into the paving, adding individual words at the edges of the site'.[17] Some of the 'individual words' can be seen in the foreground of the illustration, and they seem indicative of how stone poems often use words in isolation, or merely in juxtaposition, rather than in linear combination. When words do occur in sentence form, an element of the surreal or the counter-realist is quite common, as in the 'ocean of mirrors' in Hallett's piece. The isolated words, rather as in Clarke's Tonypandy piece, gesture towards the foundational or the geological, with words like 'fossil', 'moon', 'stream', 'mountain' reminding us of the chance combinations of elements and natural forces which result in the particularity of this place. In due course, they make it a fashionable spa town with a distinctive character provided by its honey-coloured stone, which is oolitic limestone from Combe Down, made up of tiny

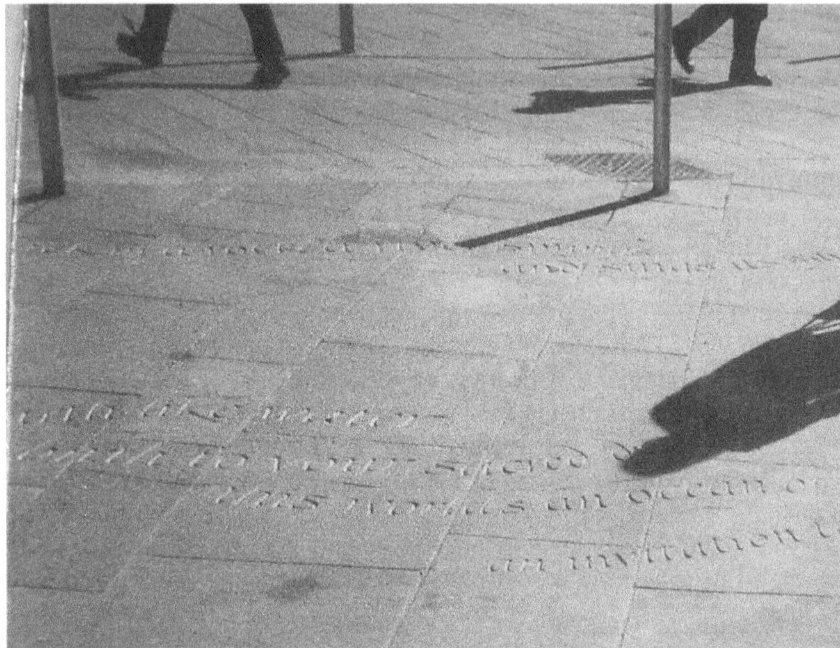

Figure 7.2　Poem by Alyson Hallett, carved by Alec Peever, Milsom Street, Bath

egg-like grains (hence 'oolitic'). The drift of the words across the gridiron of the paving seems to counterpoint rural and urban, nature and culture, encouraging a kind of *dérive* by the sacral dreamer across the main urban running-lines of passage and communication.

Street-based stone poetry has also been termed 'landmark poetry' and praised for its potentially 'infinite delivery', in the sense that once it is there, and 'set in stone' it might last nearly for ever (see Osborne 2011). Though this assumption of a degree of longevity might be justified in the case of a 'heritage' city like Bath, most city centres these days seem to be in a permanent state of 'rolling regeneration', so that landmark poems have proved vulnerable to subsequent urban development. Lemn Sissay, the official poet for the London 2012 Olympics who was elected Chancellor of Manchester University for seven years (2015–22), was first associated with the term 'landmark poem' in the late 1990s. The term 'landmark' implies something high up and visible from a distance, and the original pieces were a fairly conventional poem painted on the side of a prominent Manchester pub called Hardy's Well, and a poem called 'Rain', which looked at first sight like a giant crossword and was painted on the wall high above the Gemini Take Away in Oxford Road, Manchester. By contrast, Sissay's 'Flags' (2011) is a ground-level landmark poem which is also a stone poem, and is set into the flagstones of Tib Street in Central Manchester. This too is a collaborative work, involving an intricate meshing of individuals and organisations: the lettering was designed by local artist Tim Rushton, and is closely related to his 'Northern Quarter' street signage in Manchester, and the letters making up the words of the stone poem are each inlaid into individual tiles made at the Majolica Works in the city.[18] But the street has undergone much redevelopment, and in many places letters have become dislodged, and the spaces left have been crudely filled in with cement to keep the pavement even. As Dr Tony Shaw says on his excellent site, the result is that 'very occasionally comprehension is impossible'.[19] The scuffed and street-worn look – evidence of Macfarlane's 'foot-fall', 'wheel-roll' and 'rain-run' – is also reminiscent of the gradual erosion of the Brothers' Parting Stone, and again, sense and meaning seem to augment as the words of the poem begin to tarnish or vanish, the semantic field expanding, so to speak, as the lexical field diminishes. The fifteen 'verse panels' occur at intervals along nearly a mile of urban pavement, and the foot-fall obligingly parts around those who have stopped to read or photograph. Several verse panels have the hauntingly surreal or counter-realist tone already mentioned in connection with Hallett's Milsom Street piece. For instance, the third panel reads 'Like us they hold / the people of a / modern earth / this world / between the / windswept flags' – but the opening panel declares a polemical subtext or co-text: 'These pavement cracks / are the places where / poets pack their warrior words'. This and many other aspects of 'landmark' urban stone poems are explored in detail in chapter five of *Postcolonial Manchester* (Fowler 2013).

'And stones moved silently across the world'

The final example, which, being global in scope, is the largest-scale project of all those featured here, will be discussed in more detail, and is also by Alyson Hallett. Her website tells us that she studied at the University of East Anglia for her first degree (in comparative literature), then worked as Abbey housekeeper on the Isle of Iona in Scotland, and as a deputy project manager in Glasgow for the Richmond Fellowship (a major social-care services-provider). For two years she attended a writer's workshop run by poet, author and playwright Janet Paisley, in Pollokshields library (Glasgow), before returning to England to do an

MA in Creative Writing at Bath Spa University. The project is called 'Migrating Stones', and this is how Hallett describes its instigation on her website:[20]

> In 2001 I began to investigate the various ways in which stones move around the world. Inspired by a dream dreamed shortly after my grandmother's death; this project has evolved from an acorn of an idea conceived on the slopes of Cadair Idris [in the Snowdonia National Park, Wales] into an international public art adventure.

The italicisations in her account of the incident at Cadair Idris are mine:

> A few years ago *I* was driving through North Wales. *We* stopped for the night at the base of a mountain and pitched *our* tent in the far right-hand corner of a field where two rivers meet. Listening to the babble of water *we* watched a full moon rise between two distant hills. *I* slept well. As *we* were leaving the next morning *I* looked up at Cadair Idris and said, 'one day *I* will come back here and climb this mountain alone'.

The I/we alternation dramatises the conflicting demands of the grieving 'I' and the family unit. The great precision of the setting also seems significant – 'the far right-hand corner of a field where two rivers meet', and the 'moon ris[ing] between two distant hills' – and imparts a quasi-mystical urgency, so that the promise to return is made as if to the mountain itself, and by the singular 'I', rather than the plural 'we', as seems appropriate to the feeling of intimated-but-postponed revelation. The account continues:

> A year later, on a Wednesday afternoon in August, my maternal grandmother died. *Instinctively I knew* it was time to climb the mountain. *After a few moments of fear – I had never climbed a mountain before* and had no idea what it might involve – I hired a car, packed my bags, cancelled anything that needed cancelling and set off. [My italics again]

Here, the destined encounter with wilderness as the locale of revelation is rather like that in the medieval poem *Sir Gawain and the Green Knight*. Having encountered the Green Knight in the crowded festive hall at Christmas time, Gawain must go out into the wilderness a year later in search of the man of the man he beheaded (who immediately picked up his head and left the hall), and there receive the return blow. Like Gawain, but in hired car, rather than on horseback, Hallett sets out for the foothills:

> The foothills of Cadair Idris are beautiful beyond reckoning. Ancient oak trees, fast, gurgling stream, light flickering through a thick canopy of leaves. The further I climbed the more Wales spread out behind me, a vast array of hills, lakes every imaginable shade of green.

This is unremarkable, like the prose of an enthusiastic guidebook; then comes this:

> About half way up I came across a huge, quartz rock on the right hand side of the path. It seemed utterly out of place and I had no idea how it had come to be there. A couple of minutes later a man came alongside me. He happened to be a geologist and told me that the stone we were looking at was an erratic, a stone that had travelled across the land in a glacier, in essence, a migrating stone.

The geologist bears the visionary message promised by the mountain, which is what she came for. The way to climb a mountain is to keep going till you get to the top, but if you are a Zen Buddhist, when you get to the top of the mountain you must keep climbing, towards enlightenment. The closing in of the mist ensures this effect:

> I carried on to the top of the mountain and there, shrouded in thick cold mist and heralded by a flock of howling crows, I said farewell to my grandmother's spirit.

The narrative is powerful, and the thematising link is the erratic stone which, as the geologist is waiting to point out to her, has been carried by a glacier far from its motherbed (the technical term in geology for the erratic's point of origin). The message is that she must accept the separation from her beloved grandmother, and bid her spirit, not a pious 'goodbye' (God be with you') but a pagan 'farewell' (literally 'travel well', which is more like 'bon voyage').

When I first read about the project which resulted from the Cadair Idris experience, I thought it involved finding erratics and restoring them to their motherbeds, that is reversing their glacial migrations, and taking them home. That would have had an emotional logic, and seemed fitting, but perhaps a bit too nice and too logical. The actual project involves helping erratics to 'fare well', that is, taking them even further away from their motherbeds. They travel in a suitcase with Hallett on planes and trains, in what is essentially a combined form of land art and performance art:

> This adventure has so far involved the creation and siting of three [*sic*] stones in public places with the words 'And stones moved silently across the world' carved into them by Alec Peever. The **first** stone is in Bristol, U.K., the **second** (a 13kg piece of white limestone that I carried in my suitcase) is in a retreat centre, U.S.A., and the **third** (a 12kg piece of grey limestone which I also carried in my suitcase) is in a park at Kanahooka Point, Australia. The **4th** stone is sited on the Isle of Iona, Scotland.

Even if all the stones were not already erratics when selected, they are now. Figure 7.3 shows the fourth stone, setting out from Bristol Temple Meads Station on its journey to Iona. This stone is a 30 kg piece of limestone from a quarry near Bath. The caption tells us that 'The journey was a performance made in collaboration with Fiona Hamilton', confirming that the notion of 'performance art' is a relevant category. On its way to Iona this stone was in residence on the roof at the Laban Dance Centre (in Deptford, London) within an installation of stones from all over the world made by Hallett and international dance students (Hallett pers. com.). Plate 13 shows Stone 4's arrival on Iona, where it is 'now sited on a grassy bank next to the Iona Community's Welcome Centre' which is opposite the Abbey. Plate 14 is a close-up of the stone in position on its grassy bank. It is having a 'libation of water' from the Abbey Well poured over it as part of a small celebration and poetry reading (Hallett pers. com.).

Some inconclusive conclusions

The breadth of material discussed in this chapter is indicative of the potential scope of this topic, and I started by saying that the diversity of the field is one of its attractions. So the difficulties of generalising about it will be evident. But something has to be said to tie up the loose ends, even if only into knots. On reflection, seven themes seem to stand out: firstly, rocks and stones are the oldest objects on earth, formed in times of unimaginable remoteness by processes inconceivably slow. Whatever might be written on or about them will always be eclipsed by that fact, and that fact will be part of what they say. Hence, our own evanescence, as individuals and as a species, will always be contrastively brought to mind by any stone poem, and so all stone poems are necessarily (to use a superseded ecocritical term) 'dark green' rather than 'light green' in tendency. Another way of putting this is to say that with stone poems (to revive and adapt another old slogan) the medium is always a significant part of the message. Secondly, and paradoxically, all rocks and stones are in a state of flux and transition: they may look and feel like the Rock of Ages, but all of them bear the marks of weathering and impermanence, as they pass from state to state, animate to inanimate, liquid to solid, bending, moving, shifting, sifting, sinking, rising and so on. The ones on the seashore are rounded and egglike, others are jagged, ragged and dented – all have suffered and are suffering the forces of nature and are points in an ongoing narrative, and all this, too, is necessarily part of any narrative into which they are briefly

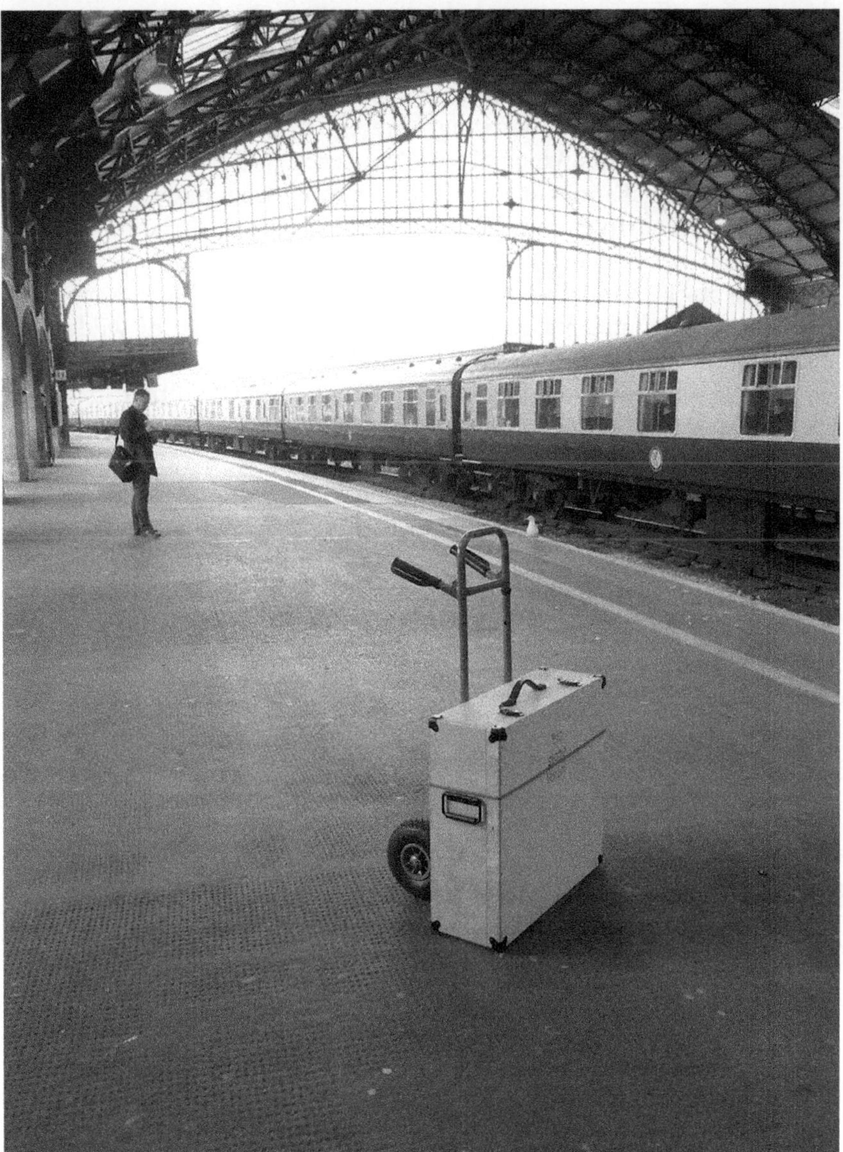

Figure 7.3 Alyson Hallett, 'Migrating Stone 4' setting out from Bristol Temple Meads Station

co-opted as stone poems. Thirdly and this probably follows from the first two, stone poems are often rather comfortless. Rocks and stones were presumably the first weapons used by humans, and overtones of violence and aggression are strongly present in some of those considered here. Hence, elements which are confrontational, difficult to contain or assimilate, or to channel in a positive way often seem part of what stone poems 'say'. Fourthly, and this is a kind of reversal of the third point, stone poems seem to embody something about creative *forces*, with the emphasis on the second word, for they work on and with an apparently recalcitrant medium, making what is a kind of essence of wilderness, wildness and beyondness into something which is assimilated into our human universe, as it might presumptively be called, so that its silence speaks, at least momentarily, with and within us. The fifth thematic point is that stone poems stimulate a kind of intimate and detailed scrutiny, evoking a passion for exactitude, and for the sustained patience of meticulous examination, as elaborated in note 1. This is a strong and long-running current of emphasis, extending at least from Ruskin to the present day. But (and this is number six), whereas that kind of intense scrutiny depends upon the presumption that the object can be isolated from all that is not the object, actually, in writing about stone poems, I have spent most of the space on what might be called 'blended stone poems' – those which are in structural partnerships with other 'sub-stances' – COR-TEN® steel, or paint on brick, or elements of perfor-mance, for instance. This is more a boast than a confession, and I cite in support of this non-purist approach Gaston Bachelard's *The New Scientific Spirit* (1985), as quoted in Hallett's *Geographical Intimacy*: 'There are no simple phenomena: every phenomenon is a fabric of rela-tions [...] a substance is a web of attributes' (2016: 17). The final point will at first seem to be the opposite to the fifth (the one about detailed scrutiny), bringing us back to the quotation from Marina Warner used at the head of this chapter. Warner, by implication, associates stone poems with precisely the opposite kind of thinking to intensity of scru-tiny, namely the kind that has an affinity with 'reverie and conjecture', and the 'shore of dreaming'. The Ruskinian intensive scrutiny is micro-specific, ultra-specialist and professional, whereas Warner's preference is for a 'laid-back', diffused thinking of a kind we might designate as goal-free, open-ended musing, like negative capability. It is like being Keats rather than Einstein, until we remember that the most world-changing scientific breakthrough moments have often been discoveries of something which the scientist was not at the time actually looking for. Perhaps it is by combining the mentalities of the 'shore of dream-ing', with the micro-specificity of professional attention and scrutiny that the most profound discoveries can be made. That seems to be the gist of the word among stones.

Acknowledgements

I am grateful for permission from Alyson Hallett, Howard Bowcott and William Welstead for their permission to use the images in this chapter and to Bill Herbert for his stimulating insights on the role of public art and its application in the North-East. I have also been much indebted, throughout this chapter, to my co-editor for many suggested parallels, connections, corrections and additional points.

Notes

1   Though differing in its underlying poetics, Ball's collection has affinities of tone and emphasis with Frances Presley's sequence 'Stone Settings', about the Neolithic upright-stone placements on Exmoor – see Presley's *Lines of Sight* (2009: 10–68). One such affinity is the emphasis on intensity of sustained attention – tactile, visual, intellectual ('noticing // careful // thinking // unhurried', Presley 2009: 12). This emphasis on closeness of attention seems pervasive in the world of stone poems, and in what is written about them, recalling a remark of Ruskin's: 'There are no natural objects out of which more can be learned than out of stones. They seem to have been created especially to reward a patient observer. Nearly all other objects in nature can be seen to some extent without patience, and are pleasant even in being half seen' (Ruskin 1906: 322). For an interesting 2006 interview with Presley, mainly about her 'Stone settings' sequence, see: http://intercapillaryspace.blogspot.co.uk/2006/10/interview-with-frances-presley.html accessed 12 September 2016.
2   For the term 'disjunctive', and an indication of its range of applicability to avant-garde poetries, see Quartermain (2009).
3   For these details see: www.isleoftiree.com/places/the-ringing-stone/ accessed 1 August 2016.
4   There are many translations of these lines: my approximation is adapted from that of the American writer Steven Pressfield (in his novel about the battle, *Gates of Fire*, 1998), which reads 'Go tell the Spartans, stranger passing by, / that here obedient to their laws we lie'.
5   To see the four-and-a-half-minute film about Little Sparta, go here: www.tate.org.uk/context-comment/video/tateshots-ian-hamilton-finlays-little-sparta accessed 12 September 2016.
6   To see the stone, visit the website, here: www.littlesparta.org.uk/ accessed 12 September 2016.
7   See the Ted Hughes Poetry Trail's website at: https://new.devon.gov.uk/stovercountrypark/ted-hughes-poetry-trail accessed 12 September 2016.

8   For 'migrating stones', see the Alyson Hallett material later in this chapter.
     The Templer Way Guidebook can be viewed at: www.devon.gov.uk/
     templer-way-guide.pdf accessed 1 August 2016. This trail, along old
     railway lines, follows the course of the River Torridge, with its *Tarka the
     Otter* associations, for part of the way (www.devon.gov.uk/tarkatrail).
     Hughes's poem '1984 on the "Tarka Trail"' refers to this (for the poem,
     see Astley (ed.) 2007: 65). In this poem Hughes was not much concerned
     with Henry Williamson's 1927 novel *Tarka the Otter*, depicting an otter's
     life in the beautiful North Devon countryside, but with the woefully-
     polluted state of the river in the 1980s. The poem mercilessly describes
     what was happening in a powerful and rightly celebrated example of the
     polemical eco-poem, showing in close-up the most horrible effects of
     uncontrolled water pollution and saying exactly who was to blame. The
     'in-your-face' poetics of extreme physical detail are similar to (for instance)
     Wilfred Owen's First World War poem 'Dulce et Decorum Est'.
9   Quotations from the Stanza Stones trail guide at: www.ilkleylitera
     turefestival.org.uk/wp-content/uploads/2012/05/Stanza-Stones-Trail-
     Guide.pdf accessed 12 September 2016.
10   *Yorkshire Post*, 10 September 2012, at: www.yorkshirepost.co.uk/news/a-
     woman-of-letters-1–4908478 accessed 12 September 2016.
11   However, AONB-status gives a measure of valuable environmental protec-
     tion to areas so designated, but unlike National Parks, AONBs do not
     have planning powers, and the designation could not prevent the building
     of Falmer Stadium (home of Brighton and Hove Albion FC) within the
     former Sussex Downs AONB (now a National Park) in 2011.
12   Marion Shoard in 2002 defined 'edgelands' as the 'apparently unplanned,
     certainly uncelebrated and largely incomprehensible territory where town
     and country meet' (Shoard 2002). The term gained currency in the UK
     with the publication of Paul Farley and Michael Symmons Roberts's *Edge-
     lands: Journeys into England's True Wilderness*, Vintage, 2012. Such
     terrain has long been a major concern of the writings of Iain Sinclair,
     notably his *London Orbital* (Penguin, 2003), describing a year's walk
     around the terrain adjoining the M25 motorway. The equivalent American
     term is Alan Berger's 'drossscape' (Berger 2007). (This note draws on the
     website for Bath Spa University's MA in Literature, Landscape and
     Environment.)
13   See the entry on the Tonypandy monument in the website of the PMSA
     (the Public Monuments & Sculpture Association) at: www.pmsa.org.uk/
     pmsa-database/11516/ accessed 12 September 2016.
14   For discussion of specular form or mirror form see http://bensonofjohn.co.uk/
     poetry/formssearch.php?searchbox=specular accessed 12 September 2016.
15   See www.ncl.ac.uk/elll/staff/profile/bill.herbert accessed 12 September
     2016.
16   For the Quakers in Darlington visit www.darlingtonquakers.org/
     darlington-s-quaker-heritage/ accessed 12 September 2016.

17 For Alyson Hallett's biography and work see her website www. thestonelibrary.com accessed 12 September 2016.

18 For a photograph from Rushdon's website showing how the tiles are formed into words within each verse frame, and then set into the pavement, see: http://cypheronline.org/publicart1–3.html accessed 12 September 2016.

19 Dr Tony Shaw's blog can be found at: http://tonyshaw3.blogspot.co.uk/2011/07/lemn-sissays-flags-tib-street.html accessed 12 September 2016.

20 www.thestonelibrary.com/ accessed 12 September 2016.

References

Astley, Neil (ed.) (2007) *Earth Shattering: Ecopoems*. Hexam: Bloodaxe.

Ball, Patricia M. (2000) *The Word Among Stones*, ed. Tony Davenport and Barbara Hardy, Royal Holloway, University of London.

Bann, Stephen (2014) *Beauty and Revolution: The Poetry and Art of Ian Hamilton Finlay*. Cambridge: Kettle's Yard [exhibition catalogue].

Berger, Alan (2007) *Drosscape: Wasting Land in Urban America*. Princeton: Princeton University Press.

Capel, Dick (ed.) (n.d.) *Poetry Path: A Year in the Life of a Hill Farmer*: Twelve poems by Meg Peacocke, lettered on stone by Pip Hall, arranged on a path in Stenkrith Park, Kirkby Stephen. Carlisle: East Cumbria Countryside Project.

Darlington Borough Council (2013) West Park: management and maintenance plan available on www.westparkdarlington.org.uk/downloads/greenflag-application-2013.pdf accessed 12 September 2016.

Fagg, M. Catherine (1997) *Rock Music*. Occasional Papers on Technology, No. 14, Pitt Rivers Museum, University of Oxford.

Farley, Paul and Michael Symmons Roberts (2012) *Edgelands: Journeys into England's True Wilderness*. London: Vintage.

Fowler, Corinne (2013) 'Rebels without Applause: Manchester's Poetry in Performance (1960s to the Present)', in Lynne Pearce, Corinne Fowler and Robert Crawshaw, *Postcolonial Manchester: Diaspora Space and the Devolution of Literary Culture*. Manchester: Manchester University Press, pp. 206–67.

Hallett, Alyson (2016) *Geographical Intimacy: Exploring the Relationship between Poet, Poetry and Place*. CreateSpace Independent Publishing Platform www.createspace.com.

Macfarlane, Robert, Stanley Donwood and Dan Richards (2013) *Holloway*. London: Faber & Faber.

MacLeish, Archibald (1990) *Collected Poems 1917–1982*. Boston, MA: Houghton Mifflin.

Osborne, Deirdre (2011) '"Set in Stone": Lemn Sissay's and SuAndi's Landmark Poetics', in C. Grabner and A. Casas (eds), *Performing Poetry: Body, Place and Rhythm in the Poetry Performance*. Amsterdam: Rodopi.

Pagan, Victoria Emma, Judith W. Page and Brigitte Weltman-Aron (eds) (2015) *Disciples of Flora: Gardens in History and Culture*. Newcastle-upon-Tyne: Cambridge Scholars Publishing.

Pollen, John Hungerford (2010 [1872]) *A Description of the Trajan Column*. Charleston, SC: Bibliobazaar.

Presley, Frances (2009) *Lines of Sight*. Bristol: Shearsman Books.

Pressfield, Steven (1998) *Gates of Fire*. New York: Doubleday.

Quartermain, Peter (2009) *Disjunctive Poetics: From Gertrude Stein and Louis Zukofsky to Susan Howe*. Cambridge: Cambridge University Press.

Royal Commission on Ancient and Historical Monuments in Scotland (1980) *Argyll: An Inventory of the Monuments Volume 3: Mull, Tiree, Coll and Northern Argyll (Excluding the Early Medieval and Later Monuments of Iona)*. Edinburgh: RCAHMS.

Ruskin, John (1906) *Modern Painters, Volume IV: Of Mountain Beauty*. London: George Allen, p. 322.

Shoard, Marion (2002) 'Edgelands', in Jennifer Jenkins (ed.), *Remaking the Landscape*. London: Profile Books.

Swaab, Peter (2014) 'Wordsworth's Elegies for John Wordsworth', *Wordsworth Circle* 45:1 (Winter). See www.questia.com/library/journal/1G1–366346800/ wordsworth-s-elegies-for-john-wordsworth accessed 12 September 2016.

Warner, Marina (2015) 'Diary', *London Review of Books*, 3 December: 46–7.

Wordsworth, Dorothy and William (1978 [1800–3]) *Home at Grasmere: Extracts from the Journal of Dorothy Wordsworth and from the Poems of William Wordsworth*, ed. Colette Clark. London: Penguin.

8

Two familiar paths well-travelled

John Darwell

As we step off the pavement and begin in earnest, a narrow path defines itself. The road disappears and we find ourselves in the bush. There is just enough bramble and dirt to ruin our shoes, enough debris strewn about to make the scene feel a little worn around the edges. Not all of these photographs are easy to understand or even necessarily likeable. Some of them seem to have been placed just to make sure we are paying attention – like a rock or a branch that catches our stride when our attention momentarily lags and we take our eyes off the path to look about. Frame and focus shift suddenly, and we need a moment to figure out what we are looking at, and why. (T. Jurovics 2010. From the introduction to *The Pond* by John Gossage)

For the past thirty years or so I have pursued photographic projects that reflect my interest in the postindustrial landscape of Britain, social history, mental health and its depiction and issues relating to humankind's impact on the environment. Projects have included explorations of the then largely disused Manchester Ship Canal, the postindustrial landscape of Sheffield's steel industry, of extractive industries in Cumbria and the Port of Liverpool. I then undertook three major bodies of work exploring global nuclear history, including visits to Hiroshima and Nagasaki, to the Chernobyl exclusion zone and to nuclear sites in Cumbria.[1]

My methodology throughout this period remained essentially unchanged. I would travel, by whatever means required, to a given location, and I would then walk, explore and evaluate what it meant to me, looking for objects or scenarios that resonated with me in terms of my reasons for being there, using the process of image production as a means of working out my feelings relating to the location. In many ways this methodology continues, but with one important change. In my early projects I would visit said locations and if feasible my dog(s) would travel with me as companions and occasionally as bodyguards. But the point being, the location came first and the dog was there as a secondary element whereas later projects were fuelled by the process of dog walking and then using that process to formulate projects.

Following on from these projects, and after an extended period of illness, I began PhD research into the visualisation of depression in *A Black Dog Came Calling* (Darwell 2008). This work had a profound effect on my practice and helped convince me as to the validity of concentrating my future work on subjects I knew, and wished to further understand in terms of their relevance to my life, and when giving talks about my work I will often describe the process as 'using photography as a means of helping me understand why I was drawn to the subject in the first place'.

My first project, following this ethos, involved an exploration of my adopted county of Cumbria for which I followed the eighty-mile coastline ('Not Starting From Here', 2005–7), photographing elements of the land and sea and the chance encounters along the way. Because of the vast scale of the Cumbrian coastline I set myself the restriction that I would produce only a photograph if I could see the sea, not necessarily in the viewfinder but within my field of vision. This project convinced me that the personal (familiar) was, for me, a more satisfactory and relevant way of working and established the template for the majority of projects that were to follow.

Within my work I am a firm believer in the power of photography to reveal far more than is present in the image and often use the mantra with my students that 'photographs should be *about* something, not just *of* something'. An example of this could be a tree: a photograph *of* a tree becomes simply about that tree with, perhaps, a wider discussion about species, location etc.; but a photograph *about* a tree takes on far greater sense of resonance, depending of course on its context. But it then becomes about strength, rootedness, longevity or any number of alternatives that a tree can symbolise. Once this is understood it frees the practitioner in so many ways in terms of the use of allegory and metaphor, and in an age where the actual production of images gets technically easier every year it is important to fully understand the meaning behind the image if one is to produce meaningful work that reaches a wider audience.

In the following section I will discuss in detail two projects that were a direct result of my developing a sense of familiarity with the subject before ever undertaking any image production, wherein the subsequent process of photographic investigation comes about as a direct result of the previous experiences associated with these particular locations or scenarios. Within this I will discuss my thought processes when undertaking the work and the key factors that initiated the projects. I will then further describe how the work fits firmly within the sense of being 'about' something and how issues raised within the work have a resonance to wider issues appertaining to environmental concerns.

1000 Yards; Or So

Over a ten-year period, twice daily (with occasional change of plan, holiday etc.) I underwent a routine that involved donning Wellington boots and waterproof jacket, and then proceeding down the lane behind my house, through the council estate (occasionally stopping to chat with a familiar face) then across the grass by the children's playground down the hill into the field by the River Petterill, a small river, averaging two to three metres wide and half a metre deep, that travels through northern Cumbria before joining the River Eden at Carlisle. For most of its length it runs through arable or pasture land but in the specific section with which I am concerned it travels, largely unnoticed, through the industrial edgelands of Carlisle where it is bordered by the M6 motorway, the main West coast railway, major housing estates, industrial units and occasional patches of parkland.

Once there my path would follow a circular route of a mile or so, without having to retrace my steps, along the river bank, upstream to the bridge then downstream back to the road (not always easy as the area was often overgrown with tree shoots or brambles) taking in the sights on display; from herons battling with eels (the heron usually pecking out the eel's eyes then leaving it as a squirming ball of slime and flesh to expire on the bank) to kingfishers darting past in a flash of blue (or if I was lucky perching on a fishing branch over the river).

Sometimes I would come upon macabre sights such as the neat pile of six yellow duckling heads left behind by a mink (later seen basking on a log by the river) or on one occasion three decapitated trout heads impaled on a barbed wire fence,[2] presumably by some fisherman or more likely the local kids who were often to be seen fishing in the more accessible stretches of the river.[3]

Other encounters included the crying woman in the middle of the field late one very wet winter's night wearing a thin white blouse, white skirt and sandals, staring into the far distance, who despite my enquiries as to her wellbeing failed to respond. This was a very unnerving moment but when I returned to check if she was still there she had disappeared, presumably to face whatever was troubling her. The situation was reported to the police but I heard no more about it. Unnerving encounters tended to be a regular occurrence and were, perhaps, linked to the river's location adjacent to a very large and notorious housing estate.

On another occasion I arrived on the river bank one January evening to find the normal blackness lit up with numerous massive spotlights, ambulance men and a large number of uniformed police. Apparently a body had been discovered on the bank that turned out to have been the result of a fatal overdose by one of the many drug users who regularly visited the river at night.

Other unsettling encounters included a large black car pulling up by the bridge over the river, where a large gentleman got out and started to unload stuffed black bin liners from the boot of the car before commencing to throw them into the river. Upon my raising concerns about this behaviour a thin grey-haired elderly man appeared from the back of the car and in a gentle almost obsequious tone asked what business it was of mine. Putting on my most official air I stated I was a solicitor for the environment agency, at which he turned and berated the larger man for his actions, they then both got back in the car and drove away, leaving me feeling quite shaken and wondering what had possessed me in terms of confronting these individuals and the possible consequences. My final recollection is of the burnt-out cars (both stolen and abandoned) that mysteriously appeared with great regularity in the field, their bodies turned to rust from the flames, a chemical reaction I always find most intriguing, whilst the interiors were reduced to grey floating ash. This daily walk, for which the catalyst was my dog Barney, a border collie of no little enthusiasm and energy when it came to walks, involved many such incidents as those described above. I calculate I walked the river's banks over ten thousand times without losing the sense of fascination such encounters held.

Looking back, and with the benefit of hindsight, I find it a little puzzling that, though I was working on numerous photography projects during this period, it was many years after I began these walks that I felt any need to actually take a camera with me on my (our) walks. I think part of the reason for this lies in the very vivid memories I have of the location: I knew it so well and in such detail I didn't feel the need to actually photograph the experience. Perhaps in some way I was conscious that the act of photographing would inevitably change my relationship with the area, and of course this is what happened. Or perhaps I had not fully recognised the area as a potential project and had therefore overlooked it for many years, its familiarity disguising the story waiting to be told.

In their book *Edgelands*, Paul Farley and Michael Symmons Roberts describe the nature of such locations:

> So much might depend on being able to *see* the edgelands. Giving them a name might help, because up until now they have been without any signifier, an incomprehensible swathe we pass through without regarding; untranslated landscape. And edgelands, by and large, are not meant to be seen, except perhaps as a blur from a car window, or as a backdrop to our most routine and mundane activities. (2012: 5. Authors' emphasis)

This description perfectly reflects the sensibility of my chosen area of exploration, a landscape of the ordinary, neither beautiful in the Kantian sense of beauty, nor sublime, just there, overlooked and peripheral (Kant 2004 [1764]). Farley and Symmons Roberts continue in their description:

> Edgelands are part of the gravitational field of all our larger urban areas, a texture we build up speed to escape as we hurry towards the country-side, the distant wilderness. The trouble is, if we can't see the edgelands, we can't imagine them, or allow them any kind of imaginative life. And so they don't really exist. The smaller identities of things in the edgelands have remained largely invisible to most of us. (2012: 5)

Much of what I had experienced on my walks was a result of serendipity, and my photographic methodology, at the time, of a large-format, heavy, film camera meant my responses had to be more measured, in terms of capturing any sense of the area, than purely allowing for the chance moments as described previously. What I aimed to visualise was the sense of the chaos of modern life where the natural and the anthropogenic clash and interact on a number of levels.

Though I adopted a more free-ranging approach and deliberately eschewed my normal tripod-based process, this brought its own challenges and revelations as, due to the usually low light levels, I often worked with a minimum depth-of-field and this led to a new kind of visualisation within my work (one I had experimented with at various points throughout my career) wherein objects were isolated against a diffused background, or foreground. An example of such images is shown at Plate 15.

Once this methodology was developed I could work on a more intuitive and free-roaming level, to explore the minutiae of detail along the river; this often involved me physically immersing myself, often to the limits of my Wellington boots, in the river as this was often the only way to get close enough to the objects I wished to photograph. My aim for the work was not to create images of a forgotten (overlooked) landscape or ecosystem per se, but was more about the experiential sensibility of being in this environment, a landscape that was very familiar, but also quite alien. For me it was not so much about getting lost in the vastness of some unknown landscape as about finding myself within the familiar – described by Bachelard (1969) as 'topophilia', a desire for the comfort of familiar spaces. Such familiar places are often edgelands.

> This is the paradox of edgelands. Feral as they are, a no-man's-land between the watched and documented territories of urban and rural, the edgelands are a passing place, backdrop for countless commuters, shoppers, rail travellers. Seen, but unseen. Looked at but not into. (Farley and Symmons Roberts 2012: 73)

I particularly like the use of the word 'feral' in the above quotation as this perfectly describes the sense of this space hovering somewhere on the edge of domesticity but remaining wild at heart, but also very vulnerable to what we do to it.

It was during this period of exploration that I became far more aware of the delicate state of the river and its misuse by both industry and the people who walked its banks. I had previously, as described with the black bag men, been aware of the litter and detritus problems afflicting the river and its banks, but somehow I hadn't taken on board fully the pressure the river was under from a variety of sources. As I explored I was drawn to a new understanding of the sheer amount of junk that found its way into the river. Not just paper and plastic blown in from the banks but also old motorcycles, children's toys, Dyson vacuums, furniture of every type, cars, either whole or parts, but also, in summer, disposable barbecues, food wrappers and beer bottles. The irony of the location being its easy accessibility,both from the housing estate and the numerous roads that ran alongside, make it an area that was regularly visited on sunny days when people would take advantage of the adjoining fields but saw little or no value in the overgrown river at the edges of their picnic sites.

Much of this junk subsequently had a tendency to end up in the river ('out of sight out of mind') and created bottlenecks when it reached overload levels and I often saw areas where the overhanging bushes trailing in the river would act as nets catching floating detritus, especially plastic bottles, creating a build-up of effluvia that began with larger objects, but, as the build-up continued, creating a situation where smaller particles filled in the gaps, thereby reducing flow and creating an ongoing cycle of build-up that would clear only during periods of increased water flow or flooding, the detritus then finding its way, eventually, to the sea, or, in this particular case, the Solway Firth.

In many respects a landscape, swamped by discarded junk, becomes something else, a different kind of place, maybe as wild and uncontrolled as nature but one defined by human detritus. Yet within this the river banks gave me a sense of exploration, of secret places that were reminiscent of the sense of adventure and dens I built as a child, and the sense of exploring secret places chimed with me on a subconscious level reminding me of those early experiences, for it is 'the tiny things we imagine simply take us back to childhood' (Bachelard 1969: 149). I also concentrated on the areas where litter, combined with the river's natural flora, pointed directly to this abuse of our natural, but undervalued, environment, the images acting as metaphors for a wider global perspective of ecological misuse and indifference.

So far I have elaborated mainly on being faced with the immediately and most obviously visible levels of detritus; what I haven't yet discussed is the more pernicious problem of industrial run-off, either from farmland, the local factories (often disused) or the proximity of the main West Coast rail line, all of which leave their detrimental traces within the river; either through storm drains that can allow highly contaminated waste and rain water (not to mention run-off from outdated industrial effluent) to enter the river system. Most of this passes by unseen, to the casual observer, owing to its lack of tangibility, for while the sight of detritus is instantly obvious, the effluvia of industry often remains largely unnoticed, its presence becoming obvious only once the effects become visible (and all the more devastating) in terms of discoloration of the watercourse, smell, or the presence of dead fish and the disappearance of invertebrates and weed that are often replaced by an explosion of algae.

In terms of my image making by combining close-up images of the detritus with mid-range images of the surrounding flora, I was inviting the viewer to follow two perspectives; one, as an explorer seeking a way through the undergrowth and, the other, having managed to navigate through, to then be faced with the sheer amount of ever accumulating rubbish present in the river. The process of photographing the area in detail allowed me to present the multifaceted nature of its structure, wherein a future audience could be guided through the work taking on board the complexity not only of the work but also, and more importantly, of the location itself. Displaying the work as a sequential journey, both physically and visually, allowed me to bring the differing elements of the environment into sharp focus, to bring into the spotlight the overlooked, or hidden, and in doing so to illuminate the many complexities that make up this ostensibly insignificant location.

Throughout this work the focus on details and the sense of journey allow the audience to be immersed in the landscape and so experience an intimate relationship with it rather than considering environmental political issues in a distanced manner. We all know places like these, and many of us spent our childhoods exploring areas not dissimilar to the one depicted in this work. The personal, experiential tone of the work brings home the fundamental point of our environment, as we live in it, not as a distanced landscape nothing to do with us personally but as something that belongs to us all and which we have a responsibility to protect.

During the production of this work I produced one image (Plate 16) that would take on particular significance, as this was the first time I came upon the phenomenon of the discarded dog shit bag (DDSB) that would later become the subject of a major (and apparently never ending) body of work. In the next section I will discuss the evolution of this particular body of work in detail.

DDSBs

As described previously, my first experience of the DDSB came whilst producing the 1000 Yards project. At that time I found the idea of bagging dog mess and then disposing of it by chucking it away into the nearest bush, tree or stream, to be quite puzzling, but I was then unaware of the significance of that first encounter. In the intervening period I began to notice their presence whenever out walking in public places such as parks, public footpaths or basically anywhere people walked their dogs, essentially the same reason I was frequenting these locations.

In many ways this was, for me, a gift of a project in that it was both available and readily accessible and yet maintained my wish to discuss issues appertaining to the environment. Also, I had consciously moved away from photographing the other, the unfamiliar, after returning from working in the Chernobyl exclusion zone. Following an article in the *Guardian* (Dauost 2001: 10–11) about my experiences within the zone, I began to develop severe misgivings about being able to drop in to such locations and then return to my 'normal' existence whilst those I had worked alongside remained in the location with no ability to escape. This had a significant effect on my future work and, after questioning the rationale of dropping in and out of such evocative locations, I felt for my own sense of integrity that I should concentrate my future efforts on subjects that were more to do with my own life or experience, and the DDSBs fitted perfectly within this.

My existence at this time involved living in rural Cumbria, teaching, and spending a good deal of my remaining time walking my dogs (my previous companion Barney, had by now passed away and I had new fellow walkers in the form of Bracken and Skye, two very smart Border Collie brothers), so it was natural to use these occasions to develop a new body of work within an environment that was both familiar and relevant. In essence an intimate perspective of this location that could be understood, by the audience, as a wider discourse on the nature of environmental degradation.

My first concern was how best to photograph these bags when I came upon them. The logical answer was carry a camera with me whenever out with the dogs. My methodology became simply a small camera bag containing a twin-lens camera, one lens, a pile of film and a small flashgun. This set-up allowed me to carry the kit without it being too demanding or impinging on my ability to walk considerable distances.

Where my original image (Plate 16) had placed the bag as a small object within the topography of the area, my new images were meant to place the discarded bag as the main or central element within the frame. The work became a typology of DDSBs where the objects were subsequently displayed in a grid (usually 8 x 8 in images) to allow the similarities of structure and form to be emphasised.[4] In many ways the works' presentation followed the classic typology structure as pioneered by the German photographers and educators Bernd and Hilla Becher, who coined the word 'Typologies' to describe their images based on the universality of objects, and how form follows function. They created photographs of artificial structures such as blast furnaces, water towers and industrial architecture, often a world apart yet maintaining a very similar appearance. Their work is often depicted in a series of photographic grids to emphasise these similarities (Becher 2000).

Very soon in the production of this work I began to realise the bags fell into various categories and largely consisted of two major supermarket brands of nappy bags (pink or yellow) or small black bags purchased specifically for the purpose. The bags began to take on characters to me and this was reflected in the titles I ascribed to the image files: 'Bunny-eared bag', 'Christmas-pudding bag', 'Black bag hanging', etc. See Plate 17 for an example of these images. This system made life easier in terms of my filing system, as, though the images were all produced on colour negative film, this was then scanned to produce digital files that then required naming, and allowed me to gain a greater sense of the patterns and similarities of structure I was encountering, as one common factor tended to be the distinctive knot each bag had, basically a reef knot with two extended ends to keep the offending contents out of sight.[5]

The idea of the DDSB raised a number of questions for me (not all of which I have resolved), not least the question, why? I can understand dog walkers picking up their dogs' mess as new law[6] took effect, but, once the nasty bit, the actual bagging, is done, why then choose to hang the offending object on any convenient fence or tree branch, throw it in the nearest bush, or throw it in the nearest river?[7] These were questions that were raised constantly throughout this project, often in conversation with curious passers-by who questioned what I was doing on my hands and knees pointing a strange-looking camera at dog poo. In many ways it became apparent that a great many people felt that in bagging the mess their responsibility for it ended and it then became someone else's (council, government?) job to dispose of the article.

So the nature of these discarded bags points to a number of contradictions that go with dog ownership. We love our pets and as such are prepared to undertake any number of fairly unpleasant acts in their service in a manner we would never consider otherwise. Cat owners engage in similar experiences in the emptying of litter trays or removal of eviscerated small mammals or birds from the living room carpets.

Clearly, this procedure brings with it various levels of revulsion (nausea) that makes for a fairly unpleasant experience. To then have to carry the bag of nastiness with you, essentially adding a negative sensibility to what is meant to be a fun experience, can make its rapid disposal a priority. The scenario then arises that there is, often, nowhere to responsibly dispose of the bag, because of either the out-of-the-way location or just a general lack of suitable bins. In my local park it was not unusual for said bins, made from plastic, to be set alight by the local kids, or for them to be overflowing with bags and remaining unemptied for weeks at a time, so it is often difficult to apportion blame purely within the more antisocial elements within the dog-walking public.

There are of course potentially serious health situations involved in leaving unbagged dog mess where it can contaminate parklands and other public areas, and each year there are a number of cases where children have become blinded as a result of coming into contact with contaminated dog mess caused by Toxocariasis, passed on by small threadworms from the larvae of dogs infected with *Toxocara canis*. Though these contaminations are relatively rare, if your child is the one infected you will undoubtedly wish for legislation to be put in place to prevent such scenarios from recurring, and here lies the problem, for such legislation, with the best of intentions, rather than solving the problem, creates other problems in its wake – partly because of lack of provision for disposal but also due to human nature, wherein such legislations are open to various levels of abuse, ignorance or just indifference and, are by their very nature extremely difficult to enforce, even with the threat of invoking anti-terror legislation and covert surveillance.

On a number of occasions I have spoken to dog wardens, usually when their curiosity has got the better of them as to what I was doing, as to the nature of DDSBs. The discussions usually following a pattern starting with the initial 'Do you mind explaining what you're doing Sir' question, then my describing my puzzlement as to why people chose to discard the bags the way they did and the general unpleasantness involved, as outlined previously. The wardens (or fellow dog walkers or curious passers-by) would then move through a process of initial suspicion followed by a general sense of bemusement as to what I was doing and how this could seriously end up displayed in a gallery or book.[8]

The discussion would then move to the fact that the majority of bags I came upon were of the standard plastic, non-biodegradable, type and I would highlight the evidence that once bagged, and thrown away, there was no chance of the contents biodegrading naturally, resulting in the bags remaining where they are for some considerable time (I photographed one bag in the same tree twice with a twelve-month interval between, yet looking at the images it is difficult to say which came first) with its ongoing dangers for farm livestock or adding to pollution levels of plastic in general. The discussion would then move to the use of maize-based biodegradable bags (handed out by the wardens) and how this solved the problem of bag longevity. In my book *DDSBs* (2013) I describe this scenario as follows:

> Biodegradable bags add another layer of complexity – what happens when the abandoned bag degrades whilst its contents were prevented from doing so? The poop falls back to the ground where it was deposited in the first place! It's a bit like time travel: the more you think about it the more complicated it gets (Darwell 2013: 2)

This could be interpreted as a tongue-in-cheek remark but in reality it raises a serious issue in terms of attempting to deal with a serious problem, for an additional, equally serious, if not worse, problem has been created and reflects on the frequent ineffectiveness of environmental legislation and the bigger picture.

In many ways this project seems to have taken on a life of its own, and I receive numerous emails on a monthly basis, with people describing their DDSB experiences or specific locations to visit that have become associated with them; and I wonder how I can further develop the project as I feel it still has a lot to say. On a recent visit to a local beauty spot I counted thirty-six DDSBs in the first fifty yards of entering the woodland, which I duly photographed. This led to a discussion about the possibility of developing the work as an online mapping project, visualising the distribution and density of DDSBs on both a national and a global basis, involving apps and GPS where the increasing use of such technologies within smart phones and the increases in quality of their built-in cameras would allow for people to post their own images from anywhere on the planet.[9] The technology involved in combating the dog-fouling problem continues as councils investigate various counter-measures including the building of DNA data bases.

As a global phenomenon I have seen DDSBs appear in the most unexpected places, from Lake District hillsides to German parklands to the beaches of Western Australia, and am now working on an ongoing project of 'International DDSBs' with the various countries tending to have their own distinctive DDSB, usually marked by differing colours: in Australia bright yellow, in Germany generally bright red. I have also been approached recently by a picture editor in the USA who was convinced my photographs were produced in his local park as he 'recognised' some of the bags and settings, which points very clearly to the universality of the DDSB.

In a recent interview for Australian magazine *Four and Sons: Where Dogs and Culture Collide*, issue 2 (2014), which featured a twelve-image grid of my DDSB images with one page of text as a Q & A under the title 'Shit Happens', I was asked a number of questions of which two in particular are relevant within the context of this chapter:

Q. What were you trying to achieve with this series?

A. In essence, the discarded bags are metaphors for many things: unenforceable laws, disregard for the environment, and the sense that it's not really my problem. So if the series can make people think twice about their actions, that's great.

Q. What do you find interesting about documenting human behaviour?

A. People are endlessly fascinating … I try to drum into my students that photographs shouldn't simply be *of* something, but rather, *about* something. Are the dog poo bags simply images of dog poo bags? I hope not. (120–1)

A major element of my practice has involved depicting the results of humankind's effects on the planet and, perhaps paradoxically, in many ways I feel the DDSB work encapsulates all this, in what could be regarded as a fairly mundane subject, yet one that addresses a huge

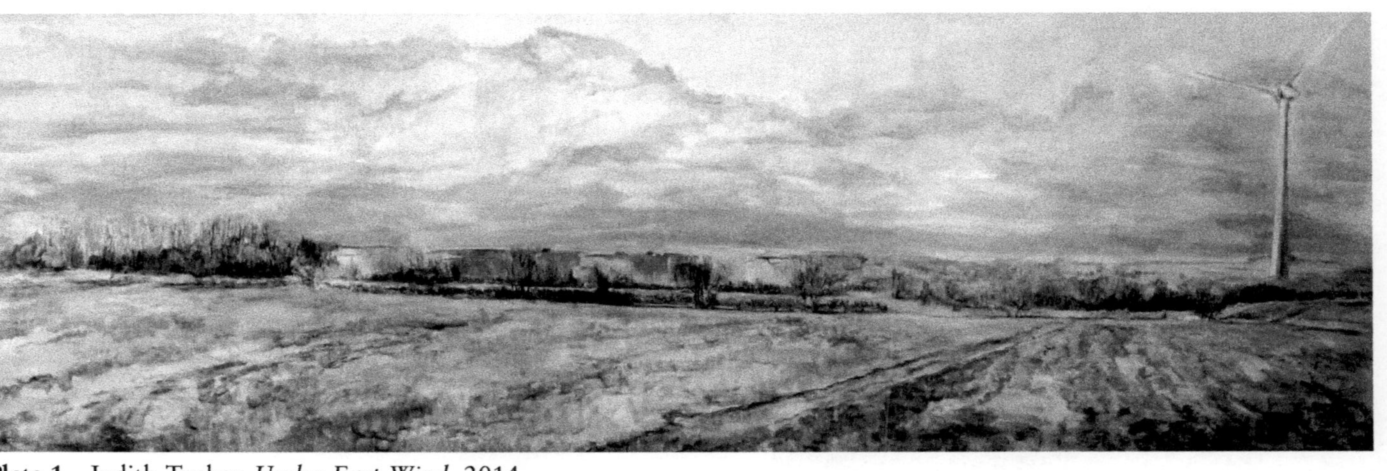

Plate 1 Judith Tucker, *Under East Wind*, 2014

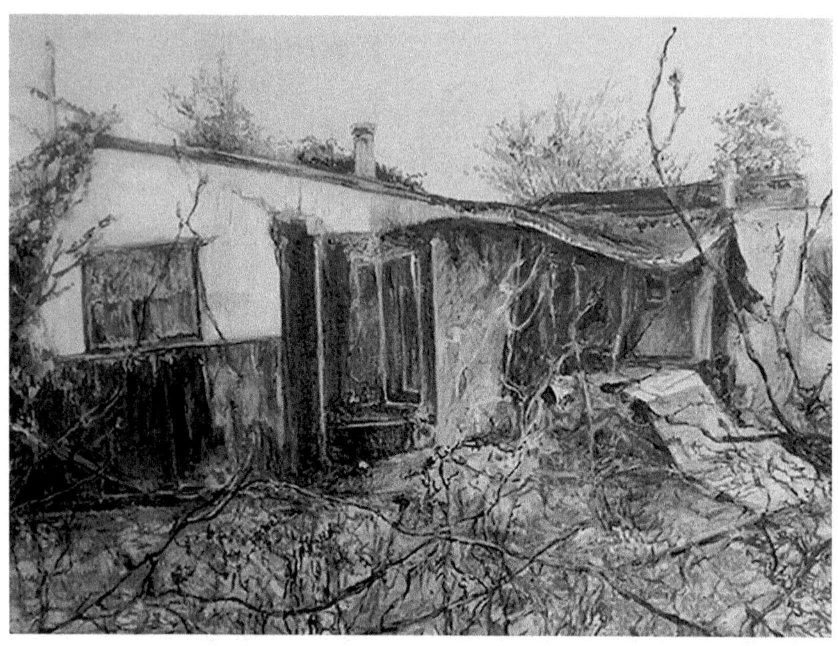

Plate 2 Judith Tucker (painting) and Harriet Tarlo (open-form poem), *Once Was Holiday,* 2015

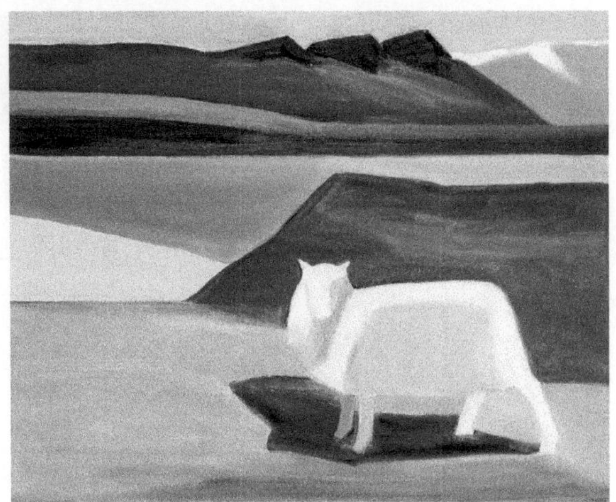

Plate 3   Louisa Matthíasdóttir, *Gul*, 1990

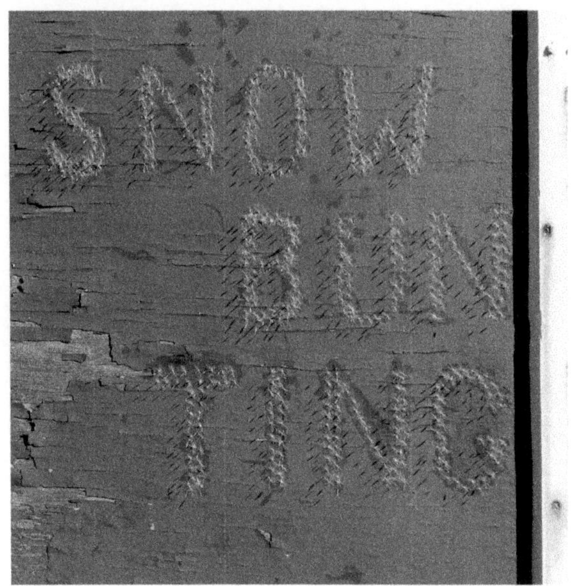

Plate 4   Julie Livsey, *Snow Bunting*, 2015. Installation view on shed wall, Flatey Island, Iceland

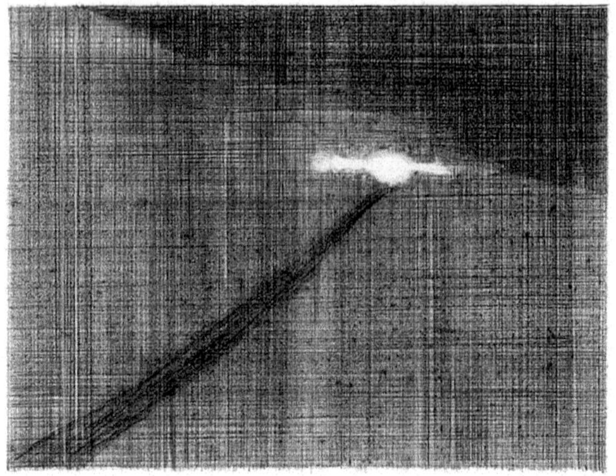

Plate 5 Lesley Hicks, *Olafsfjardarvegur-nordur*, 2015

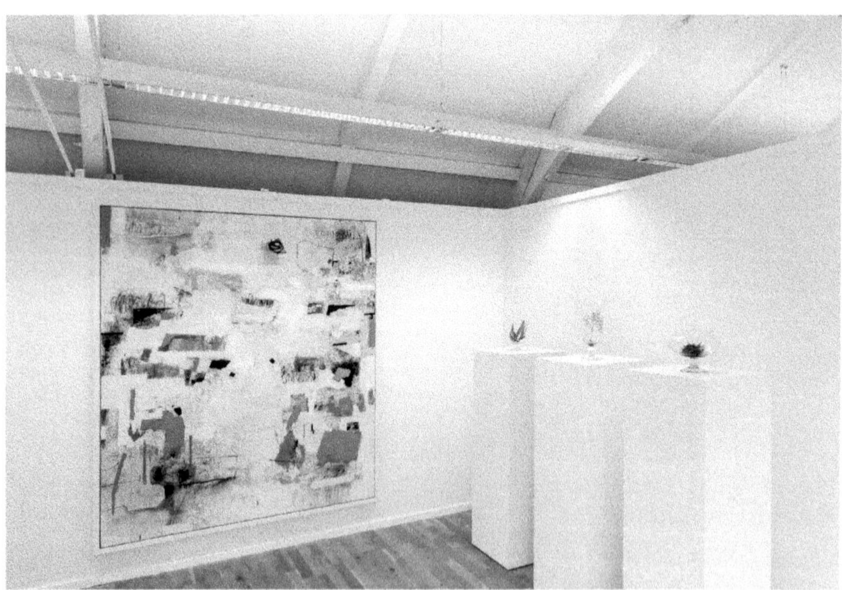

Plate 6 Patti Lean, *Snæfellsjökull (What You Have Stolen Can Never Be Yours)*, 2015

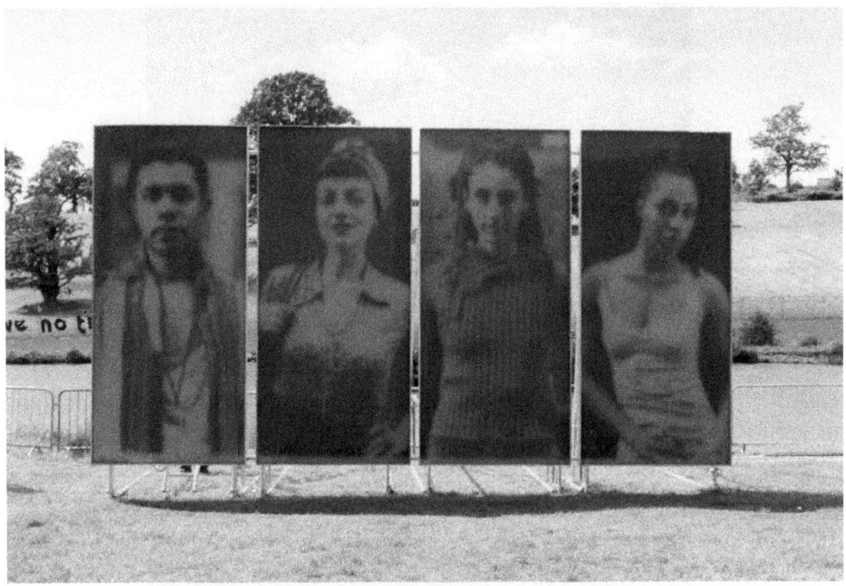

Plate 7 Ackroyd & Harvey, *Myles, Basia, Nath and Alesha*, 2007. Grass portraits installation

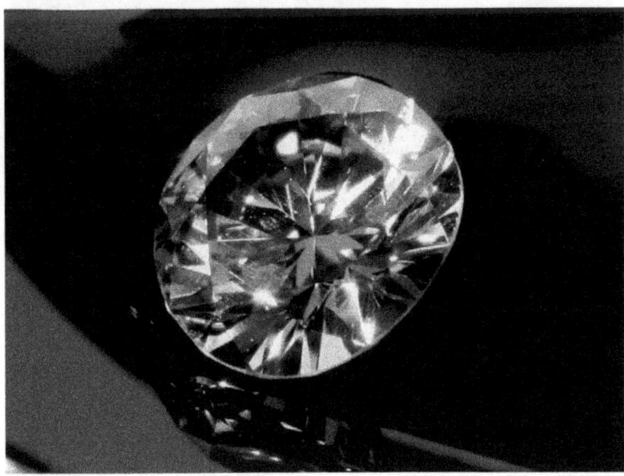

Plate 8 Ackroyd & Harvey, *Polar Diamond*, 2010. Artificial diamond made from the leg bone of a polar bear

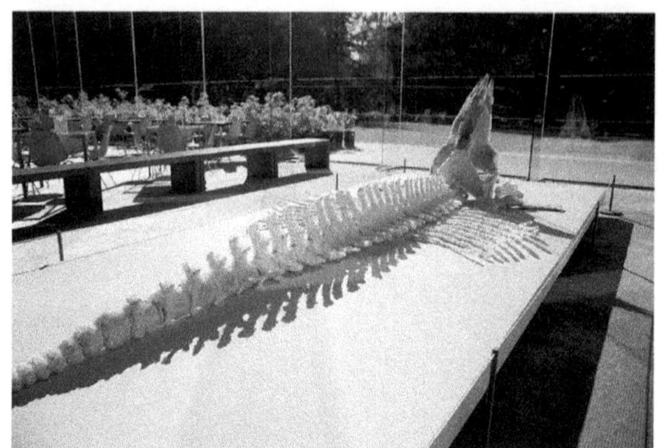

Plate 9 Ackroyd & Harvey, *Stranded,* 2006. Installation based on the skeleton of a minke whale

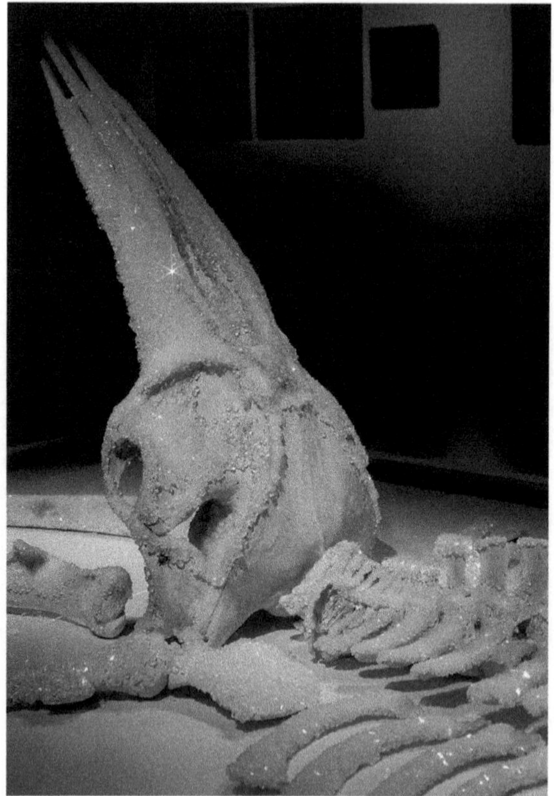

Plate 10 Ackroyd & Harvey, *Stranded* (detail), 2006. Installation based on the skeleton of a minke whale

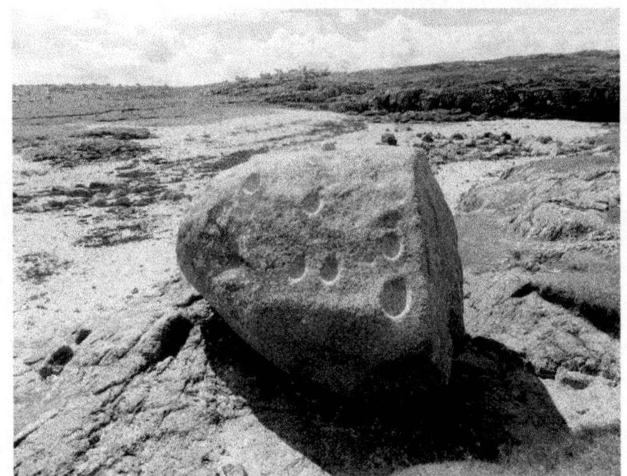

Plate 11   The Ringing Stone, Tiree

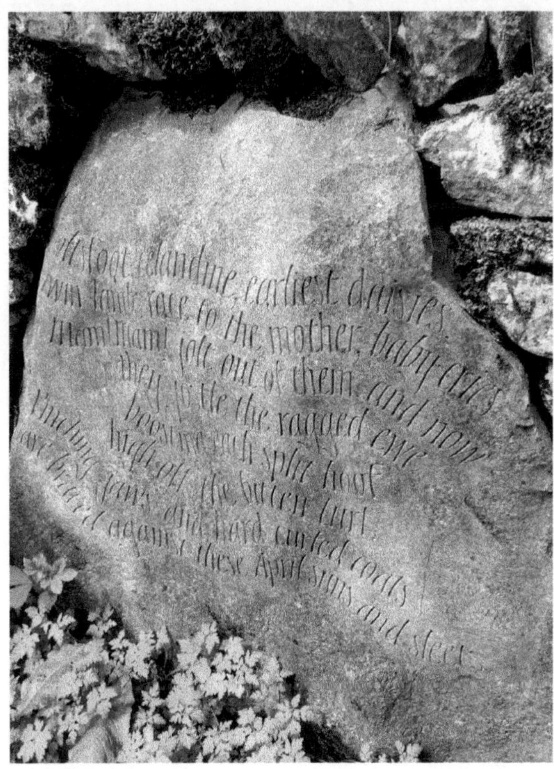

Plate 12   *April*, installation of poem by Meg Peacocke, carved on stone by Pip Hall, and placed on the Poetry Path, Kirkby Stephen

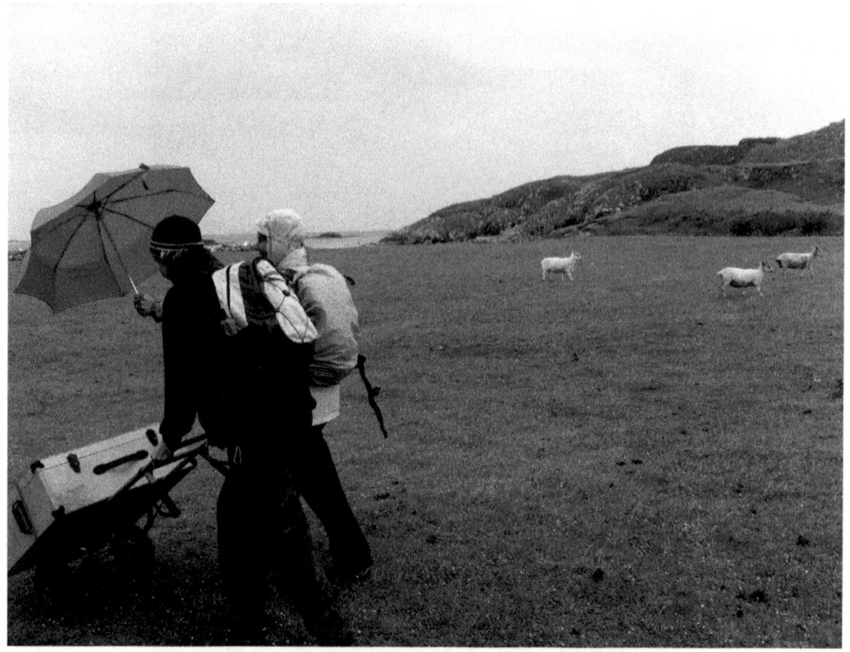

Plate 13   Alyson Hallett, Migrating Stone 4, arriving on Iona

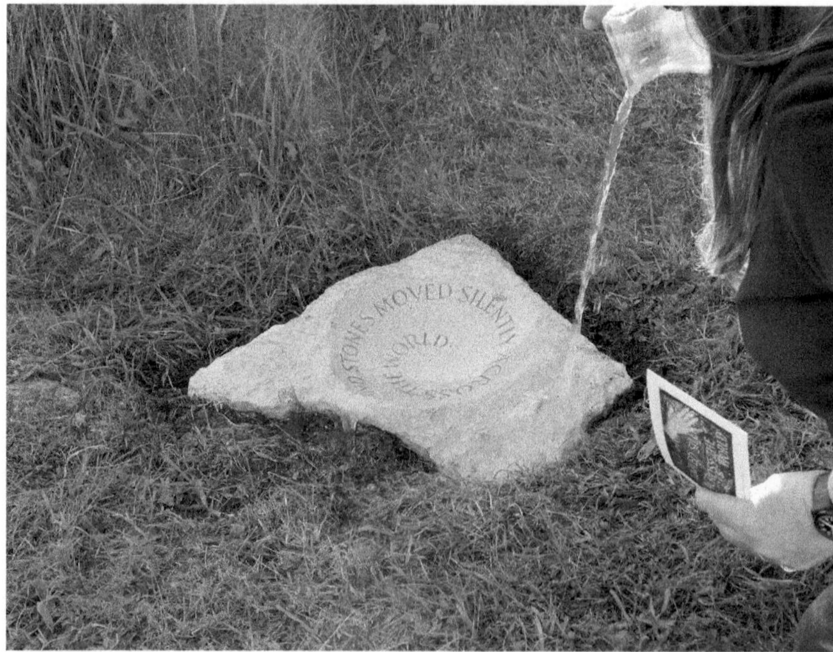

Plate 14   Alyson Hallett, Migrating Stone 4, in place on Iona with a 'libation' of water from the Abbey Well being poured over it to accompany a poetry reading

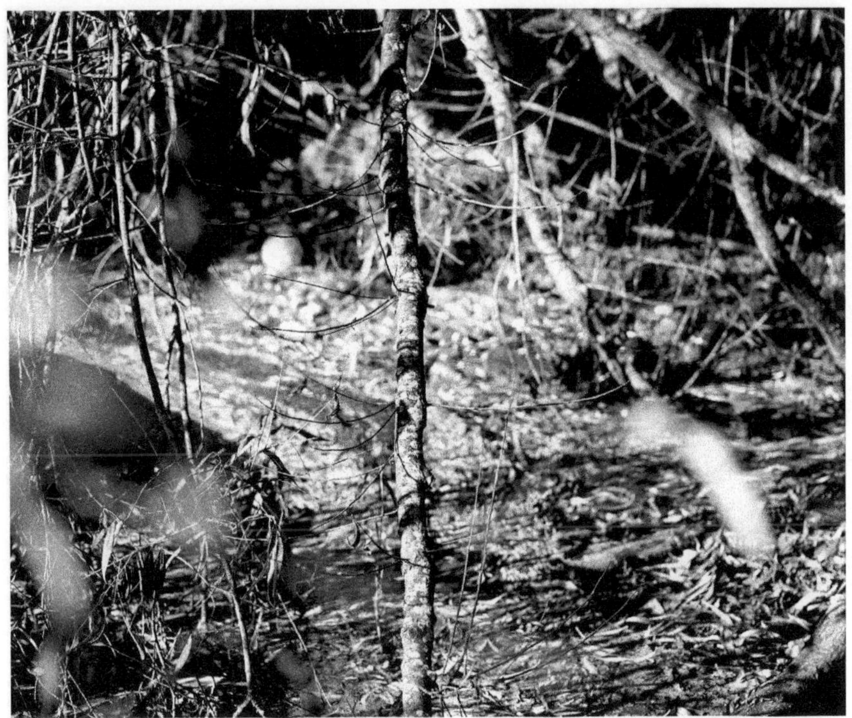

Plate 15   John Darwell, image from series '1000 Yards; Or So', 2011–20

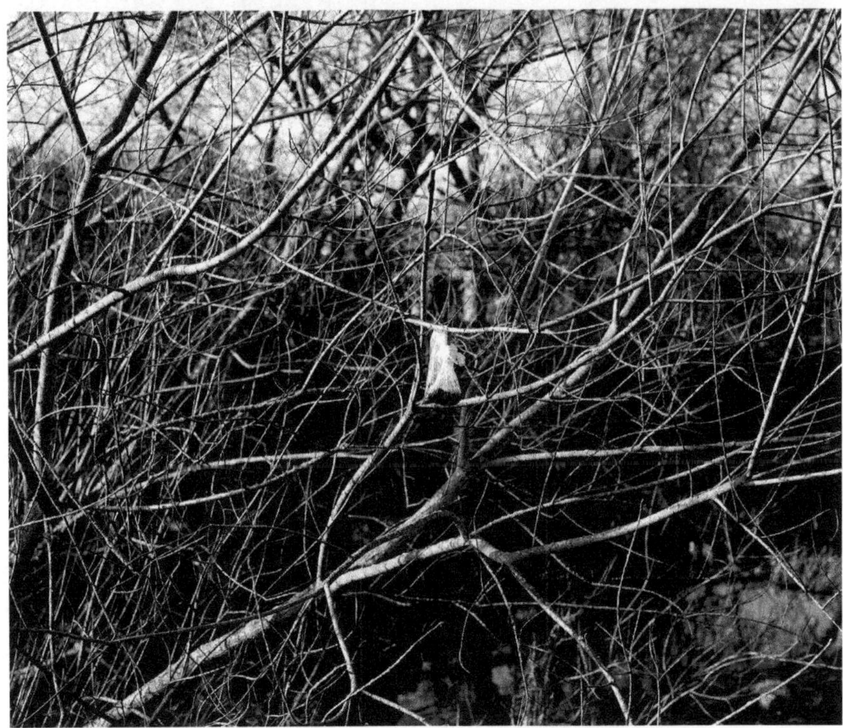

Plate 16   John Darwell, 'DDSB' from series '1000 Yards; Or So', 2011–20

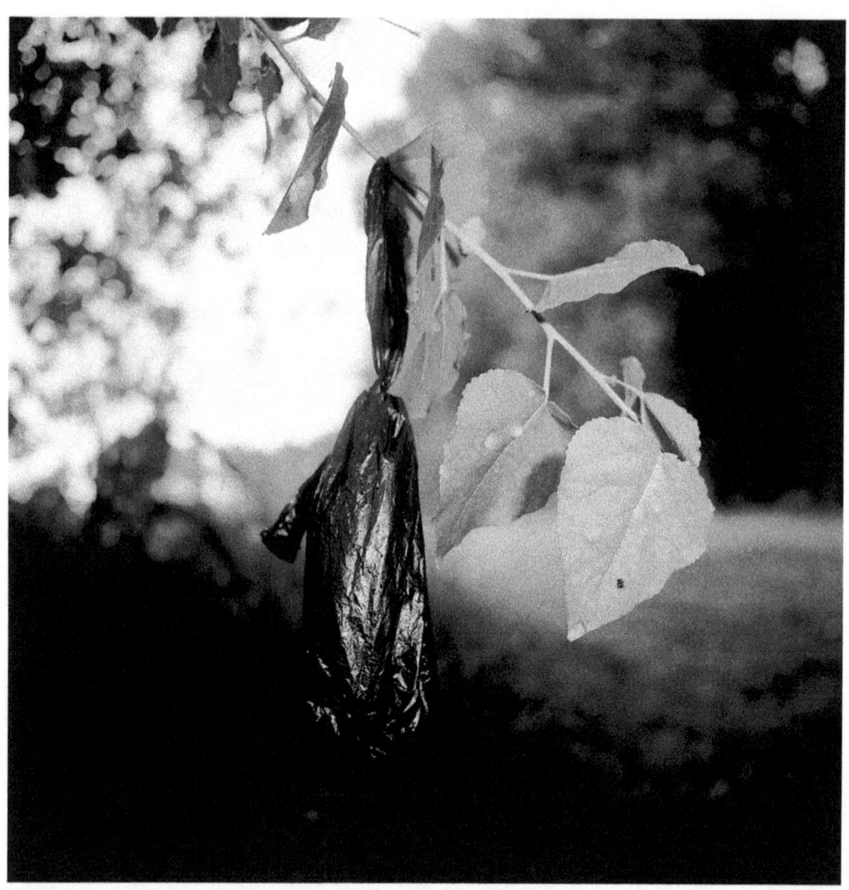

Plate 17   John Darwell, 'Black Bag Hanging' from series 'DDSBs', 2007–9

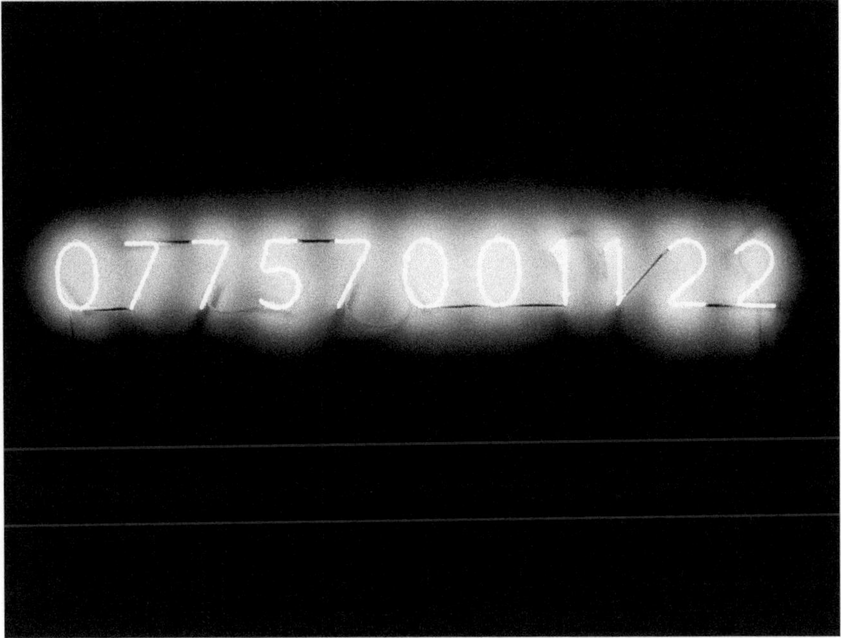

Plate 18   Katie Paterson, fluorescent tube of telephone number to ring to hear live sounds from the *Vatnajökull (the Sound of)*, Iceland, 2007–8. Installation in gallery exhibition

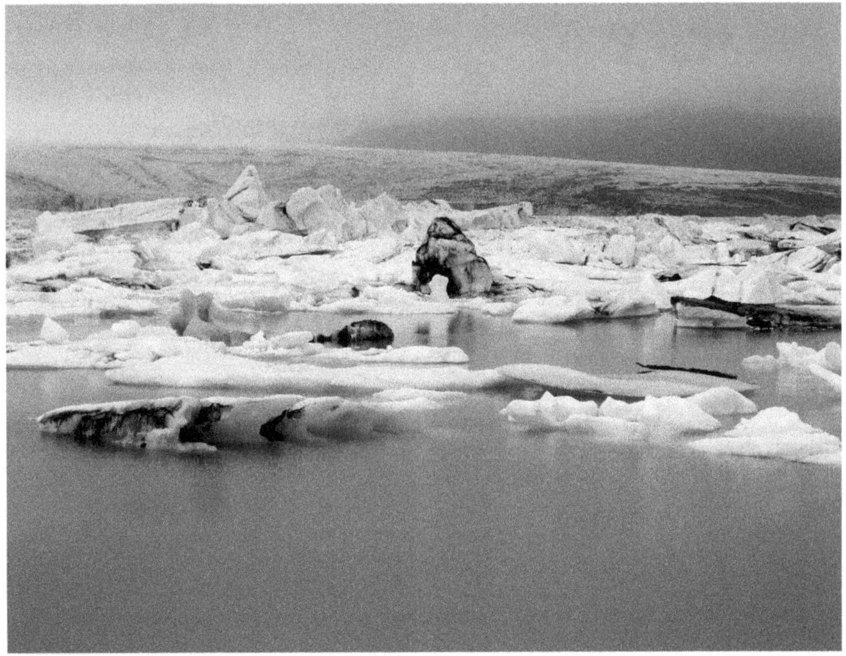

Plate 19   Katie Paterson, Photograph *Vatnajökull (the Sound of)*, Iceland, 2007–8

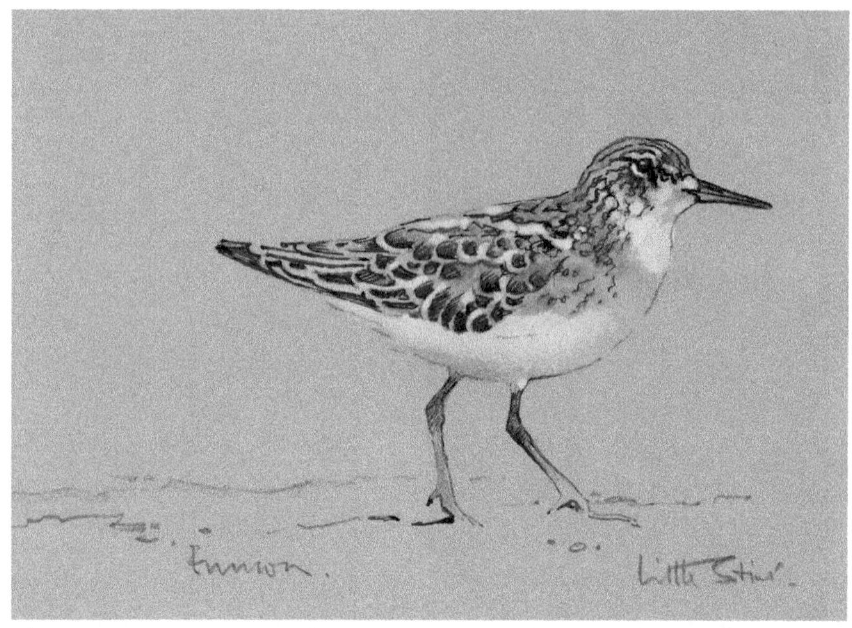

Plate 20 Eric Ennion, *Little Stint, c.* 1960

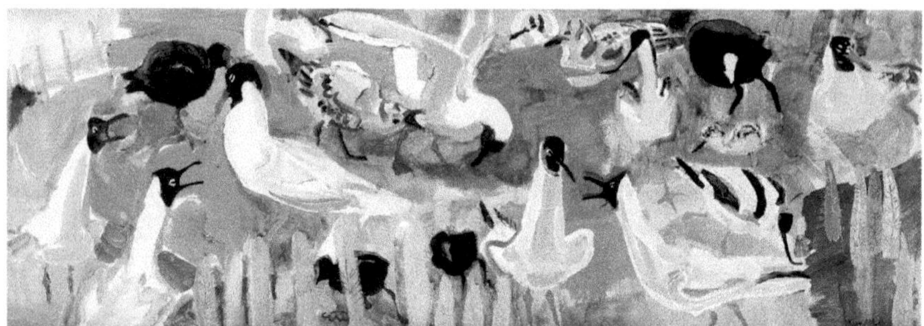

Plate 21 Kim Atkinson, *Mediterranean Gull Behaving Territorially*, 1998

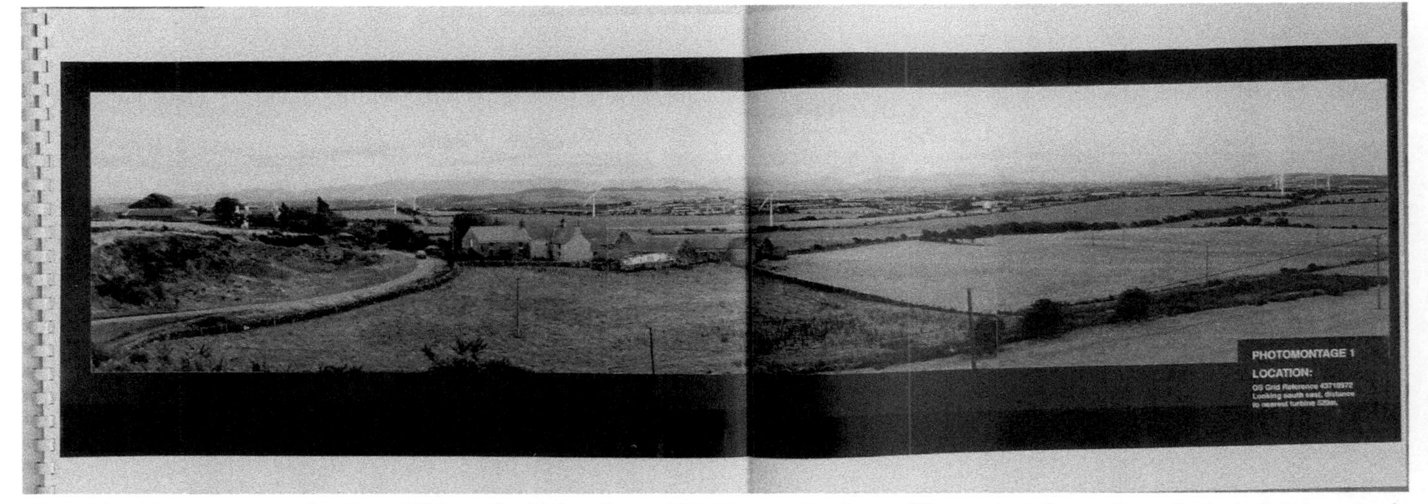

Plate 22 Photomontage by Jean Welstead of Trysglwyn Windfarm, Anglesey, illustrating the early technique joining single farm images and applying turbine transfers

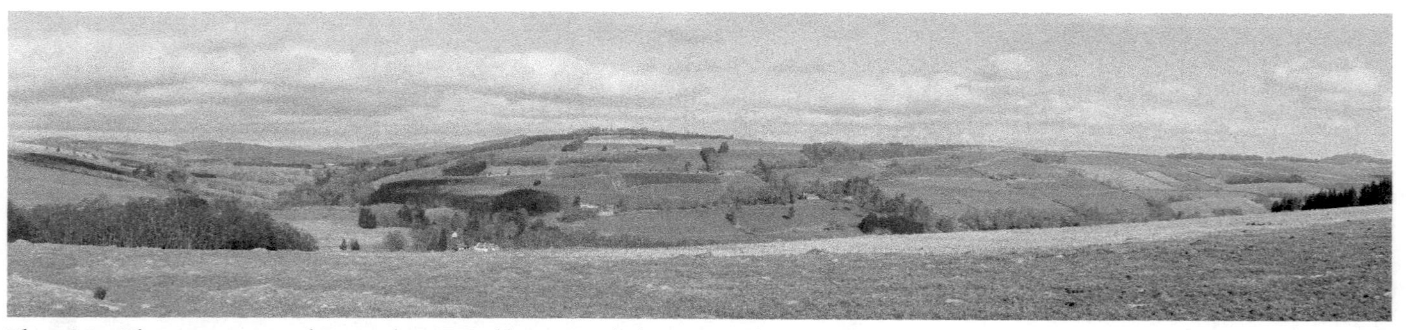

Plate 23 Photomontage of Drumderg Windfarm, Perthshire, complying with 2006 SNH guidance providing more landscape context but with the turbines appearing smaller due to linear perspective phenomenon

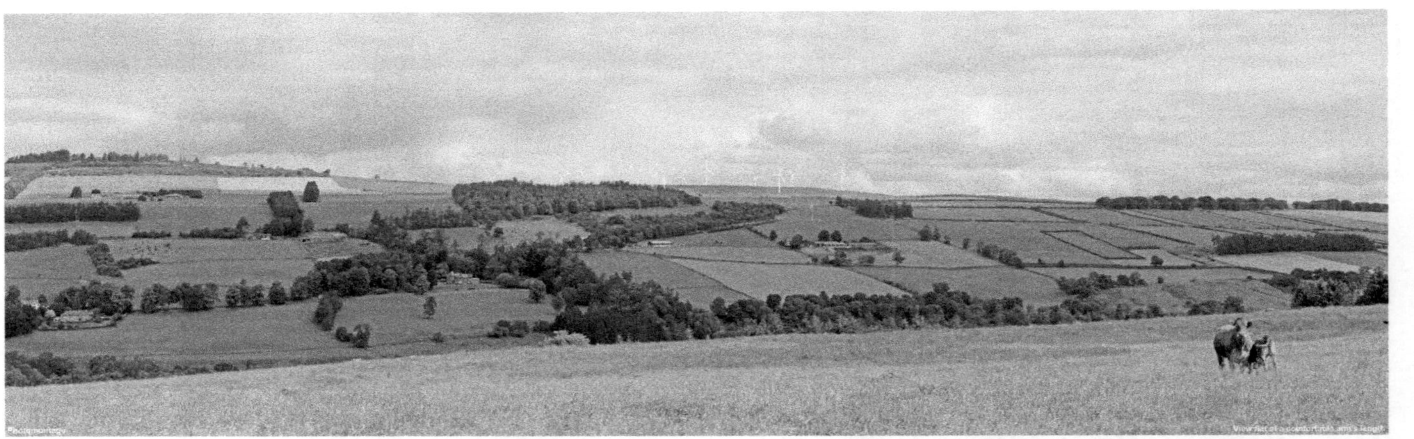

Plate 24 Photomontage of Drumderg Windfarm, Perthshire, complying with revised 2014 SNH guidance providing less landscape context but with the turbines appearing closer and larger

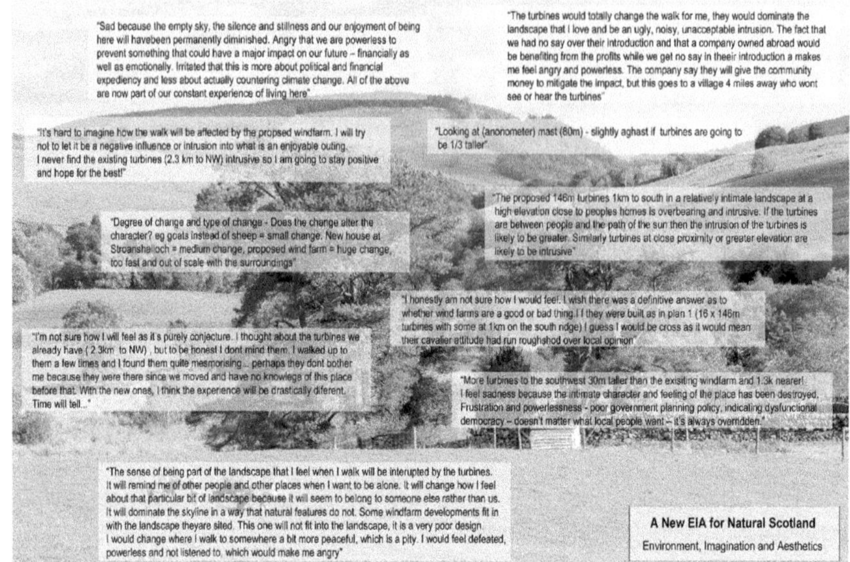

Plate 25 'Comments and observations on walk 2: imagining the proposed turbines have been built (16 m × 146 m turbines at 1 km distance)'. An annotated photomontage from 'The Missing Chapter' illustrating the feelings of participants imagining the windfarm has been built

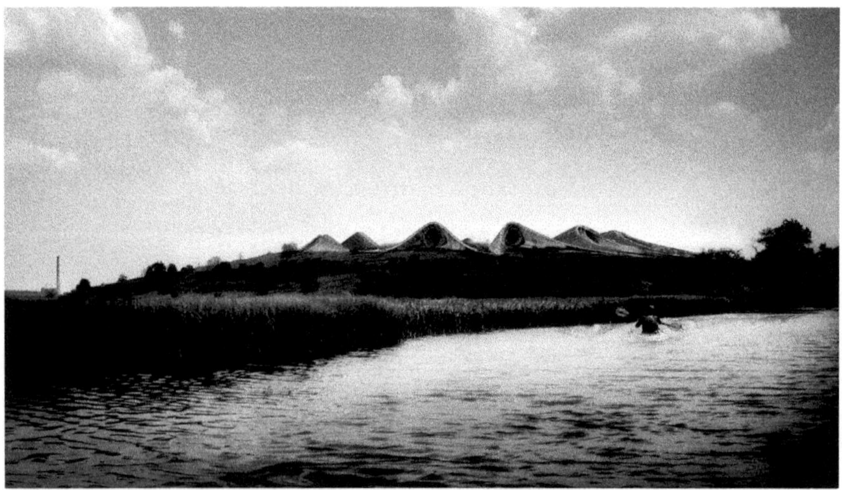

Plate 26 Artist's impression of 'Fresh Hills', an artificial landscape that lifts higher at levels of increased energy potential where more predominant wind speeds and duration exist. Uses energy technologies: WindTamerô, carbon dioxide scrubber, SmartWrapô. Annual Capacity: 238 MWh. LAGI prize winner 2012

number of issues as to how we regard, and treat, our environment and how we can, as individuals wrapped up in our personal lives, very easily turn a blind eye to misuses right under our noses, and the thought does come to me that, if we can't get to grips with such a, relatively small environmental issue, then what hope is there for dealing with the larger, potentially catastrophic, issues that face us in the years to come?

Notes

1   Further details of these projects are at my website http://johndarwell.com accessed 4 December 2015. See also Wells 2011: 178–81.
2   There could be a number of reasons for this behaviour: to display their prowess in terms of fishing ability, or possibly as a gesture to the river bailiff who was occasionally seen patrolling this stretch of river.
3   I would, and still do, pick up yards of fishing line whilst out walking the river and wonder if a system such as in Germany, where people have to undertake training in fish handling and environmental awareness, before being issued with a fishing licence, would be a good idea.
4   Described in an online article by Pete Brook (2014) as: 'This dog poop photo series is the nastiest typology you will ever see: an English photographer shoots the shit'. https://medium.com/@brookepete/this-dog-poop-bag-series-is-the-nastiest-typology-you-will-ever-seed76c58a32c14 accessed 3 December 2015.
5   There was no particular methodology in terms of exploring locations in search of the bags as after a while it became abundantly clear I could find them anywhere dog walkers were visiting. In fact it was often difficult to get away from them!
6   The Clean Neighbourhoods and Environment Act (Fouling of Land) Act 1996 requires all dog walkers to clear up after their animals, later modified in early 2005 to introduce mandatory on-the-spot fines for those who failed to do so. For a short time it was not unusual to see wardens in hi-vis jackets hiding in bushes, watching dog walkers through binoculars to ensure they adhered to the law. Added to this is the Regulation of Investigatory Powers Act (2000) to authorise the use of covert surveillance to catch terrorists and other serious organised criminals, which some authorities have invoked to catch dog foulers.
7   In all my time exploring the nature of DDSBs I have only once seen someone discard a bag. In this particular instance a little old lady quite deliberately threw the bag she was carrying into the river. Discretion being the better side of valour, I chose not to say anything to her.
8   This is an area of debate that goes way beyond my DDSB project and addresses the whole issue of where art sits and how it is perceived and the sometimes gulf between the lay observer and contemporary practice as to what is art. In my case I feel it is important to produce images that have a

strong visual appeal as this becomes the means by which I can lure the viewer into the work to then better understand the underlying message I am attempting to put across.

9 See also discussion regarding the Marine Debris Tracker. Catherine A. Novelli (2015), 'Technology has hurt our oceans, but we can also harness it to reverse the damage', *Guardian*, 9 October 2015.

References

Bachelard, G. (1969 [1958]) *The Poetics of Space: The Classic Look at How We Experience Intimate Spaces*, trans. Maria Jolas. Boston, MA: Beacon Press.

Becher, Bernd and Hilla Becher (2000) *Typologies of Industrial Buildings*. Cambridge, MA: MIT Press.

Daoust, Phil (2001) 'Atomic dustbin', *Guardian*, 12 March. www.theguardian.com/culture/2001/mar/12/artsfeature2 accessed 3 December 2015.

Darwell, J. (2008) 'A Black Dog Came Calling: a Visualisation of Depression through Contemporary Photography', unpublished PhD thesis, University of Sunderland.

Darwell, J. (2013) *DDSBs*. Carlisle: mynewtpress.

Darwell, J. (2014) Interview 'Shit happens', in *Four and Sons: Where Dogs and Culture Collide*, Issue 2 – Heel! Brisbane.

Farley, P. and M. Symmons Roberts (2012) *Edgelands: Journeys into England's True Wilderness*. London: Vintage.

Gossage, J. (2010 [1985]) *The Pond*. Second edition. New York: Aperture.

Kant, Immanual (2004 [1764]) *Observations on the Feeling of the Beautiful and the Sublime*, trans. John T. Goldthwaite. Oakland: University of California Press.

Wells, Liz (2011) *Land Matters: Landscape Photography, Culture And Identity*. London: I.B. Taurus.

9

Aesthetics as ecology, or the question of the form of eco-art

Clive Cazeaux

Although the origins of ecological art or eco-art (I shall use the latter name from here on) are relatively easy to identify, the full meaning and scope of the name are not so easy to determine. The emergence of eco-art as a visual art form is arguably the result of a number of inter-related factors in the 1960s: American and United Kingdom counter-cultures, including disillusionment with government and material wealth; conceptual art's reaction against traditional aesthetic values, especially the art work as a commodity; and the development of ecology as an empirical science, including a growing number of theoretical terms, such as 'ecosystem' and 'biosphere', that lent themselves to counterculture philosophy; and the publication in 1962 of Rachel Carson's book *Silent Spring*, a scientific study of the detrimental effects of pesticides on the environment, especially birds. More recently, fears regarding pollution, climate change, and environmental damage caused by the extraction of natural resources have made eco-art more prominent as a form of critical response.

However, while it is possible to describe succinctly the conditions that gave rise to eco-art, the forms that it has taken are manifold and pose a challenge to classification. Western visual art has always addressed the natural world either as a portrayal of the kingdom of God (an exercise in representation) or as the depiction of beauty in nature. The name 'fine art' was given to art that imitates the beautiful in nature by Charles Batteux in 1746, and the power to create beauty by *abstracting from* or *going beyond* nature became an expression of the genius or autonomy of art in nineteenth-century Romanticism.[1] But the combination of conceptual art and ecology's interest in the interconnections between organism and environment makes for a very different proposition. An art practice that is critical of traditional aesthetics and art-making practices, and open to adopting modes of expression and display from all forms of discourse, approaches nature *not to represent it* but *to work with it*. In sympathy with this openness, the natural world, once seen through the lens of ecology, stops being a static object of disinterested appreciation and becomes a set of dynamic interconnections of which one is a part and which is open to co-operation. The potential for novel, critical and political expression and intervention is therefore immense.

In this chapter, I argue that 'art' and 'ecology' are terms with broad meanings which, when combined in the concept of 'eco-art', create an overwhelming array of possibilities, and make the problem of categorisation fundamental to eco-art. I consider recent attempts to classify the field, and suggest that, while they can be helpful, the full force of the problem of categorisation is better addressed by turning to the position given to aesthetics by phenomenology. This takes the problem of categorisation down to the level of how categories can be applied to experience when conventional, subject–object frameworks have been suspended. Drawing on phenomenology, I argue that our status as Daseins, beings whose nature is always, already constructed by the environment around us, makes prominent the role of the senses, indexicality and metaphor in the organisation of experience, and provides a way of understanding aesthetics as ecology (in the broadest sense of the word). Although this leaves the classification of eco-art open, it nevertheless shows that the openness is a result of the complexities of our aesthetic rootedness in the world, where 'aesthetic' is understood in sensory, causal and metaphorical terms.

Recent attempts to classify eco-art

Linda Weintraub, in her 2012 survey of eco-art, acknowledges the variety of forms it takes and attempts to categorise them, not in the interests of identifying the essence of eco-art but in order to display the vibrancy of the genre and '[to] facilitate compare-and-contrast analysis' (Weintraub 2012: xv). She suggests four 'banner' headings that are either addressed or adopted by eco-artists – 'art genres', 'art strategies', 'eco issues' and 'eco approaches' – and which in turn subdivide into categories, as shown in Table 9.1 (Weintraub 2012: xx–xxxv).

This is not a table but a matrix. It is not the case that each row represents a particular strand of eco-art, i.e. Weintraub is not suggesting that sculpture intervenes in matters of waste with a view to promoting preservation. Rather, as a matrix, it enables her to show how a number of eco-art works address a range of issues through selected artistic strategies and, in so doing, adopt one or more eco approaches. Each of

Table 9.1   Summary of Weintraub's analysis of eco-art

art genres	art strategies	eco issues	eco approaches
paint/print	instruct	energy	conservation
sculpture	intervene	waste	preservation
performance	visualize	climate change	social ecology
photo/video	metaphorize	technology	deep ecology
bio art	activate	habitat	restoration ecology
generative art	celebrate	sustainability	urban ecology
social practice	perturb	resources	industrial ecology
digital art	dramatize	chaos/complexity	human ecology
installation	satirize	systems	ecosystem ecology
public art	investigate	reforms	sustainable
design			development

the forty-seven artworks that she discusses is prefaced by a 'schematic' diagram with lines linking all the categories that she thinks are demonstrated by the work. For example, *Greenwich Village Time Landscape* (1978–ongoing), the former 45 ft × 200 ft litter-strewn lot in downtown New York City transformed into a stretch of woodland made up of indigenous trees, flowers and grasses by Alan Sonfist, is schematised as: the art genres 'bio art', 'generative art' and 'public art'; the art strategies 'instruct', 'intervene' and 'celebrate'; the eco issues 'habitat', 'chaos/ complexity', 'systems' and 'reforms'; and the eco approaches 'preservation', 'urban ecology' and 'ecosystem ecology' (Weintraub 2012: 111).

Other recent surveys of eco-art offer different, less detailed categorisations. In *Art and Ecology Now*, Andrew Brown divides the terrain into works that: (1) visualise or call attention to ecological concerns; (2) develop through a co-operative relationship with an environment or use it as source material; (3) emerge as a result of research into physical or environmental processes; (4) critique humanity's manipulation of the planet's resources; (5) offer solutions to environmental problems; and (6) change or transform environments through 'radical interventions that have a direct impact on local and global ecosystems' (Brown 2014: 218). Although he is not explicit about them as groupings, the chapter titles used by Malcolm Miles in his *Eco-Aesthetics: art, literature and architecture in a period of climate change* effectively indicate the five areas where he thinks eco-aesthetics creates new meaning and sensibilities: (1) 'ruins and catastrophes'; (2) 'regressions and reclamations'; (3) 'representations'; (4) 'interruptions'; and (5) 'cultures and climate change' (Miles 2014). 'Representations' is possibly the one area that is additional to Weintraub's and Brown's taxonomies in Miles's account. It is the acknowledgement that aesthetic practices can complicate the representation of nature, for example, the out-of-context use of the Fibonacci pattern found in sunflower seed-heads by Peter Randall-Page's almost three metres high granite sculpture *Seed* (2007) (Miles 2014: 124). On a more critical note, Timothy Morton asserts that art focused on ideas connected with the environment has nothing to offer ecology, and 'will cease to exist at some point in the history of ecological thought'. Eco-art, he adds, is 'an art of "whateverness"' and aesthetics 'is full of emptiness – gaps and openness – rather than being a solid, plastic thing' (Morton 2010: 104–5). This is part of his project to make ecology a matter not of nature but of having connection and coexistence as the basis of thinking (Morton 2007, 2010). To be ecological as an expression of coexistence, Morton suggests, eco-art should emphasise: (1) 'automated processes such as evolution'; (2) consciousness of our condition as interconnected beings; and (3) the 'ruthlessness' with which mathematics and science model nature as a resource (Morton 2010: 105).

In the categories of eco-art offered by Weintraub, Brown, Miles and Morton, there are many overlaps, but also some differences, especially (and unsurprisingly) as a result of Morton's reorientation of ecology. It might seem ironic that art's engagement with ecology, an approach to the world that focuses on relationship, should require such efforts of classification, especially if one associates classification with the isolation of objects in containers or the bringing of particulars under a universal. But none of the authors is presenting their accounts as a definitive set of essential categories. Rather, they are simply providing critical studies that offer pathways through and comparisons across what might otherwise be a diffuse and diverse terrain. So what's the problem?

According to Garrard, the challenge for ecocriticism is 'to keep one eye on the ways in which "nature" is always in some ways culturally constructed, and the other on the fact that nature really exists, both the object and, albeit distantly, the origin of our discourse' (Garrard 2012: 10). The rub here, between one eye and the other, is the question of how we apply categories to reality, for even though reality exists independently of us, the way in which we categorise it affects the way in which we interact with it and, in turn, the forms and appearances that it presents to us in response. Ecocriticism is therefore an attentiveness to the power of categories to shape and form what is real, and a calling attention to the responsibility that comes with that power. In terms of the challenge posed to classification by eco-art, this is not just a question of finding categories with which to cut up the cake of eco-art but rather a matter of recognising how art and ecology intersect as domains whose scope is entirely open, and the scope for possibility that this creates. Instead of picturing them as domains, which implies a region that is circumscribed or defined, it might be better to think of them as horizons of possibility: conceptual art as a form that rejects art-historical genres and seeks to appropriate other, non-artistic objects and discourses, and an ecological perspective that views the world not as an object to be depicted but as a set of relations to be worked with. It is not that I think that the categories offered by Weintraub et al. are inadequate to the task of defining the various aspects eco-art can present. My point is that when one considers the possibilities that are open within conceptual art, and the possibilities that are available through exercising nature's joints, and that the two sets of possibilities will multiply, then eco-art *as the intersection where the multiplication occurs* becomes the state of constantly having to look to the categories one is reaching for, to check the categories that are introduced whenever a medium, technology or physical process is adopted, and to assess what categories might be brought to the work through audience perception and interpretation. This might imply a state of always being on one's guard with regard to how one thinks, acts, or judges, and how others do the same, but it seems to me that this is the kind of attentiveness implied by Garrard's description of the challenge of ecocriticism. What I am arguing here, and adding to the list of qualities identified by Weintraub, Brown, Miles and Morton, is that eco-art has the requirement of attentiveness to categorisation at its core.

The meaning of 'ecology'

The first step towards glimpsing the possibilities that occur at the intersection between art and ecology is to clarify the meaning of 'ecology'. In one sense, it is the name of the scientific study of the relationship between organisms and the environment in which they are set, as coined by Ernst Haeckel in his 1866 book *General Morphology of Organisms* (Haeckel 1866). (Ideas of interconnections between organisms and their environment predate this, for example, observations from Charles Darwin and Karl Möbius (to name but two) in the nineteenth century, and ultimately from the Greek philosopher Theophrastus (372–287 BC), a contemporary of Aristotle.)[2] However, the idea of interconnections between organism and environment can have the effect of turning 'ecology' into the care and consideration of organism and environment as things that are perceived to occur 'out there', in 'Nature with a capital N'.

The danger is that the focus is on environment (with networks of organisms) *as something that surrounds us* and which is therefore in some sense distinct from us, when it is arguably *the nature of relationship* per se, including the relationships formed by the way humans think about the world, that is equally deserving of attention. This is emphasised by Keller and Golley, who define ecology as the thesis that 'the essence or identity of a living thing is an expression of connections and context' (Keller and Golley 2000: 2). As indicated above, the concept of 'Nature with a capital N' is challenged by Morton. Ecological thinking, he writes, 'has set up "Nature" as a reified thing in the distance, under the sidewalk, on the other side where the grass is always greener, preferably in the mountains, in the wild', when it should be a way of thinking in which every thought has coexistence and interconnection as its foundation (Morton 2010: 8).

The idea that ecology might be interpreted not so much as a study of relationships in nature but as a theory of thinking or of being finds some support in the original meaning of the word. It is derived from the Greek *oikos*, meaning 'house', 'dwelling place', 'a place where I feel at home', 'a place where I belong' (Keller and Golley 2000: 7–8). On this basis, 'ecology' might be translated as the logic of belonging. One example of a philosophy that makes belonging a theory of being is Heidegger's phenomenology, in which human being is defined as a Da-sein, a 'being-*there*', with the crucial message being that any reference to a human being has to include the environment, the there-ness, of which they are a part (Heidegger 1996).[3] The philosophical impact of human being conceived as a Da-sein is that it opposes the Cartesian tradition of referring to the human being as a self-contained subject set against the world as a series of objects, and affirms that any identification of so-called human action has to acknowledge its embeddedness in and indebtedness to the conditions that surround and enable it. This might sound close to deep ecology, the thesis, introduced by Arne Naess, that mainstream ecology is anthropocentric, preoccupied with projects that are tied to human welfare or concepts of nature, e.g. preserving biodiversity and conserving wilderness, and therefore 'shallow' (Naess 1973). This is Morton's criticism also. He in fact acknowledges that he is joining this critical heritage, and at one point considers his approach to be '*really* deep ecology' (Morton 2007: 197–205, emphasis added). One deep ecological response has been to draw upon Heidegger's immersion of the human subject in the world as a way of ensuring that humanity is not privileged. However, I would want to argue that Heidegger's relevance for ecology goes beyond dispersing the human subject within nature or the world. This, after all, still hangs on to the concept of nature or world as an outside. Rather, the full force of what I am calling his logic of belonging can be found in the implications which Da-sein has for the way experience and the senses are understood, and specifically the way in which they might occur as forms of care (*Sorge*).[4] Experience – not just human, although admittedly this is Heidegger's focus – is shown to occur not as the *having* of impressions (the dominant view supported by empiricism and capitalism) but as an opening on to a range of possibilities made available by a set of prior conditions, e.g. a certain conceptual framework, a certain kind of body or apparatus in a certain setting, in such a way that attribution to a subject and to an object is impossible. This is a form of care in the sense that what is experienced does not simply occur as an object that I can throw away or walk away from, but occurs as an abiding part of the network of interests and concerns that defines 'my' being in the world (with 'my' in inverted commas to highlight the way in which subject–object language succeeds in reasserting itself).

The concept of 'belonging' is active in two senses here: it affirms that I as a Da-sein belong to the world in such a way that attribution of what belongs to the world and what belongs to me cannot be made. In the first sense, it is the assertion of an ontology, an expression of the fundamental nature of being as a state of immersion and entanglement that resists acts of separation and isolation. In the second, it is a component in an already-established object-centred ontology, assisting in acts of apportioning properties to one object or another. Heidegger's philosophy promotes the former, and seeks to question the latter. Although this might sound as if it makes descriptions of experience more problematic than familiar, straightforward, subject–predicate statements allow, it is just the kind of disruption to thought and language that is needed if ecology is not merely to be filed under 'environmentalism', and if ecocriticism is to call attention to the responsibility that we have for organising, categorising and, ultimately, perceiving 'nature' or reality the way we do. It turns ecology into a form of ontology, a way of thinking about the structures and divisions that organise reality and, as such, narrows the gap between ecology and ecocriticism. Although my position draws upon Heidegger, I shall not offer any detailed exposition of his phenomenology in this chapter. However, I do give an account below of how his thinking bears upon the nature of expression in eco-art.

Ecology then has a range of meanings: environment, relationships between organism and environment, thinking and being as interconnection, coexistence and belonging. If we expected a study of the possibilities between art and ecology to be simply a matter of considering those between art and environment, then we were wrong: the study has suddenly become a lot broader and a lot more complex. One point has been clarified though. There can sometimes be uncertainty over the divisions or overlaps between eco-art, environmental art and land art. What distinguishes one from the other, if anything? While the latter two declare a focus on the territory or conditions addressed by the art or in which the art is set, the range of meanings of 'ecology' confirms that eco-art has a much wider, more uncertain and almost bewildering range of possibilities. The bewilderment is on two accounts: (1) art can be anything, and (2) in its engagement with ecology it can potentially open on to anything from a relationship with an environment or a state of interconnection to a state of being situated in the world or a question of the conditions which enable the perception of reality. It has to be asked where this leaves us with the challenge of ecocriticism I took from Garrard as a preface to the question about art and ecology, namely: the challenge 'to keep one eye on the ways in which "nature" is always in some ways culturally constructed, and the other on the fact that nature really exists, both the object and, albeit distantly, the origin of our discourse' (Garrard 2012: 10). Am I now suggesting that ecocriticism has to keep additional eyes on ecology as concepts of relationship, thinking, belonging, etc.? No, my expanded list of definitions does not mean that Garrard's challenge is too narrow and that more ecocritical eyes are needed, for there is a lot of Heidegger in his formulation of the challenge. Although Garrard refers to 'nature' (admittedly in inverted commas), the emphasis he places on attentiveness to its construction and its independent existence is a fair summary of the situation we are in according to phenomenology as regards the responsibility we have for how the world makes itself manifest.

The suggestion that the relationship between art and ecology leads to a bewildering array of possibilities is understandable, and some might find it reasonable but it is arguably unhelpful, in that bewilderment does not indicate a line through the confusion to a conclusion or a position on the nature and scope of eco-art. Of course, this could be the conclusion: both concepts possess an openness or a flexibility to the degree that, when combined, no single, clear position on the nature and scope of eco-art is possible. I stated above that eco-art has at its core the need to consider how categories are applied to it, and the survey of the broader meanings of ecology means this need is now even greater, to the extent that eco-art faces an existential crisis: it is without any essence or nature that it can turn to for guidance on how it might proceed. Any attempt to offer a taxonomy of the subject is in danger of giving the impression that field has been scoped and classified, and needs to assert that the categories offered are provisional and intended to aid study through comparison and contrast, which is what Weintraub does in fact (Weintraub 2012: xv).[5] We also cannot turn to art as the source of any nature that might offer some determination. After conceptual art, the contemporary artist cannot rely upon the traditional decisions made by the histories of medium, form and style to determine the content and development of their work. Instead, any *aspect of* or *object from* or *attitude towards* life, including material or virtual possibilities, interactive technologies, and historical, theoretical and social contexts, is open to the artist.

An aesthetic response to an existential question

But I think the hollowing out of meaning is a constructive outcome. It demonstrates that the choices we *make*, whichever words, materials, technologies or contexts that we *reach for*, will be significant in that they introduce a set of concerns for exploration. The value structures that govern the definition of art and the portions of nature that warrant ecological attention have been overturned. What could be a greater indication of the potential of eco-art than the realisation that any item in the world, no matter how seemingly insignificant, can be the ground for artistic, ecological enquiry? While this presents existential crisis as a positive philosophical development, it still leaves us in the dark as to how an eco-art project might proceed. The existentialist answer is to recognise that Da-sein is a being-*there*, a being surrounded by conditions that are always, already active and under way. The problem is *not mine alone*, where '*mine*' is taken to refer to what belongs to an isolated, disembodied Cartesian mind looking for the way out of a philosophical minefield. Instead, as a Da-sein, a being who is in part constituted by the materials, technologies and communities that surround me, directions will be proposed by possibilities *that occur to me*, not in a casual, momentary, thought-bubble way but in the sense that thoughts, observations and *concerns* impress themselves upon me. 'Concerns' is italicised because it is one of the alternative translations of *Sorge*, care, in Heidegger's philosophy. It is not meant in the sense of a set of problems, although this is not excluded, but in the sense that my being is a state of active engagement with my surroundings and what the surroundings make possible. It is not that there is first a self who then looks for objects to interact with. Rather, my being as a Da-sein is the condition of being caught up in the materials, technologies, and communities that surround me, e.g. a body, the senses, contact with other beings and objects, structures that provide warmth and shelter, etc. The point is implicit in the wording of the first sentence in this paragraph: 'the choices we *make*, whichever words, materials, technologies or contexts that we *reach for*, will be significant in that they introduce a set of concerns for exploration'. 'Make' and 'reach for' affirm that, in choosing a course of action, our action can happen only because words, materials, technologies etc., surround us and sustain us, and are there to enable and articulate the action.

This is where the concept of the aesthetic is crucial. The materials, technologies and communities that surround me are aesthetic, not in the eighteenth-century sense of beauty but in the original, ancient sense of what is made manifest through the senses, the body and technology; every thing has to appear, to adopt a form. This ancient meaning has been reclaimed by phenomenology as part of its project of challenging the modern subject–object divide. It is all too easy to resort to conceptualising the senses as channels with a receiving consciousness at the end of them, but, with the subject–object divide put in question, phenomenology seeks to characterise them in terms more fundamental and ontological than mere reception. From a Heideggerian perspective, the surface of the desk at which I am sat, as I perceive it, is not mine, is not a sensation or an experience that I possess, but a care or concern in as much as it forms part of the layout of the environment in which I am situated and in which action is immediately possible. It might be useful to talk in terms of an aesthetics of care. I am not thinking of the aesthetic properties that might accompany what we ordinarily understand by care, e.g. looking after one's family, neighbours, friends, possessions, but instead the idea that those parts of life that are open, meaningful and important to us are also those that we see in detail, that take on many diverse forms, that are manifest in a variety of ways. When we look closely, what might first appear to be one thing goes on to become two, four etc.

Given the possibilities that are open between art and ecology, I am suggesting that our condition as Da-seins, beings who are situated, for whom the world is made manifest in the form of cares or concerns, offers an answer to the question of how we might understand the nature and scope of eco-art. If I am an artist, I will want to make some*thing*, and that thing won't be an object or event that comes out of nowhere or ends up residing in a vacuum, but will be nestled within a network of interests and concerns, including contender materials and technologies, and the discourses which surround them. In choosing an area for attention, all these elements have the potential to be opened up and transformed in ways that turn what originally seemed remote or beyond care into something surprising, that takes on a new appearance, with the capacity to become a care or a concern for the viewer. This happens as an extension of the aesthetics that I have already described, i.e. what is made manifest through the senses, the body and technology. It is a process I think of as 'interested signification': 'interested' because an interest or concern is present, and becomes a cognitive filter that informs interpretation of an art work, and 'signification' because all objects and appearances have the capacity to signify and evoke, more often than not in terms that go beyond an initial or familiar understanding. Three ideas from the history of aesthetics are active here: (1) *the particularising effect of the senses*: when looked at closely, in detail, all concepts and subjects have particular sensory forms that go beyond any customary, general or remote understanding of them; a concept is something which is applied, and when pictured or turned over in one's mind prior to application, will invariably involve a colour or sound or shape or situation; (2) all objects, materials and technologies have what Peirce terms '*indexicality*':[6] the capacity to leave impacts and traces in ways that are surprising as a result of the causal interaction they have with one another, meaning they can present appearances that prompt them to be seen and possibly cared for in a new light; and (3) *metaphor*: the interaction between the concepts, the sensory forms (1), and the indexical expression (2), creates the opportunity for metaphor, in which each side is revivified by the other, offering more ways in which what was originally overlooked or perceived as remote becomes surprising.[7] If eco-art can draw upon an infinite range of possibilities, then its ecological or political or philosophical value as art is that it seeks to create openings, alignments, intersections, redirections etc., that allow what are customarily regarded as 'take them or leave them' objects, i.e. they are ultimately *dis*regarded, instead to be cared for, to become *concerns* within the Da-sein of the viewer in the phenomenological sense, i.e. prospects wherein the viewer sees qualities they hadn't recognised before, and becomes inclined to consider them further. The movement from 'object' to 'care' is ecological in the phenomenological sense, for it encourages an understanding of perception that departs from the subject–object model. It could also be considered ecological in the 'environmental' sense, because it is arguably perception of the world in terms of objects that are not mine, that are expendable, whose fate is of no concern, that plays a major part in environmental destruction and neglect.

Example 1: melting glaciers

Let us look at two examples of interested signification. Two will be helpful, I think: one to indicate how my aesthetics of ecology can critique and present alternative possibilities in response to a work that is already considered eco-art; the other to show how an artist might start given the infinity of possibilities available. An advantage of the first example is that the presence of a familiar environmental cause allows me to show how my aesthetics of ecology presents an expanded notion of the form that eco-art can take. It also allows the technical terms in my aesthetics of ecology to be exercised in a context where questions of the scope of art and environmental concerns are already under way.

If one wanted to make work in response to melting glaciers, where or how would one position oneself? Does one offer a recognisable representation of a glacier or show physical properties at work through the causal, indexical trace marks that they might leave? Which technologies and which modes of presentation would one use? In Katie Paterson's installation *Vatnajökull (the Sound of)* from 2007–8, a recording of the sound of a melting glacier is made available to people if they phone a number that is presented in white neon on the gallery wall alongside photographic images of the glacier itself (see Plates 18 and 19). An excerpt from the recording can be heard via Paterson's website (Paterson 2008). The telephone number makes it possible for the observer to connect in real time with the dynamic and material reality of a melting glacier, either while they are visiting the installation or after they have left the gallery. Although we have a general sense of what 'melting ice' signifies, when it is experienced directly, in the particular, it turns out it does not have a single, fixed identity. Rather, the appearances it presents *depends upon the interested signification through which it is encountered.* The melting ice first becomes a series of particular creaking, cracking, trickling sounds that are audible at the end of a phone. This is the first, sensory aspect of interested signification. It is debatable whether a second, indexical aspect is present. An indexical sign, according to Peirce's definition, functions not through resemblance (e.g. a portrait) or convention (e.g. 'red' to signify 'stop') but through causal connection, e.g. smoke indicating fire. Arguably the sound of a melting iceberg is indexical in that the sound does not *resemble* the ice. The resemblance–index distinction is tied strongly to visual signification. The fact that the sound recording heard through the phone approximates to the sound as heard directly suggests that manipulating the power of ice or sound to have a causal impact elsewhere was not one of Paterson's intentions. But the strength of the work lies in the metaphor it creates between melting ice and a phone call, the third aspect of interested signification. As a sound, melting ice goes beyond any general sense of what we think melting ice is, and draws upon qualities in the sound (creaks, cracks, roars, trickles and other effects that are not so easily described) and the setting in which the sound is performed, in this case at the end of a phone, a situation in which one is accustomed to talking to a friend, a lover or a colleague. The iceberg-as-sound is now heard through the intimacy and other emotions that surround human contact.

What other forms might a melting iceberg adopt as eco-art? One of the arenas of possibility opened by conceptual art is the range of forms art can take and contexts in which it can sit once traditional genres have been rejected, with the suggestion that the work has a heightened autonomous, critical effect by employing forms or occurring in situations not normally associated with art. Criticality comes from the use of unfamiliar forms or situations, the argument has it, on the understanding that they are deployed in ways that put them in a new light or show them to have new effects. While having the sound of a melting glacier at the end of a phone line employs familiar sound recording technologies, i.e. causal interactions that have been established through decades of development in sound recording, a near-infinite fund of possibility remains to be explored in the causal, indexical potential of melting ice. The importance of indexical expression for my aesthetics is that it acknowledges the capacity of one object to act and leave a mark upon another independently of human interests in signification through resemblance and convention. It is recognition of the fact that objects have agency independently of human action. It is primarily discussed in aesthetics in relation to the notion of indexical drawing,[8] and is an area that is ripe for examination in terms of Latour's actor-network theory (Latour 1993, 1999) and Harman's object-oriented ontology (Harman 2005). As Harman demonstrates, metaphor is vital to appreciating the agency of objects (in addition to its role as the third aspect of interested signification), because it provides a mechanism for understanding how the properties of one object can interact with the properties of another to create something that neither object in isolation could anticipate (Harman 2005: 101–24; 141–4). In terms of the value to the ecological aesthetics I am presenting, it results in the production of forms that cannot easily be categorised, at least not in the terms of the two starting objects, and which therefore acquire an allure that makes them and possibly their starting objects new concerns for the viewer.

A work that considers the indexical potential of melting icebergs would look to the kind of setting that allows the meltwater to exert its own agency. One possibility might be the installation of monolithic blocks of ice in a series of commercial or institutional spaces, possibly selected on the basis of their carbon footprint, which are then simply allowed to melt and damage surfaces, furnishings and equipment. The meltwater would disable electronic devices, carry particles of materials it finds on its course, and leave traces of them on any trace-bearing surface, e.g. walls and carpets. The damaged items would not just be left under the heading 'damaged items' but would be documented or explored by artists in ways that pursue alternative, possible indexical or metaphorical possibilities within the objects, and allow them to present appearances that go beyond 'throw away' categories of, for example, 'stained wall', 'sodden carpet', 'short-circuited computer'. The specks, swirls, stains and ripples of colour that might be brought to what was formerly a white wall are ripe for being described in meta-phorical terms of, for example, movement, weight, tension, bodies. Drips of water landing on exposed concrete from a sodden carpet that is suspended in mid-air become very evocative. Are they footsteps? Are they distillations of former footsteps? Do the shifts in tone as the carpet changes from damp to dry make it appear map-like or sky-like? The documentation, in the form of photographs, records, installations, or other forms suggested by the damage, would be displayed in the effected space prior to or as part of the refurbishment process. Thought would be given as to whether the water used is actually from a melted iceberg or whether local tap water would do. Small-scale test-melts would be done to establish whether the different waters leave different traces, and how these differences affected interpretation. Funding would be secured to cover the cost of damage, lost productivity and health and safety administration.

It is more than likely that this will be interpreted as an act of destruc-tion executed solely in the interests of disrupting the activities of com-panies or institutions, resulting in damaged furnishings and equipment, and photographs and records of the damage. However, it is more than this, and the case for the ecological value of the work would be made in approaches to funding bodies and contender host organisations. It is a staged manifestation of the capacity of water to occupy places that most people do not want it to occupy, and to have effects in ways in which most people don't want it to have effects. The damage will obstruct the routine operation of the host organisation, not necessarily as an act of aggression but as an opportunity for staff and audience members to witness the capacity of objects to have a life or adopt a form that is other than the one into which it has been directed by design and manufacture. The effect on the working space with the water in it, and afterwards when artists are exploring the sensory, indexical and metaphorical properties of the damaged objects, would turn the working space into an art venue that not only offers an environmental message (climate change) but also demonstrates the ecological–phenomenological thesis that human being is located within a physical, technological environment that has an agency of its own. It is possible that the project would not get approval beyond a series of controlled, small-scale test-melts, and would instead become the cause of a long series of correspondence in which proposals to stage the project in the offices of selected companies are made, defended, rejected, amended, reconsidered etc. Even then, the value of the preparation and administration should not be looked. Every email and every form has an aesthetic. Such documents include categories that indicate what takes priority, and phrases that have been informed to express an institution's position on a proposal. These too can be regarded as particular, indexical expressions of the power of water.

Example 2: if I am an artist, I will want to make something

For the second example, let us consider how an artist might start given the infinity of possibilities available. It will not have the same *particular* character of the first example, as the predicament in which I am placing artists and ecocritics is one where the nature and scope of eco-art has been hollowed out, made entirely open, turned into an existential question. It is the path that is taken to choosing, forming and classifying the particular that is important, on my approach. I have suggested that, given the possibilities that are open between art and ecology, our condition as Da-seins, beings for whom the world is made manifest in the form of cares or concerns, can provide guidance on the nature and scope of eco-art. If I am an artist, I will want to make some*thing*, and this something will be set within a network of interests and concerns, including contender materials and technologies, and the discourses which surround them. It is an existential choice because art and ecology are concepts whose range is so broad that, when they are combined, no prior, stable meanings are left – for example, painting, sculpture, representation, expression, on the side of art, and nature, landscape, and environment, on the side of ecology – that can act as a point of stability, beyond the fact that we are situated beings. As far as the artist is concerned, it is going to be first and foremost a matter of their concern (repetition intended) in the phenomenological sense that, in their life, they will be inclined towards or directed towards something that is important or significant, something that stands out. This is aesthetics as ecology: in standing out, that something will have to adopt a sensory, bodily or technological form, and that form will have material or technological properties that can act upon other properties in causal, indexical and surprising ways, with the surprise feeding back to bring new, metaphorical properties to the original concern, thereby expanding the ways in which that original concern sits in the world.

So, how do I choose a concern for the purpose of the example? To suggest it is a matter of selecting an item from a shelf misses the point that, from a phenomenological perspective, concerns are always, already active as inclinations and openings that constitute one's being in the world. If the example is to occur from the point of view of the artist, then one might start from my emphasis on the aesthetic, from the something I sense I want to explore, work towards or make. This is not me smuggling in a property from the history of art after I have claimed that its nature is in question after conceptual art, for my concept situates the aesthetic as the process of disclosure whereby all things are made manifest. The main idea behind 'interested signification' is that any object or event does not have a set, intrinsic identity or essential nature. Instead, it will always appear in some form or other depending upon the faculties or interest with which it is approached. In philosophy, this is the millennia-old contest between appearances and things in themselves. Since Democritus and Plato, philosophy has maintained the idea of an object that exists in its own terms, terms that are essential, unchanging and independent of the conditions in which the object finds itself and the modes of perception introduced by a perceiver. Against this are theses from Berkeley and Kant in the eighteenth century onwards to the effect that objects always appear in specific ways according to the sensory faculties or conceptual filters that organise perception, and that concepts judged to be essential or universal are in fact inclined to accommodate the particularity of the senses.[9]

Suppose I was an artist who was also a keen cyclist, and wanted to explore the possibility of cycling as a critical art practice. What form might this take? The particularity of the aesthetic gets to work straight away, for as soon as one starts to consider the prospect, one bumps up against the question of which aspect of cycling is meant: racing, touring, commuting, mountain-biking, family, leisure, social interaction, town planning, or the fact that it is not motoring? There is also the way in which the bicycle, as a technology, changes Da-sein, the state of being in the world. When I am sitting or standing, I am aware of myself as a mass, a weight, positioned at a point, the ground a single, continuous pressure felt through my feet and legs. I can move forward by the distance permitted by the span of my legs. After each leg movement, the ground is there to meet me again, another familiar feeling of counter-pressure. As I move, the scenery changes very slightly, new sections of wall or door or greenery appearing in step with my movement. But when I sit on a bike, the world is no longer a single pressure, whether through two standing legs or one leg as the other is in motion. Instead, pressure is felt through my backside and perineum on the saddle, my hands on the handlebars and my legs on the pedals. The points of contact are also not simple acts of pressure but rather push–pull relationships on the handlebars and the pedals. When I move, when I turn the pedals, there isn't the on–off pressure of footsteps but a continuous movement in my legs, much more of a rising and falling sensation. In keeping with the continuous movement of my legs, I am carried through space in a line, not so much in a state of gliding but one where I am aware of the road as a series of pressures and bumps on scales of gentle–harsh and round–edge felt through the saddle.

One word or concern, 'cycling', opens up into a variety of aesthetic possibilities. One option might be to pay further close attention to the bodily experience of cycling and consider how this might be expressed on a public scale. Alternatively, cycling as an alternative to driving in a car might emerge as prominent, in which case thought could be given to the particularities arising from the difference between cycling and driving. One example might be the space occupied by car parks, and to recreate life-size parking lots on walls in buildings or to reproduce them through large-scale photographs, so that we are made aware of the space that is occupied by a car, and that textures in the tarmac, surface cracks, the worn white lines delineating the space and the oil stains can become objects of new and greater concern.

This might sound as if I am saying that, in terms of eco-art, anything goes. But the response makes two errors. In asserting '*anything* goes', it assumes that I am a detached, floating agent who can choose any aspect of life for the basis of an art work whatsoever, with nothing to act as a guide or an indicator as to what might warrant attention. It essentially ignores the proposal from phenomenology that, as a Da-sein, I am always, already constituted by care, concern and openness, i.e. interests that have the potential to offer direction. Also, in asserting 'anything *goes*', it assumes that I can move entirely smoothly through the network of interests, concerns, materials, technologies and communities, arranging them so they satisfy my intention, when the point of this approach is that all these elements act as a nexus of forces, of which I am a part, with openings, alignments, intersections, redirections and resistances bringing new aspects to light, i.e. allowing cares and concerns to be expanded or transformed through new forms and appearances.

Conclusion

Eco-art poses a problem to classification because its two terms have such broad meaning: after conceptual art, there are no restrictions on the material form art can take, and ecology covers notions of environment, nature, interactions with nature, interconnection and a fundamental, ontological condition of belonging. Rather than try to contain the overwhelming number of relationships and formations that are possible under 'eco-art', I accepted the existential nature of the situation and turned to Heidegger's phenomenology, a forerunner of existentialism. This presents the human as an opening in the world without an essence, whose being is constituted by the always, already active nature of sensation, the body and technology as a series of cares and concerns. What this philosophy supplies is recognition of the fact that we are always, already inclined towards portions of the world as a result of these concerns. Furthermore, it highlights that whatever we choose, reach for or make brings with it its own aesthetic qualities that offer what I termed 'interested signification', made up of: (1) particular, sensory detail; (2) properties that can create surprising effects through their causal interaction with adjacent materials; and (3) a further capacity to surprise through the metaphors that are created between these effects and the original interest. The ecological value of this process, taking 'ecology' in its broadest and oldest sense of belonging, is that objects and concepts that might ordinarily be seen as remote or unrelated to us are shown to have a power and a possibility for expression which can surprise, interrupt or present itself as an alternative to routine, object-directed, goal-directed perception.

One objection to this approach might be the point, often made against aesthetics, that whatever form is presented can be dismissed as just one more image or display or performance. The predicament is arguably becoming worse in the era of the interactive screen, when content can be dismissed with the swipe of a finger. The 'aesthetic' is customarily reserved as the adjective for describing the domain in which art is active critically, and so the political or ecological force of art is in question if an art event or proposition can be disregarded as one more 'whatever'. But on the account I have given here, the aesthetic also qualifies the way in which we are bodily and technologically situated in the world, and the way in which all concepts and concerns can be made particular through the senses. If the lack of care (in the general sense) for ecology or in what art can do in relation to ecology is the problem, then maybe a future eco-art project might have as its concern (in the phenomenological sense) the question of how to make care and its absence the subject of the senses, indexicality and metaphor.

Notes

1　O. Hanfling (1992). 'The problem of definition', in Hanfling (ed.), *Philosophical Aesthetics*. Milton Keynes and Oxford: Open University and Blackwell, pp. 1–40; this reference pp. 7–8.

2　J.D. Hughes, (1985). 'Theophrastus as ecologist', *Environmental Review* 9: 4: 296–306.

3　I have adopted the hyphenated spelling of 'Da-sein' as used by Stambaugh in her recent translation of *Being and Time* (Heidegger 1996). 'It was Heidegger's express wish', she writes, 'that in future translations the word *Dasein* should be hyphenated' (p. xiv; original italics). Heidegger's thinking, Stambaugh continues, was that, with hyphenation, 'the reader will be less prone to assume he or she understands it to refer to "existence" (which is the orthodox translation of *Dasein*) and with that translation surreptitiously bring along all sorts of psychological connotations. It was Heidegger's insight that human being is *uncanny*: we do not know who, or what, that is, although, or perhaps precisely because, we *are* it (Heidegger 1996: xiv; original italics). The hyphen in Da-sein introduces a sense of the uncanny. Rather than having Da-sein remain as a word which refers straightforwardly to human being as a clearly circumscribed thing – to existence or to the subject – the hyphen maintains the reference to us but at the same time makes it other than us. It emphasises that human being is distributed in a way that dualistic, Cartesian, subject–object terminology does not easily accommodate: a 'being there', an entity whose *being* is located and extended *in the world*.

4　For a good definition of *Sorge*, see M. Inwood (1999), *A Heidegger Dictionary*. Oxford: Blackwell, pp. 35–7.

5　However, given Weintraub's investment in the categorisation of eco-art, it is not surprising that her introduction to the survey is an account of what eco-art is and *what it is not*. Some art works that seek to be ecological by considering the interests of *nonhuman* life, she argues, end up doing so in very *human* terms. Nature is approached as 'a medium of exchange, a source of wealth, a repository of resources, and a depository for waste' (Weintraub 2012: 16). Such works, she asserts, are not eco-art. For example, Andy Warhol's 1964 lithograph *Flowers* is disregarded because its production process 'encapsulates the anthropocentric reliance upon commerce and industry' (Weintraub 2012: 11), and Walter De Maria's earth sculpture *Lightning Field* from 1977 is dismissed because the constant restoration work that is needed to maintain its four hundred steel poles after damage from lightning strikes is judged to be in defiance of the decay inherent in ecosystem dynamics (Weintraub 2012: 14). The problem with this distinction, however, is it relies on the idea that 'human' and 'nature' can be neatly separated out. It also fails to consider the critical potential of working with certain technologies to achieve aesthetic effects that call attention to the different ways in which physical forces can manifest themselves.

6   For Peirce's introduction of the concept of an indexical sign, see C.S. Peirce (1982). *The Writings of Charles S. Peirce: A Chronological Edition*, Volume 2, ed. Peirce Edition Project. Bloomington: Indiana University Press, pp. 53–6.

7   The key paper in this, the interaction theory of metaphor, is M.Black (1993). 'More about metaphor', in A. Ortony (ed.), *Metaphor and Thought* Second edition. Cambridge: Cambridge University Press, pp. 19–41.

8   A good account of indexical drawing is given by M. Iversen (2012), 'Index, diagram, graphic trace'. *Tate Papers Issue 18*. Online: www.tate.org.uk/ research/publications/tate-papers/index-diagram-graphic-trace accessed 12 November 2015.

9   For a good introduction to Berkeley's philosophy, read his own work, especially *A Treatise Concerning the Principles of Human Knowledge*, in G. Berkeley (1975). *Philosophical Works; Including the Works on Vision*, ed. M. Ayers. London: Dent. As the builder of a complex philosophical system, Kant is not so easy to read in the original. A good introduction to his epistemology and the place of the senses within it is P. Strawson, (1966), *The Bounds of Sense: An Essay on Kant's Critique of Pure Reason*. London: Methuen. The book is also good on pointing out the similarities and differences between Berkeley and Kant.

References

Brown, A. (2014) *Art and Ecology Now*. London: Thames and Hudson.

Carson, R. (1962) *Silent Spring*. New York: Houghton Mifflin.

Garrard, G. (2012) *Ecocriticism*. Abingdon: Routledge.

Haeckel, E.H. 1866. *Generelle Morphologie der Organismen*. 2 volumes. Berlin: G. Reimer.

Harman, G. (2005) *Guerrilla Metaphysics: Phenomenology and the Carpentry of Things*. Chicago: Open Court.

Heidegger, M. (1996 [1928]) *Being and Time*, trans. J. Stambaugh, New York: State University of New York.

Keller, D.R. and F.B. Golley (2000) 'Introduction: Ecology as a Science of Synthesis', in Keller and Golley (eds), *The Philosophy of Ecology: From Science to Synthesis*. Athens: University of Georgia Press.

Latour, B. (1993) *We Have Never Been Modern*, trans. C. Porter. Cambridge, MA: Harvard University Press.

Latour, B. (1999) *Pandora's Hope: Essays on the Reality of Science Studies*. Cambridge, MA: Harvard University Press.

Miles, M. (2014) *Eco-aesthetics: Art, Literature and Architecture in a Period of Climate Change*. London: Bloomsbury.

Morton, T. (2007) *Ecology Without Nature: Rethinking Environmental Aesthetics*. Cambridge, MA: Harvard University Press.
Morton, T. (2010) *The Ecological Thought*. Cambridge, MA: Harvard University Press.
Naess, A. (1973) 'The Shallow and the Deep, Long-range Ecology Movement'. *Inquiry* 16: 95–100.
Paterson, K. (2008) *Vatnajökull (the Sound of)*. Online: http://katiepaterson.org/vatnajokull/ accessed 6 January 2016.
Pignarre, P. and I. Stengers (2011) *Capitalist Sorcery: Breaking the Spell*, trans. A. Goffey. Basingstoke: Palgrave Macmillan.
Plato (1987) *Theaetetus*, trans. R. Waterfield. London: Penguin.
Weintraub, L. (2012) *To Life: Eco Art in Pursuit of a Sustainable Planet*. Berkeley: University of California Press.

10

Signs and sentiment in British wildlife art

William Welstead

It can be argued that depictions of wildlife are among the oldest extant subject matters for human creativity, going back to the cave paintings of prehistoric times. This chapter is concerned with contemporary wildlife art in Britain covering the period from the formation of the Society of Wildlife Artists (SWLA) in 1964 to the present time. Over that time a considerable body of work has been produced by SWLA artists and exhibited in the Society's annual exhibitions. This chapter considers the relevance of this creative work in ecocritical discourse, both in collaboration with literary and other creative genres and considered in its own right.

In *The Wildlife Artist's Handbook*, Jackie Garner (2013) urges those aspiring to be wildlife artists to be 'an artist first and a scientist second'. She stresses the twin pressure that these artists will face from 'wildlife enthusiasts [who] can sometimes be very critical' of images that do not convey a great deal of scientific information, and the dismissal of their work 'by the art establishment as illustration at best and "pretty pictures of animals" at worst' (2013: 13). In particular, it is evident that the picture-viewing public expects wildlife art to have a denoted meaning that relates to recognisable species. There are signs that wildlife artists are trying to break free from this straitjacket of denotation, towards a less representational form of their art. In this chapter the way that wildlife artists navigate the twin pulls of science and art is explored in the context of the task of ecocritics to read cultural works with and against discourses from ecology and environmental science.

To celebrate its fiftieth anniversary in 2014, the Society published *The Natural Eye: art book one* listing its 67 full members and illustrating examples of many of these artists' work. The SWLA annual exhibition, which since 2011 has also been called *The Natural Eye*, is open to any 'artist whose work is inspired by nature' and features all art media with the exception of photography (2013: 117). For Harriet Mead (1969–), who was elected president of the SWLA in 2009, '[a]rt can be a powerful tool for conservation, it can breathe life onto the bones of research by reminding us exactly why we should care about the increasingly gloomy news of habitat loss, climate change and extinction' (SWLA 2013: 9). This art book is a useful guide to the current practice of wildlife artists in Britain, both on their home patch and on excursions around the globe. In particular, it is an indication of how wildlife artists can use art to reconnect people to nature.

Eric Ennion (1900–81), who with Robert Gillmor (1936–) founded the SWLA, was an influential figure among wildlife artists. Although self-taught as an artist, he was himself a charismatic teacher of both artists and those interested in natural history, particularly of birds. At first he worked as a country doctor taking over his father's practice in Burwell, Cambridgeshire, but at the end of the Second World War having sold his practice, Ennion took the opportunity to become the first warden of what was the pioneering centre of the Field Studies Council based at Flatford Mill in Suffolk.[1] Here he ran courses in both art and natural history. In 1950 he purchased Monks' House between Bamburgh and Seahouses in Northumberland which for the next decade he ran as a bird-ringing (banding) observatory and study centre. The painting of a little stint at Plate 20 is from that period.

This small sandpiper is one of several small brown waders, some common and others rare, that require attention to detail to resolve into a species. Ennion captures that detail perfectly, but he also gives the bird a personality. We can see it moving purposefully in search of small invertebrates along the tideline, as this migrant bird has to if it is to replenish its fat store for the onward flight. For Tim Dee:

> Ennion was a proper birdman, a seasoned looker, and one reason why his pictures still seem fresh and valuable is that he repeatedly caught the ineffable this-ness of the birds that he painted, their quintessence, instress or jizz. (2013: 29)

The use by Dee of Gerard Manley Hopkins's term 'instress' rather than 'inscape' shows how Ennion's images offer us so much more than a faithful representation of the bird. In discussion of how Hopkins himself used these terms, Parham concludes that:

> Due to its double sided quality the concept of instress offered, simultaneously, the reinforcement of a concept of nature analogous to the ecological notion of dialectical interdependence – i.e. the idea that living forms are

'upheld' (sustained) by force or energy – and an aesthetic principle designed to convey that truth. (2010: 131)

The little stint's need to satisfy its energy requirements by foraging on the shore is conveyed to us through the aesthetic qualities of the painting. In contrast, the term 'jizz', used by birdwatchers to describe those key signs that denote the particular species, is closer in meaning to Hopkins's 'inscape' where the emphasis is placed on form. Ennion's painting is true in its denotation of the jizz of the little stint, but also conveys the energy of the bird as it works its way along the tideline.

The painting, like many that he did at this time, has a simple background, sometimes using a wash, but in this case the background is the paper itself with just a few pencil lines to anchor it to the beach. This painting, executed in thickly applied water colour and pencil, is on the inside surface of a used brown envelope. Ennion found that this recycled resource had just the right texture for this type of painting. The address and postage stamp are still on the back of the picture.

These images are instantly recognisable to the experienced field naturalist. They carry sufficient visual clues or signs to denote the species represented, but at the same time they are highly atmospheric. They also provide starting points for us to wander off on chains of connotations that complement our own experience in the field. These are not paintings for those birders whose only interest is to complete the identification of a bird to a standard where they can tick a list and move on. These are images for people who allow the birds to have a personality and agency of their own. In that respect they break down the human-species barrier and take us back to a time when field-craft and unobtrusive presence in the environment for days on end, rather than being corralled by visitor management, were the best ways to get close enough to an animal to engage with its personality.

Coming as he did from the prewar body of countrymen-naturalists, experiential involvement with nature through close encounters in the field was the foundation for Ennion's practice. Many of those who came under his influence at Flatford Mill and Monks' House were to go on to achieve eminence in ecology and biology, as well as in wildlife art, or at least to emerge trained to play a part in the development of citizen science through bird ringing (banding), recording and field survey. Artists who fell under his influence included Mary Newcomb (1922–2008), who joined him at Flatford Mill as a student helper, and John Busby (1928–2015) for whom meeting with Ennion at Monks' House resulted in his decision to follow a career as a wildlife artist. Peter Evans (1937–2001), who was to go on to have a distinguished academic career at Durham University, started to formulate his ideas on energy balance and optimal foraging strategies in shorebirds while resident at Monks' House.

Ennion's classic account of a wetland habitat, *Adventurers Fen*, illustrated by his field sketches, conveys the thrill of discovery that comes from watching the same area closely over several seasons (Ennion 1996 [1942]). These drawings and some simple paintings printed in monochrome had an immediacy that refines denotation to its bare essentials, for these are creatures not posing for portraits but going about their business that lead us to wonder what happened next.

This patch of fen close to Cambridge owes its name to the original investors, or 'adventurers', who under charter from Charles I brought experts from the Netherlands to drain the fen. Since that time the land has been exploited according to the commercial imperatives of the day. Ennion charts the move away from fen industries, including peat cutting, to agriculture in the early part of the twentieth century, and then through agricultural decline in the 1920s, reversion to fen in the 1930s. Ennion followed its development during this transition to fen as it was reinhabited by typical fenland species of birds and moths. His involvement with this place came to an abrupt end in 1941 when once more it was reclaimed to grow sugar beet, of which Ennion remarked that '[n]o crop is less in sympathy with English landscape than this alien' (1996 [1942]: Preface). Despite this loss he was phlegmatic and ends the book on a positive note:

> It [the kingfisher] would not worry overmuch to find its living gone, the pools dried out, the fen laid bare. There are little fish and broken rails to sit on in plenty of other places. It must be so. Nature cannot let sentiment usurp her laws: that is for us to feel. Adventurers Fen in all its loveliness has gone but nature goes on elsewhere. (1942: 67)

It was this confidence that there would be other places where the retreat of agriculture would allow nature to recover in some other place and time that was to be shattered by the publication of Rachel Carson's *Silent Spring* (1962). If such loveliness is to remain, nature has to be given a helping hand rather than relying on periodic fluctuations in agricultural practice to make places where wildlife can thrive. Wetland can be recreated in a relatively short time, over say decades rather than centuries, by controlling of water levels and checking the growth of vegetation. Both artists and conservationists are drawn to such wildlife-rich habitat that is still within our capability to restore and which further has the potential to mitigate some of the risks associated with climate change. Although Adventurers Fen was, at least for a time, lost physically, it persisted in Ennion's imagination. This land has now been acquired by the National Trust, which plans to restore it to fen. Ennion's writing and images have played a significant role in reinforcing our affection for such diversity.

Careful and prolonged observation and sketching of animals within their natural setting laid the foundation for Ennion to collaborate with Niko Tinbergen and Hugh Falkus in their book on animal behaviour, *Signals for Survival* (1970). This book, which is lavishly illustrated with photographs as well as Ennion's drawings and paintings, had the scholarly aim of introducing people to ethology. Tinbergen was to go on to share the 1973 Nobel Prize for Physiology or Medicine with Karl von Frisch and Konrad Lorenz for their studies 'devoted to the existence of genetically programmed behaviour patterns'.[2] Ethology as the study of animal behaviour depends on our ability to interpret the signs that animals make to one another. Ethologists act as interpreters of this *language* as explained by Julian Huxley's introduction to Konrad Lorenz's *On Aggression*:

> He has initiated a new interpretation of vertebrate behaviour. This is composed of 'behaviour units', just as anatomy is composed of structural units. These have a genetic basis, and in the course of evolutionary time have been modified by Darwinian natural selection to act as specific signals for communicating emotional states. (1967: vii)

Signals for Survival considers a single species, the lesser black-backed gull (*Larus fuscus*), with the images made in a breeding colony on Walney Island opposite Barrow-in-Furness. The cover image by Ennion is of an adult gull with three chicks begging for food. One is pecking the red-spot on the adult's lower bill, which Tinbergen's experiments had shown to happen even when chicks are hatched in an incubator and presented with a crude model with a red spot. As there would have been no time for this behaviour to be learned, the inference was that this signal (the red spot) elicited an instinctive response. The background to this painting is the industrial landscape of Barrow-in-Furness, reminding us that this is no isolated wilderness.

This image is significant in that it is very much a scientifically accurate depiction of animal communication, which in ethology is given a Neo-Darwinian explanation that would satisfy wildlife enthusiasts, even if others would criticise it for being reductionist. But it is also a work of art with considerable merit that has a cultural meaning to us as viewers. Biosemiotics has emerged over the last half century as a discipline that attempts to integrate the study of biology with that of semiotics. It extends the discipline from its basis in the study of human languages to communication between all living creatures.

Ecocritics are increasingly interested in the potential for biosemiotics to illuminate ecocritical discourse. The topic was the subject of a special edition of the journal *Green Letters* in 2015 (*Green Letters* 19:3, November 2015). In this issue Brier discusses how C.S. Peirce, the founder of semiotics, opened the way for 'living organisms [to] be described from a natural scientific as well as phenomenological-hermeneutic humanistic type of knowledge system' (2015: 280–1). It is not what we perceive but the meanings we give to that perception that are the objects of experience (2015: 286).

> Peirce develops a theory of human knowledge based on the logical quanti-ties of extension and intension associated with the symbol that is so vital for his semiotics. Thus, Peirce develops his theory of information directly from his semiotics and its most important species of sign, namely, the symbol. For Peirce, plants and animals are constrained mainly, or nearly so, to icon and indexical sign use. (2015: 287)

In *Signals for Survival* we are concerned with the accurate scientific description of what is claimed to be instinctive behaviour. However, we are also concerned with how Ennion's art work has a meaning for us that is separate from its scientific interpretation. Kalevi Kull, in his 2003 paper discussing Thomas Sebeok's pioneering role in integrating semiot-ics with biology in the new discipline of biosemiotics, notes that:

> In addition to specifically biosemiotics problems, Sebeok also touches, in some of his writings, on the area of representations of (and approaches to) nature in cultures [...]. This field, nowadays known as (cultural) *eco-semiotics*, should be taken as different from biosemiotics, because it does not deal with biological problems and belongs rather to the semiotics of culture. (original emphasis) (Kull 2003: 54)

Where an image depicts the signifying behaviour of an animal that elicits a response from an interpretant of the same species, it will have relevance both in terms of the biosemiotics of the signs given and the resulting behaviour of the animals depicted, and in terms of the ecose-miotics of the signs through which we find cultural meanings in the art itself. The next artist embodies both sets of signs in her work.

Wildlife artist Kim Atkinson (1962–) is based on the Lleyn Peninsula in North Wales.[3] She creates images outside or working in the studio. Atkinson has formal art training, but from an early age growing up on Bardsey Island in Wales she had daily contact with nature. Although the creatures and plants in her paintings are clearly recognisable for what they are, the overall effect is more abstract and impressionistic. The picture considered here, *Mediterranean Gull Displaying on Island 25* (Plate 21), was painted in July 1998 and exhibited in the Visitor Centre at the Royal Society for the Protection of Birds (RSPB) Minsmere Nature Reserve at the end of that year. For this exhibition the caption was changed from Kim Atkinson's original choice, as inscribed on the back, of *Mediterranean Gull Behaving Territorially*.

Regular art exhibitions are held in the tearoom at the reserve, with the usual format being that a group of artists is asked to interpret a theme based on wildlife that any visitor might see during a visit. The painting discussed here was produced from a few days Atkinson spent sketching on the reserve prior to a joint SWLA/RSPB group event, organised by Hilary Welch, the wife of the then warden Geoff Welch (SWLA 2013: 12). For this project six or so artists gathered together, to collaborate in the production of an artists' book. The event was organised so that, first, the artists brainstormed ideas as a group, then each wrote text from which a painting would develop. These texts were then swapped so that each artist went off to draw in the field with someone else's text. At the end of the week the group published a limited edition screen-printed book of the expedition; the text was included as an insert in the book, so that it can be read as an extended caption to the work.[4]

The success of the Minsmere reserve could be taken as endorsement of Ennion's optimism that nature will always find a place. The flat landscape behind this Suffolk beach was allowed to flood during the Second World War to discourage any invasion force from landing. In 1947 avocets, after an absence of more than a century as a British breeding bird, were found breeding here and at Havergate Island further down the coast. Although the growth of reeds discouraged them from breeding the following year, they soon returned when the surface was scraped to form the shallow lagoons they need to feed. While it was an accident that led to their return, it was the intensive management of water levels and reed removal that allowed them to remain.

One of the most popular routes through the reserve takes visitors on a high path over a reed-bed, where they will strain to see bearded tits, then along the beach behind the dunes, perhaps pausing to look at nesting little terns or stonechats, before coming to the path to the hides. As they get closer, they will hear a cacophony of calling birds; some people will be able to recognise the different calls, but to most visitors it will be confusing clamour. Once in the hide, they will settle down in the murmur of chatter from other watchers and take in the expanse of water and shingle islands in front of them. This is the view that has been captured in Kim Atkinson's painting. Five species of bird are illustrated: Mediterranean gull, black-headed gull, avocet, coot and moorhen. All are British breeding birds, although the Mediterranean gulls of the caption are at the extreme edge of their range. Kim Atkinson's original title of *Mediterranean gull behaving territorially* points to a chain of connoted meanings about the interpretation of bird behaviour, for which prior texts include the writings of pioneer ethologists Julian Huxley, Niko Tinbergen and Konrad Lorenz.

Atkinson is reading the signs from the posture and movement of the gull in the centre of the picture, as a demonstration that the gull is holding a territory, with the added connoted meaning that breeding is likely, and the right-hand bird is sitting on what might be a nest. The implication is that this artist is familiar with the behaviour patterns that denote a territorial display. It seems likely that she has acquired this knowledge through a combination of reading and field observation. For a visual artist, trained in the language of lines, the practice in ethology texts of illustrating behaviour visually, with sketches and photographs, would make them immediately accessible. This aspect of the picture records the signs made by the birds and the response that other individuals make to that display.

These signs, which are recorded impressionistically rather than with full scientific accuracy, are then given a cultural meaning as part of this work of art. Sebeok's distinction between biosemiotics and ecosemiotics is illustrated by this shift to the signifying practices in human visual culture. Each bird is shown in sufficient detail to denote its species, and would therefore qualify as an *icon* in Peirce's terminology. The two Mediterranean gulls, one in the centre and the other on the extreme right, which are the stars of this picture, are rare in Britain, with breeding success in Suffolk, in terms of the fledging of young, being confirmed only in 1999.[5] They are larger than the closely related black-headed gulls, have red beaks, a black rather than a chocolate-brown head, with the black coming further down the neck. Atkinson depicts all these features, together with the distinctive behaviour that make up the jizz of this species.

Taken together, the richness of species in the picture carries a connoted meaning of biodiversity, or in Peirce's terminology an *index* of biodiversity. For the more romantic visitor, the prior text that will come to mind is of the story of the Garden of Eden. Through careful sighting of the hide, and the use of binoculars and telescopes, it seems that people are right within the garden, but this is an illusion, for, if it is the Garden of Eden, it is after the fall, with the humans firmly fenced out of a paradise into which the view is restricted by the narrow window.

The idea that Eden can be recovered by preservationists has troubled ecocritics such as Carolyn Merchant, who questions whether such a recovery is possible (1996: 132–59).

Ecologists have been contesting how best to measure biodiversity since the term came into common usage after the Rio Earth Summit in 1992. Species richness is one facet but is far from synonymous with biodiversity. Gaston discusses how scale, time and status of species have also to be taken into account (1996: 77–113). The visual depiction of species richness in this image is therefore only one way in which we can read along the signifying chain to arrive at the abstract concept of bio-diversity, which then in Peircean terms becomes a *symbol*. In exploring contestations over biodiversity protection in forest policy in Finland, Hiedanpää and Bromley make the point that 'semiosis is "good to think with"' (2012: 357). In particular, they consider the emergence of new concepts and values through the application of Peircean semiotics:

> The theory must enable participants to grasp the intertwined roles of imagination, language and persuasion in the creation and emergence of general ideas. These aspects enable the emotional, energetic and logical interpretants to guide development toward potentially feasible possibili-ties and building blocks. The emergence of a new idea – and commitment to act accordingly – is an essential property of all inventions and innova-tions. (2012: 372–3)

The physical energy and competition implied in Atkinson's image have an echo in the contested view of what biodiversity means and how we can perceive it. While biodiversity is a policy objective for the RSPB, the artist has not manipulated the image to stress this factor. During the breeding season all these species can often be seen in the single view. The connotations we as viewers draw from the image depend on our own signifying practices and sentiments.

Management of this reserve is designed to present good views of birds through the narrow slot at the front of the hide. It may be that Atkinson has chosen the elongated frame for this picture to reflect this side-to-side view. The hide brings people close to the birds and most have binoculars or telescopes making for an even closer experience. For the visitor hoping to get close to wildlife, the rigorous management of habitat to improve the view and the tight control of visitor movements have to be unobtrusive enough to preserve the illusion that this is wild nature. The focus in the picture is on the interaction of birds on this single island, only a small area of water is shown to denote that it is an island and no sky is visible, nor are the reed-beds beyond the lagoon and the trees on the horizon.

Atkinson's painting captures the experience of confusion, diversity and abundance that is a feature of the Minsmere experience. It is a 'noisy' picture, in that the black-headed gulls are all calling in response to the Mediterranean gull's display, reflecting the range of sensory experiences in a reserve visit. Although the picture is a snapshot of action from a dynamic sequence, there are sufficient visual clues for us to read 'what happens next'. The movement of the gull to the left, already away from the centre of the picture means that we will have to adjust our own line of sight to keep it in view. A prior knowledge of the reserve in July would leave the visitor with an impression of noise and activity. The picture is therefore very suggestive of the emotional response brought on by this attack on the senses. However, given the extension of bird identification from anatomy into the whole pattern of behaviour, call and distinctive signs that make up jizz, it is difficult for a wildlife artist to let the signifier escape from what Eagleton, in discussing poetry, calls 'its grim communicative labours' (2007: 58). In addition, ecological discourse requires that species are shown within their habitat to denote the part each plays in the ecosystem. With such a heavy burden of denotation imposed by reliance on prior texts from biology and ecology, it must be questioned whether wildlife art can aspire to be eco-poetic. The richness and variety of ecological discourse that can flow from this image does, however, leave the viewer with a very broad choice of cognitive and emotional responses. Further, it should be noted that recognition of jizz is as much experiential and affective as denotative. Linda France in her poem 'Jizz' shows how to gather the signs through an immersive encounter in the field:

> Stay a while with the stretch
>
> of it, watching the way it lets
> itself go into a world of sky,
>
> releases its wings and song,
> careless of what you make it.
>
> (Lines 6–10, France 2010: 86)

A full discussion of the potential for wildlife art to be considered eco-poetic should take account of how artists learn to feel as well as to see the subjects of their work.

At the front of the picture, a line of spear-shaped plants provides a vertical structure that draws our attention upwards. These plants are a central part of the composition of the picture that reflects the language of visual art. They are horsetails, which have an important place in the discourse of evolution, where they represent an ancient taxon, which predates the evolution of modern flowering plants.[6] The plants are present here to denote the type of habitat that surrounds the island.

The red colouring of the shingle island provides a striking contrast with the white and black birds, and the artist has had to position the red bills of the Mediterranean gulls so that they do not disappear into the background. This colouring, which is an important feature of the composition of the painting, has a basis in material reality. The annual sea blite is a fleshy plant of shingle areas of saltmarsh that is closely related to the edible samphire (glasswort). At first this plant is a glaucous green colour, which gradually turns red, but the depiction of the area as continuous colour does not provide a clear enough denotation to identify this plant from the image alone, and both artist and viewer must rely on prior knowledge to associate the colour with a plant.

Kim Atkinson's picture works as an art object, in that its formal composition leads our gaze to the central part of the image of a displaying Mediterranean gull. The circle of black-headed gulls, each one calling out in protest, focuses our attention on the centre of the action, as do the vertical lines of the horsetails, which draw our attention up-and-down to counteract the side-to-side tendency brought on by the elongated shape of the frame. The image has connotations of biodiversity that can lead us into the imagery of the Garden of Eden. However, the underlying menace and dramatic tension of threatening black-headed gulls means that this is not a romantic image. Most nesting attempts result in failure that is only compensated for by the longevity of the adult birds, allowing them to try again next year. Atkinson brings her own prior reading of bird behaviour and ecology to this picture, which, given the potential for further connoted meanings for each of the individual species portrayed, allows viewers considerable scope to bring their own prior texts to an experience of the work. The picture fits within the overall narrative of the RSPB, in providing visitors with yet another sensory experience to round off their day.

Wildlife artists in Britain have always been supportive of efforts to conserve wild nature. Since 1990 there has been a formal outlet for this concern through the Artists for Nature Foundation, which was formed in the Netherlands to bring together groups of European wildlife artists to portray the beauty of a selected area as an instrument of nature conservation. The first group of such artists to work in Britain came together in 2004 and 2005 to create work inspired by the Great Fen project south of Peterborough, which is to create 3,700 hectares of traditional fenland habitat over a fifty-year timescale. The art work from the thirty artists involved in this exercise is illustrated in *The Great*

Fen (Gerrard 2006). Although this is a handsome art book, it includes chapters on the history of the area since the last ice age, the philosophy of the project and hopes for what will come in the future.

This project, which builds on the fenland management skills described by Ennion in *Adventurers Fen*, also recognises that the management of small reserves is unduly expensive and does not provide the resilience that will be necessary to mitigate the effects of climate change. Landscape-scale conservation allows for rewilding at a much more natural pace.

> Rather than focussing heavily on species and habitats, attention can be placed on processes, allowing the landscape to gently reassert itself. For parts of the Great Fen, large herbivores such as cattle and horses will be allowed to graze much more naturally than they do in traditional nature reserves, spending their whole lives out on the Fen, living off the vegetation available. This more natural management can create a diversity of habitats and vegetation heights, which will be of great value for wildlife and very attractive to visitors. (Gerrard 2006: 141)

Like Adventurers Fen, the area covered by the Great Fen was originally drained by Dutch engineers under charter from Charles I. The concept of rewilding being trialled here, which also draws on ideas developed in the Netherlands, depends on the hypothesis that much of the nature-rich landscape in Europe was produced by, now extinct, large herbivores making clearings in the closed canopy of the forest. Frans Vera at Oostvaarderplassen in the Netherlands has introduced Konik ponies, red deer and Heck cattle as being the nearest modern equivalents to maintain such an open landscape. Such is the complexity of the issues raised that the journal *British Wildlife* produced a supplement to bring together alternative views about naturalistic grazing and rewildling in Britain (2009). Papers in this supplement discuss rewilding using the Vera concepts, raise questions about whether such landscapes are really wild, defend traditional pastoral farming based on transhumance and explore the potential for carnivores such as wolves to influence the habitat. It is plain that the term rewilding covers many competing views about both its objectives and how best to achieve them.

The artists assembling to create images for the Great Fen project did so at a time when not only was the landscape about to change but the ideas that underlie these changes were still hotly contested. Not least is the question of what a natural landscape should look like. While Harris (2009: 3–15) has made the case for the role of American wildlife art in its depiction of large herbivores and wilderness as being central to the formation of national identity, the position in the Great Fen is much more confused. Here there is no grand narrative supporting an English identity, rather there are competing narratives about the value of wildness, diversity and resilience to climate change. The competing narratives about how images and texts of landscape and nature have contributed to the construction of Scottish national identity are different again and are not addressed in this chapter.

The thirty artists whose work is illustrated in *The Great Fen* have brought a wide variety of styles, some realist, others more abstract. The images in this book include those from sketchbooks, fully worked up paintings, collages and sculpture. The illustrations are arranged loosely around chapters that discuss the background to the project and where it might go in the future. The predominant land use at the start of this project is for arable cultivation by small family-run farms. Images in the chapter on 'Fenland People' include portraits of farmers, the jumble of farm buildings and abandoned structures from the old fen. Jonathan Yule's watercolour *Ploughing with Lapwing and Hare* (Gerrard 2006: 29) shows two men operating a small tractor in a field of vegetables, with two lapwings and a hare for company. There is some structure in this landscape with trees on the horizon and over it is the big East Anglian sky. In this image the arable practice is more in the pastoral tradition of small farms and non-intensive methods than the intensive monocultures illustrated by the next artist.

In contrast Carry Ackroyd (1953–) makes intensive cultivation the dominant theme in her ink and watercolour painting *A Corner of the Oasis* that illustrates the chapter on Woodwalton Fen National Nature Reserve (Gerrard 2006: 48). Intruding into this scene at the bottom of the image is a small corner of the reserve, against the background of regular fields, making a strong contrast between the rich biodiversity of the area managed for nature against the almost sterile arable. In line with her normal practice, the sky is reduced to a narrow margin at the top of the picture. In her art book celebrating the poetry of John Clare (Ackroyd 2009), she explains that portrayal of the sky as a narrow strip is out of contrariness in reaction to people expressing the view that all there was worth commenting on in the East Anglian landscape was its wonderful skies (2009: 11). She paints with a naive style that places different species across the landscape as signifiers of diversity. The birds and insects are recognisable as distinct species, but their role is to support the composition and to provide us with an overall impression of biodiversity.

Woodwalton Fen is at present isolated from Home Fen to the north and both will be incorporated into the new Great Fen, so that in time the diversity of birds and insects in this corner will extend across the whole area, thereby increasing the resilience of these species in the face of climate change. Woodwalton Fen has a special place in nature conservation in Britain. It was bought in 1910 as his own personal nature reserve by Charles Rothschild (1877–1923), who even at that early date was concerned that the rich biodiversity of such places was being lost. An earlier purchase of Wicken Fen in 1899 was given to the National Trust to become Britain's first nature reserve. He went on to found in 1919 the Society for the Promotion of Nature Reserves for Britain and Empire, which was the forerunner of the umbrella organisation for County Wildlife Trusts, now known as the Royal Society of Wildlife Trusts. These two fen reserves carry the founding narratives of English nature conservation in the same way that Yellowstone and Yosemite do for the American national parks. That this is so emphasises the difference between the soaring scale and wilderness narratives associated with American national identity and the more pastoral and small-scale nature of the English reserves. The task of artists in support of the Great Fen is to reimagine what these small-scale wilderness areas would be like if they could be enlarged to a landscape scale.

In her book of images drawing on John Clare, *'Natures Powers & Spells'*, Ackroyd adds this poet's words to her paintings. Like Clare when he was lamenting enclosure, she has been strongly influenced by loss of once common sights as a result of agricultural intensification. One serigraph 'Those Small Birds that Sing to Me' incorporates Clare's poem 'The lamentation of Round-Oak waters' into images of arable fields with just a hedgerow in the foreground rich with an improbable concentration of singing birds (Ackroyd 2009: 25). Like Clare, this artist's sadness at what is lost is balanced by joy at what remains. In the next painting, the perspective is brought down to earth as the artist has a close encounter in a fenland ditch.

In her oil on paper *Green Painting* in *The Great Fen* (Gerrard 2006: 114), Kim Atkinson offers a series of close-up images of dragonflies and vegetation. This painting is used to introduce the chapter on 'Wildlife of the ditches'. As its title suggests the colour is predominantly green, but much of the background is the black of fen mud. The painting is arranged as a series of rectangular images in a grid; some continue the image across rectangles, either vertically or horizontally, but others do not. Rather than painting a whole page of vertical reeds, she has framed the picture with images in successive grids that give some indication of the vertical structure of a *Phragmites* reed-bed, with the flowering heads all arranged in the direction of the wind at the top of the image. The centre of the painting has images in grids that explore the biodiversity of the ditch as different fen plants grow out of the water, with some rectangular sections toward the bottom of the picture depicting a surface with duckweed.

This abstract treatment of the subject brings the viewer right into the ditch. There is no long view and the focus is on the three dragonflies clinging to the vertical stems. Ecologists know that, when they get up this close, they will begin to perceive the potential of ditches as hiding places for secretive birds and habitat for a rich invertebrate community. It was this intimacy that Ennion celebrated in *Adventurers Fen* and it represents what Harriet Mead regards as important, which is 'that the artist understands their subject' (SWLA 2013: 8).

All the art works discussed here show artists with an intimate experiential knowledge of wild nature and an understanding of where this knowledge fits in scientific discourse. All the images denote at least some scientific fact, either to record signs that have behavioural significance for the individuals of the species depicted or to show those that allow us to make an accurate identification of those species. The works were all produced in response to what was happening in these environments, so as to convey narratives that acknowledge the value systems of British nature conservation. These artists have also followed artistic conventions so that their works have a place in our cultural response to the world around us. The concern of wildlife artists to make their own way in the face of demands for scientific accuracy from some viewers and for artistic values from others echoes common discourses among ecocritics. The dynamic nature of many of the images opens the way for the use of a biosemiotics model to explore the ethology displayed and shows how we recognise the jizz of a particular species. It also opens the way for an ecosemiotics model to be used to explore how wildlife art contributes to the construction of cultural meanings concerning nature, wildness and climate change. The overall conclusion is that wildlife art is a rich body of work that would merit further investigation by ecocritics.

Acknowledgements

I am grateful to the Estate of Eric Ennion and to Kim Atkinson for permission to reproduce the paintings discussed in this chapter. I am also grateful to Kim Atkinson for agreeing to an interview with me during my PhD research and for subsequent discussion of her work, and to Bob Walthew for his helpful comments on an early draft of this chapter.

Notes

1　Biographical details are from the Eric Ennion website www.ericennion.com/ accessed 7 October 2015.
2　Nobel Media AB 2014. www.nobelprize.org/nobel_prizes/medicine/laureates/ 1973/presentation-speech.html accessed 14 October 2015.
3　Discussion of this painting draws on previous work in William Welstead (2012), '"Braided Narratives": an ecocritical reading of contemporary Welsh poetry in English', unpublished PhD thesis, Aberystwyth University.
4　Interview with Kim Atkinson 30 June 2011.
5　Steve Piotrowski (2003) *Birds of Suffolk*. London: Christopher Helm (178).
6　A *taxon* is any taxonomic category such as species, genus, class etc.

References

Ackroyd, Carry (2009) *'Natures Powers & Spells': Landscape Change, John Clare and Me*. Peterborough: Langford Press.

Branson, Andrew (ed.) (2009) 'Naturalistic Grazing and Re-wilding in Britain: Perspectives from the Past and Future Direction', *British Wildlife* 20:5 (special supplement), June.

Brier, Søren (2015) 'Cybersemiotics and the Reasoning Powers of the Universe: Philosophy of Information in a Semiotic-systemic Transdisciplinary Approach', *Green Letters: Studies in Ecocriticism* 19(3): 280–92.

Dee, Tim (2013) *Four Fields*. London: Vintage.

Eagleton, Terry (2007) *How to Read a Poem*. Oxford: Blackwell.

Ennion, E.A.R. (1996 [1942]) *Adventurers Fen*. New edition. Cambridge: Colt Books.

France, Linda (2010) *You Are Her*. Todmorden: Arc.

Garner, Jackie (2013) *The Wildlife Artist's Handbook*. Marlborough: Crowood Press.

Gaston, Kevin J. (1996) 'Species Richness: Measure and Measurement', in Gaston (ed.), *Biodiversity: A Biology of Numbers and Differences*. Oxford: Blackwell.

Gerrard, Chris (text) (2006) *The Great Fen: Artists for Nature in England*. Peterborough: Langford Press.

Harris, Adam Duncan (2009) *Wildlife in American Art: Masterworks from the National Museum of Wildlife Art*. Norman: University of Oklahoma Press.

Hiedanpää, Juha and Daniel W. Bromley (2012) 'Contestations over Biodiversity Protection: Considering Peircean Semiosis', *Environmental Values* 21: 357–78.

Huxley, Julian (1967 [1963]) 'Introduction', to Konrad Lorenz, *On Aggression*. London: Methuen.

Kull, Kalevi (2003) 'Thomas Sebeok: Mister (Bio)semiotics', *Cybernetics and Human Knowing* 10:1: 47–60.

Merchant, Carolyn (1996) 'Reinventing Eden: Western Culture as Recovery Narrative', in William Cronon (ed.) *Uncommon Ground: Rethinking the Human Place in Nature*. New York and London: W.W. Norton, pp. 132–59.
Parham, John (2010) *Green Man Hopkins: Poetry and the Victorian Ecological Imagination*. Amsterdam and New York: Rodopi.
Society of Wildlife Artists (2013) *The Natural Eye: Art Book One*. Cley: Red Hare Publishing.
Tinbergen, Niko and Hugh Falkus, drawings by Eric Ennion (1970) *Signals for Survival*. Oxford: Clarendon Press.

11

Symphonic pastorals redux

Aaron S. Allen

Ecocriticism began as an endeavour rooted in text. Ecomusicology extends it to the realm of sound. For musicology, the genre or idea of the symphony is laden with prestige; for ecocriticism, the pastoral has similar stature and is a genre or mode central to the discipline. In the concise juxtaposition of these two terms, I illustrate ecomusicology, which connects ecocritical and musicological scholarship, and further outline a brief critical history of selected symphonies in relation to the pastoral. I argue that symphonies – ostensibly a textless genre of music conceived as abstract – can relate ideas about nature. Such connections between disciplines, approaches and materials contribute to the larger effort in the environmental (post)humanities to break down humans' problematic and self-destructive nature–culture binary.

The symphony as 'absolute music'?

A popular misunderstanding of the symphony is that the genre lacks the meanings conveyed in texted music such as songs and choruses. The idea of the symphony as 'absolute music' – i.e. 'abstract' or 'pure' sound, music for its own sake, in contrast to the narrativity of 'programme music' – began in the middle of the nineteenth century with the debates between Richard Wagner and Eduard Hanslick (Bonds 2014), although it is particularly notable in the thought of the twentieth-century critics Donald Tovey, Leonard Bernstein and Carl Dahlhaus.[1] Regarding Beethoven's Sixth Symphony (*Pastoral*), which I discuss below, Tovey claimed that the work would have been the same without a programme and that it was a straightforward classical (that is, absolute) symphony like Beethoven's others; Bernstein advised audiences to ignore

Beethoven's narrative and focus instead on pure musical processes, such as motivic development (see Will 2002a: 19–20). Dahlhaus argued that the symphony as a genre was 'a prototype for the development of the theory of absolute music around 1800' and that absolute music was the core of nineteenth-century aesthetics (1991: 10). In other words, these influential critics might say that the symphony is a sort of text that exists only in relation to itself, as if it were a New Critical abstraction. While the appeal and diffusion of this symphony-as-absolute-music concept have been widespread, recent scholarship has revised that history. For example, Pederson (2009) argued that Dahlhaus exaggerated the idea of absolute music; Bonds (2014) traced the millennia-long history of the contested and changing construct.

It is understandable that both highly trained critics and non-specialised audiences might construe the symphony in abstract or 'absolute' terms. After all, the symphony does not have sung text (works such as Beethoven's Ninth Symphony being exceptions). Nevertheless, aestheticians since the eighteenth century have defined the genre in relation to vocal music and poetic forms such as the Pindaric ode (see Sulzer 1771–74, Koch 1802, Jones 1973 and Bonds 1997). And contemporary critics have analysed non-vocal symphonies and provided historical, political, literary and narratological interpretations (for example, Bonds 2006 and Kraus 1991). The idea of finding interpretations relating to the environment should not be surprising for ecocriticism, although such readings are less typical in music studies; ecomusicology seeks to fill this lacuna.

As ecocriticism studies cultural texts that imagine and portray human-environment relationships, so ecomusicology 'considers musical and sonic issues, both textual and performative, related to ecology and the natural environment' (Allen 2014). As a diverse interdisciplinary field (much like ecocriticism) that engages in the study of music, culture and nature, ecomusicology can be summarized as 'the critical study of music/sound and environment [...] the coming together of music/sound studies with environmental/ecological studies and sciences' (Allen and Dawe 2016: 2). While its distinction as a field may have come about in the twenty-first century, when ecocritics began engaging with music (see Ingram 2010), the idea of ecomusicology is not new but is connected to many other intellectual pursuits through history (Allen and Dawe 2016, especially 2–4). The theoretical backgrounds for my study of symphonic pastorals come from ecocritical scholarship on the pastoral as well as musicological work on the symphony and the sublime. A brief review of each provides some necessary context.

Buell (1995) characterised the pastoral as a genre that 'may direct us toward the realm of physical nature, or it may abstract us from it' (31). Symphonic pastorals exemplify this contradictory situation: the symphonic experience is decidedly public and socially centred rather than existing in pastoral contexts (at least prior to the possibility of portable reproducible musical experiences; even then, the simultaneous experience of some pastoral nature with recorded symphonic music would be technologically mediated). Buell further observes the multiple 'ideological position[s]' possible with the (American) pastoral (1995: 44) as well as the idea of 'pastoral nationalism', which reflects both postcolonial and 'old world' tendencies that 'imagine nation in terms of country or hinterland' (Buell 2005: 144). Such nationalist endeavours are evident particularly in late nineteenth-century music, including pastoral symphonies. Gifford (1999) structures understanding of the literary pastoral in three areas: the Arcadian type involving retreat to and return from the idyll, the generalised rural with implicit or explicit comparison to the urban, and the pejorative idealisation. The idyll is particularly evident with symphonic pastorals, although the generalised rural is also present. Developed in regard to Anglo-American literature, Leo Marx's two types of pastoral, the 'popular and sentimental' and the 'imaginative and complex' (1964: 5), provide a particularly useful framework for understanding symphonic pastorals. Furthermore, contrary to Marx's opposition between low and high culture (see Ingram 2010: 54–5), both types of Marxian pastoral (and others in between) are evident in symphonies.

As with the pastoral, the aesthetics of the sublime originated in the ancient Classical era; the rhetoric of the sublime, however, matured around the same time as the genre of the symphony: in the late eighteenth century (also known in music historiography as the Classical era). As Naested (2003) explains, Edmund Burke (1757) and Immanuel Kant (1790) discussed the sublime in the context of nature; early nineteenth-century accounts by C.F. Michaelis (1805) and Friedrich Rochlitz (1830) developed the musical sublime, which applied particularly to symphonies. Philosophical descriptions and musical understandings varied, but *circa* 1800 the sublime in music could be characterised by some deviation from musical norms combined with an element of cognitive frustration (Naested 2003). Many symphonic pastorals deviated from the symphonic norm, although they simultaneously had their own pastoral-symphonic expectations. Similarly, cognitive frustration is evident in some musical elements of these works, elements that can thwart non-pastoral music expectations yet, paradoxically, come to illustrate the expected musical tropes of the pastoral.

From 'simple' pastoral idylls to a 'complex' grotesquerie: Knecht's *Portrait*, Beethoven's *Pastoral* and Berlioz's *Fantastic*

Will (2002a) has catalogued some seventy pastoral symphonies from the period *c.* 1750–1815. These works, together with other topoi that evoke military, religious or national topics, constitute the 'characteristic symphony': an instrumental piece for which text is employed to associate music with a subject. This subgenre of some 225 works pales in comparison to the abstract ideal of the symphony, represented by thousands of works in that period. As one of the most common types of characteristic symphony, pastoral works took an emotional stance to 'express pleasure in idyllic settings or shudder before storms' (Will 2002a: 2); that is, they tried to elicit pastoral and sublime emotions. Some pastorals were part of larger works, such as the 'Pifa' from G.F. Handel's *Messiah* (1742), while others such as Johann Stamitz's *Sinfonia Pastorale* (1754–57) provided merely a title and some stock musical figures (such as a quotation of a Christmas carol, simple harmonies or a common musical pastoral element: drones), which could be misconstrued as a work in a different topos, such as religious or national music. Numerous works of other genres earlier in the eighteenth century also represented nature, such as the concertos of Antonio Vivaldi's *Four Seasons* (1723–25) (see Bockmaier 1992). Two works from the period *c.* 1750–1815 stand out for their lasting recognition and for their conceptual connections regarding the pastoral: Justin Heinrich Knecht's *Le Portrait Musical de la Nature* (1785) and Ludwig van Beethoven's Sixth Symphony, Op. 68 (1808), which he titled *Sinfonia Pastorella* (referred to simply as the *Pastoral*).[2] The Knecht and Beethoven symphonies are idyllic pastorals, though of different sorts.

Knecht's *Portrait* is in three parts with five movements, numbers two through five of which are played *attacca* (without pause). Knecht provided brief descriptions for each movement: the first presents the idyllic setting, the middle three constitute a storm and the finale is the ensuing thanksgiving (see Table 11.1). Will understands the whole work to be in two parts, owing mostly to the continuous music of the latter movements (2002a: 175), but the piece is three contrasting experiences: a peaceful idyll, a stormy interruption and a thankful return to the idyll.

The main theme of Knecht's first movement is built from a horn motive, perhaps derived from what was a common compositional choice at the time: a *ranz des vaches* of the Swiss Alps (Höhnen 1984: xvii), a song that, according to Rousseau (1768), was emotionally evocative of home.[3] The invocation of the mountains with the alphorn is then followed by another common pastoral trope: birdcalls, which comprise

Table 11.1 Comparison of Beethoven's works with those of Berlioz and Knecht

Knecht *Portrait musical* (1785)	Beethoven Sixth Symphony (1808)	*Analysis of Beethoven and Berlioz*	Berlioz *Symphonie fantastique* (1830)
I. A beautiful landscape where the sun shines, the gentle breezes blow, the brooks flow through the valley; the birds warble, a purling stream descends from a height, the shepherd pipes, the lambs frolic and the sweet voice of the shepherdess is heard.	I. The Awakening of Joyous Feelings on Getting Out into the Countryside	Personal feelings / emotions	I. Daydreams – Passions
		↑ Interior World ↑	
II. The heavens darken and cloud over; every living thing is breathless and frightened. Black clouds accumulate, winds whistle, the distant thunder rumbles and the storm slowly approaches.	II. Scene by the Brook	↓ Exterior World ↓ Pastoral scene	* III. In the Fields
III. With howling winds and driving rain, the storm breaks in full fury, the treetops groan, the foaming waters rush with a dreadful noise.	III. Merry Gathering of Country People	Dance	* II. A Ball
IV. Gradually the storm subsides, the clouds disperse and the sky clears.	IV. Thunderstorm	Threatening power	IV. March to the Scaffold.
	[Nature threat]	↑ Exterior World ↑	[Social threat]
		↓ Interior World ↓	
V. Nature, transported with joy, lifts its voice to heaven and gives thanks to the Creator in soft and pleasant songs.	V. Shepherd's Song. Happy and Thankful Feelings after the Storm	Personal feelings / emotions	V. Sabbath Night's Dream
	[Positive / optimist]	Conclusion	[Negative / grotesque]

Note: * Movements eventually switched. While Table 11.1 presents the movement titles of the Knecht in comparison with those of Beethoven and Berlioz, its analytical features will be more relevant in the section discussing Berlioz. The titles are from translations in Jones (1995: 18–19), Lockwood (2003: 226) and Temperley (1971: 597–8) for Knecht, Beethoven and Berlioz, respectively.

the second idyll theme. The middle three movements entail the approach of a storm, the thunderstorm itself and the calm after the storm. The excitement of this section, which reflects the idea of the sublime, caused one nineteenth-century commentator to observe: 'One is struck by the unexpected nuances in the dynamics, by the contrasts between forte and piano, crescendo and decrescendo, and by the sudden appearance of a pianissimo after a mighty crescendo' (in Höhnen 1984: xviii). Knecht titled the final movement 'L'Inno con variazioni' (a 'Hymn with variations') and describes Nature giving thanks to the Creator. This movement is interrupted with sections that Knecht labelled 'Coro' ('Chorus'); together with the 'Inno' of the title, these terms serve to convey human emotion (Höhnen 1984: xviii), and they betray the vocal origins of the symphonic genre.

Jung (1995) interprets Knecht's *Portrait* as a theatrical piece. That perspective is based on the descriptions of natural actions and human feelings as well as Knecht's intellectual influences from the characteristic symphony and contemporaneous literature and ideas, particularly those of the poet and theatre director Christoph Martin Wieland (1733–1813), who mentored Knecht and introduced the young composer to the works of Franz Joseph Haydn and Shakespeare (Wieland's troupe staged his own translation of *The Tempest*). Höhnen (1984: xx) also observes 'the scenic-dramatic element of the theater' in the piece (which I find particularly audible in the latter half of the second movement). In a semi-dramatic move, Knecht recalls the music of the first movement at the end of the final movement, bolstering the idea that after an interruption the pastoral idyll has returned.

Beethoven's Sixth Symphony both follows and breaks from its potential model: Knecht's *Portrait*.[4] The Sixth is in five movements – like Knecht's, exceeding the symphonic norm of four. Beethoven's latter three movements are also played *attacca*, and in the middle (the fourth movement) is a storm (sometimes glossed as an extended introduction to the finale). Beethoven's descriptive titles for each movement are pithier than Knecht's (see Table 11.1); his other textual provisions include naming birds toward the end of the 'Scene by the Brook', the explanatory phrase 'More an expression of feeling than tone painting' appended to the title page of the published score, and numerous comments in his sketchbooks.

Beethoven revered nature and enjoyed his frequent trips out of Vienna and into the countryside (see Jones 1995: 19–20; Jones also provides all original German and English translations of the Beethoven texts of and comments on the Sixth). The general narrative and musical aspects of the Sixth reflect a 'Memory of Country Life' (as per Beethoven's sketch notes) and the 'joyous' and 'merry' feelings of the suspended passing of time in what was, for Beethoven, sacred territory. The interruption of the storm, which provides the dramatic and fearful sublime tension in the visit, leads to the 'thankful feelings' of the final movement. Critics have provided divergent views on both the minutiae and generalities of the Sixth for over two centuries (see Will 2002b and Jones 1995: 81ff); my intention here is simply to show the work's pastoral character and personal religiosity.

Beethoven's Sixth has at least seven musical features that reflect the idyllic pastoral. The speed of the whole is mostly moderate; the fast tempos are not too fast, slow tempos not too slow. Second, consonance and major keys are prevalent, almost to the exclusion of dissonance and minor keys. Third, harmonic motion is both prolonged – in the sense that Beethoven lingers on sonorities before changing them – and constrained, in the sense that the usual contrast of tonic relaxation with dominant tension (here, F major and C major) is rare, even though it is a hallmark of tonal music; instead, harmonic movement is mostly the more gentle contrast of tonic with subdominant (F major and B flat major). The important exception regarding these three initial features is the storm, in which the necessary contrast is provided with faster tempos and rhythmic figures, minor and dissonant harmonies, and the first use in the symphony of piccolo, trombone and timpani. Furthermore, the main harmonic area in the storm is that of the dominant, which prepares for the 'thankful' arrival of the final movement (and the tonic). Overall, however, the moderations of tempo, key and harmonic motion reflect equanimity in nature and a languid sense of time.

The fourth feature is this sense of time. Will argues that time is differentiated in the Sixth between the timelessness of the idyll and the historicity of the real world and its threats (that is, the storm). The contrasts between the two halves of the symphony – the first two movements, which are played separately and constitute a 'symphonic half', distinct from the latter three movements, which are played *attacca* and constitute a 'characteristic half' – give the sensation that '[t]ime seems to run differently' (2002a: 171, see also Will 1997). The contrast of the storm provides a kick-start to time, a reminder that interrupts the placid arrival and the daydreaming and festivities of the previous three movements (see Table 11.1). This interruption results in the final 'happy and thankful feelings', a sort of arrival on a higher appreciative plane of humility and respect for creation. The continuous flow of the final three movements both dramatises the interruption and emphasises the thankfulness. The concluding movement is a 'Shepherd's Song' intoned by the horn; it may be a secular hymn but, along with organ-like sonorities

(Will 2002b: 212), it appears nevertheless as a grateful song of praise – be it to the deity, the blue sky of the idyll or the return to the less structured time of pastoral grace.

The fifth feature is in regard to the second movement, 'Scene by the Brook', which is a popular locus for programmatic interpretation; reactions range from the picturesque images it evokes to the possibility that it reflected the moment when a goldfinch foretold Beethoven's deafness (see Jander 1993, but also the disagreement in Will 2002b and Lockwood 2003: 519). The imagery derives mostly from the continual motion in the low strings, which evoke flowing water, and the high string trills of birds; at the end of the movement, Beethoven identifies the birds: nightingale (flute), quail (oboe) and cuckoo (two clarinets). This expansion of the space between the low strings (low-lying water) and of the high strings (birds high in the trees) is reflected on the page of Beethoven's 1808 orchestral score, which followed the standard eighteenth-century convention (different from modern scores) of having the upper strings at the top of the page, followed by the winds and brass in the middle, with the low strings at the bottom (Lockwood 2003: 519). In all, this musical depiction of natural space comes closest to painting a picture of the pastoral visitor dreaming near the waterside aviary (such imagery is explored in Schmenner 1998).

The sixth aspect relates to a common feature of symphonies: the use of a stylised dance movement for the third movement. Most such movements (known as minuets or scherzos) have two main parts, the dance itself and a lighter trio, after which the dance repeats. Beethoven's 'Merry Gathering of Country People' continues the major-mode emphasis of the entire symphony, while the trio increases the joviality with an even faster, *fortissimo* dance (where a traditional minuet's trio might scale back in volume and texture, this one increases both; further, rather than usual repeats, portions of the minuet are truncated and lead more quickly into the trio). The accented drones reflect a common pastoral trope and continue the trend of slow harmonic change. The emphatic presence of festive humans in the idyll reflects a realistic view of the natural world: that is, one that is neither wild nor somehow pure, but rather one that reflects humanity's place in nature.

The final musical feature of Beethoven's symphony that relates to the pastoral is the religious aspect. Aside from general associations of the pastoral with sacred music, the religiosity of the Sixth comes out in both musical and biographical contexts. Numerous procedures and sonorities evoke relationships with Haydn's oratorios *The Creation* (1796–98) and *The Seasons* (1799–1801). The latter is an unusual example of a non-religious oratorio; librettist Baron Gottfried van Swieten based his texts about weather on the pastoral poem (1726–28) by James Thomson.

In fact, Beethoven's shepherd's horn has a melodic precedent in *The Seasons* (Jones 1995: 10–14), and it shares a resemblance with Knecht's opening theme. The repetitions of Beethoven's alphorn melody, a generic sort of *ranz des vaches*, resemble the form of a church hymn (Will 2002a: 182). In his draft sketches for the storm, Beethoven wrote 'Lord, we thank thee', and accordingly the title of the ensuing movement is often translated as 'Shepherd's *Hymn*' rather than '*Song*'. One of Beethoven's favourite books was a well-marked copy of Christoph Christian Sturm's *Reflections on the Works of God in the Realm of Nature and Providence*, which found religious ideas in all aspects of nature (see Jones 1995: 21–2). Furthermore, Will understands the arc of the symphony as transforming its 'natural paradise into a moral one' (2002a: 184, see also Will 1997). The parallel with the concluding 'Hymn' of Knecht's *Portrait* is clear, yet, rather than a public theatrical expression, Beethoven's is more a personal paean to nature.

Both Knecht's *Portrait* and Beethoven's Sixth are what Marx (1964) called simple, or 'popular and sentimental', pastorals (5). These works reflect 'the felicity represented by an image of a natural landscape, a terrain either unspoiled or, if cultivated, rural' (9). Marx's characterisation of a journey 'away from the city and toward the country' is apropos both for Beethoven's life and his Sixth Symphony. Knecht and Beethoven, however, do engage with the pastoral in different manners: the former in a public and quasi-dramatic tableau, the latter in a more personal religious experience. Other critics have interpreted the Sixth both in the heroic realm typical of Beethoven reception (that is, a generally non-programmatic plot archetype of overcoming adversity, as in Beethoven's Fifth Symphony; see, for example, Jander 1993) and in an atypical vein that sees the work apart from that heroic tradition (Jones 1995; see also Will 2002b and 2002a: 184–7, which stresses a more general humanity rather than a heroic type). Tovey and Bernstein's absolutist formulations (cited above) tried to portray the Sixth as abstract music, and Beethoven himself seems to have had some hesitance about combining programme music with the symphony. In his sketchbooks for the symphony, Beethoven wrote, 'One leaves it to the listener to discover the situations', and 'Each act of tone-painting, as soon as it is pushed too far in instrumental music, loses its force'; and then there is the sketchbook antecedent for the suggestive comment on the eventual title-page: 'The whole will be understood even without a description, as it is more feeling than tone-painting' (in Lockwood 2003: 225). The word *feeling*, here as elsewhere in Beethoven's comments, together with his hesitance in explaining too much about the symphony, resonates with Marx's observation that the simple pastoral is 'an expression less of thought than of feeling' (1964: 5). Nevertheless, Beethoven did provide titles in a narrative format and did imitate sounds of birds, a dance and a storm – all public features of the pastoral accessible to contemporaneous listeners (see Will 2002a and 2002b: 210). Moreover, listeners since have continued to find in the Sixth an idyllic pastoral inflected with personal religiosity.

Beethoven may have hesitated in his engagement with programmatic music, but Hector Berlioz was unapologetic in his fundamentally literary approach to a programme symphony, the piece that launched his career: *Épisode de la vie d'un Artiste*, more commonly known by its subtitle *Symphonie fantastique* (1830).[5] Berlioz did more than provide pithy titles or brief descriptions in this archetypal Romantic symphony: he provided a rough short story to be distributed to the audience. Berlioz's programme tells of an artist who falls in love but is rejected and overdoses on opium; he then dreams that he kills his beloved, is executed at the gallows and sees her at an orgy of witches. (Table 11.1 contains only the movement titles, as the programme is widely available, e.g. in Cone 1971, and too long to reprint in full.) Initial appearances aside, Berlioz's symphony is connected with the pastoral tradition through both a movement 'In the Fields' and the use of Beethoven's Sixth as a model. But in Berlioz's *Fantastic*, the simple pastoral takes a pessimistic and grotesque turn towards Marx's 'imaginative and complex' pastoral.

As with Beethoven's Sixth, critics such as Jacques Barzun (1950) have tried to explain away the verbal portion and argue that the *Fantastic* is absolute music, yet commentators rarely pass up the opportunity to cite the programme in discussing the work. Nicholas Temperley (1971)[6] has argued that Berlioz's music cannot be separated from the deliberately unpolished literary component that provides the essential emotional, if not narrative, corollary that allowed the composer to manipulate his audience's feelings. Berlioz knew that his method needed some explaining, as he makes clear in his introductory note, published with the score in 1846 (a text that was still, despite years of revisions to the music, substantially the same as at its premiere in 1830):[7]

> The composer's intention has been to develop, insofar as they contain musical possibilities, various situations in the life of an artist. The outline of the instrumental drama, which lacks the help of words, needs to be explained in advance. The following program should thus be considered as the spoken text of an opera, serving to introduce the musical movements, whose character and expression it motivates. (In Cone 1971: 21)

Berlioz's work has been associated with the operatic tradition (Langford 1983), and the composer's introductory note makes this parallel to aid his audience in understanding. As connective musical material to complement the programme, Berlioz employed an *idée fixe*: a melody that returns in various guises in each movement.

After the emotional turmoil, or 'le vague des passions', of the first movement when the musician 'sees for the first time a woman [...] and he falls desperately in love with her', the second movement is a dance 'in the midst of *the tumult of a party*' where 'the beloved vision appears before him and disturbs his peace of mind'. The third movement finds him in the countryside, and 'He reflects upon his isolation; he hopes that his loneliness will soon be over [...] But what if she were deceiving him!' Realising that his love is not returned, in the fourth movement he 'poisons himself with opium', but he does not manage to kill himself; rather, he only dreams 'that he has killed his beloved, that he is condemned and led to the scaffold, and that he is witnessing *his own execution*'.

The conclusion of the March to the Scaffold recalls the initial phrase (or so-called 'head') of the *idée fixe*, which the orchestra cuts off; there follow plucked strings and a triumphal conclusion in what can be interpreted as the artist's severed head falling into the guillotine basket to the roaring cheers of the crowd. The dream continues in the final movement, when he observes a gaggle of witches who have come to observe his funeral. The *idée fixe* returns in the introduction of the finale, 'but it has lost its character of nobility and shyness; it is no more than a dance tune, mean, trivial, and grotesque: it is she, coming to join the Sabbath ... A roar of joy at her arrival ... She takes part in the devilish orgy ... Funeral knell, burlesque parody of the *Dies irae, sabbath round-dance*.' (The story continues in the sequel, *Lélio, or the Return to Life*, and the work's complicated textual histories are made more complex by Berlioz's later changes to the published programme of the *Fantastic*, which, perhaps surprisingly, required no concomitant change to the music; see Temperley 1971: 598ff, and passim.)

On the surface, Berlioz's programme does not resemble Beethoven's Sixth, although some commentators hear echoes of the earlier composer in the movement 'In the Fields' (Temperley 1971: 606). But on a deeper level, and when considering one of Berlioz's drafts, their structures are remarkably similar to each other (and, to a lesser degree, to Knecht's *Portrait*). Table 11.1 separates the movements with varying types of borders, which indicate here different types of sectional divisions. The five-movement works are in three sections: an introduction that focuses on the feelings and emotions of an interior, personal world; three middle movements that present events in an exterior, social world; and a concluding movement that returns to the interior self.[8] The introduction for Beethoven is joy upon arriving in the country, while for Berlioz it is the excitement of love. The exterior world in each work is represented by a pastoral idyll, a dance and a threatening power; this last is for Beethoven a natural character (storm), while for Berlioz it is a social power (execution). In the spring of 1830, some ten months before the premiere on 5 December, Berlioz described his draft of the *Fantastic* with the second ('A Ball') and third ('In the Fields') movements switched (Cone 1971: 7–9, where the third movement is translated as 'Scene in the Country'). Berlioz's earlier version, represented in Table 11.1, parallels Beethoven's Sixth: the pastoral movements ('In the Fields' and 'Scene by the Brook', respectively) and the dance movements ('A Ball' and 'Merry Gathering of Country People') were thus in the same places. Ultimately, Berlioz switched them to their final position, perhaps to shy away from his model. The final movements of both works return to the interior world of emotion, but, where Beethoven provides a positive, optimistic outlook by thanking the creator for the return to the idyll after the storm, Berlioz instead provides a negative view – 'grotesque' as he wrote – in which his tormented love threatens him in an opium-induced nightmare.

This turn to the grotesque is evident also in the structure of Berlioz's pastoral movement, 'In the Fields', which itself mirrors the tripartite journey of Knecht and Beethoven's idyllic pastorals that came before: idyll established, idyll interrupted, idyll re-established. Berlioz's, however, departs from that model by ending with romantic torment. His pastoral movement is in three sections. First is an introduction in which the English horn and oboe – the former is a larger and lower-pitched version of the latter – pass a theme back and forth; Berlioz calls this theme a *ranz des vaches* (although it probably is not such a traditional tune) and describes it as two shepherds piping to each other across a distance. The long middle section is a series of variations on a different theme; it is interrupted by an agitated section when the *idée fixe* appears, which reflects an interior, personal storm (rather than an exterior, natural storm). The concluding section returns to the English horn melody from the opening – but the oboe is absent, and the only response is from four timpani who rumble like thunder. The shepherdess (oboe) has abandoned her loving shepherd (English horn).

At the opening of Berlioz's pastoral movement, the echo – which Marx (1964) calls a 'recurrent device in pastoral' – functions as a 'metaphor of reciprocity': the shepherd calls out to the woods, from which he hears the same 'notes of his pipe' respond and 'echo back' (23). But the reciprocal love of the outset is altered; both Berlioz's 'In the Fields' and the *Fantastic* as a whole are complex pastorals.

Marx uses Nathaniel Hawthorne's observations of Sleepy Hollow to establish the 'metaphoric design' or 'paradigm' for the complex pastoral: 'What begins as a conventional tribute to the pleasures of withdrawal from the world – a simple pleasure fantasy – is transformed by the interruption of the machine into a far more complex state of mind' (15). The machine for Hawthorne was the train, represented only by its sound. For Berlioz – the 'poet in disguise', as 'Tityrus represents Virgil himself' in the *Ecologues* (22) – it is not a machine that interrupts his pastoral; rather, the 'counterforce' (Marx's term for the disruptive or threatening power) is the artist's own internal nature of doubt: an interior storm that builds as the artist fears his love is deceiving him, as represented by the sound of an agitated *idée fixe*. Thus, Berlioz's pastoral scene questions, as Marx put it, 'the illusion of peace and harmony in a green pasture' (24). While the calm returns in the latter portion of the second section of 'In the Fields', thus seeming to reconcile that interior turmoil, the third and concluding part of the movement – which in good Romantic fashion cycles back to the opening idea – thwarts such a reading: the shepherd's pipe returns, but the only response is thunder. In neither this thunderous lack of response nor the stormy emotional reflection is the storm merely a sublime interlude that allows for a return to an earlier idyll; rather, the course of the narrative is fundamentally altered.

In part, it is the use of nature, both internal and external, to disrupt the pastoral that makes Berlioz's pastoral grotesque; in part, it is the artist's own transformation of his beloved (as represented by the *idée fixe*) from an image of desperate love to an agitating presence and, further, to a witch at an orgy. But Berlioz also twists typical pastoral gender roles. As Marx understands the pastoral, the counterforce that intrudes 'upon a fantasy of idyllic satisfaction [...] invariably is associated with crude, masculine aggressiveness in contrast with the tender, feminine, and submissive attitudes traditionally attached to the landscape' (29). For Berlioz, however, the artist's landscape is masculine, and the counterforce is the female love interest – over whom the composer eventually reasserts his dominance by writing her into a grotesque orgy that he watches while on an opium high, or as Marx puts it, in a 'complex state of mind' (15).

From romantic to rupture: Brahms's First and Second Symphonies, and Mahler's Third Symphony

In contrast to Berlioz's *Fantastic*, Johannes Brahms treats the subject of love more kindly in his First Symphony (1862–77).[9] Brahms had a long and productive friendship with Clara Schumann, the wife of one of his greatest supporters, Robert Schumann. While speculation and gossip have long surrounded Clara and Johannes's relationship, most scholars agree that their love was never consummated but remained platonic: that of friends with deep and lasting artistic, professional and personal connections (see Berry 2007, Reich 2001, 169ff and Avins and Eisinger 2001: 757ff). Their feelings were exchanged and preserved in an extensive epistolary exchange, because for much of their lives they lived in distant locales. In a sense, their relationship could be paralleled with the mature, respectful and longing love of the Troubadours and Trouvères. Such distant but deep emotions are expressed in Brahms's First Symphony in the context of the pastoral.

The usual interpretations of Brahms's First are of struggle, of overcoming the shadow of Beethoven, and/or of the debate (prompted by Richard Wagner's music and writings) over the role of voices in the symphony (see, for example, Bonds 1996, which incorporates Harold Bloom's theory of misprision). Brahms did indeed struggle mightily with his first symphonic work, for he took over two decades to complete it. And Brahms himself acknowledged (more than once) the anxiety over Beethoven; the principal theme of the fourth movement is modelled on the 'Ode to Joy' theme of Beethoven's Ninth Symphony, and, as Brahms reportedly quipped, 'every jackass notices it at once' (in Bonds 1996: 1). Such wilful paraphrase associates the music with Beethoven's text: Schiller's *Ode an die Freude*, which lauds universal brotherhood and the joy of love.

Reinhold Brinkmann has argued that, through Brahms's misreading of Beethoven's Ninth in Brahms's First, the subtext of that *Ode* – 'the humanist fervor of freedom and brotherliness' – is rejected in favour of religion and nature (1995: 32–53, 47, 45). Brahms takes the historical moment of Beethoven (the desire for peace in late eighteenth-century Vienna) and replaces it with his perception of those transhistorical needs. Brahms achieves this end by giving the impression that his 'Beethoven theme' will return at the end of the movement (which is the end of the symphony), yet he avoids a full recapitulation and provides only a fragmented version of part of the tune. Furthermore, he provides two interruptions introduced initially in the slow introduction to the fourth movement: a brass chorale ('religion') and an alphorn melody ('nature'). No explicit text is invoked here; as Brinkmann, paraphrasing Arnold Schoenberg, put it: 'form is "used" to state a meaning in notes' (37). In essence, the struggle of Brahms's First is resolved not with brotherhood or societal actions but through religion and nature.

In the context of the pastoral, Brahms evokes Clara. On 12 September 1868, Brahms sent a postcard to Clara, saying 'Thus blew the shepherd's horn today', and he notated what would later be the alphorn melody with the underlying text, 'High up in the mountain, deep down in the wold, I greet you, I greet you a thousandfold' ('Hoch auf'm Berg, tief im Tal, gruß ich dich viel tausend mal') (in Litzmann 1973: 231). As the violins foreshadow the 'Beethoven theme' in the opening measures of the fourth movement, so too do the woodwinds foreshadow the alphorn theme just before its arrival in the horn; Brahms indicates that this, Clara's, theme should be played 'always loud and impassioned' ('*f*[*orte*] *sempre e passionato*'). Shortly thereafter we hear the chorale, intoned by three trombones and three bassoons. Amidst the variations on the primary ('Beethoven') theme, the alphorn interrupts twice at moments of high tension. The concluding coda builds tension, furthering the impression that the 'Beethoven theme' will return, but all the way to the end of the work Brahms obsessively varies just one short motive of it – essentially making what was once vocal into an instrumental tune. The chorale theme interrupts again, this time with more clarion horns and trumpets along with the trombones. Clara's theme does not return. The previous interruptions, the unfilled return of the Beethoven theme and the building tension and increase in tempo of the concluding *stringendo* and *più animato* all leave us expectant (much the way, perhaps, we have been wondering if Brahms and Clara ever consummated their love). But here, Brahms does no more than provide subtle clues to his beliefs in religion and nature as suprahuman, and to the deep friendship he communicated to Clara from afar amidst pastoral Alpine and musical landscapes.

On the one hand, Brahms's pastoral interjections reflect Marx's (1964) sentimental pastoral: a sort of shepherd longing for an unattainable love. On the other hand, the pastoral moments reflect a more ideological use of the pastoral, not so much in Buell's conception of protesting injustice (2005: 15) but more in promoting an idea of what the symphony can be: alive after Beethoven, yes, and certainly not a vocal work (as Wagner proposed), but also a genre that can be comfortable in the pastoral mode. This latter position may have been somewhat unsettling for Beethoven, but Brahms took it on confidently in his next symphonic effort.

Brahms's Second Symphony (1877–78) is usually seen as a lyrical, pastoral relaxation after the toil of his First. But in Brinkmann's interpretation (1995), it is a 'late idyll', a melancholic pastoral. The music reflects this apparent opposition, while some biographical elements and the work's reception bolster such a reading.

As an idyll, Brahms's Second begins with musical features of the pastoral, or, as Brinkmann puts it, the 'entrance of nature' (1995: 195). Over a string drone, the initial horn solo uses the unaltered (natural) notes of the instrument, providing a serene melody that resembles the Catholic Marian hymn *Milde Königin gedenke* (76). The woodwinds enter occasionally, providing brighter moments, and all this occurs in regular four-square phrases. This is 'manifestly a world without conflicts. The romantic nature-topos is patent' (54). Elsewhere, pastoral elements return, as with the drone and woodwind sonorities in the trio of the third movement. In performances recorded throughout the twentieth century, the first movement is played markedly slower than at the premiere and than indicated in the score; in fact, considering fourteen recordings between 1940 and 1983, Brinkmann finds that the symphony 'is conceived as going entirely at a medium tempo', thus providing a 'reflection of a serene and tranquil pastoral atmosphere' (30–1).

Since the first performances of Brahms's Second, critical reactions have emphasised the pastoral. After the premiere, Ferdinand Pohl wrote to Brahms's friend and publisher Fritz Simrock, 'Such music can only be composed in the country, in the midst of nature'; Simrock in turn wrote to Brahms that the four-hand piano reduction was 'full of sunshine' (Brinkmann 1995: 15–16). Theodor Billroth wrote to Brahms that '[a] happy, blissful atmosphere pervades the whole', exclaiming: 'Why, it is all blue sky, babbling of streams, sunshine and cool green shade!' Brahms himself even said in a letter to Adolf Schubring in November 1877: 'it's a quite innocent, cheerful little thing'. Yet some observers also reacted to the unusual moments; the anonymous reviewer of a January 1878 performance said that the first movement 'strikes up such an endearing and cheerful pastoral tone, and although this is supplanted at times by the solemn sounds of trombones, like storms erupting over the calm, magnificent spring landscape, it always regains the upper hand, so that one imagines oneself transported back in time to the age of the idyll, which no savage passions were tearing apart' (all translated in Brinkmann 1995: 13–16, 199).

The trombones are not the only cloud to darken the idyll. The slow tempo and timpani undertones of the second movement, Brahms's only symphonic adagio, add a contrasting heaviness to the otherwise typically light inner movements of a symphony. The dark trombones (plus, in some cases, a tuba that Brahms added in the late stages of his composition; see Brinkmann 1995: 22–6) interrupt the pastoral quality of the beginning of the first movement and darken the lightness of the ending of the fourth movement, while also framing the symphony as a whole. Such dark bookends are also reflected in comments Brahms made about his composition to Simrock in November 1877: 'The new symphony is so melancholy that you won't stand it. I have never written anything so sad [...] the score must appear with a black border.' He also wrote to Elisabet Von Herzogenberg in December 1877, 'Here the musicians are playing my latest with mourning bands because it sounds so woeful; it will be printed with a black border'. Again he wrote to Simrock in December 1877: 'But you must put a black border round the score so that it also shows its melancholy outwardly!' (In Brinkmann 1995: 13–15).

These issues come together in a revealing exchange of letters between Brahms and Vincenz Lachner in August 1879. Lachner was critical of the darkening: 'Why do you throw into the idyllically serene atmosphere with which the first movement begins the rumbling kettledrum, the gloomy lugubrious tones of the trombones and tuba?' Brahms replied:

> I very much wanted to manage in that first movement without using trombones, and tried to. [...] But their first entrance, that's mine, and I can't get along without it and thus the trombones. Were I to defend the passage, I would have to be long-winded.
>
> I would have to confess that I am, by the by, a severely melancholic person, that black wings are constantly flapping above us. (In Brinkmann 1995: 128)

Also critical of an unusual, dissonant harmonic combination in the coda of the first movement, Lachner wrote: 'Maybe people will tolerate this kind of thing in future, perhaps finding pleasure in it, but my ear is too old for such things.' Brahms replied: 'But as for the note *a* that goes with the G minor in the coda, I'd like to defend that! For me it is a gorgeously beautiful sound' (in Brinkmann 1995: 127–9).

These are rare confessions by Brahms. He may have been being ironic, as his 'black border' and 'black wings' statements contradicted his earlier expression about how 'cheerful' the Second was. Yet while the music may not be depressing or brooding, it does reflect the shadows in life, even as Brahms does not emphasise them. Brinkmann situates Brahms, along with other artists, in a 'late' era, one that was historically self-conscious and excluded from innocence. We can find insight in Brahms's irony, however: this mixture of the pastoral with the melancholic may represent Brahms's 'fractured relationship with serenity' (28). Brinkmann sees this represented in the very opening of the symphony: amidst the apparent pastoral idyll, tension and disruption lurk. Nevertheless, despite the interruptions and darkenings, Brahms's Second ends positively, problematising Brinkmann's reading, as he recognises (203ff).

Some reactions to and characterisations of Brahms's Second may make it appear to fit into Marx's (1964) category of the 'popular' or simple pastoral. Brahms's take on the idyll may superficially resemble Knecht's and Beethoven's three-part journeys, but his Second is less narratological, less teleological and more jaded in its unfolding. The dark sounds of the brass interjections might suggest Marx's 'imaginative and complex' pastoral, but the counterforce is not entirely manifest. Thus Brinkmann's 'late idyll' is useful as a sort of middle ground between Marx's two categories. In Brahms's Second there are menacing shadows in otherwise peaceful pastoral glades.

Gustav Mahler's symphonic output engages with this very perspective but takes it further into the realm of Marx's complex pastoral. Mahler had an abiding interest in nature: he retreated to the Alps to compose, his scores use similes such as 'like a sound of nature', and the pastoral is a common topos in his music. Nature played a significant role in how Mahler conceived his own Romantic or artistic autobiography (Birchler 1991). But Mahler also had a fraught relationship with the modern city that breaks into his music (Peattie 2002a), for as he said: 'a symphony must be like the world; it must contain everything' – both the good and the bad. One of many examples, the Third Symphony (1893–96, revised 1906) illustrates this more pessimistic turn in the Mahlerian pastoral of fin-de-siècle Vienna.[10]

Mahler's interruptions, distorted recollections and unstable moments in his Third Symphony, particularly in the posthorn episodes of the Scherzo (the third movement of six), reflect what Thomas Peattie (2002b) has called a broken pastoral, which may be roughly equated with Marx's (1964) complex pastoral. The movement begins peacefully and sets up a series of sections that are fast-paced and in perpetual motion. A trumpet fanfare interrupts, followed by a slowing of motion; occasionally the strings and winds try to reclaim attention. The post-horn enters suddenly in this context, and immediately 'time seems to come to a standstill' (Peattie 2002b: 189): the arrival of the posthorn, its spatial separation (it is often played offstage) and the nearly static underpinning of the accompaniment all bring pastoral calm, but then echoes of the fanfare return before the posthorn moves on. The perpetual motion returns, yet the posthorn continues its varied interruptions, and the trumpet interjects its own fanfare before the scherzo continues. Peattie compares these gradual realisations to an episode in Proust's *In Search of Lost Time* (1913–27), which stresses the processes of recollection and gradual emergence: through the struggle to recall, one attains a heightened state of memory, as with the successively distorted entries of the posthorn (192). Furthermore, given Mahler's expressed ambivalent relationship with the metropolis that he needed for his career but from which he often longed to escape into more rural contexts, if the perpetual motion of the scherzo is 'an allegory of worldly bustle, it might be argued that it is this which triggers the fleeting pastoral escapes' (196). Beethoven wanted to escape Vienna for the countryside, but his response was one of personal, quasi-religious reverence, whereas Mahler finds the stark contrast worthy of distorted, or broken, recollection.

Mahler originally had a programmatic outline for the Third, but he never published it. The first movement was titled 'Pan Awakes, Summer Marches In', while the subsequent five movements all follow the formula 'What [...] Tell[s] Me', with informants ranging from flowers and animals to man, angels and Love. Movement four sets a text by Friedrich Nietzsche (from *Also sprach Zarathustra*, 1883–85), sung by an alto soloist, who, with women's and boy's choirs in movement five, sings a text from the German folk poetry collection *Des Knaben Wunderhorn* (1805–8). Add in the Schopenhauerian influence, namely his concept of the 'will' (see Starr 2004), and the work might be characterised as a philosophical pastoral. Yet, while certain ideas lean towards an idealistic view of human nature, the brooding, doubtful and pessimistic undercurrents and interruptions contribute to the overall pastoral rupture. In essence, the city functions as Marx's 'counterforce' for Mahler's complex, broken pastoral. The changes in symphonic pastorals in the long nineteenth century culminate with Mahler's fin-de-siècle take on one of the original cruxes of the pastoral mode: the conflict of city and country, or, as Buell put it, a 'representation of rusticity in contrast to and often in satire of urbanism' (2005: 144).

Continuing symphonic pastorals

Despite an understandable perception that the genre is mute or 'abstract', musical and contextual features of symphonies can convey ideas about nature. The pastoral perspectives of symphonies in the long nineteenth century were changing: from Knecht's dramatic and Beethoven's personal spiritual idylls of the simple pastoral to Berlioz's complex pastoral grotesquerie, and from Brahms's small-r romantic to his and Mahler's bleaker, more complex pastorals. While some of these works are clearly in the characteristic or programmatic subgenre, others, such as Brahms's, are what would normally be considered 'abstract' (or at least non-programmatic).

An important early voice on ecomusicological ideas, R. Murray Schafer, wrote in his seminal *Soundscapes* (1994 [1977]) that programme music is 'imitative of environment', while '[i]n absolute music composers fashion ideal soundscapes of the mind. [...] Absolute music is disengaged from the external environment[,] and its highest forms (the sonata, the quartet, the symphony) are conceived for indoor performance' (1994 [1977]: 103). While much music does exist to substantiate binary oppositions like Schafer's, some of the symphonic pastorals presented here blur and complicate such otherwise facile understandings. As 'one of the most influential concepts in the history of Western musical aesthetics', Bonds (2014) acknowledged that 'the idea of absolute music reflects the enduring Western tendency to juxtapose mind and body, reason and emotion, the spiritual and the material' (16). My hope is that this ecomusicological analysis helps make the apparently simple pastoral (and that widespread simple binary) more complex and less dichotomous (and less problematic and damaging). As such, ecomusicology is, along with ecocriticism, part of the environmental (post) humanities movement (see also Allen 2012, as well as Allen and Dawe 2016, especially 5 and 9).

Although the works I selected above provide signposts in a brief tour through the nineteenth century, they do not necessarily represent a teleological drive towards a broken modern or postmodern symphonic outlook on the pastoral. Other symphonies of the nineteenth and twentieth centuries – both programmatic and non-programmatic – would readily disrupt such a tidy (hypothetical) narrative. Even in the late eighteenth century, the pastoral had dark elements (Beckerman 1991), and considering other works would show the diversity of symphonic engagements with the pastoral. Numerous German symphonies evoke landscape and nation, reflecting Buell's concepts of 'pastoral nationalism' and 'old world tendencies' (2005: 144); for example, Mendelssohn's Fourth, *Italian* (1833) and Third, *Scottish* (1842); Schumann's First, *Frühlingssinfonie* ('Spring', 1841) and Third, *Rheinische* ('Rhenish', 1850); and Raff's Third, *Im Walde* ('In the Forests', 1869), Seventh, *In den Alpen* ('In the Alps', 1875), and Eighth through Eleventh, each based on one of the seasons (1877–83). Other national traditions include Bristow's *Arcadian* (1872) and *Niagara* (1893) symphonies (American), Orefice's *Sinfonia del Bosco* ('Symphony of the Forest', 1898) (Italian), and Dvořák's Sixth Symphony (1880) (Czech). Works of twentieth-century composers have continued to engage with pastoral topics in diverse ways, ranging from idyllic landscapes to environmentalism to post-pastoralism. For example Ives's unconventional (and unfinished) *Universe Symphony* (1915–28) exhibits the aural and emotional influences of his regular vacations in the Adirondack Mountains (Tucker 1996); Strauss's *Eine Alpensinfonie* (1911–15) reflects a journey in the Alps (see Satragni 1999, Toliver 2011); Zwilich used adult and children's choirs to exhort Thoreauvian and Biblical credos about nature and environmental stewardship in her Fourth Symphony, *The Gardens* (1999), particularly in the third movement 'A Pastoral Journey' (Von Glahn 2003); and Albert's wordless *Symphony: RiverRun* (1984) is post-pastoralist, in that it acknowledges its own participation in discourse about culture and nature (Watkins 2007). Scholars have also reconsidered claims about the apparent simplicity of British pastoralism in music: Ralph Vaughan Williams and Gustav Holst shared radical political views (Harrington 1989); Vaughan Williams's Third Symphony, *Pastoral* (1921), was not a sentimental English pastoral but rather a reflection on the ravages of the First World War (Saylor 2008).

Scholarly engagement with the literary pastoral has been a significant portion of ecocritical work. The examples illustrated and cited herein, however, show that even in a wordless and ostensibly 'abstract' genre such as the symphony, ecocritical interpretations are possible. Composers have ascribed and critics have interpreted meanings in symphonies, and ecomusicology can provide perspectives on these interrelations of music, culture and nature.

Acknowledgements

This essay is an updated and slightly revised version originally published as Allen (2011). My thanks are due to the editor of *Green Letters: Studies in Ecocriticism* and the Taylor and Francis Group for providing reproduction rights. As with my original essay, I owe continued thanks to Miranda Freeman, David Ingram, Thomas Peattie, Cody Rex, Kailan Rubinoff, Brooks Toliver, the students of my ecomusicology seminars and the anonymous reviewers of *Green Letters*. Upon completing this essay in 2010, I learned of the death of Reinhold Brinkmann (1934–2010), whose scholarly influence is most evident in the section on Brahms. I dedicate this essay (as I did with the 2011 version) to him as a token of my appreciation for his musicological passion and personal guidance, which have influenced my career and life.

Notes

1　This trend also existed in nineteenth-century America with critics such as J.S. Dwight proffering, in Von Glahn's words, 'penalties rather than rewards' for writing programme music (Von Glahn 2003: 273–4).
2　Benda (2014) is a recording of the Knecht. Numerous recordings of Beethoven's symphonies are readily available; I recommend period-instrument recordings, such as those by Norrington (1988) or Gardiner (1994).

3 Rousseau (1768: 314–15, 398) used the *ranz des vaches* as an example of a particularly suggestive music: it is a cow herders' song traditionally played on bagpipes to livestock that apparently caused Swiss troops stationed abroad to cry, desert or die because of the memories it evoked when they heard it (and thus such men were forbidden to hear it).

4 Beethoven may have known about Knecht's *Portrait*, as both men had works published by the firm of Bossler in the 1780s; furthermore, Beethoven may have seen his works listed next to those of Knecht in Traeg's catalogue of 1799 (Höhnen 1984, xvii).

5 Numerous recordings of Berlioz's *Fantastic* are available; I recommend the video recording conducted by Gardiner (2007), which uses period instruments.

6 Although an insightful account of the work from an authoritative scholar, some minor portions of Temperley's arguments would need to be updated due to recent discoveries, such as those of Macdonald (1993), who demonstrates Berlioz's recycling of old material into new works.

7 Cone (1971: 21–5) provides the originals and a translation of the programme (which exists in multiple versions); see also Temperley (1971: 597–8). In the quotations from Berlioz's programme included in this chapter, all italics and all ellipses not in brackets are Berlioz's original (as presented in Cone 1971: 21–5).

8 I am grateful to Reinhold Brinkmann for these observations. I might add that an analysis of Knecht's *Portrait* resembles vaguely the later Beethoven and Berlioz pieces: Knecht's first movement may be perceived from the interior perspectives of the shepherd and shepherdess, the middle three movements are the exterior natural events, while the final movement returns to the interiority of a prayer, albeit from the perspective of 'Nature' rather than a human.

9 The recording by Abbado (1998) is a clear articulation of some features discussed here, particularly the end of the finale.

10 The DVD by Starr (2004) provides historical, philosophical and music-analytical insights into Mahler's Third; it also provides a complete performance, with subtitles for the sung text, of the unusually long work (one of the longest in the standard repertoire).

References

Abbado, Claudio and Berlin Philharmonic Orchestra (1998) *Brahms: Symphony No. 1; Song of the Fates*. CD. Hamburg: Deutsche Grammophon.

Allen, Aaron S. (2011) 'Symphonic Pastorals', *Green Letters: Studies in Ecocriticism* 15: 22–42.

Allen, Aaron S. (2012) 'Ecomusicology: Bridging the Sciences, Arts, and Humanities', in Deborah Rigling Gallagher (ed.) *Environmental Leadership: A Reference Handbook*. Thousand Oaks: Sage Publications: Vol. 2, pp. 373–81.

Allen, Aaron S. (2014) 'Ecomusicology', in *The Grove Dictionary of American Music*. Second edition. New York: Oxford University Press.

Allen, Aaron S. and Kevin Dawe (2016) 'Ecomusicologies', in Aaron S. Allen and Kevin Dawe (eds), *Current Directions in Ecomusicology: Music, Culture, Nature*. New York and London: Routledge, pp. 1–15.

Avins, Styra and Josef Eisinger (eds) (2001 [1997]) *Johannes Brahms: Life and Letters*. New York: Oxford University Press.

Barzun, Jacques (1950) *Berlioz and the Romantic Century*. Boston, MA: Little, Brown.

Beckerman, Michael (1991) 'Mozart's Pastoral', *Mozart-Jahrbuch*: 93–102.

Benda, Christian and Orchestra Filarmonica di Torino (2014) *Le Portrait Musical de La Nature*. CD. Naxos, 8.573066.

Berry, Paul (2007) 'Old Love: Johannes Brahms, Clara Schumann, and the Poetics of Musical Memory', *The Journal of Musicology* 24:1: 72–111.

Birchler, David C. (1991) 'Nature and Autobiography in the Music of Gustav Mahler'. Unpublished PhD Dissertation, University of Wisconsin.

Bockmaier, Claus (1992) *Entfesselte Natur in der Musik des Achtzehnten Jahrhunderts*. Tutzing: H. Schneider.

Bonds, Mark Evan (1996) *After Beethoven: Imperatives of Originality in the Symphony*. Cambridge, MA: Harvard University Press.

Bonds, Mark Evan (1997) 'The Symphony as Pindaric Ode', in Elaine R. Sisman (ed.), *Haydn and His World*. Princeton: Princeton University Press, pp. 131–53.

Bonds, Mark Evan (2006) *Music as Thought: Listening to the Symphony in the Age of Beethoven*. Princeton: Princeton University Press.

Bonds, Mark Evan (2014) *Absolute Music: The History of an Idea*. New York: Oxford University Press.

Brinkmann, Reinhold (1995) *Late Idyll: The Second Symphony of Johannes Brahms*. Cambridge, MA: Harvard University Press.

Buell, Lawrence (1995) *The Environmental Imagination: Thoreau, Nature Writing, and the Formation of American Culture*. Cambridge, MA: Harvard University Press.

Buell, Lawrence (2005) *The Future of Environmental Criticism: Environmental Crisis and Literary Imagination*. Oxford: Blackwell Publishers.

Burke, Edmund (1757) *Philosophical Enquiry into the Origin of Our Ideas of the Sublime and Beautiful*. London: R. and J. Dodsley.

Cone, Edward T. (1971) *Fantastic Symphony: An Authoritative Score, Historical Background, Analysis Views, and Comments*. New York: W.W. Norton.

Dahlhaus, Carl (1991 [1978]) *The Idea of Absolute Music*, trans. Roger Lustig. Chicago: University of Chicago Press.

Gardiner, John Eliot (2007) *Berlioz Rediscovered*. DVD. London: Decca.

Gardiner, John Eliot and Orchestre Révolutionnaire et Romantique (1994) *9 Symphonies*. CD. Hamburg and New York: Archiv Produktion.

Gifford, Terry (1999) *Pastoral*. London and New York: Routledge.

Harrington, Paul (1989) 'Holst and Vaughan Williams: Radical Pastoral', in Christopher Norris (ed.), *Music and the Politics of Culture*. New York: St Martin's Press, pp. 106–27.

Höhnen, Heinz Werner (ed.) (1984) *Justin Heinrich Knecht, 'La Portrait Musicale de la Nature'*, in *The Symphony, 1720–1840, Series* C, Volume XIII. New York: Garland, pp. xi–xxiii, 1–71.

Ingram, David (2010) *The Jukebox in the Garden: Ecocriticism and American Popular Music since 1960*. Amsterdam: Rodopi.

Jander, Owen Hughes (1993) 'The Prophetic Conversation in Beethoven's "Scene by the Brook"', *The Musical Quarterly* 77:3: 508–59.

Jones, David Wyn (1995) *Beethoven: 'Pastoral Symphony'*. New York: Cambridge University Press.

Jones, Gregory Paul (1973) 'Heinrich Christoph Koch's Description of the Symphony and a Comparison with Selected Symphonies of C.P.E. Bach and Haydn', Unpublished MA Thesis, University of California, Los Angeles.

Jung, Hermann (1995) 'Zwischen "Malerey" und "Ausdruck der Empfindung": Zu den Historischen und Ästhetischen Voraussetzungen von Justin Heinrich Knechts Le portrait musical de la nature (1785)', in Annegrit Laubenthal (ed.), *Studien zur Musikgeschichte: Eine Festschrift für Ludwig Finscher*. Kassel: Bärenreiter, pp. 417–31.

Kant, Immanuel (1790) *Kritik der Urteilskraft*. Berlin and Liebau: Lagarde & Friederich.

Koch, Heinrich (1802) *Musikalisches Lexikon*. Frankfurt am Main: August Hermann.

Kraus, Joseph C. (1991) 'Tonal Plan and Narrative Plot in Tchaikovsky's Symphony No. 5 in E Minor', *Music Theory Spectrum* 13:1 (Spring): 21–47.

Langford, Jeffrey (1983) 'The "Dramatic Symphonies" of Berlioz as an Outgrowth of the French Operatic Tradition', *The Musical Quarterly* 69:1: 85–103.

Litzmann, Berthold (ed.) (1973) *Letters of Clara Schumann and Johannes Brahms, 1853–1896*. New York: Vienna House.

Lockwood, Lewis (2003) *Beethoven: The Music and the Life*. New York: W.W. Norton.

Macdonald, Hugh (1993) 'Berlioz's Messe Solennelle', *19th-Century Music* 16:3: 267–85.

Marx, Leo (1964) *The Machine in the Garden: Technology and the Pastoral Ideal in America*. New York: Oxford University Press.

Michaelis, Christian Friedrich (1805) 'Einige Bemerkungen über das Erhabene der Musik', *Berlinische Musikalische Zeitung* 1:46: 179–81.

Naested, Henrik (2003) 'How to Bring the Ocean into the Concert Hall: Beethoven's Third Symphony and the Aesthetics of the Sublime', *Danish Yearbook of Musicology* 31: 17–36.

Norrington, Roger and The London Classical Players (1988) *Symphony No. 1 in C major, Op. 21, Symphony no. 6 in F major, op. 68*. CD. Hayes: EMI.

Peattie, Thomas (2002a) 'The Fin-de-Siècle Metropolis, Memory, Modernity and the Music of Gustav Mahler', Unpublished PhD Dissertation, Harvard University.

Peattie, Thomas (2002b) 'In Search of Lost Time: Memory and Mahler's Broken Pastoral', in Karen Painter (ed.), *Mahler and His World*. Princeton: Princeton University Press, pp. 185–98.

Pederson, Sanna (2009) 'Defining the Term "Absolute Music" Historically', *Music and Letters* 90:2: 240–62.

Reich, Nancy B. (2001) *Clara Schumann: The Artist and the Woman*. Rev. edition. Ithaca: Cornell University Press.

Rochlitz, Friedrich (1830) *Für Freunde der Tonkunst*. Second edition. Leipzig: Cnobloch.

Rousseau, Jean-Jacques (1768) *Dictionnaire de Musique*. Paris: Duchesne.

Satragni, Giangiorgio (1999) 'Richard Strauss, die Alpensinfonie und der Mythos der Natur', in Karina Wisniewska, Erich Singer and Rudolf Bossard (eds), *Mythen in der Musik: Essays zu den Internationalen Festwochen Luzern 1999*. Wabern-Bern: Benteli, pp. 100–11.

Saylor, Eric A. (2008) '"It's Not Lambkins Frisking at All": English Pastoral Music and the Great War', *The Musical Quarterly* 91:1–2: 39–59.

Schafer, R. Murray (1994 [1977]) *The Soundscape: Our Sonic Environment and the Tuning of the World*. Rochester, VT: Destiny Books.

Schmenner, Roland (1998) *Die Pastorale: Beethoven, das Gewitter und der Blitzableiter*. Kassel and New York: Bärenreiter.

Starr, Jason (2004) *What the Universe Tells Me: Unraveling the Mysteries of Mahler's Third Symphony*. DVD. Pleasantville, NY: VAI.

Sulzer, Johann Georg (1771–74) *Allgemeine Theorie der Schönen Künste*. Leipzig: Weidemann.

Temperley, Nicholas (1971) 'The "Symphonie fantastique" and Its Program', *The Musical Quarterly* 57:4: 593–608.

Toliver, Brooks (2011) 'The Alps, Richard Strauss's *Alpine Symphony* and Environmentalism', *Green Letters: Studies in Ecocriticism* 15: 8–21.

Tucker, Mark (1996) 'Of Men and Mountains: Ives in the Adirondacks', in J. Peter Burkholder (ed.), *Charles Ives and His World*. Princeton: Princeton University Press, pp. 161–96.

Von Glahn, Denise (2003) *The Sounds of Place: Music and the American Cultural Landscape*. Boston, MA: Northeastern University Press.

Watkins, Holly (2007) 'The Pastoral After Environmentalism: Nature and Culture in Stephen Albert's *Symphony: RiverRun*', *Current Musicology* 84: 7–24.

Will, Richard (1997) 'Time, Morality, and Humanity in Beethoven's Pastoral Symphony', *Journal of the American Musicological Society* 50:2: 271–329.

Will, Richard (2002a) *The Characteristic Symphony in the Age of Haydn and Beethoven*. New York: Cambridge University Press.

Will, Richard (2002b) 'The Nature of the Pastoral Symphony (Review Essay)', *Beethoven Forum* 9:2: 205–15.

12

Treaty obligations: science and art in Antarctica

Mike Pearson

I have never been anywhere which is so obviously not made of words, not made out of human perceptions and understandings. It's itself. It stands apart from human culture. It overshadows human culture and there is something transporting and rather good for us in getting to a place so different. A place which we really cannot plausibly claim is just a subdivision of our own concerns. (Spufford 2011)

Antarctica

It is a continent of 14 million square kilometres. It is the coldest, driest, windiest place on the planet. It is 98 per cent covered in ice, on average 1.6 kilometres thick. It contains 90 per cent of Earth's ice and 70 per cent of its fresh water. It has no indigenous population; in winter, around one thousand scientists and other personnel occupy scattered research stations, their number rising to five thousand during summer months. Around forty thousand tourists visit each year on cruise ships, of whom twenty-eight thousand go ashore. It has long been a source of inspiration for the artistic imagination, albeit remotely – in Samuel Taylor Coleridge's poem *The Rime of the Ancient Mariner* (1789), in Edgar Allan Poe's novel *The Narrative of Arthur Gordon Pym of Nantucket* (1838); it is, currently, a bellwether for our planetary fate (Leane 2012).

Treaty and protocol

Antarctica is a 'global common', held in common, for the common good. Signed on 1 December 1959, the Antarctic Treaty[1] was a practical outcome of transnational scientific cooperation undertaken during

International Geophysical Year (IGY) 1957–58; the original document is in English, French, Russian and Spanish. It professes that 'it is in the interest of all mankind that Antarctica shall continue forever to be used exclusively for peaceful purposes and shall not become a scene or object of international discord'; and it espouses 'the substantial contributions to scientific knowledge resulting from international cooperation in scientific investigation in Antarctica' ('Preamble', The Antarctic Treaty 1959).

Article I affirms Antarctica's neutral status: 'There shall be prohibited, inter alia, any measures of a military nature, such as the establishment of military bases and fortifications, the carrying out of military manoeuvres, as well as the testing of any type of weapon.' Significantly, at the height of East/West 'Cold War' tensions, Article V declares: 'Any nuclear explosions in Antarctica and the disposal there of radioactive waste material shall be prohibited.' The Treaty is in effect the first non-nuclear proliferation agreement.

Article II confirms freedom of investigation, whilst emphasising prospects for collaborative research endeavours. Article III adds: 'In order to promote international co-operation information regarding plans for scientific programs are to be exchanged to permit maximum economy and efficiency of operations'; it foresees the movement of personnel between national expeditions and installations. Uniquely, under Article VII, all signatories have the right to appoint observers who shall have unfettered freedom of access and rights of inspection at any time to any or all areas of Antarctica – including all stations, ships and aircraft. At any point, a Russian scientist may enter a United States base and enquire about activities.

As an instrument of accord and non-partisan association, the Treaty is an enduring achievement that acknowledges individual limitations in comprehending the environmental particularities and extremes of Antarctica, and their wider implications. Its accent is however from the outset slewed towards science.

Under Article XIII, the Treaty is open for accession by any state that is a member of the United Nations; non-contributory signatories include Papua New Guinea and Mongolia. But Article IV remains contentious – whilst asserting that no activities constitute the basis of claims to territorial sovereignty, it ignores the extant and conflicting assertions of nations including Argentina, Chile and the United Kingdom, whose bases still shadow each other down the Antarctic Peninsula. And it allows the United States to be anywhere and everywhere, concealing 'a darker American ambition to have unfettered access to the entire continent so that any of its hidden resources might be exploited without regard to the rights of the supposedly sovereign powers' (Day 2012: 486).

Subsequent treaty articles, protocols and annexes defend and preserve the continent's ostensibly pristine condition. The Protocol on Environmental Protection (1991) aims comprehensively to protect the Antarctic environment and dependent ecosystems, 'in the interest of mankind as a whole'; to acknowledge 'the unique opportunities Antarctic offers for scientific monitoring and research essential to understanding the global environment'; and to designate Antarctica as a natural reserve.[2] Article 7 of the Protocol prohibits any activity relating to mineral resources other than scientific research; thus far, oil and mining conglomerates have been kept at bay.

Annex II, Article 3 to the Protocol protects the native fauna and flora from harmful interference; Article 4 prohibits the introduction of non-native animal or plant species, with special mention of poultry and their associated micro-organisms. Despite their key role in the practices of the so-called Heroic Era of exploration (1897–1922), all dogs were to be removed by 1 April 1 1994. Under Annex III, all wastes generated shall be returned 'to the maximum extent practicable to the country from which the activities generating the waste were organized'. Annex IV bans the discharge of oil and noxious substances and 'the disposal into the sea of all plastics, including but not limited to synthetic ropes, synthetic fishing nets, and plastic garbage bags and other garbage including paper products, rags, glass, metal, bottles, crockery, incineration ash, dunnage, lining and packing materials'.

What can and cannot be done and how it may be undertaken and achieved on the ground in Antarctica is thus strictly prescribed and proscribed, by agreement and by obligation. Simply, the effects and impacts of all practices and processes must be recoverable or reversible: Erase your footprint; take your rubbish home with you.

Thus far, the Treaty holds; and it offers a suggestive framework for broader application in environments and contexts closer to home, in 'local commons', although it does require us consider what comprises the common good.

Heritage

It was not always thus. Whether by accident or design, expeditions of the 'Heroic Era'[3] over-wintered, transporting and then abandoning what they needed, slaughtering wildlife as required to subsist, and leaving archaeological traces of their activities: contentiously, Antarctica is one of the few places in the world where the record of humanity's first encounter and habitation exist, and in some profusion. The fragmentary detritus of their exploratory exploits – dwellings, equipment and the faunal remains of both animal companions and victims – still litters the landscape, the marks of human presence often apparent as emplacements within and inscriptions upon the icy whiteness. And these remains are now themselves safeguarded in Annex V, Article 3 to the Protocol which ensures that 'Any area, including any marine area, may be designated as an Antarctic Specially Protected Area to protect outstanding environmental, scientific, historic, aesthetic or wilderness values, any combination of those values, or ongoing or planned scientific research'.

In the Ross Dependency, there are thirty-four historic sites. Chief amongst them are five wooden huts, at four locations accessible by ship: the bases of Carsten Borchgrevink (1898–1900), R.F. Scott (1901–4; 1910–13) and Ernest Shackleton (1907–9), with many of the provisions of their inhabitants still intact. Although these prefabricated buildings were temporary structures intended for habitation over one or two polar winters at most, they have survived in the exceptional and combined circumstances of isolation and arrested deterioration in the dryness and cold. They are the focus of a major international project, co-ordinated by the New Zealand-based Antarctic Heritage Trust (AHT), to survey, stabilise, conserve, restore and reconstruct the structures and their contents.[4] The AHT is further charged with their interpretation *and* display, in an address to those wealthy enough to visit them – at present at a cost in excess of US \$20,000 per head.

Ironically, the project acknowledges the kinds of profligate incursion that the later Treaty seeks to ameliorate, in its celebration of refuse and debris revalued as artefacts. But what survives is not just as it was left, as if for our future apprehension, some unique opportunity to experience the past just as it was, in a perfect snapshot of an Edwardian world. There is an apparent plenitude – huts filled with objects in concatenations of the exceptional and the familiar – contra expectation that the archaeological record is inevitably meagre, its components metonymic. And it is disconcerting: we don't expect the past to return in such sublime abundance. But what survives is of itself incomplete and deceptive. The assemblages are a combination of that which was not consumed, not intentionally cached or accidentally lost out in the field by parties. It is that surplus to requirements, or that having served its purpose; that deemed of neither further use nor value, not worth bringing back by expeditions always in parlous financial straits; that left, altruistically, for later expeditions; that remaining from the scavenging of subsequent expeditions; that which has escaped more recent pilfering; or resetting to better resemble period photographs.

These are complex places and the picture is a distorted one. Any claims to authentic restoration should be subject to critical scrutiny. In their contemporary arrangement, what principles of heritage display are the AHT employing? Is their preservation 'an important physical dimension to the foundation stories'; 'used to create and reinforce the moral claim that nations need to justify their occupation' (Day 2012: 522)? And what stories does it chose to tell here? For these were not locales solely of scientific rectitude and expeditionary zeal; as sites of confinement during winter months, they were places of leisure and entertainment, of artistic pursuits and of dreams – of film shows and debates, theatrical performances and games, celebratory dinners and evenings at the pianola and gramophone. And just how long will the will to maintain them last as, in the need for constant renovation, they recall 'Theseus's paradox': as all the structural components are successively replaced, do the huts remain fundamentally the same object?

Other historic sites are less auspicious. In June–July 1911, Edward Wilson, 'Birdie' Bowers and Apsley Cherry-Garrard, members of Scott's *Terra Nova* expedition, undertook an arduous trek in the depths of the polar winter. In near darkness and with temperatures frequently reaching minus 70° Fahrenheit, they hauled two sledges from their base at Cape Evans on Ross Island to Cape Crozier in search of emperor penguin eggs. Their object was to collect a series of embryos to provide evidence of the evolutionary sequence of reptiles and birds. Their trek is recorded in vivid detail in Cherry-Garrard's classic volume *The Worst Journey in the World* (1994 [1922]).

At the opening of chapter seven, Cherry-Garrard includes an inventory of the equipment they took with them – tools, scientific apparatus, sledging gear, 'expendable stores'. At Cape Crozier, this was stashed in a double-lined tent and in the so-called 'Wilson's igloo', a temporary structure they built from boulders and blocks of ice with a canvas roof supported on one of the sledges. His account of the subsequent disappearance of the tent and the destruction of the igloo around them in a fierce blizzard is one of the most extraordinary passages in his work. Some of the equipment they eventually retrieved and returned to their base at Cape Evans; some they purposely left at site, including one of the sledges; some they never refound, as it was scattered by the wind or hidden beneath drift. The rock walls lay as they fell, in a rough rectangle.

In 1957, Sir Edmund Hillary visited the site whilst testing tractors on the Commonwealth Trans-Antarctic Expedition. He found the sledge,

Wilson's drawing pencils, unexposed film and blubber stove. He removed nearly one hundred artefacts and distributed them amongst museums in New Zealand – there is a Thermos flask and zoological apparatus in Canterbury Museum, Christchurch, New Zealand. In 1959, remnants of the canvas roof were visible at site; in 1985, items there included a woollen sock that had perhaps been used to block a leak in the walls during the blizzard. By 1990, remaining objects – including a ball of string and a scarf – were in an advanced state of decay; in 1992, they were visible beneath a layer of ice in an interior demarcated by the collapsed walls. In 2015, rope, canvas, woollens and a penguin skin still protruded.

Wilson's party was at Cape Crozier for only ten days; the ruins of their camp are now rarely visited – doubly inaccessible because of their geographical remoteness and their proximity to a protected penguin colony: the site can now be approached only by permit. A potential moment of tension arises between the priorities of environment science – in the guise of faunal conservation – and of the humanities – as heritage conservation – under new demands for access: the desire by tourists to visit such an iconic locale, with Treaty and Protocol articles under pressure from changing realities.

Visitors

Tourists travelling to Antarctica land, in the main, for short periods at selected sites from cruise ships such as Norwegian company Hurtigruten's 276-berth MS *Fram*, on which I travelled to the Antarctic Peninsula in January 2010. Some mature voyagers are engaged in 'bucket list' ticking, or in a form of 'disaster tourism' to witness the whiteness before it is transformed; given the expense, there are few children – those who might stand face to face with penguins, in modes of encounter that might presage invigorated attitudes to the concerns of the Protocol. In order to forestall deleterious effects upon environment, codes of conduct have become necessary; the voluntary International Association of Antarctic Travel Operators (IAATO) organisation has drawn up 'General Guidelines for Visitors to the Antarctic'. By agreement, only one ship may visit a site at any one time; a maximum of one hundred passengers may be ashore (shuttled in relay in inflatable Zodiac boats); and vessels with five hundred passengers may not make landings.[5]

Some recommendations are relatively easy to comply with – difficult to imagine how 'the use of either guns or explosives' would ever be possible. Others are time-consuming in the context of mounting visitor anticipation and excitement – 'In order to prevent the introduction of non-native species and disease, carefully wash boots and clean all equipment including clothes, bags, tripods, tents and walking sticks before bringing them to Antarctica. Pay particular attention to boot treads, Velcro fastenings and pockets which could contain soil or seeds.' So, all rucksacks are vacuumed on initial embarkation; and compulsory, ship-issued wellington boots are disinfected before each landing, and upon return – to remove penguin guano.

'Keep a safe distance from dangerous wildlife like fur seals both on land and at sea'; 'Keep at least fifteen metres away, where practicable' is good advice when the blood-smeared reptilian maw of the leopard seal could easily accommodate a human head. The admonition to 'Always give them the right of way' endorses a pecking order here as gentoo penguins file purposefully up from the beach. But how does one 'maintain an appropriate distance', keeping five metres away from a curious creature that – lacking land-based predators – walks directly towards you?

Perhaps it's best to make landfall in Antarctica with nothing: 'Do not deposit any litter or garbage on land nor discard it into the sea'. And to leave with only memories and photographs: 'Do not take souvenirs, whether artificial, biological or geological items, including feathers, bones, eggs, vegetation, soil, rocks, meteorites or fossils.' Overall, this is a set of understandings and codes which have their nascence in exceptional circumstances that might inform and orientate human–environment relationships elsewhere.

One frequent port of call is the former British 'Base A' at Port Lockroy, built during the secretive Operation Tabarin in 1944 and now designated Antarctic Historic Site and Monument No. 61.[6] Here there is a post office; here, though no visa is necessary, you can have your passport stamped. Here the interior is arranged to reflect its occupancy in the 1950s. And here the impact of eighteen thousand visitors per season is closely monitored, for gentoo penguins nest directly under and around the huts, and Antarctic shags, with their enormous downy young, are close by. Here snowy (or pale-faced) sheathbills will quickly rummage through half-opened bags. Resembling a cross between a pigeon and a pullet – they are the only Antarctic birds lacking webbed feet – these white birds with pink facial skin are tame and inquisitive scavengers, devouring everything from seal placenta to penguin poop. In their strangeness, they are unexpected, uncanny, beyond one's anticipated avian checklist. And they go about their specialised everyday life and, as with all other Antarctic fauna, ambivalent towards and indifferent to our attempts to encapsulate their world for our own aesthetic consumption. Beyond the ambiguities of Treaty Article XIII, it is they who truly own Antarctica.

Ecology

We now cherish Antarctic fauna, but that was not always the case. In the early nineteenth century, seal and whale populations were drastically reduced: in the 1821–22 season, over 320,000 fur seals we killed for their pelts. Even now, in recent years, up to a hundred thousand albatrosses per annum have drowned attempting to take the bait from long-line fishing in which single lines may be 130 kilometres in length with forty thousand hooks. Thankfully, *pace* the Protocol, there is little sign yet of deaths through the consumption of plastic objects – bottle tops, toothbrushes, cigarette lighters, combs and children's toys – that are the fate of Pacific laysan albatrosses recorded in Chris Jordan's extraordinary photographs.[7]

Antarctica has a simple ecology; there are only two flowering plant species: Antarctic hair-grass and Antarctic pearlwort. But it is the physical environment itself that has become the harbinger of global change, the place where effects are immediately observable – in climatic data assiduously collected since the 1940s; in the historic record of carbon dioxide accumulation in ice cores; with the discovery in 1984 by British Antarctic Survey (BAS) scientists of the hole in the Earth's ozone layer, depleted principally by human-made chlorofluorocarbons (CFCs); in the catastrophic collapse of ice shelves such as Larsen B in 2002. 'Antarctic knowledge is suddenly urgent knowledge' (Spufford 2011).

Art and science

The Treaty and the attendant extolling of science – 'a form of symbolic capital' (Dodds 2012: 93) – is at the core of creation myths in Antarctica:

> A vision is offered up of far-sighted men (and they are all men in this story) using science and peace to construct said landmark agreement, designed to save the Antarctic from the grubby Cold War and colonial geopolitics. (50)

Science holds an unchallenged hegemonic position; the Treaty makes no acknowledgement of the arts, and the advent of tourism is unforeseen. Recent government schemes that have supported visiting artists and writers are primarily at the behest of science: to help contextualise and explicate research activities, with those of claimant nations helping play a legitimising role. The United States National Science Foundation's (NSF) Antarctic Artist's and Writer's Program serves to enhance public outreach with unambiguous purpose: 'to create images demonstrating to the American taxpayer that the funds spent on Antarctic research was worth it' (Fox 2011: 30). As much of the science is obscure, there is a bias towards the 'pictorial, representational and conventional': 'to document the physical form and conditions of the continent, and then to make it comprehensible as a sublime landscape suitable for preservation as a stage for scientific enquiry' (30). The New Zealand 'Artists to Antarctica' and later 'Community Engagement' programmes have aimed to promote 'understanding and appreciation of the values of Antarctica through the contribution of writers, artists and musicians', playing 'a crucial part in informing and influencing the public's understanding towards science and operations in Antarctica and the Southern Ocean' (Shepherd 2015: 403); the Australian Antarctic Arts Fellowship seeks to enhance 'understanding of the Antarctic environment and communicate the significance of Australia's activities there'.[8]

Early British expeditions included both amateur and professional artists. Edward Wilson on Scott's *Discovery* and *Terra Nova* was an accomplished watercolourist, and eminent photographers and cinematographers Herbert Ponting on *Terra Nova* and Frank Hurley on Shackleton's *Endurance* were charged with registering the still images and films that would redeem expeditionary debts. Many of Wilson's landscapes and faunal studies and Ponting's and Hurley's photographs of human endeavours are archived in the Polar Art Collection and Picture Library of the Scott Polar Research Institute (SPRI) in Cambridge, UK;[9] now the thousands of tourist snapshots record: 'We were there too'.

But in its primary whiteness, Antarctica resists easy visual representation. Sound – and the lack of it – is where its elemental particularity resides: to listen in Antarctica is to listen back in time, archaeologically – for its sonic composition is as it has always been. Herbert Ponting's film of the *Terra Nova* expedition is entitled *The Great White Silence* (1924). Restored in 2010 by the British Film Institute National Archive, the film is of course silent; but the new musical soundtrack by Simon Fisher Turner was inspired by a recording of the hushed interior of Scott's hut at Cape Evans made by sound artist Chris Watson whilst working on David Attenborough's BBC Television series *The Frozen Planet* (2011). Noise signals change and potential danger in Antarctica – an approaching blizzard, ice cracking beneath one's feet; Watson's own *Glacial Melt* records the calving of the Barne Glacier, a transitional event of groans and screams.[10] Ralph Vaughan Williams's score for Charles Frend's film *Scott of the Antarctic* (1948) – later his Symphony

No. 7, *Sinfonia Antartica* – is impressionistic, written from afar; even the film was shot in Pinewood Studios and on location in Norway. But Peter Maxwell Davies's Symphony No. 8, commissioned by the BAS to commemorate the fiftieth anniversary of Frend's film, was informed by personal experience; he visited Antarctica in December 1997. Two particular occurrences inspired his composition: on entering the pack by ship, that of hearing 'the ice crack and split before the bow, then roar along, keel to stern, in a tumultuous clatter of slabs and shards'; and of witnessing an avalanche in the narrow Lemaire Channel, the sound resembling 'the mightiest, gentlest, longest whisper ever. It was a sound which seemed almost quieter than the silence which surrounded it'.[11] In 2013, heavy rock group Metallica played inside a small dome at the Argentine Antarctic Base Carlini: in order to comply with local environmental etiquette, they used no amplification and the sound was transmitted to the audience through headphones.

Antarctica can be reached only by ship or aircraft through two 'gateways': via Punta Arenas (Chile) or Ushuaia (Argentina) and Christchurch (New Zealand). Given difficulty of access and the demands of life-support, few artists and writers have visited Antarctica of their own volition. Between 2001 and 2009, the BAS 'Artist's and Writer's Programme' supported painters, writers and composers; in 2011, on the centenary of the *Terra Nova* expedition, the SPRI sponsored Scott's granddaughter Dafila Scott as artist in residence aboard the Royal Navy's ice patrol vessel HMS *Scott*.[12] Significantly, there have been few examples of performative or time-based intervention. However in 2008–9, sculptor Chris Dobrowolski travelled south with a collection of objects: to the figurative 'blank canvas' of Antarctica, he decided to take the conventional art world, in the form of a number of gilt picture frames.[13] On arrival, he refashioned them into a traditionally designed sledge. He also took a number of models, toys and children's books – from Action Man to the Ladybird book *Scott of the Antarctic*. These he photographed in the Antarctic landscape, carefully using perspective and the distance between foreground and background to suggest humorously that the toy is of equal stature to its authentic counterpart – so his sledge appears to be pulled by dogs, absent on the continent since 1994.

Architecture

All creative activities must perforce conform to the Treaty and Protocol, yet few have had to address them directly within a design brief. Early expeditions constructed what shelter they needed to survive for a limited period, mainly in the form of barely adequate pre-fabricated wooden sheds. Scott's *Discovery* hut was purchased in Australia. It is the sort of spacious bungalow favoured by outlying settlers, hence its incongruous sun veranda; the assembly instructions are still visible on the outer wall. It was always cold, and used by Scott only as a storeroom, workshop, laboratory and *ad hoc* auditorium for theatrical presentations. Port Lockroy is that type of Ministry of War erection redolent of those found on Second World War airfields in the east of England.

The BAS's first Halley research station was established on the floating Brunt Ice Shelf in the Weddell Sea in January 1956 by the Royal Society, in anticipation of International Geophysical Year. At a place where there is no sun for a hundred days, where the wind causes drifting snow on about 180 days each year and any erection may soon be buried, it quickly collapsed under the accumulation of drifting snow.

One of the most immediate impacts of the strictures of environmental governance in Antarctica itself has been upon the design and construction of the BAS's latest base – Halley VI. The brief calls for a building that minimises impact and complies with the Protocol: that is functionally efficient; optimised for science rather than survival; and aesthetically stimulating – though, as ever, this in order to promote 'public engagement in science, engineering and technology, raising awareness and engaging public interest in the vital scientific work being carried out in Antarctica'. Within this straightforward appeal lies a more complex challenge for competitors: all materials had to fit the hold dimensions of one specific ship and be transportable after landing across 12 kilometres of ice shelf. The location and constraints of the site for Halley VI obliged entrants to consider quick-erect methods of construction with zero environmental impact given the limited time-windows for erection during the Antarctic summer and lack of specialist machinery, with only a specific repertoire of resources and equipment for transport and assembly, including the ubiquitous, tracked Sno-Cat. What, the BAS asks, is the appropriate architectural expression for a relatively small building in a vast and remote wilderness? Can colour, material and form contribute reassurance and good spirits in the long, cold winter months; this latter to lessen the likelihood of the cabin fever that threatened early expeditions, such as the outbreak of persecution mania on Adrien de Gerlache's *Belgica* expedition (1897–99).

The winning structure is the innovative design by Hugh Broughton Architects: a pre-formed, modular structure, painted brilliantly red and blue that resembles a child's futuristic toy, a 'Transformer'.[14] Crucially, it has ski-fitted, hydraulic legs that can be individually raised to overcome snow accumulation; and each module can be towed independently to a new location if the current site gets too close to the edge of the ice shelf during collapse: an unapologetic human inscription.

Art versus science

Mariele Neudecker's sculpture *Some Things Happen All At Once* (2013) is a scale-model of Halley VI, set in a cloudy Antarctic landscape.[15] The research station is submerged at the bottom of a water-filled tank, embedded in a downscaled and cropped manifestation of a geophysical ice shelf. It was shown at the 'Antarctopia' exhibition at the 15th Venice Biennale of Architecture 2014, curated by Nadim Samman and Alexander Ponomarev, a former officer of the Russian Navy.[16] The exhibition aimed 'to explore present and future models of living with Antarctica' beyond the functional, within an expanded Antarctic imaginary. The expressed purpose was to free the arts and humanities from their subservient role: 'The projects featured in this pavilion are testaments to the Antarctic community that would yet know itself – and the continent – in ways transcending national-scientific missions.' The scenography of the exhibition was intended to suggest the provisional nature of architecture in Antarctica – as well as the logistical reality of having to transport all building materials into the continent. A series of flight-cases, of the same kind used to transport scientific equipment, were used as plinths for maquettes by contributing architects. Most startling is the design from Zaha Hadid's studio that shows the sweeps, curves and blades that are her signature – an all-white alien spacecraft parked in Antarctica.

The ensuing Antarctica Pavilion at the fifty-sixth Venice Art Biennale challenged 'the festival's politics of territorial representation', claiming Antarctica as a cultural space.[17] In a contrarian statement, Samman and Ponomarev imagine an Antarctica intended exclusively for creativity as opposed to science – provocatively also 'in the interests of the entire mankind'. 'This white continent is like a white sheet of paper on which artists of different lands and nationalities will try to write new rules of cooperation.' Ponomarev's own installation deploys the Costa Concordia maritime disaster, specifically the broken pact between Captain Schettino and his passengers, as a provocative lens through which to view the fragility of the Antarctic Treaty. It continues by suggesting that the scale model of the grounded Concordia is 'tilting like a tipped iceberg (or perhaps a shift in the polar axis itself) and stands as an image of terrestrial re-orientation: a new worldview'.

Ponomarev has further plans for an 'Antarctic Biennale', to upset traditions of 'embedded artistic practice': 'Literary anthologies and post-colonial criticism of explorers' tales already exist, and sketches of icebergs have been made down below since 1895. Since then the depictions have kept coming, heroic dilettantes replaced by debentured creators funded by government committees.' In a scheme to travel to Antarctica on a dedicated ship, artists will be able 'to explore creative terrain further afield than the hegemonic issues of imperial conquest and ecology' though one hopes that the Protocol will still hold.

Reorientating practice

How might an appraisal of treaty obligations reorientate artistic practice, there and here?

Article 3 of the Protocol on Environmental Protection to the Antarctic Treaty concerns guiding environmental principles towards the protection of the Antarctic environment and dependent and associated ecosystems and of the intrinsic value of Antarctica, including its wilderness and aesthetic values, whilst valuing it as an area for the conduct of scientific research, 'in particular research essential to understanding the global environment' (paragraph 1). 'To this end activities in the Antarctic Treaty area shall be planned and conducted so as to limit adverse impacts, to avoid adverse effects on climate and on air and water quality; significant changes in terrestrial, glacial and marine environments; detrimental changes in the distribution, abundance or productivity of species or populations of species of fauna and flora and degradation of, or substantial risk to, areas of biological, scientific, historic, aesthetic or wilderness significance' (paragraph 2). 'Assessment of possible impacts shall take account of the scope of the activity, including its area, duration and intensity and the likely cumulative impacts; whether the activity will detrimentally affect any other activity and whether technology and procedures are available to provide for environmentally safe operations; whether there exists a capacity to respond promptly and effectively to accidents particularly those with potential environmental effects' (paragraph 2).

Environmental Evaluation (Annex I to the protocol) 'shall include a description of the proposed activity, possible alternatives to the activity, *including the alternative of not proceeding* (my italics), and the consequences of those alternatives; a description of the initial environmental reference state with which predicted changes are to be compared; [...] consideration of cumulative impacts of the proposed activity in the light of existing activities and other known planned activities; identification of measures, including monitoring programs, that could be taken to minimise or mitigate the impact of the proposed activity' (Annex I, article 3).

What if we were to regard these articles as transferable: as operative axioms, imperatives and circumscriptions for artistic practice in more familiar regional contexts? What might be the impact upon our own endeavours – in for instance site-specific performance and land art – if we were to regard the admonitions and obligations of Treaty and Protocol as universally binding?

Secondly, how might we continue to address Antarctica – a place few of us will ever visit, and perhaps fewer of us ought to visit – at a distance, through enhanced opportunities for remote engagement provided by digital technology? Designing alternative approaches to museology in relation to the 360-degree online imaging of the historic huts made available by the AHT; creating fictive audiovisual guides to inaccessible locations such as Wilson's igloo and the Cape Royds Adélie penguin rookery on Googlemaps; using laser-projected climate data as stage design – as in *2071* presented at the Royal Court Theatre in London and featuring scientist Chris Rapley speaking without notes for 75 minutes in a provocative form of science–art collaboration.[18]

Or perhaps we should just leave Antarctica alone, letting it 'stand apart' as a salutary retort to artistic hubris, resisting our urge to represent and explicate its scale and their affects: overshadowing us, sublime in its indifference and ineffability.

Notes

1 Secretariat of the Antarctic Treaty (1959) *The Antarctic Treaty*. www.ats.aq/e/ats.htm accessed 22 October 2015.
2 Secretariat of the Antarctic Treaty (1991) *Protocol on Environmental Protection to the Antarctic Treaty*. www.ats.aq/e/ep.htm accessed 22 October 2015.
3 The 'Heroic era/Age' of Antarctic exploration was between 1895 and 1917. www.nzaht.org accessed 26 December 2015.
4 New Zealand Antarctic Heritage Trust. www.nzaht.org accessed 22 October 2015.
5 International Association of Antarctic Travel Operators, 'General Guidelines for Visitors to the Antarctic'. http://iaato.org/c/document_library/get_file?uuid=aed1054d-3e63–4a17-a6cd-axisa87beb15e287&groupId=10157accessed 22 October 2015.
6 United Kingdom Antarctic Heritage Trust. www.ukaht.org accessed 22 October 2015.
7 C. Jordan, www.chrisjordan.com/gallery/midway/#CF000313%2018x24 accessed 22 November 2015.

8 Australian Antarctic Arts Fellowship. www.antarctica.gov.au/about-antarctica/antarctic-arts-fellowship accessed 15 October 2015.
9 Scott Polar Research Institute Picture Library. www.spri.cam.ac.uk/picturelibrary/ accessed 26 December 2015.
10 C. Watson, *Glacial Melt*. www.bbc.co.uk/programmes/b05n1dpv accessed 22 October 2015.
11 P. Maxwell Davies, (1997) 'Max's Antarctic diary'. www.maxopus.com/resources_detail.aspx?key=46 accessed 22 November 2015.
12 Dafila Scott, www.dafilascott.co.uk/antarcticgallery/antarctic.html and www.spri.cam.ac.uk/museum/exhibitions/dafilascott/ accessed 10 December 2015.
13 C. Dobrowolski, www.cdobo.com/default.asp?id_site=56143905&id_prime subject=2 accessed 22 November 2015.
14 Hugh Broughton Architects, www.hbarchitects.co.uk accessed 22 November 2015, and Ruth Slavid (2015).
15 M. Neudecker, www.marieleneudecker.co.uk/marieleneudec-14.html accessed 22 November 2015.
16 A. Ponomarev, 'Antarctopia' www.antarcticpavilion.com/antarctopia-concept.html accessed 22 November 2015.
17 A. Ponomarev, 'The Antarctic Pavilion'. www.antarcticpavilion.com/the-antarctic-pavilion.html accessed 22 November 2015.
18 C. Rapley, *2071*. www.royalcourttheatre.com/whats-on/2071 accessed 22 October 2015.

References

Cherry-Garrard, A. (1994 [1922]) *The Worst Journey in the World*. London: Picador.

Day, D. (2012) *Antarctica: A Biography*. Oxford: Oxford University Press.

Dodds, K. (2012) *The Antarctic: A Very Short Introduction*. Oxford: Oxford University Press.

Fox, W.L. (2011) 'Every New Thing: the Evolution of Artistic Technologies in the Antarctic – or How Land Arts Came to the Ice', in A. Polli and J. Marsching (eds), *Far Field: Digital Culture, Climate Change and the Poles*. London: Intellect, chapter 2.

Leane, E. (2012) *Antarctica in Fiction*. Cambridge: Cambridge University Press.

Shepherd, P. (2015) 'Creativity at the Frozen Frontier', in D. Liggett, B. Storey, Y. Cook and V. Meduna (eds), *Exploring the Last Continent: An Introduction to Antarctica*. New York: Springer, pp. 399–410.

Slavid, Ruth (2015) *Ice Station: The Creation of Halley VI, Britain's Pioneering Antarctic Research Station*. Chicago: University of Chicago Press.

Spufford, F. (2011) In BBC TV *Timeshift* 11:7 'Of Ice and Men'. First broadcast 3 November.

13

On-site natural heritage interpretation: an ecocritical reading

William Welstead

Visitors to the countryside are increasingly faced with a variety of panels, interpretation centres and other interventions that convey selected narratives and ways of seeing our natural heritage. This chapter explores the scope for these cultural objects to be included in ecocritical enquiry. The ubiquity and undemanding nature of many displays makes for an accessible source of information about basic ecology as filtered through the viewpoint of site managers for national and country parks, nature reserves and other protected sites. As such they make up a significant part of the 'prior reading' that informs the understanding and sensibilities of people as they come to literary, visual art and other cultural readings of the natural world.

Panels or 'wayside exhibits' are the cheapest medium for interpretation that are 'popular with funding agencies – cynics would say that this is because they display the agency's logo' (Bryant 2006: 182). Gibb refers to this as 'scent marking by various bodies', but also cautions that much of the inventory of such panels in the Highlands is 'considerably older than five years and time (and weather) had taken its toll' (Gibb 2006: 39).

Keirle discusses how the body managing a site can use the exhibits and other structures to reinforce a corporate image through 'a design style that reflects the organisation and makes the site instantly recognisable as being managed by a particular organisation'. He illustrates this point with a photograph of a Forestry Commission sign at Bwlch Nant yr Arian in mid-Wales (Keirle 2002: 106–7). This sign is appropriately made up of four timber planks fixed between wooden uprights, with the top surface of the top panel rising to an apex. Cut into this panel with a router is the Forestry Commission logo of two trees, one deciduous and the other coniferous, with 'Forestry Commission' in English and Welsh. This distinctive shape and clear logo is visible from a distance, but has caused problems in Wales where in 2013 the forestry body was merged with other countryside and environmental bodies into Natural Resources Wales. The new organisation has been at pains to impose its own corporate identity on the resources within its care. For the Tan y Coed woodland the new logo has been pasted over the old on the interpretation panels themselves, but in some places that has meant leaving the distinctive shape of the Forestry Commission boards with the associated old logo still in place. In other places on this site, the headboard has been removed altogether which removes the logo and disrupts the distinctive shape, as well as giving the board a vandalised appearance. It is evident that imposing a brand image on the countryside is far from simple and seems to be a priority that overrides all other considerations.

The creative arts are also frequently involved in making a direct contribution to interpretation projects, through literary and visual art commissions, story telling, exhibitions and public art. One example where the literary input was given a prominent role is the Tweed Rivers Interpretation Project, in which twenty-six writers and visual artists were asked to produce work based on a creative engagement with the river and its tributaries. An illustrated volume brought together the poetry, prose and visual art from this project (Cockburn and Carter 2005). The project also included on-site public art and more conventional interpretation panels exploring the ecology of selected sites. In their preface the authors state that:

> Interpretation here means encouraging people to explore, appreciate, and build their own relationship with a place. The Project has worked to bring alive the stories of various sites within the Tweed catchment, from viewpoints and Iron Age hill forts to eighteenth century follies and landmarks for local folk tales. (Cockburn and Carter 2005: 10)

The Tweed River catchment is not owned by a single body and (hence and thankfully?) there has been no attempt here to impose a unified corporate image. Individual writers and artists were given freedom to find their own stories, although a particularly long poem by Katrina Porteous had to be cut for reasons of space (Cockburn and Carter 2005: 23–30 and 163–70). Porteous's full poem 'Tweed' is reproduced in her collection *Two Countries* (Porteous 2014: 46–66). In the introduction to that collection she records how she went about this commission:

> Time was short and the river was long. I had only three months to research and write about over 100 miles of river. [...] For two months, I

squelched along as much of the Tweed as was publicly accessible (and a lot that was not). Susheila [Jamieson, the artist she was paired with] and I worked separately, I recorded interviews with shepherds, farm-managers, unemployed former mill-workers, water bailiffs, gillies, landowners in formidable castles, the last traditional salmon netsmen on the river, and a lifelong elderly poacher called Joe. Their voices all found their way into the poem, expressing the many tensions between the older and contemporary ways of life, and our differing approaches to what we mean by 'nature'. (Porteous 2014: 10–11)

In this respect, Porteous is following a similar formula to Alice Oswald in her long poem 'Dart', although it is very different in tone and effect (Oswald 2002).

Interpretation is a broad practice that embodies, creative writing and art, constructing ideas of place, explaining the natural environment and promoting a corporate identity. While projects like that on the Tweed Rivers will be immediately accessible to ecocritics, the humble but ubiquitous interpretation panel and the increasing use of technology may be more problematic. This chapter explores how all these elements fit together and the part they play in constructing our view of the natural environment.

Interpretation in the United Kingdom is now seen as a specialist activity with its own professional body, the Association for Heritage Interpretation. Many professionals, in the interpretation consultancies and working for statutory and voluntary heritage organisations, look to Freeman Tilden's *Interpreting our Heritage* as the text to inform their practice. In this book, which was published in 1957 and has remained in print for more than six decades, Tilden set down six principles and in particular stressed that '[t]he chief aim of interpretation is not instruction, but provocation' (2007 [1957]: 34–5). His ideas were developed for the United States National Park Service and reflect North American concepts of wilderness and the established role of National Parks, which date back to the designation of Yellowstone in 1872. There are now numerous handbooks and guides on how to approach interpretation, nearly all of which refer back to the principles developed by Tilden. For example Sam Ham, writing in the light of a considerable body of research showing just how important audience thinking is in interpretation, claims that 'Tilden was nearly thirty years ahead of theory and research when he made his famous claim [about provocation]' (2013: xvi).

National Parks in England and Wales were not established until 1951 and in Scotland even later (2002). The first National Nature Reserves in Scotland (1951), England (1954) and Wales (1954) were created under the same legislation that provided for National Parks (National Parks and Access to Countryside Act, 1949). Tilden developed his ideas in the context of an already mature concept of the role of National Parks in North America, but, when Tilden's book was first published, both national parks and nature reserves were only just being contemplated in the United Kingdom.

Much of the thinking about how the United Kingdom should protect its natural heritage took place during the Second World War. Particularly influential was the plant ecologist Arthur Tansley, who set down his proposals in a short book published on off-white wartime paper as *Our Heritage of Wild Nature* (1945). The chapter on education is only three pages long, but in it he takes a somewhat different approach to Tilden. He looked to the teaching of nature study to younger pupils and, while regretting that 'it is very limited in scope', he thought that, if merged with the 'regional geography' taught to secondary schools, it could get pupils thinking about ecology through 'the botany of crop plants, their relation to climate and soil, and the weeds of arable land [which] are all good subjects for nature study' (Tansley 1945: 60). While the 'appreciation of the character and beauty of unspoiled country is widespread' he felt that a 'more widespread knowledge and a deeper understanding of the different types of country, their physical features and their characteristic vegetation, are just what is required to build up a discriminating appreciation of rural beauty and an enthusiasm for its preservation'. He notes that 'owing to the development of motor traffic large numbers of city dwellers are able to visit the country more easily and to range much further', which offered more people the opportunity to develop their appreciation of natural and beautiful regions (61). Tansley advocated preparing attractive booklets that would cover the ecology of the region as well as the history of its towns and villages. Such booklets should avoid technical detail and could 'introduce anti-litter propaganda and discourage the defacement of nature by indiscriminate plucking of wild flowers and foliage and the uprooting of plants' (62).

In contrast to car-based tourism to areas of particular beauty, Tansley saw the role of nature reserves as primarily educational. Reserves with rare species should not be publicised and others should be centres for education in field natural history. Pamphlets for sale at reserves should be more detailed and 'serve as handbooks to the reserves for all who used them' (62). This divergence between considerations of beauty and the scientific interest of particular sites was to be embodied in the 1947 act so that National Parks and National Nature Reserves followed quite different paths until the late 1980s.

Although British National Parks were able to build on the experience in North America, practice lagged behind the innovative ways in which many museums and heritage sites were engaging with the public. For Bryant, the interpretation in the national parks 'remained information-led, formulaic and uninspiring'. There was a lack of resources and of a coherent policy for interpretation (Bryant 2006: 173), and a need for the national parks to resolve the conflict between conservation and recreational access. This issue was resolved in favour of 'Tilden's interpretation-to-protection formula [...] as a means of promoting both conservation and visitor enjoyment' (Bryant 2006: 176). This concept is consistent with Tansley's vision that visitors to national parks would understand at least some of the ecology of the landscape and become advocates for its protection.

Tansley has noted that appreciation of beauty is widespread and that increased personal mobility through car ownership has given people greater access to the countryside, but did not relate how these two factors had emerged together. Alexandra Harris in *Romantic Moderns* (2010) has shown how in the 1930s Shell-Mex commissioned contemporary artists and writers to design posters to advertise their petrol. Harris notes that 'country views in advertising are common enough but rarely do they define a whole new view of England. These posters, however, have a distinctive and coherent modern look' (Harris 2010: 217). Shell-Mex also sponsored the Shell Country Guides with John Betjeman as editor. Harris illustrates the wide ambition of Shell's advertising director:

> By the mid-thirties it seems everyone was out gazeteering; Betjeman in Cornwall and Devon, Paul Nash in Dorset, John Nash in Buckinghamshire, John Piper in Oxfordshire, Robert Byron in Wiltshire (though the excellent Wiltshire gazetteer was provided by Edith Oliver and became a model for all the others). (Harris 2010: 218)

After the Second World War, the motoring industry continued to deploy artists and writers to direct motorists both how to read the countryside and where to go to experience these insights for themselves.

Helen Macdonald, author *of H Is for Hawk*, lists the *AA Book of the Countryside* (1973) as one of the six books that made her: 'when I was a child I wasn't sure what the AA was, but in a part the organisation made the countryside for me'. However she goes on to see this 1970s picture as 'a painful record of what has disappeared. Since its publication we've lost more than 420 million birds from Europe' (*Guardian*, 31 January 2015). While artists and writers gave the motoring public a way of seeing the countryside, Tansley hoped that interest could be generated to show the part ecology plays in the formation of landscape character. However, in the immediate postwar period, ecology remained a specialist subject and scientists and amateur naturalists were wary of attracting widespread attention to what were seen as fragile and special sites. The return of the osprey to Scotland as a breeding bird in 1954 after an absence of half a century was to force a change from this secretive approach, so that wild nature could be presented to large numbers of people.

When ospreys were first found to be breeding again in the Cairngorms, the Royal Society for the Protection of Birds (RSPB) mounted a commando-style operation to guard the nest and to keep it secret. Philip Brown who played a major role in this exercise gave a detailed account of the drama of this return and the measures taken to give the birds the best chance to breed successfully in *The Return of the Osprey* (1962). In 1958 an egg collector managed to steal the eggs from the nest despite round-the-clock guarding. This event was given wide publicity in the press and public opinion came round strongly in support of the preservation efforts. The decision was taken 'to make the whole matter public and make it possible for people to watch the birds from a special observation hide established at a safe distance from the eyrie' (Brown 1962: 62). The back of the dust cover on this book shows an AA sign directing motorists to the Loch Garten site. The large car park at the site today reflects its continuing attraction for motorists as a destination for nature-based tourism.

In 2014 Loch Garten celebrated the sixty years since ospreys first returned to breed in Scotland. The visitor and interpretation facilities have been enlarged and modernised at frequent intervals over the last six decades. Visitors arrive at the large car park where an interpretation board provides an indication of what they might hope to see after they have paid to enter the observation centre. There are two logos on the board, one for the RSPB and the other the general logo for a Scottish National Nature Reserve. The RSPB logo shows a stylised image of an avocet. This species returned to breed in Suffolk in 1947 after an absence of more than a hundred years. This re-establishment as a breeding bird was regarded as a success, to rank alongside the return of the osprey, and the avocet was adopted as the symbol for the RSPB and was being reproduced on the society's tie from 1955.[1] Since then, the changing nature of the avocet depiction marks its transition from a signifier of membership to the marketing logo of a highly commercial organisation.

The avocet logo appears again on the modular interpretation board at the entrance to the Osprey Centre, where it is shown twice, once on the wooden frame at the top of the board together with the national nature reserve logo and again on one of the panels where the strapline text 'Giving Nature a Home' is positioned alongside the image. The difference between the two logos is subtle, with just a single line removed from the image and the RSPB rendered now in lower case. Such rebranding, itself a signifier of active brand management, is made more difficult where, as with the Forestry Commission in Wales, the logo is carved in the wooden frame. The paper panels in the modular board can be replaced more easily. The RSPB and national nature reserve are not the only logos on the modular interpretation panel.

A separate panel records thanks to funders by displaying the logos of Scottish Natural Heritage, EU Life, BP and the Forestry Commission. The presence of the BP logo signifies the continuing interest by the petroleum companies in being associated with preserving the natural heritage. With some irony, the panel to the right of this record of thanks is headed 'Greening your travel' to encourage visitors to move away from dependency on the car. The BP logo is itself controversial; in a 2008 article Fred Pearce dismissed BP's sunflower-like logo with its tagline 'Beyond Petroleum' as greenwash. Pearce notes that 'sheltering in the alternative energy division is BP's "emissions assets business", which makes money out of carbon trading, and a venture capital unit' (*Guardian*, 20 November 2008). BP's involvement in the Abernethy National Nature Reserve derives from its leadership of the Scottish Forest Alliance together with the Forestry Commission, RSPB and the Woodland Trust with a particular emphasis on the role of forests in carbon sequestration.[2] Not all the logos on interpretation boards are as controversial as the BP logo.

The Osprey Centre at Loch Garten is within the Abernethy National Nature Reserve which since 2003 is in turn within the much larger area designated as the Cairngorms National Park. The logo adopted for the National Park is an osprey carrying a fish. This is not the logo for the statutory park authority, but it signifies the 'park brand' and can be used by businesses, organisations and communities working within the Cairngorms area. The logo can be used in connection with guidance on interpretation developed by James Carter and Andy Ford (2008). This guidance is non-prescriptive and is based on modern best practice developed in the UK and North America. Sam Ham, a specialist in interpretative practice from the University of Idaho, in a foreword stresses that:

> The themes that are outlined in this document provide an all-important *starting point*, allowing every land manager and every community to find its own way to each theme, deciding how to express it, how to tease

from it the nuances that connect most strongly or resonate most loudly in each case and for each audience. [original emphasis] (Carter and Ford 2008: 3)

Nethy Bridge, a village within the national park and bordering the national nature reserve, has put this approach into practice.

In the centre of the village is a large 'kiosk' style interpretation display shown at Figure 13.1. The Cairngorms National Park logo is shown prominently linking the display to the park brand, but otherwise the marketing message is low-key in directing people to lists of accommodation and events within the village. Each of the four large panels develops a different theme. Counting from the left, in the first panel the narrative is that Nethy Bridge is the perfect place from which to 'discover what makes the National Park so special', contrasting the remote Arctic mountain tops with the broad flat valley of Strathspey where traditional management of fields supports the biodiversity and character of the countryside. Although the high Cairngorm plateau has the feel of a wilderness, the second panel headed 'Man Made Majesty' also stresses

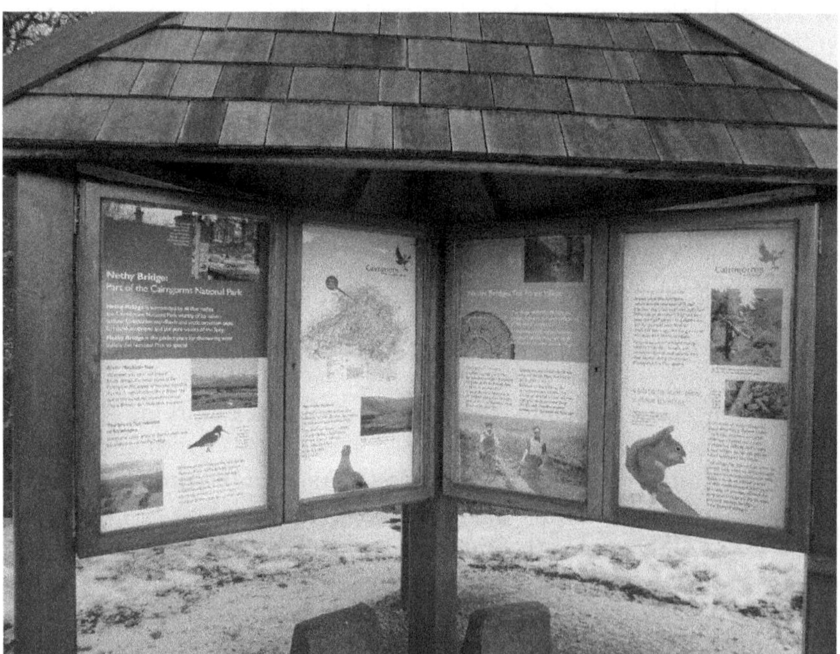

Figure 13.1   Kiosk-style interpretation display at Nethy Bridge

the part played by human activity, in this case to encourage grouse. In contrast to the parks established in North America more than a century ago, where concepts of wilderness prevailed, those in much of Europe owe their scenic and nature value to centuries of low-intensity agriculture. Sam Ham sees the approach taken by Scots as 'a new and enlightened way of understanding the role of National Parks in contemporary society'. Some sixteen thousand people live within the boundaries of the Cairngorms National Park (Carter and Ford 2008: 2). The narrative on the role of human activity in this interpretative display echoes that developed by Kate Rigby and Axel Goodbody (2011) in seeking to define 'European ecocriticism': they note that 'it is likely to be primarily concerned with cultural landscapes, with pastoral rather than wilderness' (Rigby and Goodbody 2011: 2–3). The next two panels explore two parts of the environmental history of this area.

The first identifies Nethy Bridge as 'the forest village' from the time when trees were harvested to support the early stages of the industrial revolution to the current involvement of many living in the village in the management of this important fragment of Caledonian pine forest for conservation and recreation. This is contrasted with its history in Victorian times when wealthy landowners cleared people from the land to keep up with the Royal sporting estates. Although there is more information here than on many panels, the complexity of the narrative leaves room for a variety of meanings, some of which, for example around land ownership by conservation organisations and private estates, the degree to which new plantations can be seen as natural and the continuing practice of grouse shooting over the fragile uplands are likely to be contentious.

Although Nethy Bridge uses the osprey logo of the Cairngorms National Park, the text on this display makes no reference to the bird for which Abernethy is famous. By identifying as the 'forest village' it aligns itself with the idea of the Caledonian pine forest and the associated narrative that values the cultural and wildlife potential of the woodland habitat in supporting rare species, including the red squirrel and the capercaillie. This narrative tends towards that advocated by organisations concerned with the restoration of Caledonian pine woods, such as the organisation 'Trees for Life' which has as its long-term goals 'to create a mature, healthy forest and to reintroduce missing species of wildlife, such as the beaver, wild boar, lynx and wolf'.[3]

Osprey-based tourism is now a major business, as by 2014 the population of breeding pairs in Britain had reached 200–50, with viewing opportunities in Scotland, Wales and England.[4] Vigilance is still required to protect the birds from theft of eggs or young. Armitage describes how volunteers from the military have been called upon to bring their expertise and surveillance equipment to the Loch of the Lowes site in Perthshire (Armitage 2011: 34 and 106). Ospreys started breeding here soon after the site was bought by the Scottish Wildlife Trust in 1969. When technology became available, CCTV was used first to monitor activity at the nest in its surveillance role; later it was used to collect scientific data and to present visitors with high-quality images of the birds they have come to see. Armchair ecotourists can now watch live webcam images of ospreys on the nest with no need to visit the sites concerned, so that each moment in the life cycle has a devoted audience. Tagged birds can now be tracked, when away from the nest and during migration to their winter feeding grounds in West Africa. This information is made available on the reserve website.

That the surveillance society has extended into the natural world raises questions for ecocritics. Ray has explored the issues in the context of a Canadian interactive documentary, *Bear 71*, that provides viewers with film and live 'crittercam' images of a radio-collared grizzly bear near Banff. For Ray:

> As wildlife enters the panopticon, we have to come to terms with the fact that technology is not just about producing scientific knowledge. It is becoming a tool of biopolitics. The various dissonances between technology and the wild in the webdoc's content and form, and our attempt to square this with Allison's view [about the loss of wilderness], all call for a more complicated sense of technology's ethical potential. (Ray 2014: 247)

Just as the technology of the motor car has brought nature tourists in increasing numbers into the countryside, so the technology of mass surveillance now covers the activities of wild creatures as well as humans.

As we come to terms with our own existence in the surveillance society, we have to establish how its extension to wild nature will affect our own understanding of relationships with other species. Ray concludes that:

> To recognise the social constructedness of nature is not necessarily to be anthropocentric, to use animals as mere data machines or sources of voyeuristic pleasure. Rather to recognise the social constructedness of both wild animals and spaces is to be accountable to them while allowing for their own subjectivity and agency. (Ray 2014: 252)

The influence of technology in osprey protection offers great opportunities for scientists and for the development of innovative interpretative media. However, it raises philosophical issues that would merit further investigation by ecocritics. There is still a demand for site-based tourism to see ospreys nesting and, once there, visitors can be offered interpretative materials that reflect the wider nature-interest of the site.

It was satellite tracking technology that first alerted Montgomery Wildlife Trust to the potential of its Cors Dyfi Nature Reserve near Machynlleth to attract this crowd-pleasing bird to this wetland reserve. Even without ospreys, Cors Dyfi would be an important reserve as an example of what can be done to restore a degraded habitat. Formerly grazing marsh, the area was planted with Sitka spruce trees in the early 1960s, but that crop failed. This reserve has been under the management of the Montgomery Wildlife Trust since the 1990s and owned by that body since 2005. The trust clear-felled the trees and set about restoring the area as wetland habitat to increase the biodiversity. The first indication that ospreys could be attracted to the area was in 2004 when a Scottish radio-tagged osprey gave a transmission showing she was passing the Dyfi estuary. In response in 2007 the Wildlife Trust placed an artificial nest in the reserve with the hope that ospreys could be attracted to the site. The nest was occupied every year since, but it was not until 2011 that breeding was successful.[5]

This success had a marked effect on the economic fortunes of this reserve, so that in 2013 the trust was able to attract Lottery funding for an ambitious interpretation project where, after viewing the live web-camera images of the nest and surrounding area, visitors are able to cross the reserve on a boardwalk to a '360° observatory' where they can watch the birds through binoculars. The time people spend on the boardwalk is an opportunity for them to pause at the wayside exhibits that introduce them to the wider ecological significance of this wetland reserve.

The first board that visitors come to, headed 'Discover with us', illustrated at Figure 13.2, is divided into three sections. That on the left, with a circular border, places the Dyfi UNESCO Biosphere within the global networks of biospheres which are to be 'learning sites' that 'encourage best practice for people and nature to live together'. A line on the globe connects to the second panel which shows a panoramic view of the Dyfi catchment and identifies Cors Dyfi as being within the core area of the biosphere. This map identifies three habitat types – saltmarsh, blanket bog and moorland – and also includes the 'townscape' around Machynlleth because 'people live in the townscape too [and] benefit from access to the countryside and living close to nature'. Pointing to 'you are here', the text notes that 'the biosphere supports recreation and tourism'. National and international designations are complex and the reason for them is often couched in technical terms. Here the narrative stresses the importance of people within the biosphere and the importance of

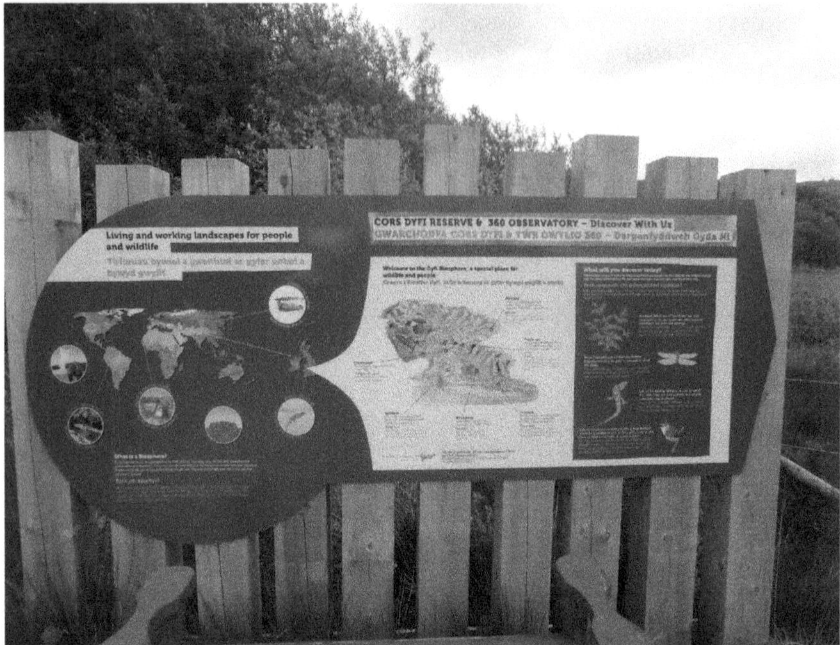

Figure 13.2 Interpretation exhibit at the start of the boardwalk at Cors Dyfi nature reserve, Wales

the natural environment for recreation and enjoyment. The third panel, headed 'what will you discover today', offers four examples of species that may be seen and urges people to 'keep their eyes and ears open and enjoy [their] visit'. This exhortation is in accord with Tilden's principle to 'provoke' interest.

During my own visit, common lizards were indeed sunning themselves on the edge of the boardwalk. Water buffaloes grazing in the marsh were a reminder that, in contrast to the desire in Scotland to extend the Caledonian pinewood, here wetland needs to be preserved by ensuring that it does not progress by ecological succession through wet willow or alder woodland to Atlantic oak wood.

Further along the boardwalk is a wooden post with a short exhortation at about child's height encouraging people to make a record of what they see and hear. This sign, headed 'Inspiring Nature', suggests that visitors make a record by taking a photograph, making a picture or writing about what they have seen. This suggestion would not be out of place in a 'creative writing field trip'. For example Terry Gifford describes the output he expects from students after such a trip to the Lake District:

> A Journal will be required to be submitted two weeks after the trip. Its form is appropriately undefined, but could contain photographs, drawings, and documentary material. It must, however, contain at least two types of material. Required are poetry from the trip and reflections on two themes: the cultural construction of the Lake District [...] and the cultural construction of Wordsworth historic sites. (Gifford 2006: 123)

This exhibit also leaves form as 'appropriately undefined', but it seems more likely that its purpose is to reintroduce the art of making 'field notes'. Canfield (2011) in *Field Notes for Science and Nature* makes the point that:

> Meticulous record keeping is at the heart of good science, and this is especially true for field scientists and naturalists. However, the status of field record keeping has come into question in the recent age of technological proliferation, and the first principles of field recording are rarely taught. Little guidance exists to help individuals develop this foundational skill, except perhaps for the ample and often accessible examples of notable nineteenth- and twentieth-century scientists. (Canfield 2011: 1–2)

Canfield goes on to cite writers like Charles Darwin and Henry Walter Bates.

It is particularly appropriate that record keeping should be advocated by a wildlife trust, for these bodies had their origin in the naturalists working with the county recorders to record the occurrence and distribution of species within a county, or, in the case of large counties, vice-county area. Montgomeryshire is one such recording area. Field trips for creative writers to such places as the Burren in Ireland have much in common with those made by ecology students and amateur naturalists to the same area. There would seem to be scope for some cross-fertilisation as both types of students should be sensitive to the cultural construction underlying the narratives embedded in the interpretation displays in natural areas.

About halfway along, the boardwalk opens out into a platform, illustrated at Figure 13.3, with two panels looking over a pool in the wetland. The left-hand panel, headed 'Life in Wetland', asks the question: 'how many species can you spot?' This now familiar narrative develops the theme that wetlands are important for a large number of species, even if they are difficult to spot. The image seems to be teeming with life while the real situation can at first sight seem rather dull. The

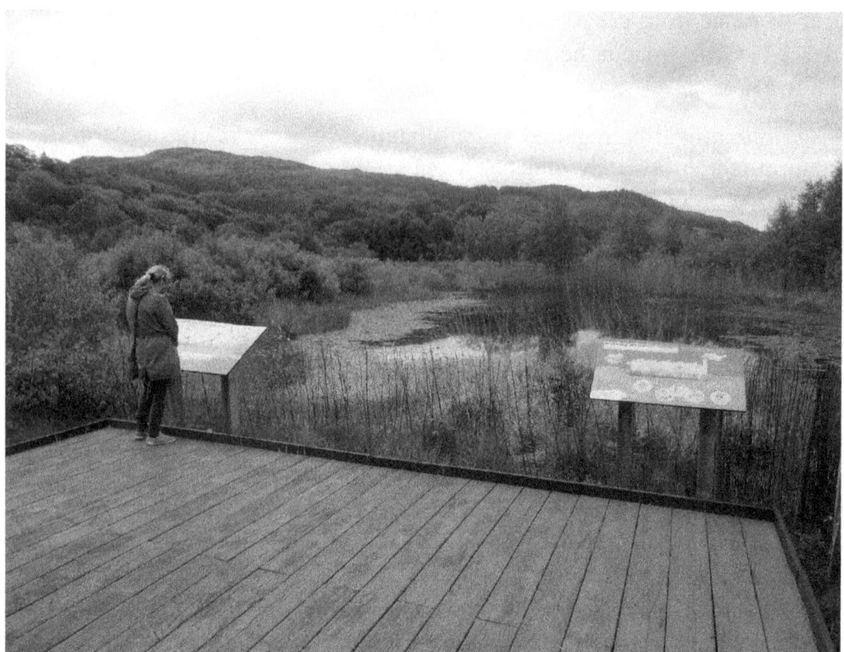

Figure 13.3 Wayside panels at Cors Dyfi nature reserve, Wales

species depicted are not named, but there is a list at the bottom of the exhibit of the species shown. The tension between trying to recognise the images, match them with the list below and trying to see at least some in the area in front of them does seem to meet Tilden's idea that exhibits should provoke. What is not said is that to see most of these species requires a long time in the field, preferably at dawn or dusk when the reserve is closed, and at a variety of seasons of the year. This type of natural history requires much more patience than the almost guaranteed view of the osprey on its nest once the visitor reaches the 360° observatory. The panel to the right of this platform takes a very different approach to the value of wetland, rather than seeing it as existing purely for the biodiversity of the habitat. With the subheading 'saving us £billions every year', this exhibit develops the idea of *ecosystem services*, using an analogy of a factory to represent the ecosystem that takes in carbon dioxide and dirty water and gives us back oxygen and clean water. Linked to this system are circles illustrating the other services supplied, which include flood control, recreation, medicines, food and materials. Wetlands are valued, and valuable, in many different ways. Helen Phillips, Chief Executive of Natural England, points out that:

> Healthy wetlands make an important contribution to our quality of life, they are important natural flood defenses [*sic*] that also help to filter and clean water supplies. Peat bogs also lock up dangerous greenhouse-gas emissions that contribute to climate change. (cited by Senior 2009: 400)

Although this exhibit does not use the term *ecosystem services*, the narrative for the benefits that flow from the wetland ecosystem together with that for carbon sequestration in Caledonian pinewoods discussed earlier in this chapter is consistent with this concept and is widely used to justify investment in habitat restoration.

Towards the end of the boardwalk there is a panel that looks back the way we have come and shows a panorama of the Cambrian Mountains on the horizon above this valley reserve. The heading 'Pumlumon – Living Landscape' is supported by only brief illustration and text. Perhaps the expectation is that by now people will want to reach their destination in the 360° observatory. The Pumlumon range is culturally important as the watershed where the Severn, Wye and Rheidol have their sources and it has been a destination for poets and writers since the Mabinogion was collected from oral tradition in the twelfth and thirteenth centuries. George Monbiot's *Feral* is a highly charged manifesto for rewilding, in which he labels such landscapes as 'sheepwrecked' (Monbiot 2013: 153–66). He records that:

> I have walked these mountains for five years now, and with the exception of a few small corners, found no point of engagement with them. Whenever I venture into the Cambrian Desert I almost lose the will to live. It looks like a land in perpetual winter. (Monbiot 2013: 65)

Monbiot's hope is that farm subsidies will come to an end to allow this desert to be greened. Restoring woodland cover would allow nature to recolonise these hills and bring with it increased biodiversity (Monbiot 2013: 166).

Despite Harri Webb's use of the term 'the green desert' as the title of his 1969 *Collected Poems*, which seems to support Monbiot's bleak view of this landscape, this poet does in fact take a more nuanced view. Matthew Jarvis, citing Brian Morris, explores the 'literal and symbolic' in Webb's use of this notion in his ecocritical reading of the poem 'Above Tregaron'. The literal use of the term is that the green desert has entered common usage as the name given to the 'sparsely inhabited upland area in the Cambrian mountains between, say, Tregaron and

Carno, the last vast emptiness at the heart of Wales' (Jarvis 2008: 19).
Later in the poem, Jarvis concludes that Webb sees himself as:

> effectively a tourist who brings the 'madness' of his world with him [...]
> he is also responsible for engaging with the environment, not for his own
> sake, but for the dreams he can project upon it. Remote Welsh space is
> in other words, something to serve a cultural purpose. (Jarvis 2008: 21)

It could be argued that Monbiot is inscribing his own cultural viewpoint
on this remote area. Like John Muir and others who first established
national parks in the United States, he erases those who currently make
a living on the hills, either by reporting the experience of two friends
who 'walked across them for six days without seeing another person'
(Monbiot 2013: 65) or by belittling these unseen farmers for the subsidies they receive (Monbiot 2013: 161).

Nelson deconstructs John Muir's similar rhetoric against domestic
sheep, by comparison with Mary Austin's more accommodating view
of domestic animals (Nelson 2000: 74–91). She argues that:

> Through the wild/domestic sheep dichotomy Muir supported a wilderness-
> is-better hierarchy, valuing all things wild over all things domestic, in
> order to develop tourism. His views represented an elitist and constructed
> hierarchy of western land value and use. Through sheep, Austin, as true
> leveller, struggles to understand the complexities of ecological dependence
> and equality. (Nelson 2000: 23)

This author invokes Edward Said's concept of 'orientalism' in claiming
that 'many of the most insidious myths about rural people and domestic
animals were created not within the vernacular regional cultures but by
urban writers who "Orientalized" the place and the people and animals
who live there' (Nelson 2000: 17). There is certainly scope for a postcolonial reading of the tropes deployed by Monbiot in his campaign for
rewilding this landscape.

The interpretation panel looking out to Pumlumon takes a different
approach to this contested landscape. It stresses the contribution of
generations of farmers, illustrated by a wall-builder, and describes it as
a 'living and working landscape', illustrated by one of the sheep that
are so much hated by Monbiot. The 'Living Landscapes' initiative is
not a statutory designation, but rather a series of projects led by the
Wildlife Trusts with the aim of restoring the landscape and making it
more resilient in the face of climate change. It will do this by working
with the current landowners and farmers. Only small parts of the
40,000 ha within the scope of this particular project are owned by
conservation bodies. Montgomeryshire Wildlife Trust gives its vision

for this area as to champion 'ecosystem services' that will reduce flood risk, improve water quality and bury atmospheric carbon.[6]

However, 'ecosystem services' is a problematic concept. Lant, Ruhl and Kraft explore some of the problems with the term. These authors build on Garret Hardin's widely cited 1968 essay 'The Tragedy of the Commons' and call their own paper 'The Tragedy of Ecosystem Services'. They draw a distinction between 'common property' and 'common pool' resources. 'For a common-pool resource it is difficult to deny potential beneficiaries the use of the resource once it has been created by society or by nature; it is therefore "non-excludable"'. Thus the clean water and oxygen restored to the atmosphere by a wetland are available to all. 'In contrast, common property refers to a property rights regime that determines the rules under which members of a community may access and use a common-pool resource' (Lant et al. 2008: 970). It is appropriate that this complex issue of *ecosystem services* should be addressed in the context of the UNESCO Dyfi biosphere in its role as a learning environment within which to explore how people live with nature. Ecocritics will need to navigate through the cultural values that are projected on to these mountains and the polemic of the rewilding lobby.

The concept of a market in *ecosystem services*, based as it is in neo-liberal market ideologies, will be problematic for some ecocritics and, as yet another payment to upland farmers to maintain a cultural landscape, is unlikely to satisfy those who would rewild the uplands so that they in turn can construct a landscape within which humans can find their place in nature. Although the exhibits on this reserve provoke rather than instruct, they carry sufficient of what is a mainstream narrative to include at least an element of propaganda for the environmental message.

There are many more exhibits along the boardwalk, but most people will press on to the observatory at its end. Whereas the wayside exhibits along the way have to stand on their own merits, the observatory has wall posters with attendant volunteers ready to engage visitors in conversation. The observatory, illustrated at Figure 13.4, offers a view over the reserve in all directions, but most visitors are looking in the direction of the osprey nest. From this vantage point it is possible to see the osprey sitting on the nest. Although binoculars are a help, this lacks the screens that gave such a wonderful detailed view of the bird on the nest at the reception to the reserve. From here it is possible to feel something of what it is like to see a wild creature within its habitat, even though it is sitting on an artificial nest on top of a telegraph pole. The design of this observatory has a modern feel, but, although the 360° view has a

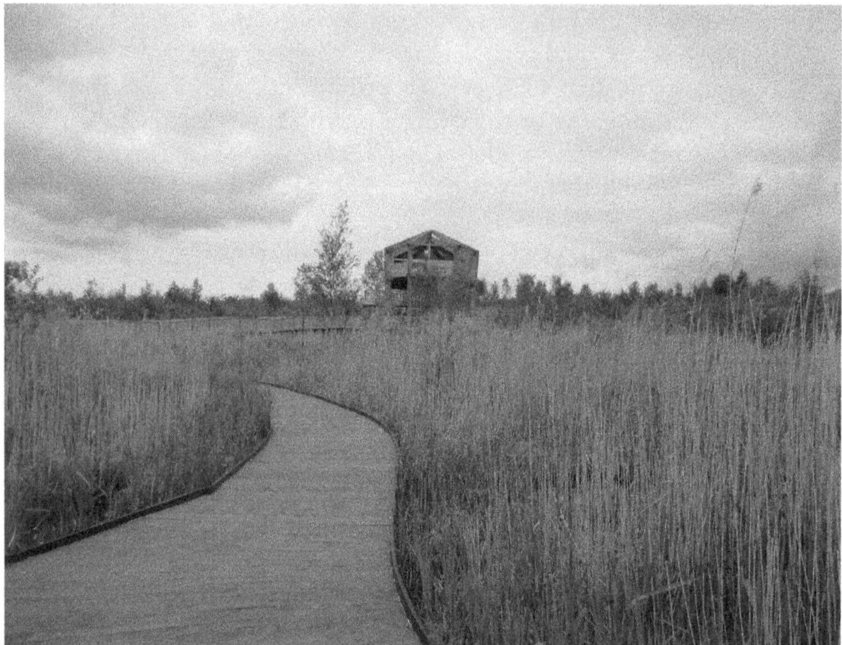

Figure 13.4   Approaching the 360° observatory at Cors Dyfi nature reserve, Wales

marked resemblance to the watch tower at the centre of Jeremy Bentham's panopticon, it is far removed from the 'wired wilderness' discussed by Ray.

The ambitions of those designing interpretation programmes are wide. They can cover brand management to education, propaganda for political viewpoints to neo-Darwinian explanations of ecosystems, creative writing and visual art to wildlife spectacle. All of these aspects have relevance to ecocriticism as we explore what wildness means and our part in the biosphere, against the disconcerting background of mass extinction, population growth and climate change.

Notes

1 Dates relating to the RSPB are taken from RSPB Milestones at www. rspb.org.uk/whatwedo/history/milestones.aspx accessed 24 August 2015.
2 Institute of Environmental Management & Assessment, 'Scottish Forest Alliance – carbon sequestration through tree planting'. http://iema.net/

event-reports/scottish-forest-alliance-carbon-sequestration-through-tree-planting accessed 24 August 2015.
3 http://treesforlife.org.uk/about/who-we-are accessed 28 August 2015.
4 Natural England, Press Release: 'First successful breeding record of ospreys at National Nature Reserve', 20 August 2014.
5 Montgomeryshire Wildlife Trust, 'Ospreys on the Dyfi'. www.dyfiospreyproject.com/history-of-british-ospreys/ospreys accessed 28 August 2015.
6 Wildlife Trusts Wales, *The Pumlumon Living Landscape* (undated). www.wtwales.org/sites/default/files/montgomeryshire_pulumon.pdf accessed 29 October 2015.

References

Armitage, Helen (2011) *Lady of the Loch: The Incredible Story of Britain's Oldest Osprey*. London: Constable.

Brown, Philip (1962) 'The Return of the Osprey', in Philip Brown and George Waterson, *The Return of the Osprey*. London: Collins, pp. 17–64.

Bryant, Margi (2006) 'Tilden's Children: Interpretation in Britain's National Parks', in Alison Hems and Marion Blockley (eds), *Heritage Interpretation*. London: Routledge, pp. 173–88.

Canfield, Michael R. (2011) 'Introduction', in Canfield (ed.), *Field Notes on Science and Nature*. Cambridge, MA: Harvard University Press, pp. 1–18.

Carter, James and Andy Ford (2008) *Sharing the Stories of the Cairngorms National Park: A Guide to Interpreting the Area's Distinct Character and Coherent Identity*. Grantown on Spey: Cairngorms National Park Authority.

Cockburn, Ken and James Carter (eds) (2005) *Tweed Rivers*. Edinburgh: Luath Press.

Gibb, Rona (2006) 'Highland Interpretive Strategy Project', in Alison Hems and Marion Blockley (eds), *Heritage Interpretation*. London: Routledge, pp. 33–40.

Gifford, Terry (2006) *Reconnecting with John Muir: Essays in Post-pastoral Practice*, Athens: University of Georgia Press.

Gross, Michael, Ron Zimmerman and Jim Buchholz (2006 [1992]) *Signs, Trails and Wayside Exhibits: Connecting People and Places*. Third edition. Stevens Point, WI: UW-SP Foundation Press.

Ham, Sam (2013) *Interpretation: Making a Difference on Purpose*. Golden, CO: Fulcrum.

Harris, Alexandra (2010) *Romantic Moderns: English Writers, Artists and the Imagination from Virginia Woolf to John Piper*. London: Thames and Hudson.

Jarvis, Matthew (2008) *Welsh Environments in Contemporary Poetry*. Cardiff: University of Wales Press.

Keirle, Ian (2002) *Countryside Recreation Site Management: A Marketing Approach*. London and New York: Routledge.

Lant, Christopher, J.B. Ruhl and Steven E. Kraft (2008) 'The Tragedy of Eco-system Services', *BioScience* 58:10: 969–74.

MacDonald, Helen (2015) 'The six books that made me', *Guardian*, 31 January, Review, 4–5.

Monbiot, George (2013) *Feral: Rewilding the Land, Sea and Human Life*. London: Allen Lane.

Nelson, Barney (2000) *The Wild and the Domestic: Animal Representation, Ecocriticism, and Western American Literature*. Reno: University of Nevada Press.

Oswald, Alice (2002) *Dart*. London: Faber and Faber.

Pearce, Fred (2008) 'Greenwash: BP and the myth of a world "Beyond Petroleum"', *Guardian*, 20 November.

Porteous, Katrina (2014) *Two Countries*. Hexham: Bloodaxe.

Ray, Sarah Jaquette (2014) 'Rub Trees, Crittercams and GIS: the Wired Wilderness of Leanne Allison and Jeremy Medes' *Bear 71*', *Green Letters: Studies in Ecocriticism* 18:3 (November): 236–53.

Rigby, Kate and Axel Goodbody (2011) 'Introduction', in Axel Goodbody and Kate Rigby *Ecocritical Theory: New European Approaches*. Charlottesville: University of Virginia Press, pp. 1–14.

Senior, Kathryn (2009) 'UK Spends Millions on Wetland Reclamation', *Frontiers in Ecology and the Environment* 7:8: 400.

Tansley, A.G. (1945) *Our Heritage of Wild Nature: A Plea for Organised Nature Conservation*. Cambridge: Cambridge University Press.

Tilden, Freeman (2007 [1957]) *Interpreting Our Heritage*. Fourth edition, edited and updated by R. Bruce Craig. Chapel Hill: University of North Carolina Press.

14

A seamless image: the role of photomontage in the meaning-making of windfarm development

Jean Welstead

Commercial windfarms first became evident in British landscapes in the early 1990s. From the outset the visual appearance of multiple turbines in the landscape divided opinion, sparking a conflict between ideas of sustainability and ideas of aesthetics, between concepts of wild land and the built environment.

The majority of windfarms require professional assessment for their likely landscape and visual impact in order to gain planning permission. One aspect of this is the production of a photomontage to show how the proposed windfarm may be seen from different viewpoints within a specified (typically 35 km) radius of the site. From the humble beginnings of a handmade assemblage of photographs and turbine images, the photomontage becomes a seamless image digitally produced to specific guidelines. The collections of photomontages presented for each proposed windfarm development are in themselves central to the visual meaning-making process of a new project and a pivotal reference point in the negotiation of a proposed new reality by the developer, the community, the regulators and the consenting body.

This chapter explores the role of photomontage in the development of windfarms over the last quarter century in Britain, and how the production of such an image contributes to the meaning-making and ontology of a new windfarm. It links the trajectory of the development of windfarm photomontage with insights from ecocriticism, an academic discipline which reads environmental texts with and against literary and artistic works and has developed contemporaneously, gradually widening in scope and praxis (Glotfelty 2003: 33–5). So far, although travelling in a similar direction and considering some of the same issues, the relationship between these two areas of thinking and practice has remained unexplored.

In examining the role and development of photomontage over this period I first explore the policy and regulatory context for the environmental assessment of landscape and the visual assessment of windfarms. I then look at the development of photomontage as a technique before discussing some of the complexities of our responses to changes in the landscape, the influence of the underlying narrative, and at the acquired aesthetic and ecocritical responses to energy infrastructure. This leads to two innovative examples, one in terms of process and one of design, before I summarise the potential role of the photomontage in the meaning-making of windfarm development.

Early windfarm development

The Centre for Alternative Technology (CAT) in mid-Wales was established in 1973 and pioneered a plethora of sustainable energy technologies including solar, wind and water energy. In 1984 on private land above CAT's Llwyngwern Quarry site the first wind turbine of any significant scale at the time, a grand 15 kw, was installed.

Five years later the 1989 Electricity Act, sections 32 and 33, introduced the Non-Fossil Fuel Obligation and implemented this over the next decade through two Electricity Orders, one for nuclear and one for Renewable Energy Sources in the form of Statutory Instruments. This government support provided a significant impetus to the small and committed renewable energy sector at the time, enabling the commercial development of windfarms.

Environmental Impact Assessment

Environmental Impact Assessment (EIA) was formally introduced into the UK in 1988 to comply with the European EIA Directive (85/337/EEC). The principal aims are to ensure that the environmental consequences of new development are known and taken into account before any consent is granted; and to encourage developers to consider environmental concerns from the earliest stage of project planning and design, when potentially adverse effects can be most effectively and economically addressed. From the outset EIA focused on biophysical effects on the environment rather than the interaction between culture and nature:

> If there is such a thing as European ecocriticism, its distinctive features might be sought in a number of dimensions. First, geographically, in that it is primarily to be concerned with cultural landscapes, with pastoral

rather than wilderness, given the shaping impact of relatively dense populations on land over centuries, and hence with a largely domesticated and, in places such as the Low Countries, even 'artificial' nature dependent for its survival on human agency. (Rigby and Goodbody 2011: 2–3)

The majority of windfarms have been developed on the edges of the pastoral landscape, allowing for suitable distance from dwellings, sufficient wind speeds and accessible routes for the power generated to be connected to the national electricity grid. As such they are located within the cultural landscape rather than one of mainly biophysical dimensions.

Landscape and Visual Impact Assessment

A critical component of the EIA is the Landscape and Visual Impact Assessment (LVIA). This can usefully contribute to pre-planning activities appraising development proposals and informing the design process at an early stage. It is defined as:

> a tool used to identify and assess the significance of the effects of change resulting from developments in both the landscape as an environmental resource in its own right and on people's views and visual amenity. (Landscape Institute 2013: 4)

The Landscape Institute (LI) was set up in 1929 as the professional body for landscape architecture in the UK. The LI upholds standards, oversees the qualifications of new landscape architects and promotes the profession of landscape architecture. Originally, when looking to create an association for garden architects, the founders changed the emphasis from garden design to landscape architecture to pre-empt the impending transition from private patronage of garden design to public patronage in the form of public amenity, town planning and urban design. The LI's focus in the 1970s was on landscape design, management and science. However, the major growth areas since then have been landscape planning, urban design, environmental assessment and garden design.

The LI responded to the need for assessment guidelines within the first phase of commercial windfarm developments. The third edition of this guidance (*GLVIA3*) recommends: that a more proportional approach is taken to ensure the relevant weight is given to the most important landscape elements; that professional judgements are made more transparent, relying more on the landscape-professional's skill and experience, rather than taking a prescriptive approach; and that the outcome of the work is presented and communicated in more accessible and understandable ways to the reader.

Of particular importance here is the separation that *GLVIA3* (LI 2013) recommends between landscape effects and visual effects, defining the two as follows:

> An assessment of landscape effects deals with the effects of change and development on landscape as a resource [whereas] an assessment of visual effects deals with the effects of change and development on the views available to people and their visual amenity. (LI 2013)

The 2013 guidance notes the significant changes to the environmental framework within which LVIA is now undertaken, particularly since the UK's ratification of the European Landscape Convention (ELC) that became binding in Britain in 2007. The ELC aims to provide a people-centred and forward-looking way to reconcile environmental management with the socio-economic challenges of the twenty-first century and to help people and communities to reconnect with place. Environmental psychologists considering the public's response to wind energy note that 'Place is implicated in becoming aware of and interpreting change' (Devine-Wright 2009: 433) in that place attachment and disruption of place can affect people's response to new developments.

The *GLVIA3*'s distinction between landscape effects and visual effects also indicates the dissimilarity between the 'cognitive view' and the 'immersed view' which is of particular interest when considering the issues of social acceptance of new energy infrastructure in the landscape. In the context of this chapter the cognitive view is used as a term to denote the more objective knowledge-based view used by professionals to conduct the LVIA and assess changes to the landscape as a resource in its own right. The immersed view refers to the more subjective and affective view that might be held by those living and working within and enjoying the landscape. The terms are not mutually exclusive but the difference is one of emphasis. However, applying only a cognitive view will not capture the relationship with place experienced by those already immersed in the landscape. The immersed view is also not the immersive view referred to when using virtual reality computer visualisations, but one where people directly experience the surrounding landscape. Svabo and Ekelund (2015: 6–7) explore this distinction when examining environmental aesthetics and its contribution to ecological design. They identify Saito's green design strategies as promoting a bridging approach to bring together the knowledge-based environmental aesthetic with the non-cognitive approach based on the art aesthetic, emotion and the aesthetics of engagement (Saito 2007: 88ff). Such a bringing together achieves a balance which avoids encouraging an environmental determinism where any object that is given ecological value, for example through environmental assessment, may also be awarded aesthetic value. This approach introduces the everyday aesthetic and therefore the more immersed view which is much closer to the real-life experience of people and communities.

The assessment of landscape effects is extensively based on the use of Landscape Character Assessments (LCA) as baseline information against which to assess landscape change. The first comprehensive landscape character review of Scotland (1994 and 1999) provided a standard methodology for identifying describing, classifying and mapping what is distinctive about our landscapes. Epistemologically it attempted to establish what we know and understand about different landscapes, and in that sense it presents a cognitive view and informed perception of the landscape as an independent resource. Furthermore, it standardised our knowledge and enabled LVIAs to be mainly, and more cost-effectively, conducted as desk-based exercises with limited site visits, revisits and/or working within the landscape. The cognitive nature of the LCA approach may be seen as in contrast to communities of locality who live and work in the area and communities of interest, for example, for recreation or creative practice, both of whom by the nature of their activity are likely to experience a more immersed and engaged relationship with the landscape. From an ecocritical perspective, walking within the landscape is increasingly being proactively used by the interdisciplinary approaches of creative practice and for understanding felt responses to the landscape. For example, creative practitioners are making repeat visits to the same location to develop a deeper understanding and connection.

The bringing together of the cognitive and immersive views presents a challenge within the LVIA process. How can what is known about the landscape be balanced with how people perceive and experience it? Landscape consultants aim to provide an objective assessment within the context of a process that stresses the natural environment by assessing biophysical aspects such as ecology, hydrology and geology. This combined with LVIA practitioners' training in landscape design aesthetics may obstruct the potentially beneficial incorporation of an everyday aesthetic within the assessment process.

The development of photomontage as an EIA tool

Visualisations of windfarms most commonly comprise photographs, wireline diagrams, photomontages, sketches and diagrams (Scottish National Heritage 2014: 23). They aim to represent the appearance of the windfarm in the landscape and form one component of the LVIA.

An example from early practice provides a useful starting point from which to examine the development of photomontage for windfarms.

National Wind Power Ltd applied for planning consent for Trysglwyn windfarm, Anglesey, in 1992. The LVIA chapter submitted by Dulas Engineering Ltd on National Wind Power's behalf consisted of just over two pages of A4 text and two more substantial A3 appendices. In describing the potential effect on landscape character it states:

> The landscape shows in its openness and in the remnants of other windmills, together with the wind-sculptured nature of the vegetation, a natural aptitude for the harnessing of this form of renewable energy, and this will, in some respects, confirm the appropriateness of the proposals.
>
> The Wind Turbine Generators (WTGs) themselves are elegant, aerodynamic structures, which do not necessarily blight or diminish the quality of a landscape, but can, in fact, endorse and emphasise its visual characteristics. It is the juxtaposition of manmade objects of a well-designed quality, with natural landforms and within appropriate views that can draw from each other and yield a composition of greater quality. (Donaldson and Edwards Partnership in association with Dulas Engineering Ltd, 1992: sections 8.2 and 8.3)

The Visual Studies appendix prepared by Dulas Engineering Ltd consisted of a map indicating the five photomontage viewpoints, a photomontage of each viewpoint including grid reference, direction of view and distance to the nearest turbine. The photographs were taken from each viewpoint using a 35 mm camera and 50 mm lens with colour negative film. The printed photographs were then arranged on two horizontally adjacent sheets of A3 paper to form a panoramic view, taped in place and photocopied to create one image. This one colour image was then used as a base to carefully place Letraset transfers of the wind turbines (scaled for different distances from the viewpoint) in the landscape. The completed image was colour photocopied again to prevent loss of any of the turbine transfers through handling. The resulting photomontage provided an approximate representation of the windfarm, retaining a handmade appearance through the visible joins of single frame photographs. An example of this can be seen at Plate 22.

In light of the *GLVIA3* discussion above, the case study provides a few points of note. Firstly, the landscape effects and visual effects are assessed separately; however, the latter assessment provides no explanation of the methodology applied, and at the time consultation with the community using the photomontages would have been fairly minimal, possibly only with the landowners. Secondly, the final assessment is written in the first person, stating the landscape architect's professional judgement rather than setting out a possibly more detached account of compliance with official guidance. Thirdly, the photomontages presented were extremely basic yet possibly more transparent in their simplicity compared to those produced today; they still served to support the planning authority's decision albeit within a pioneering context and subject to less organised opposition to wind energy.

Photomontage as applied to windfarms has travelled its own trajectory of improvement since the early 1990s. At that time semi-manual techniques such as the method used for Trysglwyn windfarm were quite widely applied. However, through the mid-1990s more sophisticated computer-generated techniques were developed to produce wirelines and associated photomontages. Leading Scottish companies such as Envision developed their own software programs (LANDVU) and superimposed turbines using Adobe Photoshop. The turbines were rendered using TrueSpace. A major driver for this was the requirement to develop computer-based photomontage techniques for power lines, as semi-manual techniques were not amenable to the scale and detail required for pylons and conductors.

At much the same time Edinburgh College of Art School of Landscape Architecture was undertaking a series of environmental studies, including one on the location and design of windfarms (Stanton 1996). Realising the critical nature of incorporating wind energy into the Scottish landscape, Scottish Natural Heritage (SNH) began to investigate the development of visualisation techniques. In the early 2000s SNH commissioned Professor John Benson of the University of Newcastle to conduct further research. This included site visits to existing windfarms in Scotland and the development of recommendations for visualisations of proposed projects. Contemporaneously, traditional film-based photography began to be replaced by digital, offering much greater flexibility and closer integration with computer-based techniques. By the mid-2000s new rendering computer programs such as POVray replaced TrueSpace and professional practice continued to develop. However, the variable nature of the windfarm visualisations being produced was problematic, and SNH was called upon to develop more specific guidance.

A steering group was set up by SNH to develop the new guidance, building on the work of Professor Benson. The revised guidance, published in 2006, provided substantial technical detail over nearly two hundred pages. Recognising that technology was changing, especially due to the introduction of digital cameras, the main aim of the guidance was to set a minimum standard but to encourage practitioners to 'do the best you can'. Its publication raised the bar considerably in the development of photomontages for windfarms. An example of photomontage applying the 2006 guidance is provided at Plate 23. In addition to the photomontage the following information is included: Ordnance Survey (OS) reference, height of eye level, Azimuth to site centre, camera height, distance to nearest turbine, type of camera, focal length, date, time, distance from which to view the photomontage and a location map. In comparison to the 1992 example, this photomontage provided a completely seamless image, as if the windfarm already existed. It is only the contextual detail and presentation that implies that it is part of a planning application for a future development.

Professional practice consistently applied this guidance, but questions remained about the visualisation method being used for windfarms and whether the resulting photomontages were underrepresenting the size of the proposed wind turbines in planning applications. This apparent underrepresentation was further exacerbated by the bringing together, through advances in computer science and photography, of the landscape and visual assessments and presentation of panoramic views as one seamless '50 mm' photomontage rather than single-frame images, the result being that the images appear foreshortened due to the linear perspective. The greater the distance of the viewpoint from the site, the more predominant this effect is. There had been complaints received from members of the public that turbines, once installed, were larger than anticipated, which led to accusations that the photomontages were misleading, resulting, in some quarters, in a breakdown of trust in the development process for proposed windfarms.

To address the issues raised, the process of constructing the visualisations required re-examination, and an alternative method was proposed. Two key publications contributed to the debate: first, a paper, 'The Visual Issue' (Macdonald 2007), which explained why panoramic photomontages were potentially misleading, and, secondly, the book *Windfarm Visualisation: Perspective or Perception?* (Macdonald 2012). On checking the 'visual issue' with the Center for Visual Science, Rochester, USA, Macdonald received the following response:

> Even if the images were viewed at the correct distance, they would still under-represent the scale of more distant objects because our brain takes into account distance in the real world to recalibrate their perceived size, a phenomenon known as 'size-constancy'. The problem with viewing photographs involving considerable distances is that our perception of depth is invariably shrunk because we are looking at a flat image with no distance information, so more distant objects appear smaller than they do in real life. (Macdonald 2012: 6)

When viewing the landscape directly we use depth cues, for example a building, a tree, a bridge the size of which we have some idea of, to estimate the size of an unfamiliar feature further in the distance. In the flat photomontage this is more difficult to judge. Other practical limitations of the photomontage have also been raised. The Environmental Statements are expensive and bulky documents and therefore not very accessible to members of the public. If one wishes to view the photomontage *in situ* this may not be affordable, but also the physical size of the printed panoramic photomontage makes it difficult to hold on site and compare directly with the landscape.

In 2011 SNH was asked by Scottish Government to review the visualisation guidance in light of the issues raised. The 2006 guidance was based on perspective geometry and viewing distance that aimed at creating a correct perspective and faithful representation. However, the change from the original (see Trysglwyn example, Plate 22) visibly stitched together 50 mm single frames to the seamless '50 mm' vertically shortened panorama may also have lost some transparency of process to the viewer. Visualisations based on both the 2006 guidance and the newly proposed methods were tested in the field against the now built Drumderg windfarm and it was found that the turbines still looked too small using the 2006 method, due to the 'linear perspective phenomenon' where the scale of an object diminishes as the distance increases. Plates 23 and 24 illustrate the difference between the two sets of guidance (2006 and 2014) from the same viewpoint, using photographs taken on different dates. It is clear in Plate 24 that the turbines, using the 2014 guidance, are more prominent, but the photomontage provides less landscape and visual context. SNH felt that there was enough of a difference to justify changing the guidance.

The revised guidance (SNH 2014) replaces that of 2006 and embraces the changes required. Additional information is provided with the image including: direction of view, horizontal field of view, principal distance, paper size (half A1) and correct printed image size. There is a new standardised photographic requirement (changed from 50 mm to 75 mm camera lens) and a format for production that includes the baseline image, wireline and a viewpoint pack. The viewpoint pack includes single frame images that can be used at the viewpoint where the viewer is immersed in the landscape and visual context. However, away from the site at a public meeting or planning committee the use of panoramas is advised to provide the landscape context. Some regional differences remain, especially in the application of a single frame image. In October 2015 SNH commissioned research to assess the response to the new guidance. Internationally, debates continue on the assessment, appropriate design and governance of emerging energy landscapes that include renewable energy and further exploitation of land-based fossil fuels.

The Landscape Research Group conference in September 2015 explored many aspects of this, including the use of tablets and immersive computer programs to help visualise proposals.[1]

The repeated revising and reissuing of guidance constitutes an epistemological and collective process in pursuit of good practice. However, once practice guidelines are in place, the scientific norms of scepticism and scrutiny may be put to one side and an advocacy or 'near-advocacy' role taken on as the practitioner enters the public arena (Callison 2014: 247–8) with, for example, their visualisations of the windfarm. It could be that although checks and balances will continue to be required, the 'near-advocacy' role is a necessity if the proposed windfarm is to become a reality.

The role of photomontage in making real the possible

The photomontage is often the most looked-at element of the Environmental Statement, with viewers wishing to ascertain the scale of the windfarm and its effect on their landscape values to help measure how acceptable it will be. As such, the photomontage is one of the sense-giving activities in the process of gaining permission to build the development. Corvellec and Risberg (2007: 306–7) explore this in terms of the notion of '*mise-en-sens*', a neologism that alludes to the performing-art term of *mise-en-scène*, or stage setting, while also indicating meaning and direction through the French term *sens*. They distinguish between sense-making, which is concerned with collective construction and reconstruction to develop a meaningful framework, and sense-giving, seen as the process of attempting to influence the sense-making and meaning construction of others towards a preferred reality (Gioia and Chittipeddi 1991, cited in Corvellec and Risberg 2007: 307). Renewable energy deployment is an example of such a preferred strategic reality. The giving and making of meaning is an iterative process similar to the EIA process. However, it may not be symmetrical, with more sense-giving than sense-making, so giving more agency to the developer at the expense of the community. Corvellec and Risberg (2007: 309) identify three main descriptive categories of *mise-en-sens*, or meaning management, for windfarm development: contextualising the project, ontologising its characteristics and neutralising any criticism.

Contextualising the project may be done through the context of energy policy at national and local level, technically through developing more efficient turbines and using co-texts to reference selected texts and activate selected pre-understandings and knowledge in the audience to give the application a specific direction. An early example of this can be seen in the Trysglywn case study which refers to the 'wind sculptured nature of vegetation, a natural aptitude for harnessing this form of renewable energy', confirming the 'appropriateness of the proposals' (Donaldson and Edwards Partnership in association with Dulas Engineering Ltd, 1992: section 8.2).

Developers may borrow from their own and other narratives to give meaning and direction to the project through the EIA process and through directly providing public information. By framing the project in this way, its meaning and momentum is sustained. In the detailed descriptions by the objective and the professional, often to saturation point, and usually excluding the subjective and affective views of the local community, there is an attempt to ontologise the project and endow it with an intrinsic character. By defining the project as a composite set of features and visualising it through photomontage they move towards turning something that is possible into something that is acceptable and thereafter existing. This, as Corvellec and Risberg (2007: 316) explain, is a meaning-management exercise in the strategic realisation of the virtual.

The momentum required by a project means that developers and their consultants are always pushing on to the next stage. 'Show-stoppers' are to be avoided and ontological features built up in a careful, acceptable way. Existing guidelines are complied with, but there is little time or appetite for the potential risk of fundamentally questioning methodologies if the *mise-en-sens* of windfarm development is to be maintained.

Social acceptance and community support

It is perhaps no surprise, therefore, that visualisations of windfarms have been central to issues of their social acceptance and community support. Social acceptance, now recognised as one of the major challenges for the deployment of energy infrastructure, comprises socio-political acceptance, market acceptance and community acceptance. Community acceptance has been defined as 'the specific acceptance of siting decisions and renewable energy projects by local stakeholders, particularly residents and local authorities' (Wustenhagen et al. 2007: 2685).

Research appears to confirm that community acceptance is in part driven by impacts on place and issues of justice. Impacts on place include health and environmental impacts, such as visual intrusion, noise, biodiversity and wellbeing. Issues of justice, which are starting to have an increasing resonance with ecocritics, include procedural justice and distributional justice. The former refers to the perceived fairness of the decision-making process, of which the environmental assessment is a central element. The *mise-en-sens* aspect of projects may also confine the project, to the extent that communities feel that they are either within or without the process. To be within it, contributing to collective sense-making and negotiating changes, can require a huge amount of energy and organisation, often with limited resources over long periods of time. Distributional justice concerns the even-handedness of developments: the realisation, for example, that local communities bear the visual impacts on place, whereas external bodies, particularly developers, accrue most of the benefits.

Fair processes have been identified as vitally important in shaping acceptance of the project as a whole, for example, people feeling that they are included in open decision-making procedures in which they have a legitimate role (Wolsink 2007: 2692), that their issues are taken seriously (Haggett 2010: 10) and that there is a balanced relationship between 'experts' and communities (Aitken 2009: 49). The photomontage in its now expert production may be missing an opportunity to involve the community more effectively and thereby improve the quality of participation (Berry and Higgs 2012: 230).

Moving forward

In present practice, photomontages, in offering a medium of addressing aesthetics, cultural appreciation of the landscape and feeling for place, are the closest to representing an ecocritical view of a proposed windfarm of any of the material produced in the EIA process. Paradoxically, however, although more accurate, and while remaining the most viewed element of the assessment, the photomontages seem to have become increasingly sterile and seamless in production. Driven by the expansion of windfarm development and the demands for more information, the emerging practice of EIA has become ever more extensive. However, it has been recognised by communities, practitioners and academics that the people and community aspect of a new development is possibly receiving less attention than it warrants. As Gifford (2013: 173) claims, there is a need for the passion, polemic and participation invoked by literature emerging from similar landscapes to those where windfarms may be sited. Socio-economic impact assessment (SIA) methodologies have been further developed and linked to aspects of social acceptance over recent years yet the deeper connection that lies between people, place and community remains relatively unexplored.

Considering the possible need for an additional EIA chapter, an environmental sociologist and two artists, Dr Claire Haggett, Robbie

Coleman and Jo Hodges, sought to address this through a project designed to gain new insights into how we as a society assign values to the interface between landscape and community. Working closely with a participating community, they developed a new EIA methodology, called 'The Missing Chapter: People, Place and Community'. The project was enabled by the participation of members of a community in Dumfries and Galloway, Scotland. The project was part of a larger research initiative, 'Imagining Natural Scotland' funded by SNH, The National Lottery and Creative Scotland and supported by the developer Infinergy.[2] The project used 'windfarms as a context in which to reimagine current land-use planning processes to include considerations of beauty, naturalness and impact on people, place and community' (Haggett et al. 2014: 1).

The biophysical focus of EIA does not fully account for the complex interrelated factors, including people, birds, livelihoods and archaeology that shape the landscape. The island of Tiree provides a good example of how closely interwoven socio-economic and ecological diversity can be. In consultations (2009–10) regarding the proposed offshore windfarm, the Argyll Array, residents explained their concerns that if the visual impact deterred tourists this could negatively impact on crofters who have diversified into tourism to support their business. If this jeopardised the crofting business it would also change the habitat, especially if crofting were to cease to be viable, which in turn would impact on the wildlife and ornithology of the island, themselves supporting other livelihoods (SQW 2011: 52). This concern for the intricate tapestry of local life unravelling due to the impacts of a new development illustrates the importance of understanding the local narrative running beneath the view of the landscape and appreciating the depth and nuances of this gaze. The 'Missing Chapter' project looks to address the lack of tools in the EIA process to understand the widely 'felt' nature of our environment and how people who live and work in the landscape experience and value it.

In order to create a chapter that would fit into an Environmental Statement and be presented in an effective way to planners and policy makers, the 'Missing Chapter' follows the format, principle and language of EIA but develops some novel methodologies. Its purpose is to add depth and character to visual descriptions of place by adding detailed individual and community narrative.

In addition to expanding beyond the 'dry, reductive lens of planning', in creative terms, the work aims to 'adjust the refractive index of that lens so that its depth of field was deeper, its sensitivity to colour and texture was intensified and its focus wider' (Haggett et al. 2014: 1). The

'Missing Chapter' introduces an action research approach to a series of studies to capture the key characteristics of the relationship between people and location, including:

1. a study to capture a sense of meaning and value – what the place means, why people have chosen to live there, and how they use and experience the place
2. a study to identify the type of impact the proposed scheme may have on the people and their relationship to that place
3. a study to assess the impact of change; and
4. a study to assess the role of mitigation.

In keeping with the format of EIA the first task (after scoping) was to establish the baseline for the study area. The study area already had an existing windfarm of sixteen turbines of 91 metres height 2.3 km away and in view of the community. In addition, there were two further windfarms proposed 1 km away consisting of sixteen larger (146 m tall) turbines. The community therefore had existing experience of a windfarm within their landscape and the possibility of two further windfarms in the vicinity which were in the process of developing site design and photomontages to be viewed in public consultations with the community.

A range of participatory appraisal methods was developed and used to understand landscape value and the meaning that certain places have to the local community. The project participants attended a series of events where the different exercises were employed, and active discussion and involvement were encouraged at all times. In reviewing the work it is evident that the project engaged participants in an interesting journey to explore, articulate and share their feelings. This in itself had an effect of developing community cohesion and shared understanding of the meaning of place. Exercises included:

- Journey to place – exploring where people had come from to the area and how long they had stayed. This included mapping the journeys people had made to reach the community.
- Reason, meaning and value – asking why people are here and what they value about the place. This gave voice and a sense of personal stories using postcards linking landscape and self.
- Land use – mapping and photographing activities on participants' own land and that to which they have access, which revealed multilevel use of the same place not to be readily obvious to outsiders.
- Favourite views – photographing and mapping location and direction of favourite views and creating a postcard set using their own

images, words and interpretations. The map was overlaid with an 'Angle of Gaze' to capture key connections to place.

- Significant places – by renaming significant places participants made apparent their own narrative of the landscape.
- Film posters – creating a community narrative through individual and collective connection to place. For example, 'They came to bury a friend and stayed to create a future' and 'Landscape and love, from frozen tundra to the hills of home'.
- Community radio station – creating a day-long localised broadcast to extend the community bonds by sharing participants' choice of music that they associated with the area.

These activities reached out to all the senses and developed an articulated view of the participants' sense of place before then assessing the impact of the proposed project. Of particular relevance here is the project's exploration of the meanings behind the view and responses to proposed change that are provided as annotations to the photomontage. This breaks down the perfected look and accuracy of the photomontage and interrupts it with the feelings of local people as shown in Plate 25.

The 'Missing Chapter' project connected with the community in a way that the usual assessment process has difficulty achieving. It was an important exercise in exploring the collective understanding or narrative that lies beneath the surface of the landscape as depicted in the photomontage. It gives voice to the people who cannot walk away from the pictured landscape and treat it as a framed picture or tourist viewpoint (Cosgrove 1984: 16) and offers a more profound visual reading for the viewer.

Landscape – the underlying narrative and acquired aesthetic

The installation of wind turbines within landscapes has presented fundamental questions in terms of how we value and appreciate our landscape. The photomontage has been an almost silent partner in this, driven by the due diligent approach to present accurate images of the prospective windfarm. Yet it has the potential to be part of a more transparent meaning-making process in the development of low carbon landscapes. Landscape research has sought, using phenomenological approaches, to interpret hidden meanings, stories, memories and associated values, in a similar way to the 'Missing Chapter' example, which insiders and outsiders can decode as the underlying narrative of a landscape. By understanding the cogency of the underlying low carbon narrative, society may slowly learn to embrace the changes to the landscape demanded by such an energy transition (Selman 2010: 161).

Historically, the British landscape has been changing since the end of the last Ice Age some ten thousand years ago and the 'underlying narrative' presents a palimpsest that reflects the different phases of economic and social development over this time. The industrial revolution and the 'Great Acceleration' since the 1950s have been so significant in terms of human impact that this period is now referred to as the Anthropocene era. Improvements in agriculture since the eighteenth century, including new crop rotations, new breeds of livestock and parliamentary enclosure, have also had an impact on the visual character of much of England and southern Scotland. In upland Scotland improvement was associated with the Highland clearances and the replacement of crofting with large sheep farms and sporting estates. Ecocritics have explored how such changes in land use and industrialisation have been received by writers and artists. The ecocritical discourse emerging from the creative processes could in itself form a type of stewardship of our collective feelings towards the landscape, something that is currently largely missing from the environmental assessment process.

Artists and architects in the eighteenth and nineteenth centuries contributed further to the transformation of the landscape with Arcadian-style commissioned works. Competing concepts such as the sublime and the picturesque further illustrate the close interaction of society, culture and nature. Improvement of the landscape around the great country houses continued to manicure the landscape, on the basis of principles of Humphrey Repton and Capability Brown. Literature at the time indicates that there was some resistance to the insensitivities of such developments.

John Muir (1838–1914), the Scottish-born American advocate for wilderness protection, has been particularly influential among ecocritics. Terry Gifford (2013), in discussing novels by John Buchan and Andrew Greig, brings Muir's philosophy into consideration of issues of ownership and access. Gifford argues that:

> because these novels value, at heart, the experience of contact with highland land, they are reminders of the need to continue to debate the nature of that experience against the pressure of contemporary capitalism. (Gifford 2013: 173)

Learning to love low carbon rural landscapes is a complex challenge; the Arcadian landscape is revered, there are moves to protect wild lands and there are issues of ownership and access. Gifford (2013: 166) argues that, in the long term, access may be more important than ownership. The requirement for electricity generation may mean there is an inevitable tension between the need to access such energy resources and the land over which they exist. It is likely that a balance between local attachment to place and a more eco-cosmopolitan view may be required (Heise 2008: 6–7).

In towns and cities there has been a different storyline and aesthetic, as, prior to the national grid, electricity was generated close to the end-user to ensure efficiency of distribution. The buildings that housed power stations were designed by architects and integrated into the city or townscape. Many of these buildings have now been converted and repurposed, such as the redundant Bankside Power Station (constructed 1947–63), which was designed by Sir Giles Gilbert Scott (1880–1960) and later, as an indication of its aesthetic value, converted into the Tate Modern art gallery.

Another example of this close link between urban community and electricity generation is the Portobello power station built by the Edinburgh Corporation in 1923. In addition to domestic requirements, the electricity generated lit the streets and powered the trams and the local swimming pool's wave machine. The power station is no longer the appreciated landmark seen from miles around but the palimpsest layers continue in the markers for new housing developments with street names such as Electra Place.

Renewable energy schemes, particularly wind energy, have typically not benefited from this close cultural or historical integration with the existing land, sea or townscape. Nor have they, in general, been developed adjacent to the major demands for electricity where upgrades of the grid system, such as Beauly Denny, have been a necessity. Improved grid infrastructure has been the subject of much debate and tension. Ecocritical responses through poetry and photography to the steel and concrete structures of the grid seek to see and hear these changes in our landscape more deeply.

Liz Wells discusses how photographers are questioning the effects of aesthetic strategies and how the 'industrial sublime' has become a familiar feature in exhibitions. One example is the work of John Darwell, whose postindustrial documentary work has included photographs of 'nuclear power stations [which] are carefully composed to heighten the pictorial landscape of which they now seem to form a part' (Wells 2011: 178–9).

More recently, Philip Gross has collaborated in *I Spy Pinhole Eye* with photographer Simon Dennison in a sequence of poems that speak to pinhole camera images of pylon footings. In one poem 'Yggdrasil', which takes its title from the Norse myth of the 'world tree' stretching between heaven and hell, Gross writes:

> Planted here (where else?), the world-
> tree, its roots in a boule of concrete,
> its planet of boulder, the split nut
> from which it is sprouted, its tendrils unfurled
>
> (Gross and Dennison 2009: 19)

In this image Gross plays with industrial aesthetics by deploying both myth and an organic image of tendrils that is almost Gothic.[3]

Windfarms as the predominant renewable energy development to date may be inherently difficult to integrate with the cultural landscape due to their current technology design, and the approval process for them has often been fraught with difficulty. Responding to social resistance to the increasing cumulative impact of windfarms, a new initiative seeking to bring back a more positive, creative and artistic vision of our requirement for energy generation has emerged.

The Land Art Generator Initiative (LAGI) was set up in 2010 to invite innovative designers to submit their ideas for public art installations that have the added benefit of providing utility-scale clean energy generation. The designs deliver a combination of technological ingenuity, aesthetic delight and sufficient scale to meet energy requirements in a much more discreet manner. The proposed designs show promise of embodying an ecocritical conversation with the landscape, reflecting a smart, passionate, value-driven response to our need for sustainable energy sources.

One example of this is a US competition entry entitled 'Fresh Hills' that has been designed to emerge from the landscape as natural undulations, whilst simultaneously generating energy from the wind.[4] This created landscape rises at levels of increased energy potential where more predominant wind speeds and duration exist. It illustrates a direct relationship between energy and land, the design being determined by the local wind speeds. The structure, illustrated at Plate 26, guides the airflow, creating a low-pressure system on the other side of the mounds resulting in a pastoral central plaza. As if standing at the eye of a storm, the central hub becomes a place to gather, reflect, play and explore. At the same time, the hub acts as a departure point guiding the visitor through its valleys to the extending vista platforms with site lines that extend all the way to the Manhattan skyline.

Conclusion

In summary, photomontage is a tool that has been adapted over the last quarter-century to produce increasingly accurate visualisations of proposed windfarms. It is the centrepiece in making the possible move closer to becoming a reality, as it depicts the composite features of a windfarm within the landscape. In terms of *mise-en-sens* it gives meaning and direction to the project and provides a method of comparison once fully constructed and operational. Improving the principles and methodology behind the photomontage has been subject to much debate, tension and hard work over this period. The main driver has been to create and deliver accuracy rather than engage creative or participatory practice to construct what, on the surface, could be taken as an artist's impression. However, from an ecocritical and social-acceptance perspective, the photomontage could beneficially be used to develop deeper understanding of the meaning of place in the local community, using methods such as those applied through the 'Missing Chapter' project. This may disrupt the smooth surface of the computer-generated photomontage with a variety of different contributions and 'immersed views', but as a whole it may generate a greater sense of procedural justice and make plain the distributional impacts by enabling articulation of what matters to the local community.

Since the early 1990s the underlying narrative for wind energy in the UK has often been subject to political and economic uncertainty. However, it remains an important contributor to decarbonising our electricity supply and complying with the Climate Agreements reached at the UN Conference on Climate Change (COP21 2015).[5] In terms of the 'acquired aesthetic' (Bourdieu 1984, cited in Selman 2010: 160) claims that the process generally takes one or two generations to adapt seem justified. If the early 1990s are viewed as the beginning of our transition to a low-carbon landscape, then we have experienced approximately one generation's worth of effort. Along with the inevitable imperfections of the development process over this time, an enormous amount of momentum has been gained and collective learning achieved. In addition, there is a growing recognition that the landscape will be different if we are to achieve the energy transition required.

The visual impact of windfarms and development of the photomontage as a tool to visualise this became an issue just as ecocriticism was making headway in academia. They have both been actively pursued in the context of growing interest in sustainable development, biological diversity and climate change. In terms of practice, just as ecocriticism is widening its scope, so visual representation of wind turbines has now to allow for a better understanding of how people perceive the landscape and move around in it. Photomontage, as part of the EIA, is a medium within which we can collectively negotiate our low-carbon landscape values and drive forward innovative thinking such as LAGI in terms of design, and of the 'Missing Chapter' in terms of process.

Acknowledgements

I am very grateful to Brendan Turvey, Scottish National Heritage, for his time discussing the history of photomontage and for providing the images for Plates 23 and 24. I am also grateful to Robbie Coleman, Dr Claire Haggett and Jo Hodges for permission to publish the image at Plate 25 and to Robert Ferry and Elizabeth Monoian of LAGI for permission to publish the 'Fresh Hills' image on Plate 26. I thank Caroline Stanton and Ian Macaulay for providing information on the development of photomontage techniques and Lindsey Guthrie and Brendan Turvey who have read and commented on earlier drafts of this chapter. The ideas and views expressed in this chapter are entirely my own responsibility.

Notes

1 Energy Landscapes, Perception, Planning, Participation, Power, 16–18 September 2015, Dresden, Germany. http://lrg2015.ioer.info/index.html accessed 3 May 2016.
2 http://imaginingnaturalscotland.org.uk/ accessed 3 May 2016.
3 See for example John Ruskin (2004 [1853]: 47): 'The affectionate observation of the grace and outward character of vegetation is the sure sign of a more tranquil and gentle existence, sustained by the gifts and gladdened by the splendour, of the earth.'
4 LAGI second prize winner 2012. Artists: Matthew Rosenberg, Matt Melnyk, Emmy Maruta, Robbie Eleazer, Los Angeles (CA), USA. Energy Technologies: WindTamerô, carbon dioxide scrubber, SmartWrapô, annual capacity: 238 MWh.
5 United Nations conference on climate change (COP21) www.cop21.gouv.fr/en/ accessed 6 January 2016.

References

Aitken, Mhairi (2009) 'Wind Power Planning Controversies and the Construction of "Expert" and "Lay" Knowledges', *Science as Culture* 18:1: 47–64.

Berry, R. and G. Higgs (2012) 'Gauging Levels of Public Acceptance of the Use of Visualisation Tools in Promoting Public Participation: a Case Study of Windfarm Planning in South Wales, UK', *Journal of Environmental Planning and Management* 55:2: 229–51.

Bourdieu, P. (1984) *Distinction: A Social Critique of the Judgment of Taste*. London: Routledge.

Callison, C. (2014) *How Climate Change Comes to Matter: The Communal Life of Facts*. Durham, NC, and London: Duke University Press.

Corvellec, H. and A. Risberg (2007) 'Sense Giving as Mise-en-sens – the Case of Wind Power Development'. *Scandinavian Journal of Management* 23: 306–26.

Cosgrove, D. (1984) *Social Formation and Symbolic Landscape*. London: Croom Helm.

Devine-Wright, P. (2009) 'Rethinking NIMBYism: The role of Place Attachment and Place Identity in Explaining Place-protective Action', *Journal of Community & Applied Social Psychology* 19: 426–41. Published online 5 January in Wiley InterScience www.interscience.wiley.com accessed 19 April 2016.

Donaldson and Edwards in association with Dulas Engineering Ltd (1992) *Tryslgwyn Windfarm Environmental Statement*. Manchester: National Wind Power.

Gifford, T (2013) 'Ownership and Access in the Work of John Muir, John Buchan and Andrew Greig', *Green Letters: Studies in Ecocriticism* 17:2: 164–74.

Gioia, D.A. and K. Chittipeddi (1991) 'Sensemaking and Sensegiving in Strategic Change Initiation', *Strategic Management Journal* 12:6: 433–48.

Glotfelty, Cheryll (2003), 'A Guided Tour of Ecocriticism, with Excursions towards Catherland', in Susan J. Rosowski (ed.), *Willa Cather's Ecological Imagination*, Cather Sudies 5. Lincoln, NE, and London: University of Nebraska Press. www.unl.edu/cs005_glotfelty.html accessed 6 December 2015.

Gross, Philip and Simon Dennison (2009), *I Spy Pinhole Eye*. Blaenau Ffestiniog: Cinnamon.

Haggett. C. (2010) 'The Principles, Procedures, and Pitfalls of Public Engagement in Decision-making about Renewable Energy', in P. Devine-Wright (ed.), *Renewable Energy and the Public*. London: Earthscan.

Haggett, C., R. Coleman and J. Hodges (2014) 'A New Environmental Impact Assessment for Natural Scotland: Environment, Imagination and Aesthetics'. *The Missing Chapter: People, Place and Community*. http:// imaginingnaturalscotland.org.uk/the-projects/a-new-eia-for-natural-scotland/ accessed 19 April 2016.

Heise, U. (2008) *Sense of Place and Sense of Planet: The Environmental Imagination of the Global*. Oxford sand New York: Oxford University Press.

Landscape Institute (2013) *Guidelines for Landscape and Visual Impact Assessment*. Third edition. Abingdon: Routledge. www.landscapeinstitute.org/ knowledge/GLVIA.php accessed 19 April 2016.

Macdonald, A. (2007) *The Visual Issue. An Investigation into the Techniques and Methodology Used in Windfarm Computer Visualisations*. Inverness: Architech Animation Studios.

Macdonald, A. (2012) *Windfarm Visualisation: Perspective or Perception?* Dunbeath: Whittles Publishing.

Rigby, Kate and Axel Goodbody (2011), 'Introduction', in Axel Goodbody and Kate Rigby (eds), *Ecocritical Theory: New European Approaches*. Charlottesville, VA, and London: University of Virginia Press.

Ruskin, John (2004 [1853]) *On Art and Life*. London: Penguin.

Saito, Yuriko (2007) *Everyday Aesthetics*. Oxford: Oxford University Press.

Scottish Natural Heritage (2014) *Visual Representation of Windfarms*. www.snh.gov.uk/planning-and-development/renewable-energy/visual-representation/ accessed 19 April 2016.

Selman, P. (2010) 'Learning to Love the Landscapes of Carbon Neutrality', *Landscape Research* 35:2, 157–71.

SQW (2011) *Phase 2 Socio-Economic Report*, Argyll Renewables Communities, Islay Energy Trust, https://islayenergytrust.files.wordpress.com/2011/12/arc-phase-2-socio-economic-report-final-28–11–11.pdf accessed 19 April 2016.

SQW and Queen's University Belfast (2012) *A Review of the Context for Enhancing Community Acceptance of Wind Energy in Ireland*. Sustainable Energy Authority Ireland. www.seai.ie/Renewables/Wind_Energy/Attitudes_towards_Wind_Energy_in_Ireland/ accessed 3 May 2016.

Stanton, C. (1996) 'The Landscape Impact and Visual Design of Windfarms'. *Landscape Publication* No. LP/9603. Edinburgh: Edinburgh College of Art.

Svabo, C. and K. Ekelund (2015) 'Environmental Aesthetics: Notes for Design Ecology'. *Design Ecologies No. 6*. Stockholm: Nordes 2015: Design Ecologies (www.nordes.org).

Wells, Liz (2011), *Land Matters: Landscape Photography, Culture and Identity*. London and New York: I.B. Taurus.

Wolsink, M. (2007) 'Planning of Renewable Schemes: Deliberate and Fair Decision-making on Landscape Issues instead of Reproachful Accusations of Non-cooperation', *Energy Policy* 35: 2692–704.

Wustenhagen, Rolf, Maarten Wolsink and Mary Jean Bürer (2007) 'Social Acceptance of Renewable Energy Innovation: an Introduction to the Concept', *Energy Policy* 5:5: 2683–91.

Index

'pl.' before a number indicates an image in the plates section

EU authorised representative for GPSR:
Easy Access System Europe, Mustamäe tee 50,
10621 Tallinn, Estonia
gpsr.requests@easproject.com

www.ingramcontent.com/pod-product-compliance
Ingram Content Group UK Ltd.
Pitfield, Milton Keynes, MK11 3LW, UK
UKHW020955170726
7214IPUK00039B/344